D1448031

# MacRoberts on
# Scottish Building Contracts

**Second Edition**

## MacRoberts
Solicitors

**Foreword by**
**The Rt. Hon. Lord Hamilton**

**Blackwell**
Publishing

© 1999, 2008 by Blackwell Publishing Ltd

Blackwell Publishing editorial offices:
Blackwell Publishing Ltd, 9600 Garsington Road, Oxford OX4 2DQ, UK
Tel: +44 (0)1865 776868
Blackwell Publishing Inc., 350 Main Street, Malden, MA 02148-5020, USA
Tel: +1 781 388 8250
Blackwell Publishing Asia Pty Ltd, 550 Swanston Street, Carlton, Victoria 3053, Australia
Tel: +61 (0)3 8359 1011

The right of the Author to be identified as the Author of this Work has been asserted in accordance with the Copyright, Designs and Patents Act 1988.

All rights reserved. No part of this publication may be reproduced, stored in a retrieval system, or transmitted, in any form or by any means, electronic, mechanical, photocopying, recording or otherwise, except as permitted by the UK Copyright, Designs and Patents Act 1988, without the prior permission of the publisher.

Designations used by companies to distinguish their products are often claimed as trademarks. All brand names and product names used in this book are trade names, service marks, trademarks or registered trademarks of their respective owners. The Publisher is not associated with any product or vendor mentioned in this book.

This publication is designed to provide accurate and authoritative information in regard to the subject matter covered. It is sold on the understanding that the Publisher is not engaged in rendering professional services. If professional advice or other expert assistance is required, the services of a competent professional should be sought.

First published 2008 by Blackwell Publishing Ltd

2  2009

*Library of Congress Cataloging-in-Publication Data*

MacRoberts on Scottish building contracts / MacRoberts Solicitors; foreword by the Rt. Hon. Lord Hamilton.–2nd ed.
p.  cm.
Includes bibliographical references and index.
ISBN 978-1-4051-2973-2 (hardback : alk. paper)
1. Construction contracts–Scotland.  I. MacRoberts (Firm)
KDC501.M33 2008
343.411′078624–dc22
2007027071

A catalogue record for this title is available from the British Library

Set in 10/12pt Palatino by SNP Best-set Typesetter Ltd., Hong Kong
Printed and bound in Singapore by Fabulous Printers Pte Ltd

The publisher's policy is to use permanent paper from mills that operate a sustainable forestry policy, and which has been manufactured from pulp processed using acid-free and elementary chlorine-free practices. Furthermore, the publisher ensures that the text paper and cover board used have met acceptable environmental accreditation standards.

For further information on Blackwell Publishing, visit our website:
www.blackwellpublishing.com/construction

# Contents

# Foreword

The Rt. Hon. Lord Hamilton

When in 1999 Lord Hope of Craighead penned the Foreword to the first edition of this work, he wished it a long life and every success in the important task of providing practical advice in its chosen field – namely, to serve as a companion volume for use with the SBCC forms and to deal with general principles which are relevant to building contracts of all kinds. He also expressed the hope that it might be possible for it, like the forms, to be kept up to date by the issuing of revised editions at appropriate intervals.

Much has happened in that field since the publication of the first edition. In 2005 the JCT carried out a comprehensive revision of the whole suite of its contract forms. The SBCC is producing Scottish versions of the majority of these forms. The latter are now 'stand alone' contracts, rather than the traditional English Conditions with Scottish Supplements. New contract forms have been added, among them forms which include design obligations. This edition provides a commentary to the latest version of the Standard Building Contract for use in Scotland and to the parallel Design and Build Contract.

It goes much further. When the last edition was published, Part II of the Housing Grants, Construction and Regeneration Act 1996 had only recently come into force. There was little practical experience of its operation and even less judicial interpretation of it. All that has changed. Adjudication has become a major feature of the practical implementation of construction contracts and there is a wealth of judicial observation on the relevant legislation. The authors devote a whole chapter (Chapter 16) to that aspect of dispute resolution. Although arbitration has in recent years become less popular as a forum for resolving construction contract disputes, it is still of relevance and a chapter is devoted to that subject (Chapter 17). As is illustrated by the substantial number of recent judicial decisions cited, the courts have become an increasingly important forum. Their decisions (both from Scotland and from England) are noted and commented on. A separate chapter (Chapter 19) is now devoted to health and safety aspects and a quite new discussion (Chapter 18) addresses taxation issues. An added chapter (Chapter 2) deals with the rules on procurement against their E.U. background.

The law relating to construction contracts, while having its own specialties, must be seen in the context of the general law of contract and related topics. That context is well-addressed by the authors. Specifically Scottish topics (such as prescription and the Scottish approach to unjust enrichment) are admirably dealt with. The authors do a service to all those who practice in or have dealings with this field of economic activity, which is of the first importance to the commercial life of Scotland.

Arthur Hamilton

# Preface

When, in about 1996, we embarked upon the preparation of the first edition of this book, the first dedicated text on Scottish building contracts, neither of us considered the possibility of a second edition. Indeed, if asked upon publication of the first edition, we suspect that we would have kindly declined the invitation, notwithstanding Lord Hope of Craighead's kind words in his Foreword. Nevertheless, the invitation came and we accepted, the trials and tribulations of the first edition being but a distant memory.

In the Preface to the first edition we said that the object of the book was to bring some light to the darkness of the law of Scotland in relation to building contracts. That remains our goal. The landscape has changed significantly since 1999. The most obvious example of this is adjudication. The first edition devoted only two pages to this subject and had no cases to refer to. This edition has a chapter devoted to adjudication with numerous case references. That is not the only change. As highlighted by the Lord President, in his kind Foreword, there are new chapters on Procurement, Tax and Health and Safety. Arbitration now merits a chapter in its own right; and many of the other chapters have been significantly expanded.

We noted in the Preface to the first edition the close relationship between the law of Scotland and the law of England in the area of construction and engineering law. That remains the case today. In this edition we highlight certain notable developments, including those relative to novation arising from the decision in *Blyth & Blyth Ltd* v. *Carillion Construction Ltd*; those relative to global claims arising from the decision in *John Doyle Construction Ltd* v. *Laing Management (Scotland) Ltd*; and the first decision by the House of Lords in a case under the 1996 Act, namely, *Melville Dundas Ltd* v. *George Wimpey UK Ltd*.

MacRoberts were fortunate to be instructed in each of those cases. We hope that the insight we offer in relation to these, and many other notable decisions, provides some practical assistance.

As with the first edition, there have been a number of individual contributors. Only David Arnott, Richard Barrie, Shona Frame, Neil Kelly and ourselves remain since the first edition, in this edition we have been joined by our colleagues Mike Barlow, Michael Drysdale, Julie Hamilton, Alison Horner, Isobel d'Inverno, Alison Keith, Colette McGinley, Jennifer McKay, Barbara Mitchell, Duncan Osler, Sarah Pengelly, Anne Struckmeier, Gavin Thomson, Catherine Thompson, Laura Wilkinson, David Wilson and

Christine Worthington and our now former colleagues Craig Bradshaw, Karen Cameron and Craig Morrison.

The invaluable contribution made by our Library Information Officer, Alan McAdams, deserves special mention. It would appear that no level of obscure query is beyond Alan. In addition to answering numerous questions, he carried out countless hours of research, provided helpful comments on the text and generally made life far easier than it might have been for many of the contributors.

Marie Clare Clezy had the unenviable task of sorting out the tables and, as with the first edition, David Flint provided valuable assistance in the preparation of the index, as did Lynn Barker, Martin Barr and Elora Mukherjee. Each of the secretaries who participated in putting the chapters in to a presentable form deserves our thanks, particularly Jennifer Kennedy who, as well as her work on a number of chapters, put this edition in to a form that could be submitted to the publishers. We must also thank Lucy Alexander and her colleagues at Wiley-Blackwell for their forbearance and assistance.

Finally, we are indebted to Robert Howie QC for taking the time to read over the text and for the helpful observations he offered. Ultimately, of course, responsibility for any errors or omissions rests entirely with the contributors and ourselves, as editors!

We have endeavoured to state the law as at 1$^{st}$ October 2007.

David Henderson
Craig Turnbull

MacRoberts
152 Bath Street
Glasgow

# Chapter 1
# Building Contracts in General

## 1.1 Introduction

Numerous books have been written on the subject of building contracts. However, many of those are of a specialist nature and most are written from the perspective of English law. The aim of this book is to provide a practical guide to building contracts governed by the law of Scotland.

Building contracts are the cornerstones of an increasingly expanding industry. The very size of the construction industry means that it is of huge significance to the economy. The construction industry contributes more than £12 billion to the Scottish economy every year. That is nearly 10 per cent of Scotland's total economic output. The latest statistics show that 200,000 people work in construction meaning the industry accounts for one of every 11 jobs across the country.

## 1.2 Definition of a building contract

### 1.2.1 General

The definition of a building contract is not straightforward. The construction industry encompasses building and engineering projects which differ enormously in nature, size and complexity. The terms 'building contract' and 'construction contract' are often used interchangeably. The term 'construction contract' was given a statutory meaning for the first time by section 104 of the Housing Grants, Construction and Regeneration Act 1996 ('the 1996 Act') and the breadth of the definition illustrates the wide-ranging nature of building contracts. A construction contract for the purposes of the 1996 Act must be in writing, however a building contract can be wholly oral.

### 1.2.2 Construction contracts under the 1996 Act

In defining a building contract, considerable assistance can be derived from the 1996 Act. Part II applies to 'construction contracts', being agreements in relation to 'construction operations'. These terms are defined respectively by sections 104 and 105. By virtue of section 107 the agreement must be in writing.

Section 104 provides as follows:

(1)   In this Part a 'construction contract' means an agreement with a person for any of the following –

   (a)  the carrying out of construction operations;
   (b)  arranging for the carrying out of construction operations by others, whether under sub-contract to him or otherwise;
   (c)  providing his own labour, or the labour of others, for the carrying out of construction operations.

(2)   References in this Part to a construction contract include an agreement –

   (a)  to do architectural, design or surveying work, or
   (b)  to provide advice on building, engineering, interior or exterior decoration or on the laying-out of landscape, in relation to construction operations.

(3)   References in this Part to a construction contract do not include a contract of employment (within the meaning of the Employment Rights Act 1996).

(4)   The Secretary of State may by order add to, amend or repeal any of the provisions of subsection (1), (2) or (3) as to the agreements which are construction contracts for the purposes of this Part or are to be taken or not to be taken as included in references to such contracts . . .

It will be noted that the 1996 Act applies to matters beyond the carrying out of building works. It applies to architectural, design and surveying works and to advising on building, engineering, interior or exterior decoration or on the laying-out of landscape in relation to construction operations.

The definition of 'construction operations' is central to Part II. This term is defined by section 105(1) which provides as follows:

(1)   In this Part 'construction operations' means, subject as follows, operations of any of the following descriptions –

   (a)  construction, alteration, repair, maintenance, extension, demolition or dismantling of buildings, or structures forming, or to form, part of the land (whether permanent or not);
   (b)  construction, alteration, repair, maintenance, extension, demolition or dismantling of any works forming, or to form, part of the land, including (without prejudice to the foregoing) walls, roadworks, power-lines, electronic communications apparatus, aircraft runways, docks and harbours, railways, inland waterways,

pipe-lines, reservoirs, water-mains, wells, sewers, industrial plant and installations for purposes of land drainage, coast protection or defence;

(c) installation in any building or structure of fittings forming part of the land, including (without prejudice to the foregoing) systems of heating, lighting, air-conditioning, ventilation, power supply, drainage, sanitation, water supply or fire protection, or security or communications systems;

(d) external or internal cleaning of buildings and structures, so far as carried out in the course of their construction, alteration, repair, extension or restoration;

(e) operations which form an integral part of, or are preparatory to, or are for rendering complete, such operations as are previously described in this subsection, including site clearance, earth-moving, excavation, tunnelling and boring, laying of foundations, erection, maintenance or dismantling of scaffolding, site restoration, landscaping and the provision of roadways and other access works;

(f) painting or decorating the internal or external surfaces of any building or structure.

Section 105(2) details a number of operations that are not construction operations for the purposes of Part II. The exceptions relate to oil and gas and mining, both underground and opencast; nuclear processing, power generation, water or effluent treatment and the production, transmission, processing or bulk storage (other than warehousing) of chemicals, pharmaceuticals, oil, gas, steel or food and drink; the manufacture or delivery to site of components or equipment where the contract does not also provide for their installation; and the making, installation and repair of wholly artistic works.

## 1.2.3 Excluded contracts

Section 106 provides that Contracts with residential occupiers are excluded from the operation of Part II of the 1996 Act, as is any other description of construction contract excluded by order of the Secretary of State.

A construction contract with a residential occupier is one which principally relates to operations on a dwelling which one of the parties to the contract occupies, or intends to occupy, as his residence.

The term 'dwelling' means a dwelling-house or a flat; and for s.106(2) 'dwelling-house' does not include a building containing a flat and 'flat' means separate and self-contained premises constructed or adapted for use for residential purposes and forming part of a building from some other part of which the premises are divided horizontally. In itself, section 106 is self-explanatory. However, it should be noted that a residential occupier cannot be a limited company for the purposes of this section, see *Absolute Rentals Ltd* v. *Gencor Enterprises Ltd* (2001).

The Construction Contracts (Scotland) Exclusion Order 1998 ('the 1998 Order') came into force with Part II of the 1996 Act on 1 May 1998. This excluded from the scope of Part II of the 1996 Act project agreements under the Private Finance Initiative (provided certain criteria were met) but not sub-contracts such as the construction contract and facilities management or operation and maintenance contract.

Certain development agreements are also excluded from the operation of Part II under article 6 of the 1998 Order. A contract is a development agreement if it includes provision for the grant or disposal of a relevant interest in the land on which take place the principal construction operations to which the contract relates.

A relevant interest in land means either ownership; or a tenant's interest under a lease for a period which is to expire not earlier than 12 months after the completion of the construction operations under the contract.

In *Captiva Estates Ltd* v. *Rybarn Ltd (In Administration)* (2006) Captiva entered into a contract with Rybarn to construct 28 flats. Captiva owned the land on which the development was to take place. The contract provided that, as consideration for the works, Captiva would pay Rybarn and would also grant to Rybarn an option to purchase leases in respect of 7 of the 28 flats. The question arose as to whether the contract was a development agreement within the meaning of the English equivalent to the 1998 Order. The court held that the definition of a 'development agreement' in the 1998 Order is wide and the contract was caught by it.

### 1.2.4 Agreements in writing

Section 107 of the 1996 Act provides that Part II only applies to agreements in writing or evidenced in writing or recorded by one of the parties or a third party who has been duly authorised to do so.

In *RJT Consulting Engineers Ltd* v. *DM Engineering (Northern Ireland) Ltd* (2002) the Court of Appeal held that what has to be evidenced in writing is, literally, the agreement, which means all of it, not part of it. A record of the agreement also suggests a complete agreement, not a partial one. The only exception to the generality of that construction is the instance falling within s.107(5) where the material or relevant parts are alleged and not denied in written submissions in adjudication or other defined proceedings.

This case was followed in *Redworth Construction Ltd* v. *Brookdale Healthcare Ltd* (2006). It is important to highlight that the contract itself does not have to be in writing, simply that the terms must be evidenced in writing.

## 1.3 *Parties involved in a building project*

The number and identity of the persons involved in a building project can vary considerably depending on the nature and complexity of the project. At one end of the scale a private individual may engage a joiner, electrician or builder to carry out work to his home. In such an instance, the employment of anyone other than the tradesman or builder may not be necessary. At the other end of the scale, major projects, such as the construction of public buildings, motorways, hotels or power stations, can involve a considerable number of parties from different professional and non-professional disciplines. It is therefore crucial to identify, particularly in a large project, the parties involved in that project, the terms of their respective appointments, the scope of each individual's involvement, and their roles within the project. The following parties are commonly involved in building projects:

### 1.3.1 Employer

The term 'employer' is used throughout this book as meaning the party for whose benefit the building works are being carried out. The term 'employer' is adopted for the reason that it is the term generally used in the standard form building contracts and associated documentation. However, other terms are in general use, such as 'the owner', 'the client' or 'the authority'. It is the employer who usually assembles a team to advise him. There is no obligation or requirement upon an employer to do so. The obligations of employers under a building contract are considered below in Chapter 4. Smaller projects often do not require the involvement of anyone other than the employer and the contractor. The nature of the team varies depending upon the nature of the project. The employer's team in a large project may consist of an architect and/or an engineer, a quantity surveyor, one or more specialist consultants and, possibly, a project manager and a clerk of works. The terms of appointment of each member of the team are very important. Each individual is required to have a clear understanding of his obligations and the inter-relationship of those obligations with the other parties involved in the project. If the scope of each individual's obligations is not clearly defined by the employer then difficulties can arise with unnecessary overlap of work or, more importantly, in crucial issues failing to be addressed by any of the members of the team for the reason that each thought that another was responsible for the unaddressed issue. An example of the type of problem that can arise is to be found in the case of *Chesham Properties Ltd* v. *Bucknall Austin Project Management Services Ltd and Others* (1997).

This book will only address the relationship between the employer and the chosen contractor. The relationship and contractual arrangements between the employer and others such as, for example, the architect, engineer and specialist consultants will not be considered in detail.

### 1.3.2 Architect

In traditional contracting, the architect is the individual who usually has overall responsibility for the project from its conception to its conclusion. In order for an architect to become a chartered architect he or she must have completed a seven-year course in the design, specification and erection of buildings. When this has been completed they will appear on the register of the Architects Registration Board (ARB) and can apply for membership of the chartered professional bodies. The architect is the agent of the employer and the general law of Scotland in relation to agency applies to their actions. The scope of their actual authority depends upon the terms of their agreement, or appointment, with their client, the employer.

Chartered architects in Scotland can be members of the Royal Incorporation of Architects in Scotland (RIAS) and/or the Royal Institute of British Architects (RIBA). The RIAS is a charitable organisation founded in 1916 as a professional body for all chartered architects in Scotland. It produces a suite of standard forms of appointment to be used depending on whether it is traditional or design and build method of procurement. The most recent appointments under traditional procurement are SLA/2000 (Jan 2005 revision) and ASP/2005 (Small Project) while a design and build version, DBC/2000 (May 2006 revision), is for use where the architect's client is the building contractor.

### 1.3.3 Quantity surveyor

A quantity surveyor may be engaged by the employer or the architect to discharge specific functions. The functions tend to be of a financial nature and can include, for example, preparing bills of quantities, valuing work done and ascertaining direct loss and expense under the provisions of the building contract. Like architects, chartered surveyors are members of a professional organisation, in this case the Royal Institution of Chartered Surveyors (RICS). The RICS produces sets of documents relating to the appointment of a quantity surveyor. 'Appointing a Quantity Surveyor in Scotland', published in July 1999, includes a 'Form of Enquiry', a 'Schedule of Services', a 'Fee Offer', a 'Form of Agreement' and 'Terms of Appointment'. 'Appointing a Building Surveyor', published in 2001 includes 'Conditions of Engagement', a 'Project Brief Checklist', 'Scopes of Service' and a separate 'Appointment Agreement for Building Surveying Services' for use in Scotland, as well as one for England and Wales.

### 1.3.4 Engineer

In an engineering contract, the engineer normally stands in a similar role to that of the architect under a building contract. The relevant professional organisation is the Institute of Civil Engineers (ICE). The ICE produces a range of publications, some in conjunction with other organisations, including conditions of contract, an adjudication procedure, an appendix to the Scottish Arbitration Code and guidance notes. There are also trade associations. The Association for Consultancy and Engineering (ACE) (formerly the Association of Consulting Engineers) is a trade association for firms of consulting engineers. The ACE is a member of the European Federation of Engineering Consultancy Associations (EFCA) and is affiliated to the International Federation of Consulting Engineers, or Federation Internationale des Ingenieurs-Conseils (FIDIC). The ACE produces publications including guidance notes, standard agreements, conditions of contract and a directory of ACE firms, as well as documents in conjunction with other bodies, including the ICE, EFCA, the Institute of Mechanical Engineers (IMechE) and Institution of Engineering and Technology (IET) (formerly the Institution of Electrical Engineers (IEE). Notable examples are the IMechE, IEE and ACE model forms of general conditions of contract.

The Civil Engineering Contractors Association (CECA) is a trade association for civil engineering contractors. The CECA in Scotland represents over 80 civil engineering contractors ranging in size from small rural contractors to multi-nationals. It too produces a series of publications, including forms of sub-contract, some in conjunction with other organisations.

### 1.3.5 Specialist consultants

In large building projects employers often employ specialist consultants to advise on specific areas, for example, mechanical and electrical works or heating and ventilation works. Architects and engineers may be employed in a specific limited role to advise on an area in which they hold themselves out as specialists.

### 1.3.6 Project manager

Depending upon the size of the building contract and the method of procurement, the employer may decide to engage a project manager. A project manager is a particular feature of a management contract. The project manager's role tends to be organisational but it is important to define his exact relationship with the other members of the team. It should be noted that contractors can employ a person to organise the implementation of the contract and this individual can sometimes also be termed the project manager.

### 1.3.7 Clerk of works

A clerk of works is the individual on site who is generally employed by either the employer or the architect to oversee the execution of the works and to report back to the employer or architect.

### 1.3.8  Contractor

Once an employer has decided upon the nature and extent of the work which they wish carried out (possibly with the assistance of the architect and quantity surveyor), they will usually invite one or more contractors to tender for the work. The term 'contractor' is used throughout this book as representing the individual, firm or company responsible for carrying out the building works for the benefit of the employer. It is adopted for the reason that it is the term most commonly used in the standard form building contracts and associated documentation (although the term 'constructor' is used, for example, in PPC 2000). The obligations of contractors under a building contract are considered below in Chapter 5.

### 1.3.9  Sub-contractors

In practice, elements of the work are often executed not by the main contractor but by sub-contractors or even sub-sub-contractors. These may include 'nominated sub-contractors' (chosen by the employer or his agent according to special contractual rules); 'domestic sub-contractors' (chosen by the main contractor normally with the employer's consent); or 'works contractors' (under a management contract).

The position of sub-contractors under a building contract is considered below in Chapter 11.

In addition to the principal parties referred to above, it must be appreciated that other parties can have a role in a building project such as suppliers, insurers, funders, prospective tenants and purchasers of the building.

### 1.3.10  Experts

Some specialist consultants may be considered experts in their field. The use of expert witnesses in complex construction disputes is not unusual. An expert should act objectively and independently to avoid being viewed as no more than a hired gun. The expert witness or, to give him his proper title under Scots law, the 'skilled witness', is a person who through practice or study, or both, is specially qualified in a recognised branch of knowledge.

The duties and responsibilities of experts in civil cases in England were set out in detail by Mr Justice Cresswell in *National Justice Compania Naviera SA* v. *Prudential Assurance Co. Ltd ('The Ikarian Reefer') (No.1)* (1993). The duties and responsibilities of expert witnesses in civil cases include the following:

- Expert evidence presented to the court should be, and should be seen to be, the independent product of the expert uninfluenced as to form or content by the exigencies of litigation, see *Whitehouse* v. *Jordan* (1981).
- An expert witness should provide independent assistance to the court by way of objective, unbiased opinion in relation to matters within his expertise, see *Polivitte Ltd* v. *Commercial Union Assurance Co. Plc* (1987) and *Re J (Child Abuse: Expert Guidance)* (1991). An expert witness should never assume the role of an advocate.
- An expert witness should state the facts or assumption upon which his opinion is based. He should not omit to consider material facts which could detract from his concluded opinion, see *Re J* (1991).
- An expert witness should make it clear when a particular question or issue falls outside his expertise.
- If an expert's opinion is not properly researched because he considers that insufficient data is available, this must be stated with an indication that the opinion is no more than a provisional one, see *Re J* (1991). In cases where an expert witness who has prepared a report could not assert that the report contained the truth, the whole truth and nothing but the truth without some qualification, that qualification should be stated in the report, see *Derby & Co. Ltd and Others* v. *Weldon and Others (No. 9)* (1990).
- If, after exchange of reports, an expert witness changes his view on a material matter having read the other side's expert's report or for any other reason, such change of view should be communicated (through legal representatives) to the other side without delay and when appropriate to the court.
- Where expert evidence refers to photographs, plans, calculations, analyses, measurements, survey reports or other similar documents, these must be provided to the opposite party at the same time as the exchange of reports.

These principles were subsequently approved by the Court of Appeal in *Stanton* v. *Callaghan* (2000). In England guidelines in respect of expert witnesses are now embodied in Part 35 of the Civil Procedure Rules and the relative Practice Direction.

In Scotland, there are presently no court rules in relation to the conduct of expert witnesses. The principles set out in the *National Justice Compania Naviera SA* case have been referred to by the Scottish courts, with approval, in *Elf Caledonia Ltd* v. *London Bridge Engineering Ltd and Others* (1997) (one of the cases arising from The Piper Alpha disaster). Lord Caplan described the formulation of an expert's duties in *National Justice Compania Naviera SA* as being helpful and correct. Certain observations, consistent with the principles set out in the *National Justice Compania Naviera SA* case, were also made in *McTear* v. *Imperial Tobacco Ltd* (2005). Certain professional bodies, for example, the RICS in Scotland, produce guidance for their members when acting as expert witnesses.

## 1.4 Types of building contract

Once the employer has assembled his team, he needs to enter into a contract for the execution of the works. The contract documents are generally prepared on the advice of the architect and possibly the quantity surveyor. The employer and the other party to the contract, generally the contractor, are free to negotiate and thereafter determine the terms upon which they will contract with each other. This is considered in more detail below in Chapter 3. In practice, the parties seldom have equal negotiating power and one party can often impose its terms upon the other with little, or even no, negotiation.

### 1.4.1 Procurement routes

There are many different types of contractual arrangement which can be entered into. In smaller projects there may only be a quotation by the contractor which is accepted, with or without qualification, by the employer. The quotation may, or may not, have standard terms and conditions attached to it. The parties may negotiate over the incorporation of all, or part of, the standard terms and conditions into their contract. Projects of a larger nature have now become more complex since, in recent years, an increasing number of contractual arrangements have become more common, particularly with regard to the responsibility for design and management of the project. The type of contract will to a large extent depend on the employer's key priorities, and the particular circumstances of the proposed project, such as speed, certainty of cost, and status of design.

Under traditional procurement the design process remains separate from the construction process. The contractor usually has no design responsibility and its obligations are limited to the execution of the works and the provision of materials to a design provided by the employer unless it is contracted to design a specific part of the works, known as a Contractor's Designed Portion. The contract is usually administered by the employer's professional team.

Nowadays, a more common type of procurement route in major projects is design and build in which the contractor undertakes both the design and the construction of the works in return for a lump sum price. The contractor usually appoints his own design team although often their appointments will initially have been made with the employer and then novated to the contractor.

The third main type of procurement route is 'management' which can be one of, or a combination of, management contracting, construction management and 'design and manage'. Under management contracting, the overall design of the works is the responsibility of the employer's design team. The employer appoints a management contractor who is responsible for managing the carrying out of the works by works contractors appointed by the management contractor under a number of works contracts for the various packages comprised in the works. The management contractor manages the overall process. Normally the management contracting route is used to allow a contract to be let where design is at an early stage so that design and construction can proceed in parallel along with the procurement of the works packages as and when appropriate in accordance with the programme. This normally means a loss of cost certainty for the employer, even although the works packages will be procured competitively. Under construction management, the employer appoints a design team and a construction manager. Unlike a management contractor, a construction manager does not appoint the contractors who actually carry out the works; instead those contractors (known as trade contractors) are appointed by the employer. The management of the construction process is performed by the construction manager on the employer's behalf. Under 'design and manage' procurement, the management contractor is not only responsible for managing the works packages but also for the design team.

### 1.4.2 Lump sum contracts

A lump sum contract is a contract in which the contractor agrees with the employer to carry out the building works for a pre-agreed price. The price is only subject to adjustment in certain limited circumstances such as variations and fluctuations in costs. The characteristics of a lump sum contract can apply to both design and build and traditional contracts. A contract using bills of quantities will be a lump sum contract if the bills are fully measured at the time the contract is entered into.

### 1.4.3 Measurement contracts

In this type of contract the sum which the employer pays the contractor is determined by measuring the work done on completion of the project and by applying quantities to agreed rates or some other form of valuation. An example is a contract based on bills of approximate quantities, where the bills of quantities cannot be accurately measured in advance of the contract being entered into.

### 1.4.4 Cost reimbursement and prime cost contracts

There are different types of such contracts such as cost contracts, cost plus contracts and prime cost contracts but the common feature of these types of contract is that the sum which the employer pays the contractor is not a pre-agreed sum but a sum calculated by reference to the actual cost of the works carried out, generally with the addition of an amount to cover profit and a management fee. This may be a predetermined percentage of the costs, a predetermined fixed fee or a variable fee calculated according to a predetermined formula.


### 1.4.5  Turnkey contracts

This term is sometimes used in the context of design and build contracts. The contractor may undertake to provide a building ready for use, perhaps taking responsibility not only for the construction of the building but also for the procurement of the site and possibly even furnishing the building. It has been suggested that the term is intended to indicate that on completion of the project the key can be turned and the building will be ready for use. The phrase can also be used to refer to specific contract conditions. The European International Contractors (EIC) published the EIC Turnkey Contract in May 1994. FIDIC has also published turnkey contracts, beginning in 1995 with its 'Orange Book' entitled *Conditions of Contract for Design-Build and Turnkey*. This was replaced in 1999 by the 'Yellow Book' and the 'Silver Book'.


### 1.4.6  Two-stage tendering

This method of procurement is becoming more prevalent and its key characteristic is to involve the contractor at an early stage before completion of the design and before fully priced tenders have been obtained. The intention is to allow the contractor to collaborate with the employer and their consultants in the design and procurement process. This procurement method is normally only used with design and build contracts. The first stage tender is based on an outline design by the employer's professional team and the competitive element relates to the amount of preliminaries, the overhead and profit percentage and the pre-contract fee. Normally, the preferred bidder will enter into a pre-contract agreement to include the development of design and procurement of sub-contract packages. Ideally the tenderers should be committed to the amount of the tendered preliminaries etc. and the work packages are then procured competitively and transparently so that there is no scope for negotiation. The risk for the employer is that the outstanding matters cannot be agreed during the second stage with the result that the process must be commenced from scratch. The two-stage tendering process may be combined with a form of guaranteed maximum price ('GMP'), where the Contractor bids the GMP and takes the risk of the total amount of work packages subsequently exceeding that GMP. While two-stage tendering is often used in public sector contracts, care needs to be taken to follow the EU public procurement rules, particularly if the restricted procedure applies, as the contracting authority cannot allow the second stage to develop into a negotiation. This would clearly infringe the requirements of the restricted procedure. Procurement is considered below in Chapter 2.

### 1.4.7 Joint ventures

This type of arrangement is now a very common method of procurement. A special purpose company or partnership is created by two or more parties (often a land owner and a developer) each contributing their respective assets, funds and/or skills with a view to procuring a construction project. The joint venture company/partnership will become the employer for the purposes of the building contract.

### 1.4.8 Partnering

Over the last few years there has been a perceived desire within the construction industry to move away from a confrontational and adversarial culture to a collaboration culture, with the objective to create common goals between parties to the project and an understanding of each party's expectations and values. This is largely a product of two ground-breaking reports of the 1990s, 'Constructing the Team' by Sir Michael Latham in 1993, and 'Rethinking Construction' by a committee chaired by Sir John Egan in 1998. This has in turn led to a movement towards partnering contracts. Generally speaking, partnering aims to foster a sense of commitment to a project, to emphasise mutual goals and objectives, and to promote equity, trust, co-operation and fair dealing. The supposed consequential benefits of partnering include savings in time and cost, improved quality and fewer defects, and reduced risk of disputes. It is probably fair to say that partnering was initially regarded with some scepticism due to the arguably vague targets often included in partnering 'charters' and the somewhat aspirational wording used in these charters, which in most cases were non-binding. However, since the introduction in September 2000 of the ACA Standard Form of Contract for Project Partnering ('PPC 2000'), which was the first standard form of project partnering contract, the tendency has been for partnering concepts to be incorporated as part of the contract itself rather than as a procedural overlay (as in the case of a partnering charter). A Scottish supplement has been published to accompany PPC 2000 and PPC 2000 was itself revised in 2003. The key features of PPC 2000 are as follows:

- PPC 2000 is a multi-party contract; not only do the client and the contractor enter into the contract, but also the client's representative and any consultants appointed by the client, and possibly certain specialists (who are sub-contractors appointed by the contractor).
- PPC 2000 contains various processes covering the period prior to construction on site, and assumes a selection of the contractor on the basis of

quality rather than a lump sum price. Indeed the parties are obliged to work together to arrive at an agreed maximum price, rather than a lump sum price being fixed at the very outset.

- PPC 2000 provides for the supply chain to be finalised, so far as possible, on an open book basis, encouraging partnering relationships with the specialist appointed by the contractor. Those specialists may themselves become full members of the partnering team, in which case they execute a joining agreement.
- The contractor is obliged to submit a business case to the client in respect of those parts of the work that it wishes to undertake directly by package or by the appointment of a specialist.
- PPC 2000 provides for a core group to be established, comprising key individuals representing partnering team members, who undertake regular previews of progress and performance and make decisions on certain matters.

Other standard form partnering contracts include:

- TPC 2005 (published by ACA and similar to PPC 2000, but for use with term contracts);
- Public Sector Partnering Contract ('PSPC') promoted by 'Perform 21';
- ECC Secondary Option Clause X12 : Partnering;
- JCT Constructing Excellence Contract 2006.

### 1.4.9  NEC Engineering & Construction Contract

The NEC family of documents has become increasingly popular and is no longer considered the 'new engineering contract'. The NEC Engineering and Construction Contract can be used for a wide range of different procurement routes and comprises nine Core clauses, with six Main Option clauses, two Dispute Resolution clauses and eighteen Secondary Options clauses. The main options are as follows:

- Option A: Priced Contract with Activity Schedule;
- Option B: Priced Contract with Bills of Quantities;
- Option C: Target Contract with Activity Schedule;
- Option D: Target Contract with Bills of Quantities;
- Option E: Cost Reimbursable Contract;
- Option F: Management Contract.

### 1.4.10  Other forms

In addition to the foregoing, a number of other bodies within the construction industry produce their own standard forms of contracts and associated documentation. For example, the Institution of Civil Engineers has for many years published forms of contract for used in civil engineering works, while the 'GC/Works' family of contracts remains widely used by the public sector. An examination of these is beyond the scope of this book but such documentation may well be appropriate depending upon the nature of the project in question. In any event, before using any standard form users should ensure that it meets the employer's needs and is properly integrated with the other documents forming the contract.

### 1.4.11 PFI and PPP

Although the Private Finance Initiative and Public Private Partnerships are beyond the scope of this book, it must be recognised that there has been a rapid growth in this method of procurement of public sector building and infrastructure works since the mid-1990s. The construction contracts forming part of the package of project documents are normally bespoke contracts, the form and terms of which are largely dictated by a pass-through of the obligations under the overarching project agreement. The funding and risk transfer features of such projects, coupled with the construction/operational interface, have lead to the development of practices and principles peculiar to the construction contracts used in these projects. As a result such contracts need to be regarded as a quite distinct category of construction contract.

## 1.5 SBCC forms of building contract

In Scotland many building contracts are entered into on the Scottish Building Contract Committee (SBCC) standard forms. The constituent of bodies of SBCC are currently the Association of Consultancy and Engineering, the Association of Scottish Chambers of Commerce, the Convention of Scottish Local Authorities, the National Specialist Contractors Council – Scottish Committee, the Royal Incorporation of Architects in Scotland, the Royal Institution of Chartered Surveyors in Scotland, Scottish Building, Scottish Casec, the Scottish Executive – Building Division and The Law Society of Scotland.

The SBCC has produced standard forms since 1964. Over the years, the number of standard forms has increased and numerous revisions and amendments have been issued. These can make it difficult to identify the precise terms upon which parties have contracted. Matters are often further complicated by the attempts of employers and contractors to modify the provisions of the standard form contracts which can result in unforeseen consequences for both the employer and the contractor.

JCT carries out, from time to time, a revision of its Standard Conditions. It carried out a major revision to the main standard forms in 1980 ('JCT 80'), followed by numerous Amendments. The form was then reprinted as a

1998 edition ('JCT 98'), again followed by various Amendments. 2005 saw the launch of new editions of practically every JCT contract. This has been the most comprehensive revision of the whole suite of JCT contracts for many years.

The overhaul of the JCT contracts in 2005 was in response to calls for change following market research. The JCT found that the industry expressed a preference for integrated documents for use rather than core documents with a series of supplements. There was uncertainty of what form to use and what supplement was appropriate with each form.

The JCT's aim was to present contracts in a user friendly way. It achieves that by producing stand-alone contracts without the use of supplements. Each contract contains information about the circumstances in which it is suitable for use and many have their own Guides containing additional explanatory information.

The structure of the contracts has been substantially overhauled with clauses being grouped into sections such as 'Payment' and 'Control of the Works', renumbered and the wording substantially revised in line with an aim to use plainer, non-legalistic language.

Many clauses have been shortened and simplified, sometimes by defining terms which tend to require long explanation (such as 'Interest' and 'Insolvency') and sometimes by incorporation by reference of statutory provisions (such as the CDM Regulations and VAT legislation) or procedural rules (such as the adjudication provisions in the Scheme for Construction Contracts and arbitration rules).

Articles and Contract Particulars are all located at the front of the contract so that all project specific sections which require to be filled in are grouped together. A number of default provisions are contained so that if the particulars are not properly completed, this does not leave a gap but the default situation is automatically applied.

Certain provisions have been deleted – Nominated Sub-Contractors and Suppliers, Performance Specified Work, Contractors Price Statement and Insurance for Employer's Loss of Liquidated Damages no longer appear in the standard form. There are optional provisions to be chosen as required, such as sectional completion and Contractor's Designed Portion. These are provided for within the wording of the standard form without the need for separate supplements to be read into the main contract form.

The position in Scotland is that the SBCC are producing Scottish versions of the majority of the JCT forms. These are no longer published as Scottish Supplements to be read into the JCT form, but as stand-alone contract documents. The changes between the JCT and SBCC versions are only those required to bring the JCT contracts in line with Scots law and procedure. All section and clause numbering is common as between equivalent JCT and SBCC contract forms.

The principal areas of difference as between JCT and SBCC are the third party rights and the arbitration provisions.

Third party rights relates to the ability to confer benefits on a person who is not party to the contract and would typically be used in a construction context where collateral warranties would otherwise be required. In England this is governed by the Contracts (Rights of Third Parties) Act 1999. This Act does not apply in Scotland. In Scotland the equivalent is the *jus quaesitum tertio*, a common law right. The contract contains provisions to make an election as to whether warranties are to be provided or whether this will be dealt with by way of third party rights.

In relation to arbitration, the difference between JCT and SBCC relates to the procedural rules incorporated.

There is a wide variety of SBCC standard forms of contract available and the Standard Building Contract Guide (SBC/G/Scot) identifies the documents published by the SBCC.

New contracts have been added to the suite of standard forms for both the JCT and SBCC including Design and Build, Minor Works with Contractor's Design, Framework Agreement, and Sub-Contract Forms (SBCSub, SBCSub/D, DBSub) covering the situations where there is no design element in the sub-contract, where the main contractor is to design parts of the main contract works and the sub-contractor is to design all or part of the sub-contract works and, for use with the design and build main contract, whether or not the sub-contract works include design by the sub-contractor.

In this book, references to clauses are (unless the text expressly specifies otherwise) to those in the Standard Building Contract With Quantities for use in Scotland, SBC/Q/Scot (revised May 2006). This contract is referred to in this book as 'the SBC'. In view of the growing popularity of design and build as a method of procurement, this book also focuses on the relevant provisions of the Design and Build Contract for use in Scotland, DB/Scot 2005 (revised May 2006), which is referred to for convenience as 'the SBC/DB'. In the sections which consider the relevant provisions of the SBC and the SBC/DB, we use the defined terms set out in those contracts.

# Chapter 2
# Procurement

## 2.1 Introduction

This chapter describes an increasingly important element of law relating to construction, namely the requirements in relation to contracts which require to be awarded, in accordance with the Public Contracts (Scotland) Regulations 2006 (in this chapter, referred to as 'the Regulations'), by public bodies which are subject to those Regulations.

This chapter briefly introduces the European Union's public procurement regime, and explains some features which are significant in relation to construction contracting.

The Regulations implement the public contracts Directive 2004/18/EC in Scotland ('the Directive'). This is known as the Classic Directive. Prior to the coming into force of the Regulations three sets of UK Regulations implemented into UK law corresponding EU Directives in relation to services, supplies and works contracts, namely, the Public Services Contract Regulations 1993, the Public Supply Contract Regulations 1995 and the Public Works Contracts Regulations 1991. The Directive was designed to modernise and update the procedures in relation to the awarding of contracts in the public sector originally established by Directives 92/50/EEC, 93/36/EEC and 93/37/EEC. There are corresponding Regulations for England, Wales and Northern Ireland. This chapter refers to the provisions of the Regulations, unless otherwise indicated.

Procurement by entities operating in the water, energy, transport and postal services sectors has, from 31 January 2006, been subject to Directive 2004/17/EC, which was implemented into Scots law by the Utilities Contracts (Scotland) Regulations 2006. These Regulations apply to relevant procurement contracts entered into by utilities in relation to the activity for which they are a specified utility.

The public procurement legislation referred to above essentially comprises procedural rules founded with economic purpose, to ensure that a level playing field across the EU is put in place for those competing for public sector contracts.

## 2.2 EU public procurement regime and EU economic and legal principles

The founding economic objectives of the European Union include providing for the free movement of labour, capital, goods and services throughout EU member States in a free internal market. Accordingly, barriers to trade such as restrictions on the use of foreign products, quota systems and subsidies to domestic industry, are contrary to EU (and national) law. Various Articles of the Treaty establishing the European Community are relevant to public procurement law, but (i) Article 28 EC prohibits quantitative restrictions on imports and all measures having equivalent effect between member States (the free movement of goods), (ii) Article 43 EC prohibits restrictions on freedom to provide services within the Community in respect of nationals of member States (the right of establishment), and (iii) Article 12 EC prohibits discrimination on grounds of nationality. In addition, and depending on how it is conducted, the award by government bodies of contracts to third parties, or 'public procurement', may also act as a barrier to trade by hindering equal market access and fair competition between all EU undertakings to such contracting opportunities.

In response, EU legislation has been introduced to co-ordinate and converge the public procurement procedures in EU countries. Consistent with their origins in the Treaty establishing the European Community, the primary objectives of these rules are economic, to create circumstances where economic operators may compete for public contracts on a level playing field in economic terms. Corresponding economic principles predict the benefits of these circumstances; they dictate that the number of market participants competing for such contracts should thereby increase, so creating competitive tension during public procurement competitions and causing bidders to reduce prices and increase the quality of their proposals.

A complex framework of legislation governing public procurement has been enacted to achieve these economic aims. In addition, the case law of the European Court of Justice has established legally binding principles relevant to public procurement, the most important of which are prescribed by regulation 4 of the Regulations, which requires (when those Regulations apply) that a contracting authority (i) must not treat a person who is not a national of a relevant State and established in a relevant State more favourably than one who is; (ii) must treat economic operators equally and without discrimination; and (iii) must act in a transparent and proportionate manner. Each of these principles merits some further comment:

### 2.2.1 Transparency

Contracting authorities must ensure that information on procurement opportunities and on relevant rules, policy and practice is made available to all interested parties, notably potential works contractors, suppliers and service providers. These interested parties have extensive rights of access to such information and, according to the European Court of Justice, a company which is closely involved in the tendering procedure (including the successful tenderer) must receive, without delay, precise information concerning the conduct of the entire procedure, see *Embassy Limousines & Services* v. *European Parliament* (1998).

### 2.2.2 Non-discrimination

Contracting authorities must not discriminate against contractors or providers from other EU countries compared to domestic undertakings, and must not discriminate between domestic and imported products or services. Contracting authorities should not impose conditions on non-domestic bidders which are different to or more demanding than conditions imposed on domestic bidders. In relation to conditions of tendering, the European Court of Justice has declared that observance of the principle of equal treatment of tenderers requires that all the tenders comply with the tender conditions so as to ensure an objective comparison of the tenders submitted by the various tenderers, see *European Commission* v. *Kingdom of Denmark* (1993).

### 2.2.3 Equality

Contracting authorities may not impose conditions on some bidders and not on others unless (exceptionally) there is reasonable justification for such treatment. All enquiries and requests for information or other assistance must be treated fairly and equally.

### 2.2.4 Mutual recognition

Contracting authorities must accept technical specifications, diplomas and qualifications if supplied by undertakings from other EU countries when they are generally recognised as being equivalent to those required or recognised in the UK, see regulation 9(15) of the Regulations.

### 2.2.5 Proportionality

This principle requires that a contracting authority's definition of performance and technical specifications is necessary and appropriate in relation to the objectives to be reached by the awarding body, i.e. that contracting authorities do not apply excessive and disproportionate technical, professional or financial conditions when selecting candidates for a procurement.

It is important to note that the Regulations implement the Directive into Scots law and must be interpreted purposively in accordance with that Directive and other applicable EU legislation and case law, notably the EU legal principles referred to above, see *Von Colson* v. *Land Nordrhein-Westfalen* (1984) and *Marleasing SA* v. *La Comercial Internacional de Alimentacion SA* (1990). This, in turn, means that even if the terms of the Regulations are clear, they may need to be interpreted not strictly in accordance with that clear meaning. It is possible that a court applying a purposive interpretation of the Regulations may re-write all or part of them, changing their meaning and the implications, to an extent consistent with the purposes of the relevant EU rules.

The legal principles outlined above are also important from the contracting authority's perspective, because complying with them will allow it to create strong competitive conditions.

## 2.3 Beyond the EU

The EU public procurement regime does not only offer protection to nationals (including legal and natural persons) of EU member States, in respect of contracts being awarded by EU public bodies. By virtue of certain international agreements, there are also some protections for EU nationals in tendering for contracts outside the EU, and for non-EU nationals tendering within the EU.

Firstly, the European Economic Area Agreement ('the EEA Agreement') is intended to promote trade between the European Free Trade Association ('EFTA') and the EU, and application of the EU public procurement procedures is extended to three EFTA member States (Iceland, Liechtenstein and Norway). The EEA Agreement establishes public procurement principles and procedures in these EFTA States which are similar to the EU public procurement position. Application of the EEA Agreement by these EFTA States is monitored by the EFTA Surveillance Authority and the EFTA Court. The European Commission and the European Court of Justice ('ECJ') monitor application within the EU.

Secondly, the EU and EU member States entered into a number of 'Europe Agreements' with certain States of Central and Eastern Europe, many of who have since become EU member States. These agreements provide for access by undertakings of the relevant State to Community contracts on terms not less favourable than those applied to EU nationals.

Thirdly, the Government Procurement Agreement ('GPA'), which forms part of the World Trade Organisation Agreement, has coverage in parallel with the EU procurement provisions. As well as giving rights to EU-based tenderers, it applies to contracting authorities in GPA States outside the EU, thereby affording EU and non-EU tenderers protections outside the EU as well as within.

The GPA largely conforms to the same principles as the EU procurement regime and signatories undertake to treat each other on the basis of mutual reciprocity and provide guaranteed market access to specified listed areas. Similarly to the EU procurement regime, the GPA is designed to make laws, regulations, procedures and practices relating to government procurement more transparent and to guard against discrimination against foreign products or suppliers. As with the EU public procurement regime, the GPA imposes deadlines, prohibits the splitting of contracts and establishes detailed rules on the content of tender documentation and the contract award process. The post-award information and publication requirements in the GPA require suppliers from GPA States to receive prompt information on contracting authorities' procurement practices, an explanation of why the supplier's application to qualify was rejected, why its existing qualification to tender was brought to an end, and information on the characteristics and relevant advantages of the tender selected, see Article XVIII of the GPA. The GPA requires States bound by the GPA to provide aggrieved parties with effective procedures to challenge alleged breaches of the GPA, either in the courts or to an impartial and independent review body, see Articles XX and XXII of the GPA. Disputes between GPA Parties are subject to the procedures of the WTO Understanding on Rules and Procedures Governing the Settlement of Disputes. They constitute separate requirements, but the similarities between the EU and GPA procedures are such that by complying with the Directive and the Regulations, a contracting authority should also be in compliance with the GPA.

## 2.4 Conditions for application of the procurement rules

The Regulations only apply to the procurement and award of contracts if certain pre-conditions are met. In summary, these pre-conditions are as follows:

- that the body awarding the contract is a contracting authority;
- that the object of the contract falls within the scope of 'works', 'services' or 'supplies' as defined in the Regulations;
- that the value of the works, services or supplies under the proposed contract is in excess of the relevant financial threshold set out in the Regulations (although regard should be had to section 2.17 below in relation to the advertising of lower-value contracts).

## 2.5 Who must comply with the Regulations?

A body is required to follow procedures under the Regulations for the award of relevant contracts if it falls within the definition of contracting authority in regulation 3 of the Regulations. Regulation 3 lists a number of central and local government bodies, and a wider category of what are known as bodies governed by public law, being a corporation established, or a group of individuals appointed to act together, for the specific purposes of meeting needs in the general interest, not having an industrial or commercial character, and

- financed wholly or mainly by another contracting authority, or
- subject to management supervision by another contracting authority, or
- more than half of the board of directors or members of which, or, in the case of a group of individuals, more than half of those individuals, are appointed by another contracting authority.

There is considerable case law in relation to the various elements of this definition. In *Mannesmann Anlagenbau Austria AG* v. *Strohal Rotationsdruck GmbH* (1998), the ECJ held that the body in question had to have been established to meet needs in the general interest not having an industrial or commercial character and the fact that it also carried out other, commercial, activities was irrelevant, but see also *Universale-Bau AG* v. *Entsorgungsbetriebe Simmering GesmbH* (2002), *Adolf Truly GmbH* v. *Bestattung Wien GmbH* (2003) and *Arkkitehtuuritoimisto Riitta Korhonen Oy* v. *Varkauden Taitotalo Oy* (2003).

The requirement of being financed wholly or mainly by another contracting authority was clarified in *R* v. *HM Treasury, ex parte University of Cambridge* (2000). The expression 'for the most part' has its ordinary meaning of 'more than half', and that the decision as to whether a university is a contracting authority should be made annually, with the budgetary year during which the procurement procedure was begun being the most appropriate period for calculating how it was financed.

It may be clear that certain purchasing bodies constitute contracting authorities for the purposes of the Regulations, but for other bodies the procurement position may need to be considered more closely. In a construction and major projects context, care may need to be taken, for example where a joint venture includes a public sector party, to ensure that where the joint venture body does fall within regulation 3(1)(aa) of the Regulations, it complies with the Regulations in awarding relevant contracts.

## 2.6 Treatment of a proposed contract as a works contract, supply contract or a services contract

The original EU public procurement legislation, which was consolidated into the Directive, comprised separate Directives in respect of works contracts, supply contracts and services contracts. Accordingly, central to the scope of application of each of these Directives, and also the UK implementing Regulations, were the definitions of a public works contract, a public supply contract and a public services contract. In addition there are specific rules in relation to the treatment of contracts for a combination of works, supplies and/or services (mixed contracts).

### 2.6.1  What is a works contract?

A contract will be a works contract to be awarded under the Regulations if it is a 'public works contract', defined by regulation 2(1) of the Regulations as a contract, in writing, for consideration (whatever the nature of the consideration):

- for the carrying out of a work or works for a contracting authority, or
- under which a contracting authority engages a person to procure by any means the carrying out for the contracting authority of a work corresponding to specified requirements.

A subsidised public works contract is one for which a contracting authority undertakes to contribute more than half of the consideration to be, or expected to be, paid under a contract, but which has been or is to be entered into by another person (the subsidised body), see Regulation 34(1) of the Regulations. Depending on the subject matter, there is a requirement on the contracting authority to impose a condition of making such a contribution that the subsidised body complies with the Regulations in relation to that contract as if it were a contracting authority itself, and either to ensure that the subsidised body does so comply or to recover the contribution, see regulation 34(2) of the Regulations. This requirement applies to public works contracts for any of the civil engineering activities specified in Schedule 2 to the Regulations, and to building work for hospitals, facilities intended for sports, recreation and leisure, school and university buildings or buildings for administrative purposes, see regulation 34(2)(a) of the Regulations. It also applies to public services contracts covered by the Regulations for providing services in connection with such subsidised public works contracts, see regulation 34(2)(b) of the Regulations.

### 2.6.2  What are works?

Works are defined under the Works Regulations as any activities specified in Schedule 2 to the Regulations. This long list specifies works on a broad basis and includes:

- Construction of new buildings and works and restoring and common repairs;
- Site preparation (demolition and wrecking of buildings, earth moving and site clearing, building site drainage and drainage of agricultural or forestry land);

- Test drilling, boring and core sampling for construction, geophysical, geological or similar purposes;
- General construction of buildings and civil engineering works (including bridges, pipelines, power lines and assembly and erection of prefabricated constructions on site);
- Construction of highways, roads, airfields, sports facilities and water projects;
- Other construction work involving special trades (pile driving, water well drilling and construction, shaft sinking, steel bending, bricklaying and stone setting, scaffold erecting and dismantling, including renting of scaffolds);
- Installation of electrical wiring and fittings (including telecommunications and electrical heating systems, residential antennas and aerials, fire alarms, burglar alarm systems, lifts and escalators);
- Insulation work activities (thermal, sound or vibration);
- Plumbing (installation of plumbing and sanitary equipment, gas fittings, heating, ventilation, refrigeration or air-conditioning equipment and sprinkler systems);
- Other building installation (illumination and signalling systems for roads, railways, airports and harbours);
- Building completion (plastering, joinery installation, floor and wall covering, painting and glazing); and
- Renting of construction or demolition equipment with operator.

### 2.6.3 What is a supply contract?

A contract will be a supply contract to be awarded under the Regulations if it is a 'public supply contract', defined by regulation 2(1) of the Regulations, as a contract, in writing, for consideration (whatever the nature of the consideration):

- for the purchase of goods (whether or not the consideration is given in instalments and whether or not the purchase is conditional upon the occurrence of a particular event); or
- for the hire of goods by a contracting authority (both where the contracting authority becomes the owner of the goods after the end of the period of hire and where it does not);

and for any siting or installation of those goods.

In relation to a contract which has both supply and services elements, that contract shall only be a public supply contract where the value of the consideration attributable to the goods and any siting or installation of the goods is equal to or greater than the value attributable to the services, see Definition of 'public supply contract' in regulation 2(1) of the Regulations.

### 2.6.4 What is a services contract?

A contract will be a services contract to be awarded under the Regulations if it is a 'public services contract', defined as a contract, in writing, for consideration (whatever the nature of the consideration) under which a contracting authority engages a person to provide services but does not include a public works contract or a public supply contract. The definition of 'public services contract' is to be found in regulation 2(1) of the Regulations.

### 2.6.5 Mixed Contracts

The Regulations address the possibility of contracts being for mixed requirements. Thus a contract both for supply of goods and of services shall be considered to be a public services contract if the value attributable to those services exceeds that of the goods covered by the contract.

A contract for services which includes works elements (i.e. activities specified in Schedule 2 to the Regulations) that are only incidental to the principal object of the contract shall be considered to be a public services contract. This is similar to the test developed by the ECJ in its judgments on certain public procurement cases under the preceding Directives, see *Telaustria Verlags GmbH* v. *Telecom Austria AG (2000)*, and *Gestion Hotelera Internacional SA* v. *Comunidad Autonama de Canarias* (1994).

### 2.6.6 Part A and Part B Services

The procedures which must be followed under the Regulations differ according to whether a contract for Part A Services or Part B Services is to be awarded. In terms of the Regulations, a Part A services contract is a contract under which services under Part A of Schedule 3 are to be provided. Similarly, a Part B services contract is a contract under which services specified in Part B of Schedule 3 are to be provided. The full procedures apply in respect of Part A Services (commonly referred to as 'priority' services) but do not apply to Part B Services (commonly referred to as 'residual' services). Each of these two categories contains a number of different types of services; for example, legal services are a Part B (residual) service.

A single contract for services specified in both Parts A and B of Schedule 3 to the Regulations is required to be treated as

- a Part A services contract if the value of the consideration attributable to the services specified in Part A is greater than that attributable to those specified in Part B; and
- a Part B services contract if the value of the consideration attributable to the services specified in Part B is equal to or greater than that attributable to those specified in Part A.

## 2.7 *What are the relevant financial thresholds?*

The Regulations only require to be followed by contracting authorities for certain contracts whose estimated value (net of VAT) exceeds a particular threshold amount, see Regulation 8(1) of the Regulations.

In respect of the award of public works contracts and subsidised public works contracts, the Regulations apply to contracts to be awarded by a contracting authority which have an estimated value which is expected to exceed a threshold currently of £3,611,319 (€5,278,000), see regulation 8(2) of the Regulations.

For public supply contracts or public services contracts a distinction must be made between two categories of public sector bodies, see regulation 8(3) and regulation 8(4) of the Regulations. Schedule 1 to the Regulations lists central government bodies which are subject to the World Trade Organisation Government Procurement Agreement. The Regulations apply to contracts to be awarded by these bodies with an estimated value which is expected to exceed a threshold currently of £93,738 (€137,000) in relation to public supply contracts or public services contracts, with the exception of Part B (residual) services, Research & Development Services, certain Telecommunications services in Category 5 and subsidised services contracts. These have a threshold currently of £144,371 (€211,000). A higher threshold applies in respect of other public sector contracting authorities; the Regulations apply where public supply contracts and public services contracts are to be awarded by a contracting authority which is not listed in Schedule 1 to those Regulations, if the estimated value is expected to exceed currently £144,371 (€211,000).

The estimated value of a public contract shall be the value of the total consideration payable, net of value added tax, which the contracting authority expects to be payable under the contract, and any form of option, renewal of the contract, fees or commissions which are to be included in the calculation, see regulation 8(7) and regulation 8(8) of the Regulations.

A specific aggregation rule requires a contracting authority which has a single requirement for goods, services or works and enters (or proposes to enter) into a number of contracts, to aggregate for the purposes of regulation 8(1) the consideration expected to be payable under each of those contracts, see regulation 8(11) of the Regulations.

Regulation 8 of the Regulations contains a number of other relevant considerations and requirements in relation to contract value thresholds, but importantly provides that a contracting authority shall not enter into separate contracts nor exercise a choice under a valuation method with the intention of avoiding the application of the Regulations, see regulation 8(19).

## 2.8 *Is there an applicable exclusion?*

The Regulations do not apply to the seeking of offers in relation to a proposed public contract, framework agreement or dynamic purchasing system where the contracting authority is a utility within the meaning of the Utilities Contracts (Scotland) Regulations 2006, nor to other contracts which meet certain other conditions, see regulation 6(1) of the Regulations. Regulation 6(2) contains certain other exemptions, for contracts:

- in relation to telecommunications;
- which are secret or require special security measures;
- for the acquisition of land, including existing buildings, land covered with water and any estate, interest, easement, servitude or right in or over land;
- in relation to broadcasting;
- for arbitration or conciliation services;
- for certain financial services;
- for central banking services;
- for research and development services (unless certain conditions are fulfilled);
- under which services are to be provided by a contracting authority because that contracting authority or person has an exclusive right to provide the services; or which is necessary for the provision of the services; and
- for a services concession, subject to regulation 46 which provides a duty of non-discrimination in certain circumstances.

## 2.9  Types of procurement procedure

The Regulations provide for four main types of competitive procedure which a contracting authority may follow. Three of these, the open procedure, the restricted procedure, and the competitive negotiated procedure, were established in Directives 92/50/EEC, 93/36/EEC and 93/37/EEC. The fourth procedure, the competitive dialogue procedure, was introduced by the Directive.

The detailed rules applying to each of these procedures differ. The competitive dialogue and competitive negotiated procedures may only be used in specified limited circumstances. A contracting authority should carefully consider which procedure is appropriate and document its reasons for the decision it takes in this regard.

## 2.10  The open procedure

The stages of the open procedure (in which all interested parties may submit proposals), are set out in regulation 15 of the Regulations and in summary are set out below:

### Step 1: Advertising

The contracting authority must send to the Official Journal a contract notice submission in prescribed form under regulation 15(2). The contracting authority must send this as soon as possible after forming the intention to seek offers, and must use the form of the contract notice in Annex II to Commission Regulation (EC) No. 1564/2005, colloquially known as an OJEU Notice (OJEU being *The Official Journal of the European Union*). This advertises the contracting authority's requirement and gives interested potential bidders details of how to obtain further information. In completing a contract notice submission, the contracting authority is required to provide a range of information about its contract requirements and about the procedure being conducted. Although there is no pre-qualification stage under the open procedure, the contracting authority may require an economic operator to satisfy minimum levels of economic and financial standing and/or technical or professional ability if they are specified in the contract notice and are related and proportionate to the subject matter of the contract, see regulation 15(12).

**Step 2: Tender period**

A period of not less than 52 days (the tender period) must be allowed to enable interested parties to prepare and submit tenders, although that time limit can be reduced further if a Prior Information Notice has been issued, if the award notice has been sent electronically and if the contracting authority has given unrestricted and full direct access by electronic means to the contract documents.

Periods for taking action under the Regulations run from the day after the day on which the action is taken, and shall be extended where necessary to include two working days or to end on a working day, see regulation 2(4).

In the open procedure, except for minor clarifications, the contracting authority must choose between tenders as they are bid, although in limited circumstances bidders may be asked to re-tender.

**Step 3: Evaluation**

The contracting authority must evaluate all bids either on the basis of lowest cost or most economically advantageous tender, see regulation 30(1).

**Step 4: Contract award**

Following evaluation, a contracting authority may decide to award a contract (as described in more detail below in relation to the restricted procedure) and must publish a contract award notice in the Official Journal within 48 days, see regulation 31(1).

## 2.11 The restricted procedure

The stages of a restricted procedure are set out in regulation 16 of the Regulations and include an additional stage, namely the contracting authority making a preliminary assessment of those who express an interest in the procurement, as to whether they should pre-qualify for the tender competition (pre-qualification). In summary the stages in a restricted procedure are as follows:

### Step 1: Advertising

The contracting authority must send to the Official Journal a contract notice application in prescribed form, see under regulation 16(2). The contracting authority must send this as soon as possible after forming the intention to seek offers. As in the open procedure, this advertises the contracting authority's requirement and gives details of how interested parties may obtain further information.

### Step 2: Pre-qualification stage

Interested parties must have (at least) 37 days from the date of dispatch of the contract notice, within which to notify the contracting authority that they wish to be invited to tender, see regulation 16(3) and regulation 16(5). However, that limit can be reduced further if the award notice has been sent electronically or where the minimum time limit is rendered impractical by reason of urgency. See as follows:

- regulation 16(5): where the contract notice is submitted by electronic means in accordance with Annex VIII of the Directive, the time limit may be reduced by seven days;
- regulation 16(6)(a): a time limit of not less than 15 days from dispatch of the OJEU Notice for reasons of urgency;
- regulation 16(6)(b): a time limit of not less than ten days where the contract notice has been submitted by electronic means in accordance with regulation 16(5) and compliance with the minimum time limit of 37 days is rendered impractical for reasons of urgency.

The contracting authority must select tenderers in accordance with regulations 23, 24, 25 and 26 of the Regulations. An economic operator can only be excluded from the group of economic operators from which a contracting authority is to select those to be invited to tender, on the grounds for exclusion set out in regulation 23 (such as on insolvency or conviction of a criminal offence), or if the economic operator fails to satisfy minimum standards of economic and financial standing or technical or professional ability, see regulation 16(7).

The number of persons which the contracting authority can invite to tender must be sufficient to ensure genuine competition and must at least be equal to any minimum number which may have been specified in the contract notice, see regulation 16(10). Where there is a sufficient number of economic operators suitable to be invited to tender, the contracting authority may limit the number which it intends to invite, but the contract notice must have specified the objective and non discriminatory criteria which would be applied in so doing, and must also have specified the minimum number (which shall be not less than five) and (where appropriate) the maximum number of economic operators which the contracting authority intends to invite to tender.

No price or other bidding indications may be asked for at this stage, nor considered if voluntarily provided by an economic operator. The criteria used for the selection of tenderers do not apply to the award of a public contract. In pre-qualification, the contracting authority is selecting tenderers whereas after pre-qualification and during the tender stage it is evaluating tenders. This is an important distinction to maintain during public procurements.

**Step 3: Tender period**

Those selected to tender by the contracting authority will usually be sent a formal invitation to tender (or 'ITT') by the contracting authority which must be accompanied by the contract documents, see regulation 16(13). A period of not less than 40 days (the tender period) must be allowed to enable interested parties to prepare and submit tenders, see regulation 16(16). However that time limit can be reduced further for reasons of urgency, if a Prior Information Notice has been issued and if the contracting authority has given unrestricted and full direct access by electronic means to the contract documents. See as follows:

- regulation 16(17): a time limit of not less than ten days from the date of dispatch of the invitation where the minimum time limit of 40 days is rendered impractical for reasons of urgency;
- regulation 16(18): generally to be not less than 36 days but in any event not less than 22 days, if a prior information notice was submitted to the Official Journal between at least 52 days and no more than 12 months prior to the dispatch of the OJEU Notice;
- regulation 16(19): the time limits may be reduced by five days, provided that the authority offers unrestricted and full direct access to the contract documents by electronic means and the contract notice specifies the internet address at which the contract documents are available.

In the restricted procedure, and in common with the open procedure, the contracting authority must choose between tenders as they are bid, although it is possible to seek clarification of the terms of bidders' proposals, and in certain circumstances bidders may be asked to submit further tenders.

**Step 4: Evaluation**

The contracting authority must evaluate all bids either on the basis of lowest cost or most economically advantageous tender, see regulation 30(1). When using the latter basis of evaluation, the contracting authority must state the weighting which it gives to each of the criteria chosen in the contract notice or in the contract documents, which helps bidders to understand how they might make their proposals as attractive as possible, see regulation 30(3).

**Step 5: Contract award**

Following evaluation a contracting authority may make a contract award decision, and on doing so must then provide bidders and those who applied to be selected to tender, as soon as possible after the contract award decision is made, with relevant information. Section 2.15.2 below describes these requirements in more detail. Subject to those requirements, a contracting authority may proceed to award a contract after evaluating bids, and must publish a contract award notice in the Official Journal within 48 days containing specified details about the contract awarded, the successful contractor and also about the procurement competition, see regulation 31(1).

## 2.12 The negotiated procedure with advertisement

### 2.12.1

A significant feature of the negotiated procedure with advertisement is that it allows a contracting authority to negotiate commercial and pricing proposals and contract terms with bidders, which is not possible under either the open procedure or the restricted procedure.

The negotiated procedure with advertisement is set out in regulation 17 of the Regulations. In summary the stages in a negotiated procedure with advertisement are as follows:

**Step 1: Advertising**

The contracting authority must send to the Official Journal a contract notice submission in prescribed form (see under regulation 17(3) of the Regulations), and the contracting authority must send this as soon as possible after forming the intention to seek offers, and must use the form of the contract notice in Annex II to Commission Regulation (EC) No. 1564/2005. As in the open and restricted procedures, this advertises the contracting authority's requirement and gives details of how interested parties may obtain further information.

### Step 2: Pre-qualification stage

Interested parties must have (at least) 37 days from the date of dispatch of the contract notice within which to notify the contracting authority that they wish to be selected to negotiate, see regulation 17(5). That limit can be reduced further if the award notice had been sent electronically or where the minimum time limit is rendered impractical for reasons of urgency. See as follows:

- regulation 17(5): where the contract notice is submitted by electronic means in accordance with Annex VIII of the Directive the time limit may be reduced by seven days;
- regulation 17(8)(a): a time limit of not less than 15 days from dispatch of the OJEU Notice for reasons of urgency;
- regulation 17(8)(b): a time limit of not less than ten days where the contract notice has been submitted by electronic means in accordance with regulation 17(5) and compliance with the minimum time limit of 37 days is rendered impractical for reasons of urgency.

The contracting authority must select tenderers in accordance with regulations 23, 24, 25 and 26 of the Regulations. An economic operator can only be excluded from the group of economic operators from which a contracting authority selects those to be invited to tender on the grounds for exclusion set out in regulation 23 (such as on insolvency or conviction of a criminal offence), or if the economic operator fails to satisfy minimum standards of economic and financial standing or technical or professional ability, see regulation 17(7).

The number of persons selected to negotiate must be sufficient to ensure genuine competition and must at least be equal to any minimum number which may have been specified in the contract notice, see regulation 17(12). Where there is a sufficient number of economic operators suitable to be selected to negotiate (see regulation 17(11)), the contracting authority may limit the number which it intends to select to negotiate, but the contract notice must have specified (i) the objective and non-discriminatory criteria which would be applied in so doing; (ii) the minimum number, to be not less than three, and (iii) where appropriate, the maximum number of economic operators which the contracting authority intends to invite to negotiate.

In pre-qualification, the contracting authority is selecting parties to negotiate whereas after pre-qualification and during the negotiation tender stage it is evaluating proposals. No price or other bidding indications may be asked for or taken into account at the pre-qualification stage, nor may they be considered if voluntarily provided to the contracting authority, see regulation 17(9). The criteria used for selection of tenderers do not apply to the award of a public contract, see regulation 30(1).

**Step 3: Tender and negotiation period, leading to evaluation and contract award**

Those selected to negotiate by the contracting authority will usually be sent a formal invitation to negotiate (or 'ITN') by the contracting authority which must be accompanied by the contract documents, see regulation 17(15).

Conduct of this phase has a very significant bearing on the outcome of the procurement and, as a minimum, the following key points should be borne in mind in relation to bid preparation and communication during the tender period.

For the contracting authority the priority should be to ensure that all tenderers clearly understand in detail the requirements which it wishes to be met through the contract it proposes to award. Public sector bodies may have multiple policy objectives. For example, a national health service contracting authority may have clinical, financial and health and safety objectives for the same procurement. These may compete in priority terms, or even conflict. In such circumstances, it may not be possible for tenderers fully to understand the contracting authority's requirements unless they are told the relative importance of such competing or conflicting requirements. Economic operators preparing proposals will be particularly concerned to understand how these proposals will be evaluated, hence the important requirements for the contracting authority to provide evaluation criteria and weighting information. It will also be important to the contracting authority to ensure proposals received meet its expectations and requirements. Providing tenderers with clear details in relation to evaluation should assist in this.

The contracting authority must evaluate all bids either on the basis of lowest cost or most economically advantageous tender, see regulation 30(1). In the negotiated procedure, as well as seeking clarification of proposals, the contracting authority is permitted also to negotiate with tenderers. The Regulations provide that, where it needs to identify the best tender in order to award the public contract, the contracting authority is obliged to negotiate with economic operators which have submitted tenders with the aim of adapting the tenders to the requirements specified in the contract documents, see regulation 17(20).

**Step 4: Contract award**

Following evaluation, a contracting authority may decide to award a contract (as described in more detail above in relation to the restricted procedure), and must publish a contract award notice in the Official Journal within 48 days, see regulation 31(1).

### 2.12.2 Restrictions on using the negotiated procedure

The negotiated procedure with advertisement can only be used in specified circumstances, namely: (i) because of irregular or unacceptable tenders pursuant to an open procedure or restricted procedure, but only if the terms of contract used for that earlier procurement are not substantially altered in the negotiated procedure; (ii) exceptionally, when the nature of the work or works to be carried out, the goods to be purchased or the services to be provided or the risks attaching to them, are such as not to permit overall pricing; (iii) for a public services contract, when the nature of services to be provided (in particular intellectual services) is such that specifications cannot be drawn up with sufficient precision to permit award of the contract using the open or restricted procedure; and (iv) for a public works contract, when the nature of services to be provided (in particular intellectual services) is such that specifications cannot be drawn up with sufficient precision to permit the award of the contract using the open or restricted procedure.

The precise conditions in which a contracting authority should regard itself as being permitted to use the negotiated procedure have been under close scrutiny. For complex procurements such as PPP projects, the European Commission developed the competitive dialogue procedure described below in preference to widespread use of the negotiated procedure. Contracting authorities should only use the negotiated procedure where there is clear justification for doing so. Choice of procurement procedure is discussed further in sections 2.13.1 and 2.13.2 below.

## 2.13 *The competitive dialogue procedure*

The new competitive dialogue procedure is intended for use in the award of 'particularly complex' contracts, where there is a need for contracting authorities to discuss their requirements with shortlisted candidates before final written tenders are received. The Recitals to the Directive describe the purpose as providing 'a flexible approach', preserving competition between operators and permitting discussion of 'all aspects' of the contract with each candidate.

The stages of the competitive dialogue procedure are set out in regulation 18 of the Regulations. In summary the stages are as follows:

### Step 1: Advertising

The contracting authority must send to the Official Journal a contract notice submission in the prescribed form, see under regulation 18(4) of the

Regulations. The contracting authority must send this as soon as possible after forming the intention to seek offers, and must use the form of the contract notice in Annex II to Commission Regulation (EC) No. 1564/2005. As in the open, restricted and negotiated procedures, this advertises the contracting authority's requirement and gives details of how interested parties may obtain further information.

### Step 2: Pre-qualification

Interested parties must have (at least) 37 days from the date of dispatch of the contract notice, within which to notify the contracting authority that they wish to be selected to participate, see regulation 18(7). However, that limit can be reduced further if the award notice had been sent electronically, see regulation 18(9).

The contracting authority must select participants for the competitive dialogue in accordance with regulations 23, 24, 25 and 26 of the Regulations. An economic operator can only be excluded from the group of economic operators from which a contracting authority selects those to be invited to tender on the grounds for exclusion set out in regulation 23 (such as on insolvency or conviction of a criminal offence), or if the economic operator fails to satisfy minimum standards of economic and financial standing or technical or professional ability, see regulation 18(10) and regulation 18(11).

The number of persons selected to participate in the dialogue must be sufficient to ensure genuine competition and must at least be equal to any minimum number specified in the contract notice, see regulation 18(13). Where there is a sufficient number of economic operators suitable to be selected to participate in the dialogue (see regulation 18(12)), the contracting authority may limit the number which it intends to invite to participate in the dialogue, but the contract notice must have specified: (i) the objective and non-discriminatory criteria to be applied to limit that number, (ii) the minimum number, to be not less than three, and (iii) where appropriate, the maximum number that the contracting authority intends to invite to participate in the dialogue.

No price or other bidding indications may be asked for or taken into account at this stage, or considered if voluntarily provided, see regulation 18(11). The criteria used for selection of tenderers do not apply to the award of a public services contract, see regulation 30(1).

### Step 3: Dialogue phase

Tenderers participate in competitive dialogue with the contracting authority, in response to an invitation to participate. The contracting authority's required aims during the dialogue are to identify and define how its needs can best be satisfied, in consultation with the participants, see regulation 18(20).

The contracting authority may discuss 'all aspects of the contract', but shall ensure equality of treatment amongst all participants', see regulation 18(21). A concern for participants is that others could acquire and exploit their proprietary ideas, and so proposed solutions or confidential information are not to be divulged to other candidates without consent, see regulation 18(21). The competitive dialogue procedure is to continue until one or more comparable solutions can be identified which are capable of meeting the contracting authority's needs, see regulation 18(24).

The procedure may be conducted in successive stages, permitting stage by stage the reduction of solutions, but enough bidders must remain to ensure genuine competition at tender stage, see regulation 18(23).

**Step 4: Post-dialogue tender stage**

The contracting authority may continue the dialogue until it can identify one or more solutions capable of meeting its needs, if necessary after comparing them, and should formally declare the dialogue concluded, see regulation 18(24) and regulation 18(25). Contracting authorities should consider carefully when this declaration should be made as it marks an important transition during the procedure.

Once the dialogue is concluded the contracting authority invites each participant to submit a final tender on the basis of any solution or solutions presented and specified (not necessarily by that tenderer) during the dialogue, see regulation 18(25). The contracting authority cannot invite fewer than three tenderers to do so, provided a sufficient number of candidates satisfy the qualitative selection criteria.

**Step 5: Evaluation and fine-tuning to award**

Tenders are then evaluated on the basis of the award criteria and the contracting authority shall award the contract to the participant which submits the most economically advantageous tender, see regulation 18(27). Importantly, at this stage there is no further scope for dialogue or negotiation and tenderers can only be asked to clarify, specify or fine-tune their proposals, see regulation 18(26).

**2.13.1 How complex is particularly complex?**

The competitive dialogue procedure is confined to 'particularly complex' contracts, defined as contracts where the contracting authority is not objectively able to:

- define the technical means capable of satisfying its needs or objectives; or
- specify either or both of the legal and financial make-up of a project, see regulation 18(1).

This definition lacks clarity. The first limb refers to an inability to define the 'technical means' for meeting the contracting authority's needs. Although not clearly defined in the Regulations, this may be interpreted as referring to the skills, knowledge, technology or methods capable of realising the contracting authority's overall objectives.

The second limb of the definition of 'particularly complex' is equally unclear. The term 'legal and/or financial make-up' is not defined further although it may refer to difficulties in predetermining the contractual structure and terms (including funding arrangements). In the initial stages of major projects there is likely to be some uncertainty in this regard, but it is not clear to what degree the contracting authority must be unable to specify either the legal or financial make-up of a project in order to justify using the competitive dialogue.

A competitive dialogue is permitted where contracting authorities consider that the use of the open or restricted procedure will not allow award of the contract. This suggests a degree of discretion but a contracting authority would need to establish that it is not 'objectively able' to define or specify the required information. Recital 31 to the Directive describes the circumstances for which competitive dialogue is intended as being when it is objectively impossible to define the means of satisfying the contracting authority's needs, or of assessing what the market can offer in the way of technical solutions and/or financial/legal solutions. Those recitals do state that projects for integrated transport infrastructure or for large computer networks may be regarded as 'particularly complex' and do refer to projects involving 'structured financing', which may include most PPP/PFI projects.

### 2.13.2 Interaction between the competitive dialogue and the open, restricted and negotiated procedures

Dialogue between the contracting authority and bidders to identify and define how the authority's needs can best be satisfied is not part of the open procedure, nor is it part of the restricted procedure. It is pre-supposed, for both of these procedures, that the contracting authority's requirement has been accurately described in advance. In contrast, two existing grounds for using the negotiated procedure assume the contracting authority's requirement is not entirely clear, namely, when:

- exceptionally, the nature of the works or services or the risks attaching to them are such as not to permit overall pricing, see regulation 13(b); or

- for public services contracts, the nature of the services is such that the specification cannot be established with sufficient precision to permit award by open or restricted procedures, see regulation 13(c).

Accordingly there is some overlap between when the competitive dialogue procedure and the existing competitive negotiated procedure can be used. An inability to predetermine technical means (competitive dialogue) is similar to an inability to establish contract specifications with sufficient precision (negotiated procedure), and difficulty in specifying the 'financial make-up' of a project (competitive dialogue) may be a reason why 'prior overall pricing' is not possible (negotiated procedure).

Although the former practice was to use the negotiated procedure where available for complex projects such as PFI or PPP, Office of Government Commerce ('OGC') guidance on the Competitive Dialogue Procedure issued in January 2006 repeats the Commission's view that the 'prior overall pricing' ground is not available for 'ordinary PPPs'. It is therefore to be expected that contracting authorities will use the competitive dialogue procedure for complex procurements.

### 2.13.3 Practical issues in conducting a competitive dialogue

#### Strategies for dialogue

Contracting authorities must not reveal one participant's proposed solution to another participant without consent, see regulation 18(21)(c). That right to confidentiality sits uneasily with the intention through competitive dialogue to encourage innovation towards best solutions. Participants may take different approaches to the dialogue, including on how early and in how much detail to share their proposals with the contracting authority. As a result, the contracting authority may receive rudimentary proposals with high potential as well as better developed proposals with less potential; if so, it may be difficult for a contracting authority to compare them fairly and objectively.

#### No 'cherry-picking'

A participant may fear other participants exploiting or 'cherry-picking' its ideas, and may object to the contracting authority disclosing to other participants a solution it proposes. The concern may be particularly great in relation to a solution which includes proprietary technology or intellectual property. The perceived risk of participants having such concerns may lead a contracting authority to require each bidder to submit a tender based on its own proposal for a solution, see regulation 18(25). However, that may prevent or restrict participants from competing on the basis of the contracting authority's favoured solution, in turn potentially impairing the contracting authority's ability to obtain best value for money from the procedure.

### Clarification and fine-tuning

Final tenders can be clarified and fine-tuned but this shall 'not involve changes to the basic features of the tender … when those variations are likely to distort competition or have a discriminatory effect', see regulation 18(26).

Those familiar with PPP/PFI and major construction projects will appreciate how hard it would be in practice to avoid negotiation completely in the lead-up to conclusion of contract or financial close. But according to OGC guidance, work can be done with all bidders at preferred bidder stage (just as under the negotiated procedure), and should not be regarded as distorting competition, as it would need to be done with whichever bidder is appointed.

The Scottish Procurement Directorate has issued a number of Notes in relation to public procurement. Although not legally binding, this and other central government guidance is relevant to public procurement, and compliance may be a pre-condition for contracting authorities to receive funding and approval for contract award.

In reality it may be hard for one participant closely to scrutinise others' dialogue with the contracting authority on specifications or terms. Rights of confidentiality may make it difficult for participants to know precisely what was discussed with the successful tenderer, both before and after tenders were invited.

## 2.14  *Awarding the contract*

It is essential that a contracting authority develops a robust evaluation model including evaluation criteria and evaluation weightings to enable it to assess bids, just as with any public procurement procedure.

### 2.14.1  Criteria for the award of the contract

The contracting authority shall award a public contract on the basis of the offer which:

• is the most economically advantageous to the contracting authority, or
• offers the lowest price.

This is intended to ensure that contracting authorities take decisions to award contracts on the basis of objective (commercial) criteria.

Using lowest price may be unduly restrictive for a procurement if proposals received offer economic advantages for the contracting authority other than in terms of the price payable. In choosing to make its evaluation assessment based on what is most economically advantageous, the contracting authority can take into consideration other factors as well as price, e.g. programme to completion or delivery, quality, environmental characteristics, design and aesthetic characteristics, functional features and technical assistance.

### 2.14.2 The most economically advantageous tender

The Regulations provide a non-exhaustive list of the type of factors that may be taken into account in assessing what is most economically advantageous. The Regulations provide that the criteria must be 'linked to the subject matter of the contract', see regulation 30(2).

An authority must disclose its chosen evaluation criteria for assessing what is most economically advantageous in the OJEU Contract Notice or contract documents, or in the case of the competitive dialogue procedure, in the descriptive document, see regulation 30(3). Further, the contracting authority should state the weighting which it gives to each of the chosen criteria. If the contracting authority does not believe that it is possible to allocate weightings, it must indicate the criteria in descending order of importance, see regulation 30(5).

If a contracting authority fails to state the relevant award criteria or fails to state them clearly in the OJEU Contract Notice (or in the contract documents), it will be required to award the contract on the basis of the lowest price, see *R* v. *Portsmouth City Council, ex parte Coles Colwick Builders Ltd and George Austin Ltd* (1997).

## 2.15 *The Alcatel mandatory standstill period*

Under the EC Directives providing for procurement remedies ('Remedies Directives'), EU Directives 89/665 and 92/13, once a public contract had been awarded to a successful tenderer the only statutory procurement remedy available to unsuccessful tenderers was to seek damages from the contracting authority for any alleged breach. Prior to contract award, interim remedies other than damages were (and still are) available, as described in section 2.16 below. The ECJ decision in *Alcatel Austria* v. *Bundesministerium fur Wissenschaft und Verkehr* (1999) found that the Remedies Directives are intended to protect tenderers against arbitrary decisions by contracting authorities, in particular at the stage where infringements can still be rectified, but such protection cannot be effective if the tenderer is not able to rely on these rules against the contracting authority. Instead effective legal protection pre-supposes, first, an obligation to inform all tenderers of the award decision, so that each has a genuine possibility of raising proceedings and exercising their remedies. In addition it must be possible for the unsuccessful tenderer to examine in sufficient time the validity of the award decision; a reasonable period must therefore elapse between the time when the award decision is communicated to unsuccessful tenderers and conclusion of the contract.

### 2.15.1 The ten-day standstill period

In order to give effect to the terms of the ECJ judgment in *Alcatel*, the Regulations provide for a 'standstill' period between when an award decision for a contract awarded under those Regulations is notified to bidders, and the date on which that contract is to be entered into, see regulation 32(3).

A mandatory period of a minimum of ten days is required between a contracting authority communicating an award decision to all tenderers and actually concluding the contract (i.e. confirming the award and thus proceeding with the purchase). The Regulations also allow for an additional de-briefing if requested by unsuccessful tenderers (see regulation 32(4)) and apply strict deadlines to both the tenderer's request and the authority's response in accordance with the following summary timetable:

### Day 0

Notice of award decision to be sent (email or fax) to all tenderers.

### Day 2

Deadline (by midnight at end of Day 2) for unsuccessful tenderers to request additional de-briefing.

### Day 3 to Day 7

Contracting authority to respond to de-briefing requests (by the end of Day 7 at the latest to ensure there are at least three working days between the last de-brief and the end of the standstill period), failing which the standstill period should be extended.

### Day 10

End of standstill period.

**Day 11**

Final award (and execution) of contract, assuming no legal challenge.

These standstill requirements do not apply where there is only one tenderer following the extreme urgency provision under the negotiated procedure, see regulation 32(6).

In protracted procurements which follow the negotiated procedure or competitive dialogue procedure (including PPP/PFI procurements) the OGC has proposed that the standstill period may, if appropriate, apply from the point at which the contracting authority ceases dialogue or discussions with other bidder(s) and announces the appointment of a preferred bidder. The rationale behind this is that the announcement of the preferred bidder effectively brings an end to the competitive stage of the award process.

### 2.15.2 Information to be provided about award decisions

The following information must be provided by a contracting authority when notifying the award decision to unsuccessful suppliers as soon as possible after the contract award decision is made:

- the award criteria;
- the score obtained by both the winning tenderer and the unsuccessful tenderer; and
- the name of the winning tenderer.

Where additional de-briefing is requested in writing by an unsuccessful tenderer, in accordance with the Regulations, the contracting authority shall inform the tenderer of the characteristics and relative advantages of the successful tender at least three working days before the end of the standstill period. Where a request is not made under regulation 32(4) of the Regulations, a contracting authority shall within 15 days of the date on which it receives a written request from an unsuccessful tenderer inform the tenderer as to why it was unsuccessful. Further, when the unsuccessful tenderer submitted an admissible tender the contracting authority shall inform the unsuccessful tenderer of the characteristics and relative advantages of the winning tenderer and their name, see regulation 32(9)(b).

Requests for additional de-briefing within the mandatory standstill period may alter the duration of the standstill period. Therefore, to avoid as much uncertainty as possible as to the contract commencement date, authorities may wish when calculating the standstill period to make allowance for time needed to conduct additional de-briefing(s), or to provide the additional de-brief information to all unsuccessful tenderers at the time of contract award decision notification.

Importantly, one key European Commission proposal to amend the existing Remedies Directives, Directives 89/665/EC and 92/13/EC, is that contracts entered into following breach of the mandatory standstill requirements in the Regulations would be invalid. However, to date the European Commission's proposals have still to undergo European legislative scrutiny (co-decision procedure) and may change prior to enactment.

If the requirements of the standstill rules have been followed by the contracting authority and tenderer, and a legal challenge is brought within the ten-day period, then the contract must not be concluded prior to the outcome of such legal challenge, even if the tenderer's application to the court is likely to be unsuccessful.

## 2.16  Remedies against contracting authorities (bidder grievances and complaints)

The number of formal complaints and successful court actions concerning claimed breaches of EU public procurement law is perhaps lower than the number and scale of contract awards under the EU public procurement regime might suggest should be the case. This section explains the legal position in some detail. However, in addition it may be that contractors choose not to pursue legal remedies (regardless of the merit of their claim) partly because they may be concerned that doing so could affect their prospects of winning contracts under subsequent procurement competitions. Such concerns appear founded in the perception, which may or may not be accurate, that some contracting authorities do not comply fully with the public procurement requirements of equality and non-discrimination at all times.

### 2.16.1  Contracting authority duty to comply with the Regulations

Regulation 47(1) of the Regulations provides that a contracting authority owes a duty to 'economic operators' (including bidders, would-be bidders and interested parties), to comply with the provisions of those Regulations and with any enforceable Community obligation in respect of a public contract. For breach of that duty, economic operators suffering loss may pursue express statutory remedies of (i) interim suspension of the procurement procedure or decisions under it, (ii) setting aside of the procurement procedure or decisions under it and/or (iii) damages, see regulation 47(8).

### 2.16.2  The Remedies Directives

The substantive procurement rules in the Regulations implement Council Directives 89/665/EEC and 92/13/EEC (the 'Remedies Directives') which apply in relation to public procurement covered by the Directive.

The Remedies Directives require each EU member State to ensure that effective remedies and means of enforcement are available to suppliers, contractors and service providers who believe that they have been harmed as a consequence of a breach of their respective public procurement rules.

The rights of action laid down in the Regulations are available to any person who sought to tender for a relevant contract. Accordingly, the remedies are potentially available to any economic operator who had an interest in being engaged to perform the contract in question. The complainant must be an economics operator from an EU country or from a country which is a signatory to the GPA.

### 2.16.3 What statutory remedies are provided?

#### Interim measures

A variety of remedies are available to an aggrieved party. The complainant may ask the court to issue an interim order, which suspends the allegedly defective award or suspends the implementation of any decision or action taken by the awarding authority in the course of such a procedure.

#### Set-aside and amendment orders

The court may also set aside any decision or act taken unlawfully in a procurement procedure and to order the awarding authority to amend any documents. Set-aside and amendment orders, like interim measures, may only be granted if the contract in question has not been entered into.

#### Damages

Under regulation 47(8) of the Regulations, a remedy in damages is also available to a complainant, regardless of whether or not the contract in question has been entered into.

Damages are available to an economic operator who has suffered loss or damage as a consequence of a breach of the Regulations, which do not expand upon the principles governing the availability and amount of damages in proceedings under Scots law. Potentially, however, proceedings may lead to significant financial liabilities for the contracting authority, where economic operators become entitled to damages as a result of its failure to comply with the Regulations on a procurement.

#### European remedies – corrective procedure

As well as (or instead of) bringing an action before a national court, aggrieved parties may also lodge complaints with the European Commission. Once such a complaint is lodged, the European Commission may initiate what is known as 'corrective' procedure if it is satisfied that a clear and manifest breach of public procurement rules has been committed during a contract award procedure, see EC Directive 92/13, Chapter III.

### 2.16.4 Bringing proceedings under regulation 47

The Regulations provide that proceedings may not be brought against a contracting authority unless that contracting authority is informed of the breach or apprehended breach and the complainant's intention to bring proceedings, see regulation 47(7)(a). Such proceedings must be brought promptly, and in any event within three months from the date when the grounds for bringing first arose unless the court believes there is good reason to extend this period, see regulation 47(7)(b).

Case law indicates that complainants may be required to bring proceedings 'promptly', see *M Holleran Ltd* v. *Severn Trent Water Ltd* (2005) before they have properly considered the merits of their actions and even before they know they have been unsuccessful in the procurement. The judge in *M Holleran Ltd* case emphasised the importance of the letter before action in any proceedings, which should be sent 'pre-promptly' in order to give a contracting authority an opportunity to remedy the defect. *KeyMed (Medical and Industrial Equipment) Ltd* v. *Forest Healthcare NHS Trust* (1998) established that the three-month period commences when the grounds first arise for the breach/apprehended breach and that this could be before a complainant has any knowledge of the facts.

### 2.16.5 Proposals to amend the Remedies Directives

The European Commission has put forward a proposal for a new Directive, amending the Remedies Directives, with the aim of improving the effectiveness of review procedures for the award of public contracts.

The European Parliament agreed at first reading of the Commission's proposals and the new Directive is expected to be adopted by the Council by the end of 2007. The new Directive is to introduce, amongst other things, a mandatory standstill period similar to that found in the Regulations (see section 2.15 above), to give tenderers an effective review procedure at a time when infringements can still be corrected.

## 2.17 *Awarding low-value contracts fairly*

The Regulations and the preceding legislation set out the procedures to be followed in the award of public contracts valued above a certain threshold, but for some time it has been unclear as to what obligations apply to the award of certain public contracts to which those Regulations do not apply. On 24 July 2006 the European Commission issued an interpretative communication on the Community law applicable to contract awards not (or not fully) subject to the provisions of the Public Procurement Directives (the 'Communication'). This seeks to clarify the rules which apply to such public contracts, e.g. contracts valued at below the threshold for application of the Regulations and Part B contracts. The terms of the Communication may assist in interpreting one novel requirement in the Regulations which was not contained in Directives 92/50/EEC, 93/36/EEC and 93/37/EEC, as follows. A contracting authority proposing to award a public contract with an estimated value below the relevant threshold, or a proposed public contract which is otherwise exempt from the requirement to be advertised, if required by its general Community obligations, for the benefit of any potential economic operator, must ensure a degree of advertising sufficient to enable open competition and meet the requirements of the principles of equal treatment, non-discrimination and transparency, see regulation 8(21).

The Communication does not contain new legislative rules but provides Commission guidance on the application of the minimum standards of equal treatment, non-discrimination and transparency derived from the EC Treaty in the award of below-threshold public contracts. The requirement for transparency consists in ensuring, for the benefit of any potential tenderer, a degree of advertising sufficient to enable the services market to be opened up to competition and the impartiality of the procedures to be reviewed.

Importantly, the contracting authority must first decide if the public contract in question would be of interest to economic operators located in other EU member States. The Communication proposes that in making such a decision a contracting authority must be guided by an assessment of the relevance of that contract to the internal market on the basis of its subject matter, value and customary practices in the relevant sector.

Should the contracting authority decide that a public contract might be of interest to economic operators located in other EU member States, the Communication provides guidance under three distinct heads – advertising, contract award and review procedures.

In relation to advertising, an undertaking located in an EU member State must have access to appropriate information regarding a public contract before it is awarded, to allow it to be in a position to express its interest in that contract. In order to satisfy this requirement the Commission is of the view that a contracting authority must publish a sufficiently accessible advertisement prior to the award of the contract, and lists optional means of publication. The Communication states that the greater the interest of the contract to potential bidders from other EU member States, the wider the coverage should be. The advertisement should provide as much information as an economic operator from another EU member State will reasonably need to make a decision on whether to express interest in the procurement procedure.

# Chapter 3
# Entering into a Building Contract

## 3.1 Introduction

Many people may not realise the frequency with which they enter into a contract whilst going about their everyday business. For example, purchasing a train ticket constitutes the formation of a contract between the railway company and the passenger. Few people recognise that this is a formal legal arrangement which imposes rights and obligations on both the passenger and the railway company. In reality, contractual relationships of one nature or another hold the very fabric of the commercial world together, including the construction industry. Without the certainty that a contract provides, the resulting chaos would inevitably render the conduct of business, in any meaningful sense of the term, impossible.

## 3.2 Essentials of written and oral contracts

### 3.2.1 Agreement

A contract is essentially an agreement, expressed either in writing or verbally, between a number of parties (not necessarily restricted to two) regarding the same subject matter. The law relating to the formation of contracts is of general application notwithstanding the diversity of subject matter which may constitute the agreement between the parties. In this regard there is little distinction between, for example, a contract for the sale of goods and a building contract. The essentials of formation for both are identical.

A contract is formed when the parties to it reach agreement as to the essential elements of the transaction. There must be what is termed *consensus in idem*, the literal meaning of which is 'agreement in the same thing'. There is no need for consensus between the parties in relation to every detail of the transaction – the test is an objective one. It was held in the case of *Muirhead & Turnbull* v. *Dickson* (1905) that:

> 'commercial contracts cannot be arranged by what people think in their inmost minds. Commercial contracts are made according to what people say.'

This does not mean that the courts will always disregard the presumed intention of the parties at the time the contract was entered into. In *Bank of*

*Scotland* v. *Dunedin Property Investment Co. Ltd* (1998), the court held that in order to interpret a contract the court was entitled to have regard to discussions between the parties in order to establish the parties' knowledge of the circumstances with reference to which particular terms were used in a contract. Only if both parties had something in their contemplation at the time the terms of the contract were agreed would the court have regard to such matters.

There are certain exceptions to the general principle that a contract can only be construed by reference to what it actually says. Implied terms are considered below in section 3.4. There have also been statutory inroads. Sections 8 and 9 of the Law Reform (Miscellaneous Provisions) (Scotland) Act, 1985 provide that the court may rectify a document which fails to express accurately the common intention of the parties at the time the agreement was made. It is important to note that for an application for rectification to be successful, an underlying agreement and common intention must be demonstrated. In other words *consensus in idem* must be established. Further, in terms of section 1 of the Contracts (Scotland) Act 1997, contrary evidence may be led to show that there are additional terms to an apparently complete document (save where the document expressly states that that comprises the whole terms of the contract).

Even where the parties to a contract do not think that they have reached agreement, the court may consider that they have. In *Uniroyal Ltd* v. *Miller & Co. Ltd* (1985) it was held that, in establishing whether parties had entered into a contract, the fundamental principle to be applied is to consider whether or not, and when, there has been *consensus in idem* between parties. In that case there was no agreement regarding the price of goods to be supplied under the contract and it was held that such lack of consensus was fatal. The court held that there was no contract between the parties as, in this particular instance, price was a fundamental and essential part of the contract.

Performance of a purported contract in the mere belief by the parties to it that it was binding and where none of the essentials had been agreed will generally not be sufficient to enable the courts to conclude that there is *consensus in idem*. In *Mathieson Gee (Ayrshire) Ltd* v. *Quigley* (1952) it was held that it is not enough for the parties to agree that there was a concluded contract if there was otherwise lack of agreement on essentials.

Even where there appears, on the face of it, to be no agreement there may still be a concluded contract as a result of the actions of the parties. In *Roofcare Ltd* v. *Gillies* (1984) the pursuers submitted a tender to carry out repairs to the roof of the defender's property. Their offer was made subject to the condition that the quotation was 'subject to the undernoted terms and conditions and no alterations, exclusions, additions, or qualifications to the quotation and specification will be made unless confirmed in writing by Roofcare'. The defender accepted the quotation, confirming that the pursuers should proceed with the repair work to the roof 'making same wind and watertight'. The pursuers did not reply to this qualification. The defender then allowed the work to proceed and the pursuers sued the defender for payment. The defender contended that there was no *consensus in idem* due to the wind and watertight qualification not being accepted by the pursuers, and so there was no contract. The Sheriff Principal held that there had indeed been consensus. The pursuers had presented an offer that was the only basis upon which they would carry out the contract unless otherwise agreed in writing. The defender, who knew of that condition, added his qualification knowing that if it was to be accepted the pursuers would do so in writing. The pursuers did not accept the condition in writing. Despite this, the defender allowed the work to proceed. By his actions the defender was held to have accepted that the wind and watertight qualification did not apply and that there was a contract between him and the pursuers.

### 3.2.2 Offer and acceptance

Offers should be contrasted with 'invitations to treat', where a party demonstrates by words or by conduct a willingness to negotiate a contract. In a construction context, where tenders are invited these constitute invitations to treat. The tender that is submitted by the contractor in response constitutes an offer which is available for acceptance by the employer.

An offer must be communicated to the party to whom it is made, see *Thomson* v. *James* (1855). It is thought that where an offer is communicated by a third party (unless an authorised agent of the offerer, for example, a solicitor) it cannot be accepted. Only where the offer is communicated by the party making it can it be accepted.

A simple, unconditional offer may be revoked at any time before acceptance, see *Thomson*. The revocation must be communicated to the recipient of the offer before it has any effect. Thus, offerers may change their mind at any time prior to acceptance. On the other hand, if an offer is stated to be irrevocable for a certain period it cannot be withdrawn during that time. However, the period during which a firm offer is to be kept open cannot be vague or it is unenforceable, see *Flaws* v. *International Oil Pollution Compensation Fund* (2001).

Where a time limit for acceptance is specified within the offer and no acceptance is received within that time, the offer will fall unless the offerer extends the time limit for acceptance. In *Thomson* it was held that an offer, pure and unconditional, puts it in the power of the party to whom it was addressed to accept the offer, until by the lapse of reasonable time he has lost the right. What constitutes a reasonable time will depend on the facts and circumstances of each case.

A simple offer made without limit of time may lapse where there is a material change of circumstances after the offer has been made. In *McRae* v. *Edinburgh Street Tramways Co.* (1885) it was held by Lord President Inglis that the change of circumstances must render the offer 'unsuitable and absurd' before it will lapse.

Where an offer is made and has not lapsed due to any of the above factors the contract will be concluded, provided there is agreement between the parties, when the offer is accepted. Acceptance can be express or it can be implied from the actions of the recipient of the offer. Again, it is essential that the acceptance is communicated to the offerer.

There is a general rule in Scots law that silence by the recipient of the offer does not imply acceptance of the offer, subject to two exceptions (see below). In *Wylie & Lochhead* v. *McElroy & Sons* (1873) it was held that the contention by the pursuers that the offerees' silence inferred acceptance was a most unreasonable one. Actions on the part of the offeree may be sufficient to infer that they have accepted the offer. In *Gordon Adams & Partners* v. *Jessop* (1987) the defender instructed the pursuers to place his property on a list of properties for sale. The pursuers, after inspection of the premises, wrote to the defender stating that the property was placed with them on a 'sole agency' basis. The defender's solicitor wrote to the pursuers stating that while the pursuers were instructed to place the property on the list, they were not appointed as sole agents. The pursuers responded that they would not accept property unless it was on a sole agency basis. The defender did not respond to that but allowed the pursuers to continue to place the property on their list. It was held that a contract existed between the parties. The defender, in the full knowledge that the pursuers were insisting that they were sole agents, allowed the pursuers to place the property on their list. In the light of the defender's actions the pursuers' belief that there was a contract between the parties was a reasonable one, induced by the defender's behaviour.

There are two exceptions to the general rule that silence does not constitute acceptance of an offer:

- unilateral or 'if' contracts where uncommunicated acts of the party accepting the offer may be sufficient to conclude the contract (see *Carlill* v. *Carbolic Smokeball Company* (1893)); and
- the postal acceptance rule (see section 3.2.3 below).

Acceptance can be verbal, written or implied from the conduct of the parties. Above all, the acceptance must meet the offer. An acceptance which does not accept all of the parts to the offer or which tries to incorporate conditions or qualifications into the offer is not an acceptance at all but a counter-offer, see *Wolf & Wolf* v. *Forfar Potato Co.* (1984). In general, the effect of a counter-offer is to refuse the original offer, which will then fall and can no longer be accepted. Where a counter-offer is accepted unconditionally by the original offerer then the contract will be concluded.

Acceptance of an offer must be communicated to the offerer before the contract is concluded. There are exceptions to this general rule, for example, where the contract is concluded as a result of the actions of the parties and where acceptance is made by post. The offer may stipulate the method of acceptance, for example, by post, telex, fax or telephone. Where the method of acceptance is stipulated, communication of the acceptance must be made by that method or it will be invalid. Where no method of acceptance is stipulated, the acceptance is valid provided it is made in a competent manner. Particular rules apply regarding postal communications.

### 3.2.3 The postal acceptance rule

The case of *Thomson* v. *James* (1855) sets out the principles of the postal acceptance rule. In that case the offer was posted to the offeree. The offeree posted his acceptance and, on the same day, the offerer posted a letter withdrawing the offer. Both letters arrived at their respective destinations on the same day. The question for the court was which letter took effect first – was there a concluded contract or did the letter withdrawing the offer take effect before the letter accepting the offer? Obviously, if the retraction was effective first, then the offer no longer existed and could not be accepted.

It was held by the court that the acceptance was effective and that, therefore, there was a concluded bargain between the parties which could not be affected by the letter of revocation. The rationale was that an acceptance is effective when physically posted whereas a letter revoking an offer is not effective until it actually becomes known to the offeree.

Where the offer specifies a time limit within which it must be accepted, acceptance will be effective provided the acceptance is posted within the time limit. It is of no consequence to establishing whether there is a concluded contract if the acceptance is not actually received until a few days after the time limit expires, provided it is posted before the time limit expires, see *Jacobsen, Sons & Co.* v. *Underwood & Sons* (1894).

The courts may, in very exceptional circumstances, depart from a strict application of the postal acceptance rule if to apply it would lead to an absurd result, see for example *Burnley* v. *Alford* (1919).

Where acceptance is made by telex transmission it has been held in the English case of *Brinkibon Ltd* v. *Stahag Stahl* (1983) that the postal rule does not apply – telex is a method of instantaneous communication and is therefore treated in the same way as an oral communication. A telex acceptance was held to be effective when printed out at the offerer's end.

It is likely that facsimile transmissions would be treated in exactly the same way as telex transmissions. The position regarding emails is less certain. Email communications are not necessarily instantaneous and may take some time to reach their recipient. This might lead to a conclusion that the general postal acceptance rule should apply. The 'control' argument also favours this conclusion; once the email has been sent, the sender has no control over ensuring it reaches its recipient.

There is, however, the counter-argument that, generally speaking, emails do reach their recipients quickly and it is possible to track receipt of emails whether electronically or by telephoning the recipient to ensure successful receipt. The origin of the postal rule was to create certainty at a time when post was the only form of communication and was generally slow.

There is also uncertainty over how the courts would treat the recipient of a fax or email who does not activate the means of accessing the communication within a reasonable time. It may be that the courts will consider this to be similar to the circumstances in *Burnley* v. *Alford* (1919), holding that the communication becomes effective when it ought, in the ordinary course of business, to have been read.

Regulation 11 of the Electronic Commerce (EC Directive) Regulations 2002, whilst not resolving the point completely, states that orders (including contractual offers) and acknowledgements of receipt 'will be deemed to be received when the parties to whom they are addressed are able to access them'. Regulation 11 applies to parties who are not consumers.

### 3.2.4 Battle of the forms

It is common within the construction industry for offers to be made subject to the offerer's standard conditions of contract (frequently printed on the reverse side of the offer or appended thereto). Difficulties arise where the offeree accepts the offer subject to the qualification that the offeree's standard conditions will apply. In the ordinary course of events this would undoubtedly constitute a counter-offer requiring the offerer's acceptance. Where, however, work is commenced prior to the counter-offer being accepted, a question arises as to whether there was, in fact, a contract and if so on whose terms. Whilst it has often been said of this scenario that the person firing the last shot will be successful, it has also been commented that it may be more helpful to look at the documents as a whole to determine whether the parties have reached agreement on essential points, notwithstanding differences between the forms, see *Butler Machine Tool Co. Ltd* v. *Ex-Cell-O Corporation* (1979). Ultimately, the issue will be decided on the basis of an objective assessment of what the parties agreed, looking at the evidence in the particular circumstances of the case.

## 3.3 *Capacity to contract*

Special rules apply to the capacity of certain categories of persons to enter into contracts. The main categories are as follows.

### 3.3.1 Young persons

The Age of Legal Capacity (Scotland) Act 1991 makes a distinction between two groups of young people, namely, those under the age of sixteen and those aged between sixteen and eighteen. With limited exceptions, a person under the age of sixteen has no legal capacity to enter into any transaction (s.1(1)(a)).

A person over the age of sixteen has legal capacity to enter into contracts. However, a person who enters into a contract between the ages of sixteen and eighteen can, in certain circumstances, apply to the court to set aside the contract if it is shown to be prejudicial and provided that such an application is made before the person concerned attains the age of twenty-one (section 3).

### 3.3.2  Insanity

It is a general principle of Scots law that an insane person has no power to contract and any contracts which such a person purports to enter into are void, see for example *Gall* v. *Bird* (1855). In addition, such contracts are generally void even although the other party may not have known that he was dealing with a person of unsound mind at the time that the contract was entered into, see *Loudon* v. *Elder's Curator* (1923). However, continuing contracts in which a party has entered into whilst they were sane are not necessarily rendered void by that party's subsequent insanity, see *Howie* v. *CGU Insurance plc* (2005).

### 3.3.3  Aliens

It is the position in Scots Law that, conforming to the Rome Convention, a contract made during a period of residence in Scotland cannot be set aside on the ground that one of the parties was an alien who lacked contractual capacity under his or her own legal system unless it is proved that the other party knew of the incapacity or was negligently unaware of it. This principle is incorporated into the Scottish legal system by section 2 of the Contracts (Applicable Law) Act 1990.

### 3.3.4  Corporate bodies

A corporate body is a distinct legal entity which is entirely separate from the members of the corporation. A corporate body can enter into contracts and can sue and be sued. Corporate bodies will contract through their agents. The agent must have express or ostensible authority to bind the corporation to the contract he purports to make. Directors of companies have ostensible power and authority to bind the company in transactions.

A corporate body created by statute, or exercising statutory powers, cannot enter into any contract or dispose of its funds in any way which is not authorised by the statute or reasonably incidental to the powers conferred. To do so would be *ultra vires*, i.e. beyond its powers. Where a party is dealing with a company incorporated under the Companies Acts the position regarding *ultra vires* has been simplified. Following implementation of the Companies Act 2006 (due to come into force on a series of implementation dates those being 1 October 2007, 6 April 2008 and 1 October 2008) both new and existing companies will have one main constitutional document, that being articles of association. A deeming provision will transfer an existing company's memorandum of association into its articles (see section 28 of the Companies Act 2006). In terms of section 31 of the Companies Act 2006, unless a company's articles specifically restrict the objects of the company, its objects are unrestricted. Where a company deals with a person in good faith, the power of the directors to bind the company, or to authorise others to do so, is currently deemed to be free of any limitation under the company's memorandum and articles of association, see s.35A of the Companies Act 1985 (restated by section 40 of the Companies Act 2006 which comes into effect on 1 October 2008). A person is not to be regarded as acting in bad faith by reason only of their knowing that an act is beyond the powers of directors under the memorandum and articles of association of the company. In addition, a person is presumed to have acted in good faith unless the contrary is proved, see s.35A(2) of the Companies Act 1985 (restated by s.40(2) of the Companies Act 2006). Further, a party to a transaction with a company is not bound to enquire as to whether the transaction is permitted by the company's memorandum or as to any limitation on the powers of the board of directors to bind the company or to authorise others to do so, see s.35B of the Companies Act 1985 (restated by s.40(2) of the Companies Act 2006).

### 3.3.5 Limited liability partnerships

Limited liability partnerships (LLPs) were created by the Limited Liability Partnership Act 2000 and are designed to offer the organisational flexibility and tax status of partnerships combined with limited liability for its members. An LLP is a body corporate, and is a separate legal body from its members. This allows the LLP to enter into contracts and hold property. Unless provided under statute, usual partnership law shall not apply to an LLP, as LLPs are more akin to companies than partnerships. Unlike a partnership, if a member leaves the LLP, the LLP continues to exist.

Where a party contracts with the LLP rather than an individual member, any claim for breach of contract lies against the LLP, and only a claim in delict may be brought against the individual member. The members will no longer be liable jointly (and in Scotland severally also) for the debts and obligations of the LLP.

Members of the LLP may represent and act on behalf of the LLP in all its business. However the LLP will not be bound by the actions of a member where that member has no authority to act for the LLP and the person dealing with the member is aware of this or does not know or believe that the member was in fact a member of the LLP. Where a person has ceased to be a member of the LLP, he will still be regarded as a member of the LLP in a question with a person dealing with that former member, unless (a) the person dealing has had notice that the former member has ceased to be a member of the LLP or (b) notice that the former member has ceased to be a member of the LLP has been delivered to the Registrar of Companies.

## 3.4 Implied terms

Implied terms are those which may be implied into a contract to reflect either the presumed though unexpressed intention of the parties or which may be implied by statute or other rule of law irrespective of the intention of the parties, see *Morton* v. *Muir Brothers* (1907).

In relation to the former ('factual implication'), a number of tests have been devised by the courts to determine whether the implication of terms may be permissible. It goes without saying that factual implication is heavily dependent upon the facts and circumstances of the case in question.

In *The Moorcock* (1889), Lord Justice Bowen formulated a test for implying terms, which has become almost universally known as the 'business efficacy' test. He stated that:

'I believe if one were to take all the cases, and they are many, it will be found that in all of them the law is raising an implication from the presumed intention of the parties with the object of giving to the transaction such efficacy as both parties must have intended that at all events it should have.'

Another approach adopted by the courts is to apply what has become known as the 'officious bystander' test. The test derives its name from the judgment in the English case of *Shirlaw* v. *Southern Foundries* (1939). The test is essentially whether an 'officious bystander', a fictitious person who was privy to the discussions of the contracting parties, upon proposing the inclusion of a term would be 'testily suppressed with a common "Oh of course" by the parties'. Put more simply, is the term proposed by the 'officious bystander' so obvious that its intended inclusion goes without saying?

The tests are distinct, however, in either instance it is clear that the factual implication of a term must be reasonable in the circumstances, see *Morton*. However, not all terms that are reasonable may be capable of being implied. The courts, to some extent, require evidence of necessity as well, see *Liverpool City Council* v. *Irwin* (1977). The courts will not imply a term merely because to do so would be fair. The terms of a contract can be harsh and unfair, but terms will be implied only if they are necessary to make the contract work, see *Rockcliffe Estates plc* v. *Co-operative Wholesale Society Ltd* (1994).

Furthermore a term may also be implied on the basis of custom and usage, particularly in a district or trade or other context, see *Morton*. Implication under this head still requires evidence of necessity and to some extent over-laps with the officious bystander test, albeit it in a localised sense.

Implication arising by operation of a rule of law manifests itself in a number of ways. The implied duties that are incumbent upon a seller as to quality have long been elevated to statutory form and indeed still are, see the Supply of Goods and Services Act 1982. However, there are many instances where the present legislation applicable to sale is inapplicable. In such instances the courts have been willing to imply almost identical duties on the seller as those imposed under statute, simply because they are legal incidents to contracts of sale. However, in the absence of a precedent, impli-cation on this basis will seldom arise, see *Scottish Power plc* v. *Kvaerner Con-struction (Regions) Ltd* (1998) where the court found that any implication of terms should be exceptional.

The following part of this chapter is restricted to a consideration of the implication of terms into contracts within the construction industry. A more detailed appraisal of implied terms lies outwith the scope of this book.

It would appear that the presence of an alternative remedy under a con-tract (albeit less attractive than the one sought under the implied term) will generally preclude the implication of an implied term. Thus where a contract provided for works to be carried out in phases and only one phase provided for an extension of time in the event of delay, the House of Lords refused to imply an extension of time clause into another phase where delay could have been dealt with under alternative provisions of that contract, see *Trollope & Colls Ltd* v. *North West Metropolitan Regional Hospital Board* (1973). In *F Brown plc* v. *Tarmac Construction (Contracts) Ltd* (2000), the court refused to imply a term where the claim rested on express provisions which sat alongside the proposed (broader) implied term. It should be noted that a 'more tightly and precisely formulated implied term' might have been justified, if pleaded.

Over the years, the courts have become increasingly willing to imply terms which, in their most general form, have tended to require the employer and his agents (e.g. the architect or engineer) to fulfil their obligations timeously to allow a contractor to progress their works. Whilst each case will necessar-ily turn on its own facts, the following terms have been implied into main contracts by the courts:

- That the employer and its agent (in this case the engineer) were obliged to provide the contractor with all necessary details and instructions in sufficient time to enable the contractor to execute and complete the works in 'an economic and expeditious manner and/or in sufficient time to prevent the claimants being delayed in such execution and completion', see *Neodox Ltd* v. *Swinton and Pendlebury BC* (1958) and *J & J Fee Ltd* v. *The Express Lift Co. Ltd* (1993). Where the contractor has prepared a contract programme such that the programmed completion date is earlier than the date for completion stated in the contract, the contractor is entitled to complete the works in accordance with the programme. However, the employer is only obliged to act within timescales that allow the contractor to complete the works in accordance with the contractual completion date and not to the contractor's accelerated programme, and the court will not imply a term to the contrary, see *Glenlion Construction Ltd* v. *The Guinness Trust* (1986).

- Not to hinder or prevent the contractors from carrying out their obligations in accordance with their contract or from executing the works in a regular and orderly manner, and to give possession of the site within a reasonable time, see *London Borough of Merton* v. *Stanley Hugh Leach Ltd* (1982).
- The employer must take all reasonable steps to enable the contractor to discharge its obligations and to execute the works in an orderly and regular manner, including things which the architect is obliged to do to facilitate this, see *Mackay* v. *Dick and Stevenson* (1881) and *Lubenham Fidelities and Investments Co. Ltd* v. *South Pembrokeshire DC and Another* (1986).
- The employer is obliged to ensure that the architect provides the contractor with full correct information concerning the contract work, see *Lubenham Fidelities Ltd*.

In *Neodox Ltd* v. *Swinton and Pendlebury BC* (1958) the court considered 'reasonable time' in the context of the provision of information. It said:

> 'What is reasonable time does not depend solely upon the convenience and financial interest of the claimant. No doubt it is to their interest to have every detail cut and dried on the day the contract is signed, but the contract does not contemplate that. It contemplates further details and instructions being provided, and the engineer is to have a time to provide them which is reasonable having regard to the point of view of him and his staff and the point of view of . . . [the employer], as well as the point of view of the contractors.'

Similar duties to the foregoing would also appear to be incumbent upon a contractor when supplying necessary information and not hindering completion by a sub-contractor, see *J & J Fee Ltd* v. *The Express Lift Co. Ltd* (1993).

Where the parties have clearly contemplated a risk, legal implication will not be sufficient to imply a term unless it satisfies the additional test of necessity, see *Martin Grant & Co. Ltd* v. *Sir Lindsay Parkinson & Co. Ltd* (1984). In addition implication will generally be precluded where the term seeks to impose liability on a party for matters over which they have no control, see *Ductform Ventilation (Fife) Ltd* v. *Andrews-Weatherfoil Ltd* (1995). Finally, the courts have been unwilling to imply a term where the implied terms sought were at variance with the express provisions of the contract, see *Scottish Power plc* v. *Kvaerner Construction (Regions) Ltd* (1998).

Regard should also be had to any entire agreement or exclusion clauses which may preclude the inclusion of implied terms. Implied terms in respect of quality are considered below in section 4.3.

## 3.5  Letters of intent

Although best avoided, commercial necessity may demand that certain works or services are carried out before the parties are in a position to enter into the formal building contract. It is possible for design, supply and even construction to be started on the basis of a letter of intent. A 'letter of intent' is probably a misnomer for the type of document that generally goes under that description in construction projects. In certain cases, such letters may be intended to fall short of establishing a legal relationship and merely to provide comfort to the recipient. However, they are normally intended to create a binding relationship, albeit for a restricted purpose and a limited period. The expression of a future intention to contract under a letter of intent is capable of being construed as a legally enforceable promise under Scots law. Whether a letter of intent will fall short of establishing a legal relationship or constituting an enforceable promise will depend largely on the form of wording used in each case, a view supported by the court in *ERDC Group Ltd* v. *Brunel University* (2006). The phrase 'letter of intent' was said not to be a term of art, but one whose meaning and effect depend on the circumstances of each case.

A number of recent cases have reinforced the proposition that valid and enforceable contracts can be created by letters of intent, see *Hackwood Ltd* v. *Areen Design Services Limited* (2005), and *Robertson Group (Construction) Ltd* v. *Amey-Miller (Edinburgh) Joint Venture and Others* (2005) Although in the latter case, the letter of intent was agreed as being a 'stop-gap' arrangement in the context of on-going negotiations towards a formal contract, once the contractor had commenced work on the basis of the letter, it was contractually obliged to proceed with the works.

In many instances, where work has been carried out by one party pursuant to a letter of intent, the analysis of whether a contract has been formed is somewhat irrelevant; if there is no contract the party who has tendered performance will have a claim based on *quantum meruit*, i.e. reasonable payment for work done. In *ERDC Group Ltd* work proceeded on the basis of a letter of intent, with the scope of the works and the financial authority being increased by four further letters of intent. The authority in the final letter of intent expired on 1 September 2002, but the contractor continued working until the works were completed in November 2002. A formal contract was never signed, because the contractor argued that the scope of the works had changed significantly from that anticipated at the outset, and that it was therefore entitled to be paid on a *quantum meruit* basis. The court found that until 1 September 2002, there was a valid contract and payment was to be made (and had been made) in accordance with that contract. For work done after 1 September 2002, the contractor was to be paid on a *quantum meruit* basis but on the basis of the tender rates and prices as there was no reason why this original basis of payment should be different (the contractor had argued that it should be paid on a cost plus basis). The court noted the case of *Sanjay Lachhani* v. *Destination Canada (UK) Ltd* (1997) which held that a contractor should not be better off as a result of the failure to conclude a contract than they would have been if their offer had been accepted.

However, where a party who has received performance seeks damages for breach of contract, the issue is likely to be highly important. Where a letter of intent anticipates that, for example, a standard form of contract will be entered into by the parties at some future date and no such contract is subsequently entered into, the party who has received performance will be deprived of the protection which the terms of the standard form might otherwise have provided. For example, in the absence of a contract stipulating the quality of the work to be performed, the party unable to avail itself of the protection offered by the contract terms is left to argue that the *quantum meruit* claim should be reduced in light of the work performed. In the case of *Wescol Structures Ltd* v. *Miller Construction Ltd* (1998) negotiations between the sub-contractor and both main contractor and the employer's representatives proceeded on the basis of letters of intent. The sub-contractor insisted in its replies to the letter of intent that the standard DOM/2 form of sub-contract would apply, whereas the employer's representatives, who wrote the letters of intent, stated that the sub-contract would be 'back to back with the main contract' but failed to specify any specific terms. The case, which related to payment terms, was decided on the basis of the standard form even though the standard form was never entered into, partly because the employer had never challenged the sub-contractor's assumption.

English law is more developed in relation to letters of intent. The leading English authority on this point is *British Steel Corporation* v. *Cleveland Bridge & Engineering Co.* (1984). Here, where a party commenced work on the basis of the words 'pending the preparation and issuing to you of the official form of sub-contract' contained in a letter of intent, it was held that it was 'very difficult to see how [the plaintiff], by starting work, bound themselves to any contractual performance'. Here, amongst other things, neither the price, the delivery dates, nor the applicable terms of contract had been agreed. It is worth noting that the omission of agreement as to price need not be fatal, see *Amec Capital Projects Ltd* v. *Whitefriars City Estate Ltd* (2003) and *Hackwood Ltd*. The use of the word 'pending' was indicative of a state of preparation only.

In *Hackwood Ltd* the letter of intent stated that the JCT conditions 'will be' the basis of the contract, and the Technology and Construction Court held that such a reference was sufficient to incorporate the standard form save to the extent that such terms were inconsistent with the terms of the letter of intent, notwithstanding that the appendix and other project specific data were not yet agreed. If relevant information was missing (for example, the amount of liquidated damages) then that mechanism only would fall away.

Notwithstanding the analogy with promise, a letter of intent may also be construed as an offer capable of being accepted, depending on its terms, see *Uniroyal Ltd* v. *Miller & Co. Ltd* (1985) and *Mowlem plc (t/a Mowlem Marine)*

v. *Stena Line Ports Ltd* (2004). In determining whether an offer has been made the terms of the letter itself are crucial.

## 3.6 Incorporation of terms by reference to another document

Generally, reference to a particular form of contract will be sufficient to incorporate its terms. Reference can be oral, but it is preferable that it is in writing (although not conclusive, see *Kaye* v. *Bronesky* (1973)). Thus an agreement that a contractual relationship will be governed by reference to a particular form of contract will be sufficient to incorporate those terms into that contract, subject to the conditions referred to being readily identifiable or at least identifiable with reference to common industry knowledge, see *Modern Building Wales Ltd* v. *Limmer & Trinidad Co. Ltd* (1975). Thus reference to a sub-contractor's order being 'in accordance with the appropriate form for nominated sub-contractors RIBA 1965 edition' was sufficient, after evidence had been led to show that, whilst a contract formally called 'RIBA 1965 edition' did not exist, the term was commonly used in the building trade to refer to the 'green form'.

The foregoing scenario envisages, however, that the terms of any conditions referred to will be suitable in the circumstances, for example, that a sub-contract relationship will be governed by recognised sub-contract terms. What is more problematic and, indeed, a relatively common occurrence in the construction industry, is where party A attempts to impose the terms and conditions to which it is subject, for example, under a main contract, into a sub-contract which they have entered into with party B. This is commonly referred to as a 'back to back' arrangement.

This issue was considered by the Outer House of the Court of Session in *Parklea Ltd* v. *W & J R Watson Ltd* (1988). Here a sub-contract purported to incorporate the main contract conditions into the sub-contract that also contained other express terms. A dispute arose as to whether the arbitration clause in the main contract was applicable to the sub-contract. A number of principles emerge from this case which are of guidance in assessing whether such terms are capable of incorporation:

- The starting point must be to consider whether the parties have incorporated the whole of the main contract conditions; it is irrelevant that some (and not others) of the conditions would have fitted very neatly into the sub-contract conditions.
- Do the words incorporating the sub-contract conditions make clear that they are applicable to the exclusion of all other provisions? It was held that a reference to the main contract conditions 'solely regulating' the relationship between the parties was not indicative of an exclusion of all other conditions; the subsequent reference to the applicability of the main contract provisions being excluded where they conflicted

with other express terms of the sub-contract mitigated against such a construction.

- Where the purportedly incorporated terms conflict or duplicate other express terms of the sub-contract or duplicate the terms of the main contract this will militate against the conclusion that the main contract terms will exclusively regulate the parties' contractual relationship.

*Parklea Ltd* follows a line of authority whereby the Scottish courts have been reluctant to apply the terms of an arbitration clause in similar circumstances. It is interesting to note that in *Parklea Ltd* it was a matter of agreement between the parties that only wholesale incorporation of the terms of the main contract would be sufficient to incorporate the arbitration clause. It would appear that the English courts might be prepared to adopt a broader approach. They have held that where the main contractor's terms are not inconsistent with the sub-contractual relationship they could be incorporated. See *Brightside Kilpatrick Engineering Services* v. *Mitchell Construction (1973) Ltd* (1975), and, with particular regard to arbitration clauses, see also *Giffen (Electrical Contractors) Ltd* v. *Drake & Skull Engineering Ltd* (1993) and *Roche Products Ltd and Another* v. *Freeman Process Systems and Another* (1996).

More in keeping with the approach of the Scottish courts is the Canadian case of *Smith & Montgomery* v. *Johnstone Brothers and Co. Ltd* (1954) where it was held that where a contract made reference to the terms of another contract, and expressly incorporated a number of those terms, then only those expressly included will form part of that contract. Here the incorporation of an express term of a main contract, which made reference to the payment provisions in respect of nominated sub-contractors, and which was expressly incorporated into the sub-contract, was held to be valid. The English courts have also addressed the issue as to whether the words 'shall be deemed to have notice of all the provisions of the main contract' are sufficient to incorporate those terms and answered in the negative, see *Jardine Engineering Corporation* v. *Shimizu Corporation* (1992).

Incorporation of terms may be relevant when considering letters of intent as these often refer to the terms of a building contract which has not yet been finally agreed. This can be a subject of disagreement if the final contract is not executed, as often one party argues that it cannot have been the intention of the parties that the terms of a contract that was still being negotiated should govern the relationship between the parties. In *Hackwood Ltd* the Technology and Construction Court found that the object of the letter of intent was to establish an interim contract that would govern the relationship between the parties until the final contract was agreed, on terms that both parties appreciated could govern the whole of the project. In particular, the use of the future tense ('the basis of the contract will be . . .') did not indicate that the referenced terms should only apply to the final agreed contract and not the interim contract. In this case, the standard form of contract was incorporated into the interim contract, save for those terms that were inconsistent with the terms of the letter of intent.

## 3.7 *Signing a building contract*

### 3.7.1 General

The requirements of Scots law in relation to the signing of documents are set out in the Requirements of Writing (Scotland) Act 1995 ('the 1995 Act').

Writing is not required for the constitution of a contract except where the contract relates to the creation, transfer, variation or extinction of an interest in land (section 1). Although writing is not required for other forms of contract, the parties may execute their contract in such a way as to render the contract self-proving.

The 1995 Act distinguishes between a document which has been validly signed and a document which has self-proving status. A validly signed document is one which has been subscribed by the grantor (section 2). Here extrinsic evidence is necessary to confirm the validity of the signatures. However, if the requirements of the 1995 Act regarding witnessing (which will be discussed in more detail later) have been followed then the signatures of the parties will be afforded self-proving status. In effect, this means by virtue of the means of execution the signatures of the parties are presumed valid and need not be proved (section 3).

Where a contract has schedules annexed to it, the schedules will be incorporated into the contract if they are referred to in the body of the contract and it is identified on the face of the schedules that they are the schedules referred to in the contract. If this is done there is no need for the schedules to be signed (s.8(1)). It is only where a contract relates to interests in land that any schedule attached to the contract requires to be signed (s.8(2)).

The precise requirements of subscription vary depending upon the designation of those signing the contract.

### 3.7.2 Individuals

If a party to a building contract is contracting as an individual (which includes a sole trader), then that person must subscribe the contract and have their signature witnessed by one witness. If this is done, subscription by that person will be self-proving (s.3(1)).

### 3.7.3 Partnerships

In the absence of specific internal signing requirements, a contract will be validly executed on behalf of a partnership if it is signed by one partner or another authorised person (Schedule 2 paragraph 2(1)(3)). The signatory can either sign his own name or the name of the firm (Schedule 2 paragraph 3). The law regarding the power of a partner to bind a firm is set out in the Partnership Act 1890. The signature of the partner, or the authorised person, must be witnessed by one witness in order to make their subscription self-proving.

### 3.7.4 Companies

A company will validly execute a contract if it is signed by one director, the company secretary or by a person authorised to sign the contract on the company's behalf (Schedule 2 paragraph 3). Again, for the subscription to be self-proving a single witness must witness it. The contract will also be self-proving if it is signed by two directors, or a director and the company secretary or by two authorised persons (Schedule 2 paragraph 2(5)). In these circumstances there is no need for the signatures to be witnessed.

### 3.7.5 Limited liability partnerships

Signature of a document by a limited liability partnership (LLP) will be self-proving if it has been signed by a member of the LLP in front of a witness, or by two members of the LLP (Schedule 2 paragraph 3A(5)), although the document will be validly executed on behalf of the LLP if it is signed by a member of the LLP (Schedule 2 paragraph 3A(1)).

### 3.7.6 Local authorities

A contract will be validly executed by a local authority if it is signed by the proper officer, usually the chief executive, see Schedule 2 paras 4(1) and (3). A person purporting to sign as the proper officer is presumed to be the proper officer, see Schedule 2 paragraph 4(2). For the subscription to be self-proving, the contract must be subscribed by the proper officer on the local authority's behalf and either have the signature witnessed by one witness or have the contract sealed with the local authority's seal, see Schedule 2 paragraph 4(5).

### 3.7.7 Witnesses

The 1995 Act reduced the requisite number of witnesses from two to one. If more than one signatory is signing at the same time one independent person can competently witness all signatures.

Witnesses must be independent with no direct interest in the contract. In addition, witnesses must be over the age of sixteen; be of sound mind; be able to write; and not be blind.

The witness must see the signatory sign the contract or, alternatively, the signatory can sign the contract outwith the presence of the witness and thereafter show their signature on the contract to the witness and acknowledge to the witness that the signature is in fact his. The witness must know the signatory but all that is required in that regard is a reliable introduction prior to signing or acknowledging, see *Brock* v. *Brock* (1908).

It is the practice for witnesses to sign opposite the signatory's signature and customary, although not strictly necessary, for witnesses to write the word 'witness' after their signature.

### 3.7.8 Electronic signature

The Electronic Communications Act 2000 means that electronic signatures and certificates supporting them are admissible as evidence 'in relation to any question as to the authenticity of the communication or data or as to the integrity of the communication or data' (s.7(1)). The question of whether electronic form is permissible in specific areas will be addressed on a case by case basis by statutory instrument; however, it is not yet possible to dispose of heritable property electronically.

# Chapter 4
# Employers' Obligations

## 4.1 Introduction

A building contract will usually set out, in express terms, the obligations owed by the employer to the contractor. Where these are not set out, certain terms will be implied due to the nature of the contract. Implied terms have been considered in section 3.4.

All of the obligations owed by the employer, be they express or implied, would appear to fall into two main categories. Firstly, an obligation of co-operation or the requirement to do certain things to put the contractor in a position of being able to carry out their own obligations under the contract. Secondly, an obligation to make payment for the work carried out by the contractor.

Although these will be referred to as the employer's obligations, the employer commonly employs others to perform certain of these functions on their behalf, for example, the Architect/Contract Administrator under the Standard Building Contract (SBC). In this chapter, we will use the term 'Architect' rather than repeatedly refer to both terms. In a design and build contract (such as SBC/DB) the employer will normally delegate his duties to the employer's agent. The reference to the employer's obligations will therefore include the obligations which may be owed by other parties on the employer's behalf and it should be noted that breach by these parties will lead the employer to become liable for any losses suffered by the contractor as a result, see *Neodox Ltd* v. *Swinton and Pendlebury BC* (1958).

We will consider first the duties to do certain things necessary to enable the contractor to carry out his works. In *Mackay* v. *Dick and Stevenson* (1881), Lord Blackburn stated that it was:

> 'a general rule that where in a written contract it appears that both parties have agreed that something shall be done, which cannot effectually be done unless both concur in doing it, the construction of the contract is that each agrees to do all that is necessary to be done on his part for the carry-ing out of that thing, though there may be no express words to that effect. What is the part of each must depend on circumstances.'

Whilst this might be described as the positive duty flowing from the employer's obligation to do everything necessary to enable the contractor to carry out their works, another term which has been frequently implied is the obligation not to do anything which will hinder the contractor from carrying out their obligations under the contract or from executing work in a regular and diligent manner, see *London Borough of Merton* v. *Stanley Hugh Leach Ltd* (1985). In other words, the employer cannot do anything to prevent the contractor from performing his obligations under the contract.

Examples of the general obligation to do all that is necessary to enable the contractor to carry out their works are the obligation to give the contractor possession of the site; the obligation to administer the site; and the obligation to issue instructions and to provide information.

## 4.2 Possession of the site

### 4.2.1 General

In certain contracts it is an express term that the employer will give possession of the site, or the relevant part of it, to the contractor to enable him to carry out the works, see, for example, clause 2.4 of the SBC. Where this is not expressly stated it will be implied as, in the majority of contracts, a contractor cannot carry out their works unless they actually have possession of the site, see *R* v. *Walter Cabott Construction Ltd* (1975). In referring to the requirement for the employer to give the contractor possession of the site, this is not possession in its legal sense but more a right of entry or control falling short of literal possession.

The questions which then arise are: when is the employer required to give the contractor possession; what is the nature and extent of the possession which the employer requires to give the contractor (including consideration of whether or not the giving of possession implies that the contractor will have uninterrupted access to and possession of the site); and, finally, what is the duration of this obligation?

### 4.2.2 Time of possession

As stated above, the contract will often expressly state when the employer is required to give the contractor possession. Where the contract does not expressly provide for the date when possession must be given to the contractor, it will be implied that possession must be given within a reasonable time to enable the contractor to complete the works by any completion date which may exist, see *T & R Duncanson* v. *The Scottish County Investment Co. Ltd* (1915). In the case of the SBC, the actual date on which possession is to be given will be stated in the Contract Particulars. There is provision for postponement of this for a period not exceeding six weeks, or such lesser period as is stated in the Contract Particulars, see clause 2.5. An instruction given by the Architect under clause 3.15 in regard to postponement is a relevant event by virtue of clause 2.29.2.1 that may entitle the contractor to an extension of time. It is also a matter affecting the regular progress of the Works, by virtue of clause 4.24.2.1, which may entitle the contractor to loss and expense if the date of commencement of the contract is likely to have an overall effect on completion. Failure by the employer to issue an extension of time where they have delayed the commencement of the contractor's possession may result in the employer being unable to apply liquidated and ascertained damages where the contract has an expired completion date, see *Wells* v. *Army & Navy Co-operative Society Ltd* (1902).

### 4.2.3 Nature and extent of possession to be given

The contractor is normally entitled to possession of the whole site. That would appear to be what is meant by clause 2.4 of the SBC which refers to the contractor being given possession of the site on a specified date of possession. 'Site' is not a word that is defined by clause 1.1. In any case, it will be implied that the employer must make available the entire area that is necessary to enable the contractor to carry out their contract works. In some cases this has been held to extend beyond the actual area which will be occupied by the completed structure into other areas, for example, to provide working space and to enable the contractor to work efficiently and in accordance with generally accepted construction practices, see *R* v. *Walter Cabott Construction Ltd* (1975).

It is not an implied term, however, that the employer must provide work to the contractor in such a way as to enable them to carry out the work on an economic basis, see *Martin Grant & Co. Ltd* v. *Sir Lindsay Parkinson & Co. Ltd* (1984). A similar consideration arose in *Scottish Power plc* v. *Kvaerner Construction (Regions) Ltd* (1998). In that case the contract stipulated a period of 24 weeks as that allowed for the work. There was no guarantee of continuous working. The Lord Ordinary held that the defenders had power to interrupt the continuity of the period of 24 weeks. The reasoning behind that decision turns very much upon the provisions of the particular contract in question and it is submitted by the authors that the decision, which is to the effect that where there is a specified contract period and no guarantee of continuous working the employer has the right to interrupt, is not one which should be followed. If this were an absolute right, an absurd situation could arise with the employer being entitled to commence then stop the works at will.

The employer does not have any implied right to come on to site after possession has been given to the contractor. If they wish to retain the right to do so the contract should expressly provide for this. An example of this is to be found in clause 2.6 of the SBC which, with the consent in writing of the contractor, allows the employer to use or occupy the site or the Works or part of them prior to completion, whether for storage or otherwise. Where operated, this appears to effectively provide the employer with a licence from the contractor to use or occupy part of the site to the extent necessary for the particular purpose that the employer has in mind, see *Impresa Castelli SpA* v. *Cola Holdings Ltd* (2002). Further examples can be found in clauses 3.1 and 3.4 which provide for the presence on site of the Architect and clerk of works. It is submitted that possession should imply that the employer, or those employed by him, should have a right of reasonable access for the purposes of inspection, supervision and administration of the contract. Where nothing is said about possession, the contractor must be allowed use and possession of the site as required for the purposes of carrying out their works, see *Ductform Ventilation (Fife) Ltd* v. *Andrews Weatherfoil Ltd* (1995).

After starting on site, the contractor may be denied undisturbed occupation for a variety of reasons, only some of which may be the responsibility of the employer. Where another contractor or supplier, referred to in the SBC as Employer's Persons, has been employed by the employer for certain aspects of the work not covered by the contractor's scope of works, the contractor, where he has had information regarding this other work, is under an obligation to permit the execution of such work. This will imply a right for the other contractor to enter onto the site to complete their works, see, for example, clause 2.7.1. Where information in relation to such other works has not been made available to the contractor, the employer's right to have access to, and to instruct other contractors to execute works on the site, is subject to the consent of the contractor, see clause 2.7.2.

An employer will not be liable where there is unauthorised occupation by a third party such as picketers, unless they have induced or condoned the obstruction, see *London Borough of Merton* v. *Stanley Hugh Leach Ltd* (1985). The employer does not warrant that access for the contractor will not be prevented by a third party, such as a picketer, see *LRE Engineering Services Ltd* v. *Otto Simon Carves Ltd* (1981). In the case of clause 2.13.1 of the SBC, the incorporation of the standard method of measurement ('SMM 7') requires that any conditions relating to access should be stated in the bills of quantities. In certain circumstances, the employer may be liable to pay loss and expense to the contractor for failure to provide them with access to the site, see clause 4.24.5. By virtue of clauses 3.10 and 5.1.2.1, it remains open to the Architect to vary the access available to the contractor, subject always to the contractor's reasonable right to object to this.

### 4.2.4  Duration of the obligation to give the contractor possession

This obligation subsists for as long as the contract is running which will usually mean that the contractor ceases to have possession and the employer regains possession at practical completion. This is unless the contract provides for sectional completion and handover to the employer, for example, as provided for by recital 6 of the SBC. Where there is no express provision stating when the contractor is to lose possession of the site, they will be entitled to possession for so long as is necessary to allow them to perform their obligations under the contract, see *Castle Douglas and Dumfries Railway Company* v. *Lee, Son and Freeman* (1859).

Under clause 2.33 of the SBC, the Employer can, with the consent of the Contractor (which consent should not be unreasonably withheld), take possession of any part of the Works prior to practical or sectional completion (if applicable). The taking of partial possession will have important consequences for that part of the Works in respect of the practical completion date, the Rectification Period, insurance and liquidated damages, see clauses 2.34 to 2.37.

An intervening event may occur which allows the employer to take back possession of the site prior to practical completion, where for example they are entitled to terminate the contractor's employment under the contract. The Employer's grounds of termination are to be found in clauses 8.4, 8.5 and 8.6 of the SBC. In those circumstances, the Employer may take possession of the site under clause 8.7.2.1 and the contractor may be obliged to remove or have removed from the site any temporary buildings, plant, tools, equipment, goods and materials. Termination is considered below in section 9.4.

## 4.3 Administration

### 4.3.1 General

The employer is under an obligation to administer the site in such a way as to ensure that the Contractor can meet their obligations under the contract. In this chapter we will consider the obligation incumbent on the Employer under the SBC to appoint an Architect, together with the obligation not to interfere with the certifying process where a certifier, such as an architect, has been appointed and the obligation incumbent upon an employer to use his best endeavours to ensure that the architect carries out his required functions, where it appears that he may be failing to do so.

### 4.3.2 Appointment of architect and other professionals

The SBC requires the appointment of an Architect (or Contract Administrator, as the case may be) together with a Quantity Surveyor if appropriate, see Articles 3 and 4. The Architect will also be the CDM Co-ordinator for the purposes of the CDM regulations unless an alternative person is specified in article 5. The employer also has the option of appointing an employer's representative and/or clerk of works, see clauses 3.3 and 3.4. Under article 3 of SBC/DB the Employer will specify the Employer's Agent. The CDM Co-ordinator will be the contractor or such other alternative person specified in Article 5.

The architect acts in all respects as the employer's agent. Normally, the architect will have been appointed prior to the contractor tendering for the contract. Failure to appoint an architect where the employer is contractually obliged to do so is a breach of contract by the employer, see *London Borough of Merton* v. *Stanley Hugh Leach Ltd* (1985). Where the contract calls for the appointment of an architect, it may well be that this is a condition precedent to the contractor's obligation to perform the work. Contractors may, however, be personally barred from insisting on the appointment of the architect if, for example, they commence work and the contract proceeds without the appointment of an architect.

If for any reason the architect, contract administrator or quantity surveyor becomes unable to act, the employer has a duty to appoint a replacement. They should do so within a reasonable time and their refusal to do so may amount to a repudiation of the contract entitling the contractor to rescind. Repudiation and rescission are considered below in Chapter 9. Unless there is an express term to the contrary, the employer cannot appoint itself to perform the architect's, or any other professional's, certification or decision making functions part way through a building contract, see *Scheldebouw BV* v. *St James Homes (Grosvenor Dock) Ltd* (2006). The position is different under a design and build contract. There is no reason in principle why the employer cannot undertake such functions, and indeed the wording of SBC/DB suggests that it is the employer who has the primary obligation to undertake such roles, with the Employer's Agent acting in a delegated capacity.

Whilst in most contracts the identity of the architect will be expressly stated, it would be wise for the contract to be worded to refer to the appointment of the individual architect 'or such other person as may be nominated by the employer'. This is in order to avoid a situation arising where there may be confusion surrounding the existence of an obligation to appoint a successor should the appointment fail for any reason. In *Croudace Ltd* v. *London Borough of Lambeth* (1986) it was held that there had been a breach of contract on the part of the council where the architect employed by them on a contract, and who had been dealing with the contractor's claim for loss and expense, retired and the council delayed in appointing a successor. In that case, the architect named in the contract had a responsibility to ascertain the contractor's claims. There would appear to be an obligation on the employer to ensure that the successor to the original architect is reasonably competent to perform the job, see *London Borough of Merton* v. *Stanley Hugh Leach* (1985).

### 4.3.3 Nomination of sub-contractors and suppliers

An employer may decide to nominate a sub-contractor or supplier where, for example, they wish to ensure the quality of certain work that is to be performed, or the quality of certain materials that are to be supplied, or to avoid the price constraints which the contractor may be under. In these circumstances the sub-contractor/supplier is termed a nominated sub-contractor/supplier. Unlike its predecessors, the SBC does not contain any provisions allowing for nominated sub-contractors. Clause 3.8 gives the option to the Employer of listing not less than three persons in the Contract Bills to provide certain work measured or described there, however, the Contractor ultimately has the final say as to which of those persons on the list carries out that work and clause 3.8.4 makes it clear that that person remains a domestic sub-contractor as opposed to a nominated sub-contractor. As such, if the employer wishes to nominate a sub-contractor or supplier for a particular element of the works then the standard form will require to be revised. Sub-contractors and suppliers are considered below in Chapter 11.

### 4.3.4 Obligation of non-interference

The architect's role is *quasi* arbitral in nature. This is considered below in Chapter 7. Whilst he is a professional person, he is not independent. He is an agent of the employer, see *Beaufort Developments (NI) Ltd* v. *Gilbert-Ash NI Ltd and Another* (1998). The employer is nevertheless under an implied obligation not to interfere with the operation of the certification process by the architect. Employers may be open to a claim for damages should they attempt to do so. Employers owe a duty to ensure that the architect discharges his obligations properly, see *London Borough of Merton* v. *Stanley Hugh Leach Ltd* (1985). They may also owe to the contractor a duty to replace an incompetent architect where they become aware that the architect is failing to perform his functions under the contract, or is taking into account things he ought not to, having regard to the contract, see *Panamena Europea Navigacion Compania Limitada* v. *Frederick Leyland & Co. Ltd* (1947).

## 4.4 Information and instructions

The SBC provides that where not included in the Information Release Schedule, the Architect shall from time to time provide the Contractor with such further drawings or details as are reasonably necessary to explain and amplify the Contract Drawings and shall issue such instructions as are necessary to enable the Contractor to carry out and complete the Works in accordance with the Contract, see clause 2.12.1. Should the Contractor not receive information and/or instructions within the necessary time then this may be a relevant event entitling the Contractor to an extension of time, by virtue of clause 2.29.6, and also may be a matter materially affecting the regular progress of the Works which may entitle the Contractor to recover loss and expense, by virtue of clause 4.24.5. These obligations of the Employer correspond with the obligation of the Contractor, contained within clause 3.10, to comply with instructions issued by the Architect forthwith, subject to certain exceptions. The obligations of the Contractor are considered below in Chapter 5.

In *Neodox Ltd* v. *Swinton and Pendlebury BC* (1958), it was held that what was a reasonable time for the provision of details and instructions necessary for the execution of the work did not depend solely on the convenience and financial interests of the contractor. The employer, through his agents (the engineer in this case), was to have a period of time to provide the information which was reasonable having regard to the point of view of himself and his staff, as well as that of the contractor. It was held in this case that there was an implied term that details and other instructions necessary for the execution of the works should be given by the employer's agent from time to time in the course of the contract and should be given within a time reasonable in all the circumstances.

The employer, through its architect, will therefore be in breach of contract for failure to give details and information in sufficient time to enable the contractor to perform their obligations under the contract. This does not imply an obligation to provide information to contractors such that they can complete ahead of the contractually stipulated date, even if they have indicated that this is their intention, see *Glenlion Construction Ltd* v. *The Guinness Trust* (1987). As regards requests from the contractor for information and instructions required by him, it has been held that a document setting out in diagrammatic form the planned programme for the work and indicating the days by which instructions, drawings, details and levels were required, which was issued by the contractor at the commencement of the work, could amount to a specific application for information. It was held that the date specified for delivery of each set of instructions met the contractual requirement of not being unreasonably distant from nor unreasonably close to the relevant date, see *London Borough of Merton* v. *Stanley Hugh Leach Ltd* (1985).

Failure by the employer to provide the contractor with the drawings and necessary information to enable them to carry out their works may, depending on the importance of the work in question and after a reasonable request for the information by the contractor, constitute a repudiation of the contract entitling the contractor to rescind. Clause 8.9.2.2 of the SBC specifically provides that if the carrying out of the whole or substantially the whole of the uncompleted Works is suspended for a continuous period of the length specified in the Contract Particulars by reason of any impediment, prevention or default by, amongst others, the Architect, this will entitle the Contractor to terminate their employment under the contract. That clause would appear wide enough to cover suspension caused by failure to provide necessary information and/or instructions. Termination is considered below in section 9.4.

## 4.5 Variations

### 4.5.1 General

To instruct variations might be more appropriately described as a right the employer has, which imposes a corresponding obligation on the contractor to carry out the work so instructed, as well as an obligation on the employer to pay for the work instructed under the variation. The nature of variations and the treatment of them under the SBC will be considered here.

In general, neither of the parties to a building contract has an implied right to vary the works on the basis that, having entered into a contract to carry out certain works for a specific sum of money, the parties are entitled to stand by this and do no more than that which they have contracted to do. In reality, however, the work which was originally specified may have to be modified for a variety of reasons such as unexpected ground conditions or other circumstances which parties were not able to identify with any degree of certainty at the outset. This is particularly so on a major building project. In addition, the employer may wish to instruct the contractor to carry out certain extra works or, having discovered a quicker or easier way of doing something, to omit certain works that were originally included within the contract.

For these reasons, the contract, if in written form, will almost invariably entitle the employer to vary the works and a contractor will be under an obligation to carry out or omit works in accordance with a variation instruction. This is subject to the contractor's right to be paid for the work and to receive an extension of time if completion of the works is delayed as a result of the additional work instructed.

Essentially, a variation is a change in the scope of the contract works and is something that will lead to an adjustment of the contract price. Any work which the contractor is either expressly obliged to do in terms of the contract, or which is necessary by implication, falls within the contractual scope of the works and does not amount to a variation. It will therefore depend upon the terms of the contract as to whether or not an instruction to carry out certain works will amount to a variation of the contract works for which the contractor should be entitled to additional payment.

For example, in a contract which can truly be said to be lump sum there is no obligation on the employer to pay for work by way of a variation even if the work is not described or shown on drawings or if the contractor incurs additional costs due to the impracticable nature of the design. If the contract obliges the contractor to achieve a particular result, the contractor cannot claim as a variation a requirement to use more expensive materials if it becomes obvious that cheaper materials will not be appropriate. This is a risk the contractor takes in tendering a sum to achieve that end result. Contracts so far varied as to make them fundamentally different from that engaged for may give rise to a claim for pagment *quantum mercuit*, see *ERDC Construction Ltd* v. *H M Love & Co* (1995). *Quantum mercuit* is considered below in section 8.4. Likewise, if something is missing from the bills of quantities but, nevertheless, is necessary to achieve the end result, the requirement for the contractor to do that work will not amount to a variation. For example, in *Williams* v. *Fitzmaurice* (1858) a contractor was obliged to build a house which was to be ready by a specific date. The specification for the works did not include for any type of flooring and the contractor tried to state that he was entitled to extra payment for having to fix floorboards. However, as the contract was to achieve a particular result, namely, the completed house, the flooring was deemed to be included in the contract and did not amount to a variation.

The contract will often provide for the employer having power to vary the contract works (usually through the architect) and in these situations, the contractor will be obliged to comply with the instructions of the architect, which instructions, in the case of the SBC, should be in writing, see clause 3.12.1. Where an employer has varied the contract works their obligation to provide detailed drawings in respect of the varied works will be the same as their obligation to do so in relation to the contract works; that is to provide such drawings and information within a reasonable time to allow the contractor to perform their obligations in terms of the contract.

In interpreting the scope of the contract, whether or not the bills of quantities form a contract document will be of great importance. In the past, bills of quantities were considered to be only an estimate of the works that were used as a guide for the contractor. They were not contract documents and were not to be taken as having contractual effect. If more materials were required than were stated in the bills this did not amount to a variation of the contract works. Nowadays, bills of quantities may be incorporated as a means of pricing varied or omitted work that has been instructed by the architect. Where the bills of quantities are incorporated as a contract document, that is the contractor is to carry out the work stated in the bills of quantities, contract drawings and specification, then an increase in the quantities will amount to a variation. This can be the case even if the contract is said to be lump sum, see *Patman & Fotheringham Ltd* v. *Pilditch* (1904).

Where the contract gives the employer or his architect power to order variations it will specify the extent of this power and will provide that variations can be issued at any time up to completion of the works, subject to appropriate adjustments being made to the completion date and the contract price, see, for example, clauses 2.29.1 and 4.3.1.1 of the SBC respectively.

### 4.5.2 Variations under the SBC

In the SBC, the term 'variation' has a detailed definition, which is set out in clause 5.1, and has two separate meanings.

First, it means the alteration or modification of the design, quality or quantity of the works. This includes the addition, omission or substitution of any work; the alteration of the kind or standard of any of the materials or goods to be used in the works; or the removal from the site of any work executed, or materials or goods brought onto site by the contractor for the purposes of the works, other than work, materials or goods which are not in accordance with the contract.

Second, it means the imposition by the employer of any obligations or restrictions in regard to four defined matters or the addition to, or alteration or omission of, any such obligations or restrictions imposed by the employer in the contract bills in relation to the defined matters. The four defined matters are: access to the site or use of any specific parts of the site; limitations of working space; limitations of working hours; and the execution or completion of the work in any specific order. In SBC/DB the term 'Change' is used in place of 'Variation', but the meaning is the same.

The Architect's powers in respect of Variations are, largely, set out in clause 3.14. The Architect is expressly given the power to issue instructions requiring a Variation and any instruction issued by him in this regard is subject to the contractor's right of reasonable objection under clause 3.10.1, where the instruction relates to the alteration of the kind or standard of any of the materials or goods to be used in the Works. Similar powers are given to the Employer under clause 3.9 of SBC/DB. In addition to the Contractor's right of reasonable objection, clause 3.9.1 of SBC/DB provides that the Employer may not effect a Change which is, or which makes necessary, an alteration or modification in the design of the Works without the consent of the Contractor, which is not to be unreasonably withheld or delayed.

The Architect also has the power to issue instructions to expend provisional sums included in the Contract Bills or in the Employer's Requirements. The Architect is empowered to sanction in writing any Variations made by the Contractor otherwise than pursuant to an instruction of the Architect. Variations should be instructed or confirmed in writing by virtue of clause 3.12.1. If the Architect purports to issue an instruction otherwise than in writing, it will have no immediate effect. The contractor is required to confirm the instruction in writing to the Architect within seven days of receipt of that instruction and if not dissented to in writing by the Architect, it will take effect seven days after receipt of the Contractor's confirmation, see clause 3.12.2. Alternatively, the Architect can confirm the instruction in writing within seven days of giving the instruction in which case it takes effect from the date of that confirmation, see clause 3.12.3. If neither party confirms the instruction but the Contractor nevertheless complies with it, the Architect may, at any time prior to the issue of the Final Certificate, confirm the instruction in writing with retrospective effect, see clause 3.12.4. Similar provisions are contained in SBC/DB clause 3.7.

The issuing by the Architect of an instruction requiring a Variation is under clause 2.29.1 a relevant event entitling the contractor to an extension of time, but only insofar as the works have in fact been delayed by the issue of the instruction and so long as the contractor has followed the requirements of clause 2.28.6. The contractor is also entitled to payment for the work carried out in complying with the Architect's instruction and the SBC provides detailed provisions as to how such work should be valued. Those provisions are to be found in clauses 5.2 to 5.10.

The employer cannot vary the contract to the extent that it alters the fundamental nature of the contract works, see *McAlpine Humberoak Ltd* v. *McDermott International Inc* (1990). Nor can he vary the contract by omitting large aspects of it and then employing another contractor to carry out the work. That will amount to a repudiation which, in turn, entitles the contractor to rescind and seek damages, see *Commissioner for Main Roads* v. *Reed & Stuart Pty Ltd* (1974).

Although under the SBC there is a requirement for variation instructions to be in writing, this may be waived in certain circumstances. Examples of such circumstances are: where the work is of such a different character or nature that it is said to be outside the terms of the contract and forms a separate contract; where the main contract is no longer operative; where the final certificate has been issued including a sum for the variations and there is no opportunity for review of this; where an arbiter is given the power to consider whether the work is or is not a variation and he decides that the work done was a variation; or where, for any other reason, the employer is personally barred from insisting, or has waived his right to dispute, that something was properly a variation where the instruction was not in writing.

## 4.6 Other obligations

### 4.6.1 Payment

The other main obligation owed by the employer to the contractor under a building contract, as outlined at the start of this chapter, is to make payment for the works executed under the contract. The obligation incumbent on the employer to make payment to the contractor is of such significance that it is considered separately in Chapter 8. In the context of the SBC, payment is conditional upon the issue of certificates which are, therefore, also significant in the context of payment. Certification is considered below in Chapter 7.

Under SBC/DB there are two alternative mechanisms for interim payments. The appropriate alternative must be selected by an entry in the Contract Particulars. Payment may be made on the basis of stage payments (Alternative A) or on the basis of the value of work executed (Alternative B). In each case, the Contractor must make an application for interim payment. In the case of Alternative A, the application will be made following the completion of a relevant stage, while under Alternative B the applications are made at monthly intervals. Since the final date for payment is 14 days from receipt of the application, the application is, in effect, a condition precedent to an interim payment.

### 4.6.2 Insurance and indemnity

In considering the obligations incumbent upon employers under building contracts, the issues of insurance and indemnity are also worthy of mention. At common law, there is no implied obligation incumbent upon an employer, to insure, however, frequently the form of contract used by parties, such as the SBC, will include such obligations. These are considered separately in Chapter 14 below.

### 4.6.3 Health and safety

As with all other employers (in the employer/employee sense, as opposed to the building contract sense), employers owe a number of duties in respect of health and safety. Similar duties are incumbent upon contractors. In the area of building contracts such duties are, generally, more pertinent to contractors. These matters are considered below in Chapter 19.

# Chapter 5
# Contractors' Obligations

## 5.1 Introduction

As with the obligations of the employer, a building contract will ordinarily set out, in express terms, the obligations owed by the contractor to the employer. Similarly, where these are not expressed, certain terms will be implied into the parties' contract. The majority of the obligations considered in this chapter relate to the execution of the works, but it should be borne in mind that parties are free to contract in whatever manner they see fit. Accordingly, certain other types of obligation are routinely imposed upon contractors, for example, the obligation to take out and maintain insurance under the SBC.

## 5.2 Completing the works

### 5.2.1 Common law

Where a contractor is engaged to carry out specified work, they have an obligation to carry out and complete that work. This carries with it the obligation to execute the work in a good and workmanlike manner using the skill and care to be expected of a builder of ordinary competence. This involves adopting methods which are in accordance with the regular practice in the building trade at the time, see *Morrison's Associated Companies Ltd* v. *James Rome & Sons Ltd* (1964). The exception to this would be if, in particular circumstances, there was an indication of an unusual or extraordinary risk in doing the work in the normal manner. In these circumstances, the contractor would be required to carry out the works in a different way or else would run the risk of being found negligent, see *Morrison's Associated Companies Ltd*.

### 5.2.2 The SBC provisions

The SBC provisions expressly include the obligation to carry out and complete the works. This is to be found in Article 1 of the Articles of Agreement and clause 2.1 of the Conditions. The obligation is to carry out and complete the works in a proper and workmanlike manner and in accordance with the

Contract Documents (namely the Contract Drawings, the Schedule, the Contract Bills, the Agreement and the Conditions together with, where applicable, the Employer's Requirements, the Contractor's Proposals and the CDP Analysis and any other Contract Documents listed in Schedule Part 8). In relation to the particular provisions of SBC/DB, see sections 5.2.3 and 5.3.4.

As the work proceeds, the contract allows the Architect to issue instructions and the Contractor has an obligation, under clause 3.10, to comply with all instructions issued to him in regard to any matter over which the Architect has power under the contract to issue instructions. The instruction may be one which requires a Variation under clause 5.1. Variations are considered above in Chapter 4.

The Architect may, in terms of clause 5.3.1, in his instruction for a Variation state that the Contractor is to provide a 'Schedule Part 2 Quotation'. This is a reference to the procedure set out in the Schedule Part 2 for submission by the Contractor of a quotation setting out the amount of the adjustment to the Contract Sum, including the effect of the instruction on other work supported by all necessary calculations, any adjustment to the time required for completion of the Works and/or Section to the extent that this is not covered by any revision to the Completion Date already made, the amount to be paid in lieu of any ascertainment under clause 4.23 of direct loss and/or expense not already included elsewhere, a fair and reasonable amount in respect of the cost of preparing the Schedule Part 2 Quotation and indicative information on any additional resources required to carry out the Variation and the method of carrying it out.

The Quotation is to be sufficiently detailed to allow it to be evaluated by or for the Employer. Schedule Part 2 requires the Contractor to prepare such a Quotation within 21 days of being instructed to do so or of receipt of sufficient information to allow him to do so, whichever is later and is to be open for acceptance by the Employer for seven days from its receipt by the Quantity Surveyor. The Schedule then sets out the procedure for acceptance or rejection of the Quotation.

This procedure is time consuming and requires significant input from both the Architect, in terms of detailing the proposed Variation, and the Contractor in preparing the Quotation. It is therefore likely to be used only for the most significant proposed Variations.

There are sanctions available against the Contractor, in terms of clause 3.11, if he fails to comply with an instruction. These allow the Employer, if there is non-compliance within seven days after receipt of a notice, to employ and pay others to carry out the work required and provides that the Contractor is responsible for all additional costs incurred as a result. These are deducted from the Contract Sum.

A further matter arising from variations is the Contractor's entitlement to additional time. Under clause 2.27.1 the Contractor is obliged, if and when it becomes reasonably apparent that progress of the work or any section is being or is likely to be delayed, to give written notice to the Architect of the circumstances of this including the cause or causes of the delay, and to identify any event which is a Relevant Event. The contract contains a list of circumstances which are termed Relevant Events, which includes Variations (clause 2.29.1) and instructions of the Architect under certain clauses (clause 2.29.2). The Contractor is required in terms of clause 2.27.2, in respect of each event identified in the notice, either in the notice or in writing thereafter, to give particulars of its expected effects, including an estimate of the expected delay in the completion of the works or any section. The Contractor is in terms of clause 2.27.3 to notify the Architect of any material change in his estimated delay or in other particulars and to supply such further information as the Architect may reasonably require.

Upon an application by the Contractor, if the Architect considers completion of the work or any section is likely to be delayed beyond the relevant completion date, the Architect shall give an extension of time to the Contractor and fix a later date as the completion date for the works or the sections that he considers to be fair and reasonable all in terms of clause 2.28.1. Extensions of time are considered in more detail below in Chapter 6.

Finally, Variations can also give rise to loss and expense being payable to the Contractor. As soon as it has become or should reasonably have become apparent to the Contractor that regular progress of the work has been or is likely to be affected by one of the Relevant Matters listed in the contract, the Contractor can, in accordance with clause 4.23, make written application to the Architect stating that he has incurred or is likely to incur direct loss and/or expense for which he would not be reimbursed by a payment under any other provision of the contract. One of the Relevant Matters to which this applies is Variations, see clause 4.24.1. If the Architect considers that the regular progress of the works has been or is likely to be materially affected as stated in the Contractor's application, or that direct loss and/or expense has been or is likely to be incurred, he ascertains (or instructs the quantity surveyor to ascertain) the amount of direct loss and/or expense sustained by the Contractor. Any amount so ascertained falls to be added to the Contract Sum in accordance with both clauses 4.3.3.4 and 4.25.

There may be work which does not form part of the Contractor's contract which the Employer wishes to carry out himself or which he wishes others to carry out. In such cases, clause 2.7.1 provides that if the Contract Bills provide the information necessary to allow the Contractor to carry out and complete the Works in accordance with the Contract, the Contractor shall permit the execution of such work. Where the Bills do not do so, clause 2.7.2 provides that the Employer may arrange for the work to be executed, although this requires the Contractor's consent.

The Contractor has obligations in relation to the availability of Contract Documents. The Contractor is obliged, under clause 2.8.3 to keep on site and available to the Architect or his representative at all reasonable times a copy of the Contract Drawings, the unpriced bills of quantities, the Contractor's Designed Portion documents (where applicable), the descriptive Schedules or similar documents necessary for use in carrying out the Works as referred to in clause 2.9.1.1, the master programme referred to in clause 2.9.1.2 and the drawings and details referred to in clauses 2.10 and 2.12.

The obligation in relation to the master programme in clause 2.9.1.2 is that the Contractor is required, without charge, to provide to the Architect two copies of his master programme for the execution of the Works and, within 14 days of any extension of time awarded under clause 2.28.1 or of agreement of any Pre-agreed Adjustment fixing a revised Completion Date due to acceptance of a Schedule Part 2 Quotation, an amendment or revision to the programme to take account of that.

In relation to Contractor's Designed Portion Works, the Contractor is, under clause 2.9.2.1, to provide without charge to the Architect, two copies of such Contractor's Design Documents and (if requested) related calculations and information, as are reasonably necessary to explain or amplify the Contractor's Proposals and, under clause 2.9.2.2, all levels and setting out dimensions which the Contractor prepares or uses for the purposes of carrying out and completing the Contractor's Designed Portion.

The Contractor's Design Documents and other information referred to in clause 2.9.2.1 are to be provided as and when necessary and in accordance with the Contractor's Design Submission Procedure set out in Schedule Part 1 or as stated elsewhere in the Contract Documents and the Contractor is not to commence any work to which such a document relates before that procedure has been complied with, all in terms of clause 2.9.3.

The Contractor's Design Submission Procedure in Schedule Part 1 sets out in detail what documents are to be prepared and submitted by the Contractor, the format of these and their timing. It also sets out the procedure for comment by the Architect who can provide an 'A', 'B' or 'C' rating with 'A' meaning the Contractor is to carry out the work in strict accordance with the document, 'B' meaning the Contractor is to carry out the work in accordance with the document but taking on board the Architect's comments and 'C' meaning the Architect's comments are to be taken into account and the document resubmitted. Work is not to be carried out in accordance with a document marked 'C'. The Employer has no liability to pay for any work within the Contractor's Designed Portion Works executed otherwise than in accordance with Contractor's Design Documents marked 'A' or 'B'. In cases of disagreement by the Contractor with the Architect's comments, the Schedule sets out a procedure for the contractor to challenge them in which case the Architect is required to reconsider and either confirm or withdraw the comment. All of this is subject to the overriding obligation of the Contractor to ensure that the Contractor's Design Documents and the Contractor's Designed Portion Works are in accordance with the contract.

In relation to levels required for the execution of the Works, the Architect is, in terms of clause 2.10, to provide these in the form of accurately dimensioned drawings containing the information required to allow the Contractor to set out the Works. This does not apply to Contractor's Designed Portion Works. The Contractor is responsible under clause 2.10 for amending any errors arising from his own inaccurate setting out at no cost to the Employer, that is unless the Architect instructs that such errors are to remain but, if they do, then a deduction is made from the Contract Sum.

The Architect has obligations in terms of clause 2.12.1 to provide further drawings or details as are reasonably necessary to explain and amplify the Contract Drawings. These are, under clause 2.12.2, to be provided at the time it is reasonably necessary for the Contractor to receive them having regard to the progress of the Works. The Contractor's obligation in relation to this is, in terms of clause 2.12.3, where the Contractor has reason to believe the Architect is not aware of the time by which the Contractor needs the information, to advise the Architect sufficiently in advance to allow him to comply with his clause 2.12 obligations. In this way, whilst the primary obligation is on the Architect, there is still a secondary obligation on the Contractor who, therefore, cannot simply sit back and wait for information to arrive but must proactively seek it. This is consistent with the obligation in clause 2.28.6.1 to constantly use best endeavours to prevent delay in the progress of the Works or any Section, however caused, and to prevent the completion of the Works or any Section being delayed or further delayed beyond the relevant Completion Date.

The Contractor has further obligations in relation to access to the site. In terms of clause 3.1, the Architect is to have access at all reasonable times to the Works but also to any workshop or other premises of the Contractor where work is being prepared for the contract. If work is being prepared by sub-contractors then the Contractor is to include a provision in the sub-contract to secure a similar right of access to the sub-contractor's premises and is to do 'all things reasonably necessary' to make that right effective. Such rights of access are subject to reasonable restrictions which are necessary to protect proprietary rights in the property.

In terms of the Contractor's representatives on site, the Contractor's obligation is, under clause 3.2, to ensure that at all times he has on site a competent person-in-charge. Any instructions or directions issued to that person are deemed to be issued to the Contractor. The Employer can also appoint representatives who can include a clerk of works. The Contractor is required, under clause 3.4, to allow any clerk of works to carry out his duty of acting as inspector on behalf of the Employer. The Contractor's obligation to carry out and complete the Works in accordance with the contract Conditions does not alter, as provided by clause 3.6, regardless of any such inspections by the clerk of works or the Architect.

Sub-contracting of parts of the Works is commonplace but contractors are, in terms of clause 3.7.1, not to sub-let the whole or any part of the works without the written consent of the Architect. The same applies under clause 3.7.2, where there is a Contractor's Designed Portion, to sub-letting of the design work. The Contractor maintains his obligation to carry out and complete the works and other contractual obligations regardless of any subletting. The position in relation to sub-contractors and suppliers is dealt with in more detail in Chapter 11.

As the work progresses, the Contractor may find fossils, antiquities and other objects of interest or value on the site. On making such a discovery the Contractor is obliged in terms of clause 3.22 to use best endeavours not to disturb the discovered item and to cease work insofar as continuing with the work would endanger the item or prevent or impede its excavation or removal, to take steps to preserve the item in the exact position and condition in which it was found and to inform the Architect of its discovery. The Architect may issue instructions in relation to the item in terms of clause 3.23. The Contractor does have a corresponding right in terms of clause 3.24 if compliance with such obligations involves the contractor in incurring loss and/or expense for which he would not be reimbursed under any other provision of the contract. Compliance with instructions issued under clause 3.23 is also a Relevant Event for the purposes of the extension of time provisions in clause 2.28.

The SBC defines completion of the works or section of work as being when in the opinion of the Architect practical completion of the works or a section is achieved and the Contractor has complied sufficiently with the requirements of clauses 2.40 and 3.25.3. These relate to the provision of the Contractor's Design Documents showing or describing the Contractor's Designed Portion as built, where the contract includes a Contractor's Designed Portion, and the provision of information for the Health and Safety file that is required by the CDM Regulations. At this date the Architect issues the Practical Completion Certificate under clause 2.30. This has been taken as meaning that the works have been completed for all practical purposes and the Employer could take them over and use them for their intended purpose, see *Borders Regional Council* v. *J Smart & Co. (Contractors) Ltd* (1983). The issue of the Practical Completion Certificate triggers the release of the first half of the retention fund under clauses 4.20.2 and 4.20.3.

The Employer may take possession of the works once practical completion has been achieved. This does not put an end to the Contractors' obligations. They remain responsible for remedying any defects, shrinkages or other faults which may appear during the Rectification Period and which are due to materials or workmanship not in accordance with the contract or any failure of the Contractor to comply with his obligations in respect of the Contractor's Designed Portion, see clause 2.38. This is more fully dealt with in section 5.3 below.

Once the defects, shrinkages and other faults as specified in the schedule of defects have been made good, the architect issues a Certificate of Making Good under clause 2.39. This triggers the release of the second half of the retention fund under clause 4.20.3.

### 5.2.3 The SBC Design and Build Contract

The SBC/DB is a stand-alone document and adopts the same format as the other SBC 2005 forms (although the clause numbering is not identical).

Save in certain specific respects, referred to in more detail below, it does not depart significantly from the Scottish Supplement to JCT Standard Form of Building Contract With Contractor's Design 1998 Edition ('WCD 98').

The SBC/DB generally follows the principles of the SBC where there is a Contractor's Designed Portion, with the design requirements being set out in the Employer's Requirements and the Contractor's Proposals. The relationship between the Employer's Requirements and the Contractor's Proposals inherent in WCD 98 is maintained, i.e. that the Contractor's Proposals are intended to constitute the Contractor's response to the Employer's design requirements. As stated in the SBCC Guide to the SBC/DB:

'Depending upon the procurement approach adopted, the level of detail within the Employer's Requirements may vary between a performance orientated statement of objectives and a detailed and prescriptive statement of what the Contractor is to provide. Similarly, and responding to the degree of detail within the Employer's Requirements, the Contractor's Proposals may contain the result of substantial design development work or may simply be a reiteration of the Employer's Requirements'.

The break-down of the lump sum contract price is contained in the Contract Sum Analysis and this should be in sufficient detail to allow for monthly interim valuations where Alternative B of the SBC/DB clause 4.9 has been selected. The contract is administered on behalf of the Employer by the Employer's Agent rather than by an architect or contract administrator. Broadly, the duties carried out by the Architect/Contract Administrator under the other SBC forms are carried out under the SBC/DB by the Employer and, in practice, these duties will be delegated to the Employer's Agent. The Articles of Agreement provide that, save to the extent otherwise specified by written notice by the Employer, the Employer's Agent shall have full authority to receive and issue applications, consents, instructions, notices, requests or statements and otherwise to act for the Employer under any of the conditions. Thus it will be the Employer's Agent who will, for example, issue valuations for payment, issue the practical completion statement, issue instructions, and determine applications for extensions of time and loss and expense. Other significant features of the SBC/DB are:

- The inclusion of a Contractor's Design Submission Procedure similar to that in the SBC where there is a Contractor's Designed Portion (see description in section 5.2.2 above).
- Collateral Warranties or Third Party Rights from the Contractor to purchasers, tenants and funders and collateral warranties from relevant Sub-Contractors, including warranties to the Employer (see Chapter 13).
- A requirement on the Contractor to maintain professional indemnity insurance.

- The retention of the term 'change' as opposed to 'variation' (the latter being used in the other SBC forms).
- The use of the terms 'Practical Completion Statement' and 'Notice of Completion of Making Good' instead of the 'certificate' terminology used in the other SBC forms.
- Express limitations on the Contractor's responsibility for the Employer's Requirements which did not previously appear in WCD 98 (see section 5.3.4 below).
- Clause 3.9 provides that the Employer may not instruct a Change which is, or makes necessary, an alteration or modification in the design of the Works, without the consent of the Contractor, which is not to be unreasonably withheld or delayed.

## 5.3 Quality of the work

### 5.3.1 Workmanship and design at common law

As far as workmanship is concerned, at common law, the contractor has an obligation to execute the work in a good and workmanlike manner using the skill and care to be expected of a builder of ordinary competence. This obligation subsists whilst the works are being carried out, it does not only arise at completion, see *Surrey Heath Borough Council* v. *Lovell Construction Ltd and Another* (1998).

The test of what constitutes such skill and care is the standard of the ordinary skilled contractor exercising and professing to have that particular skill. It is not necessary to possess the highest expert skill but is sufficient to exercise the ordinary skill of an ordinary competent contractor exercising the particular skill, see *Bolam* v. *Friern Hospital Management Committee* (1957).

It may not be sufficient to show the contractor did the same as other contractors if it can be shown the generally accepted practice is not correct, see *Sidaway* v. *Board of Governors of the Bethem Royal Hospital and the Maudsley Hospital* (1985).

The obligation may go further than simply carrying out the work as it is contained on drawings or in other design information provided by the design team.

In a case where the contractor was to provide all materials and perform all work shown on an architect's drawings, but where they were not supervised by an architect or engineer, it was found that the contractor had accepted that the employer was relying on their skill as contractors. There were defects in the plans provided to the contractor. The contractor ought to have recognised the defects and, since they were being relied on by the employer, had a duty to warn the employer of the defects in the plans and the difficulties which would arise if the plans were followed, see *Brunswick Construction Ltd* v. *Nowlan & Others* (1974).

The courts have been willing to imply a term into a contract requiring a contractor to warn of design defects as soon as the contractor came to be aware that they existed. In a case where the court considered it must have become apparent during construction work that the design of curtain walling was unbuildable, it was found this should have been reported. This was on the basis that if, on examining the drawings or as a result of experience on site, a contractor formed the opinion that in some respect the design would not work, or would not work satisfactorily, it would be absurd for them to carry on building in accordance with it. The contractor was found to have a duty of care to warn the employer and architect of design defects known to them, see *Equitable Debenture Assets Corporation Ltd* v. *William Moss Group Ltd and Others* (1984).

The duty to warn goes further. A term has been implied into a contract requiring the contractor to warn the architect of defects in the design which they believe to exist. This does not oblige the contractor to carry out a critical examination of the drawings, bills and specifications looking for mistakes. The contractor's primary duty is to build not to scrutinise the design. The obligation to warn arises when, in the light of their general knowledge and practical experience, the contractor believes or comes to believe that an aspect of the design is wrong, see *Victoria University of Manchester* v. *Hugh Wilson & Others* (1984).

Even though the contractor has to be satisfied that the design is satisfactory or suitable, the work is still required to be carried out in accordance with good building practice. A contractor cannot rely on drawings or designs produced by a surveyor to relieve them of this duty, see *Mackay* v. *Stitt* (1988). The contractor, if not satisfied with a design that is produced to him, has a duty to raise any queries with the design team. Even if the contractors are given such assurances they may, if still not satisfied, need to take precautions against failure of the design. If they do not do so then they may be found to have acted with less care than is to be expected of an ordinary competent builder, see *Edward Lindenberg* v. *Joe Canning and Others* (1992).

Where there are health and safety considerations, the duty to warn can go further. In a case where temporary support was to be provided to roof trusses, the sub-contractor considered the propping as designed to be inadequate. They advised the designer but did not follow up their objections. The propping failed, causing the roof to collapse. It was found that the sub-contractor ought to have pressed its objections on safety grounds and made these progressively more formal and insistent including putting them into writing, approaching higher levels of management, threatening to or actually reporting the problem to the regulatory authorities and, ultimately, suspending work, see *Plant Construction plc* v. *Clive Adams Associates and Others* (2000).

The courts have, however, refused to extend the duty to warn to cover a situation where a design and construct contractor who was being advised by structural engineers claimed that specialist underpinning contractors ought to have advised them of the need for temporary lateral support to be provided while the basement was being excavated. This claim was made on the basis that it was said the underpinning contractor knew and/or it was obvious that there was a significant danger the design and construct contractor might excavate the basement without providing such support. Given the danger of the excavation proceeding without the support it was said it could not be assumed by the underpinning contractor that the excavation would be carried out safely. The court accepted that if the underpinning contractor had been instructed to carry out work it knew to be unsuitable and dangerous then it would have a duty to warn the contractor, even though the contractor was itself receiving advice from a structural engineer. However, in this case, the work was to be carried out by another party in the future. The underpinning contractor did not know how the contractor intended to carry out the work. It was accepted that the method chosen by the contractor was negligent. It was considered relevant that the contractor was receiving advice from a structural engineer. In these circumstances it was considered unreasonable to impose a duty to warn on the underpinning contractor, see *Aurum Investments Ltd* v. *Avonforce Ltd (In Liquidation) and Others* (2000).

Where the contractor is not responsible for the design of a system or its integration into the works or for the selection of a proprietary system, there is no implied warranty by the contractor that the system will work, see *Greater Glasgow Health Board* v. *Keppie Henderson & Partners* (1989).

The view of what constitutes normal practice may alter depending upon the nature of the development. For example, where plumbing sub-contractors in a multi-storey flat development took the normal steps which would be taken to drain pipes of water in ordinary houses or small developments, they were found to be to blame for damage caused by burst pipes – the burst being caused by water which had not been drained from the pipes. The plumbing sub-contractors had failed to warn anyone that the pipes could not be completely drained. The normal practice of draining pipes, which resulted in some water remaining, did not apply in the face of the extent of the damage which might be expected in a multi-storey development were this to be followed, see *Holland & Hannen & Cubitts (Scotland) Ltd* v. *Alexander Macdougall & Co. (Engineers) Ltd* (1968).

Where employers make known the purpose of the building and circumstances indicate that they are relying upon the contractor's skill and judgement to provide it, there is an implied term that the works will be fit for the purpose for which they were intended. Where a contractor expressly undertakes to carry out work which will perform a certain duty or function in conformity with plans or specifications, a 'fitness for purpose' obligation, and it turns out that the works would not perform that function if the plans were followed, the contractor will be liable for the failure to perform even if the work was carried out in accordance with the plans and specifications.

In a case where contractors were employed on a design and build contract to build a new factory, warehouse and offices it was made known to the contractor that oil drums stored in the warehouse would be moved around by forklift trucks. When constructed, the movement of the forklifts caused vibrations which led to cracking of the floor. It was found that since the employer had made known to the contractor the purpose for which the building was required, they had relied on the contractor's skill and judgement. The contractor was therefore required to ensure the building was reasonably fit for its purpose, see *Greaves & Co. (Contractors) Ltd* v. *Baynham Meikle & Partners* (1975).

General observations about fitness for purpose obligations were made in a case related to the standard of duty to be implied into a town development agreement and whether an obligation was to be implied that the houses to be built were to be fit for human habitation. It was observed that where a contractor has design responsibility their duties are to carry out the work in a good and workmanlike manner, to supply good and proper materials and to provide a building reasonably fit for human habitation, see *Test Valley Borough Council* v. *Greater London Council* (1979).

In a case concerning the collapse of an aerial mast, the court said it saw no reason why if contractors contract in the course of their business to design, supply and erect a television aerial mast, they should not be under an obligation to ensure that it is reasonably fit for the purpose for which they knew it was intended. The question to be asked is whether the person for whom the mast was designed relied on the skill of the supplier to supply and design a mast fit for the purpose for which it was known to be required, see *Independent Broadcasting Authority* v. *EMI Electronics Ltd and BICC Construction Ltd* (1980).

In a case where a contractor was to design and build houses for a local authority and the authority had made known the purpose for which the work was required so as to show reliance on the contractor by the employer a term that the buildings designed by the contractor as dwellings should be fit for habitation on completion was implied into the contract, see *Basildon District Council* v. *J E Lesser Properties* (1984).

In assessing whether there is an implied fitness for purpose obligation there is no distinction to be made between reliance by the employer in relation to the quality of materials and their design, the design and specifications of the functional parts of the installation as a whole and the condition of the ground as all of these are integral parts of the whole and all are interdependent on each other. The term of reasonable fitness for purpose will be implied irrespective of whether there has been any negligence or fault or whether the unfitness results from quality of work, quality of materials or defects in the design, see *Viking Grain Storage* v. *T H White Installations Ltd* (1985).

The duty can be limited to certain aspects of the work only. In a case where an employer advised the contractor that boilers were to be installed in flats which were thereafter to be sold and the contractors recommended boilers, the employer's claim that although the boilers worked satisfactorily they resulted in lower SAP (Standard Assessment Procedure) ratings for the flats making them more difficult to sell, failed. It was found that as the employer had only given partial information to the contractor, which did not include information upon which they could form a view as to the effect of the boilers on the SAP ratings, the employer had not relied on the contractor to advise in relation to this. The contractor had only been relied on to the extent of advice as to the qualities of the boilers generally so that there was only partial reliance. The contractor's duty had been fulfilled in relation to the issue on which the employer had relied on them, see *Jewsons Ltd* v. *Leanne Boykan* (2004).

The contractor in a contract including an element of design responsibility may have an obligation to complete a design which has been commenced by others. In a case where the contractor was to design piled walls, they relied on the content of a report on ground conditions prepared by the employer's engineer. It was found that the design obligation was to complete the design of the piled walls. This meant developing the conceptual design of the engineers into a complete design capable of being constructed. Understanding the principles underlying the work and forming a view as to their sufficiency was required so that the completed design as a whole was prepared with reasonable skill and care, see *Co-operative Insurance Society Ltd* v. *Henry Boot (Scotland) Ltd* (2002). This has implications for the Contractor's responsibility for inadequacies in the Employer's Requirements under the SBC where there is a Contractor's Designed Portion and under the SBC/DB, see section 5.3.4.

The implied fitness for purpose obligations described above can, of course, be (and, more often than not, are) displaced by the express terms of the contract imposing a 'reasonable skill and care' standard, see the SBC clause 2.19.1 (where there is a Contractor's Designed Portion) and the SBC/DB clause 2.17.1, referred to in more detail in section 5.3.3 below.

### 5.3.2  Materials – common law

Until 1995 (when the relevant statute was extended to Scotland) it was the case that the common law implied into contracts that required the supply of materials, terms that the materials used would be of good quality and would be reasonably fit for the purpose for which they were used, unless it could be demonstrated that the parties' intention was to exclude the implied terms, or either of them, see *Young & Marten Ltd* v. *McManus Childs Ltd* (1968). Where the purchaser made known to the contractor the particular purpose for which the materials were required, so as to show that reliance was being placed on the contractor's skill and judgement, and where the materials were of a type which it was in the course of the contractor's business to supply, it was implied that the materials would be reasonably fit for that purpose, see *Young & Marten Ltd*.

There was a further obligation in relation to materials, namely, that they had to be free from defects which would have meant that they were not of the requisite quality. This also applies to latent defects which could have been detected using due skill and care. This did not, however, go so far as to imply a warranty by the contractor that the materials were suitable for the contract purpose in circumstances where the selection of the materials or their suitability was not a matter for the discretion of the contractor, see *Greater Glasgow Health Board* v. *Keppie Henderson & Partners* (1989).

The matter of implied terms in relation to the supply of materials is now dealt with by the Supply of Goods and Services Act 1982 which was extended to Scotland in relation to contracts made on or after 3 January 1995. Implied terms as to quality and fitness are now to be found in s.11D(2) and (6).

### 5.3.3 Workmanship, design and materials under the SBC

By virtue of clause 2.3.1 of the SBC the Contractor is obliged to use materials and goods for the Works of the kinds and standards described in the Contract Bills. Materials and goods for any Contractor's Designed Portion Works are to be of the kinds and standards described in the Employer's Requirements, Contractor's Proposals or the Contractor's Design Documents, see clause 2.3.1. The Contractor is not permitted to substitute any materials or goods without the written consent of the Architect.

There is a further provision in clause 4.1 which provides that the quality and quantity of the work included in the Contract Sum is deemed to be that set out in the Contract Bills and, where there is a Contractor's Designed Portion, in the Contractor's Designed Portion documents.

Workmanship for the Works, excluding Contractor's Designed Portion Works, is to be of the standards described in the Contract Bills. Workmanship for any Contractor's Designed Portion Works is to be of the standards described in the Employer's Requirements or Contractor's Proposals, all by virtue of clause 2.3.2.

The terms as to quality of materials or goods and standards of workmanship are subject to the proviso in clause 2.3.3 that where and to the extent that these are a matter for the opinion of the Architect, such quality and standards are to be to his reasonable satisfaction. To the extent that the quality of materials or goods or standards of workmanship are not described in the manner set out in clauses 2.3.1 and 2.3.2, nor stated to be a matter for the Architect's opinion or satisfaction, they are required, under clause 2.3.3 in the case of the Contractor's Designed Portion, to be of a standard appropriate to it and in any other case, of a standard appropriate to the Works.

The Contractor is required by clause 2.3.4, if the Architect requests, to provide reasonable proof that the materials and goods comply with clause 2.3.

The Contractor has an obligation, in terms of clause 2.3.5 to take all reasonable steps to encourage Contractor's Persons to be registered cardholders under the Construction Skills Certification Scheme (CSCS) or qualified under an equivalent recognised qualification scheme. The CSCS was set up in the mid-1990s with the aim of improving quality standards in the construction industry and reducing accidents by raising health and safety standards. It is managed by CSCS Limited whose board includes representatives of the

Construction Confederation, Federation of Master Builders, GMB Union, National Specialist Contractors Council, Transport & General Workers Union, Union of Construction, Allied Trades and Technicians, CITB – Construction Skills, Construction Industry Council and the Construction Clients Group.

If there is any discrepancy in, or divergence between, Contract Documents, clause 2.15 provides that the Contractor is required to give immediate notice to the Architect of this and the Architect is then required, by clause 2.15, to issue instructions to the Contractor as to how the discrepancy or divergence is to be dealt with.

Where any discrepancy or divergence to be notified under clause 2.15 is within or between Contractor's Designed Portion Documents other than the Employer's Requirements, the Contractor is, under clause 2.16.1, to send with his notice, or as soon as reasonably practicable thereafter, a statement setting out his proposed amendments to remove it. Where the discrepancy is within the Employer's Requirements, the Contractor's Proposals prevail. Where the Contractor's Proposals do not deal with such a discrepancy, the Contractor is to inform the Architect of their proposed amendment to deal with it. The Architect either agrees to that or decides how the discrepancy is to be dealt with and that agreement or decision is treated as a Variation, see clause 2.16.2.

If the Contractor becomes aware of any divergence between the Statutory Requirements and the Contract Documents, then, under clause 2.17.1, they are immediately to give notice to the Architect specifying the divergence and, where it is between the Statutory Requirements and any of the Contractor's Designed Portion documents, the Contractor is to inform the Architect of their proposed amendment for removing it. Under clause 2.17.2 the Architect is then to issue instructions in that regard within seven days of becoming aware of such divergence or within 14 days of receipt of the Contractor's proposed amendment, where applicable.

Clause 2.18.1 makes provision for emergency compliance with Statutory Requirements in such circumstances. If the Contractor has had to supply materials and/or execute work before receiving instructions, the Contractor is to supply such limited materials and execute such limited work as is reasonably necessary to secure immediate compliance with the Statutory Requirements. The Contractor is then obliged, in terms of clause 2.18.2, to inform the Architect of the emergency and the steps taken under clause 2.18.1.

Where there is any failure to comply with clause 2.1 in regard to the carrying out of the work in a proper and workmanlike manner and/or in accordance with the health and safety plan, clause 3.19 provides that the Architect may issue whatever instructions are reasonably necessary as a result. If this is done, the Contractor receives no addition to the Contract Sum and no extension of time for complying with such an instruction.

Where the Works include a Contractor's Designed Portion, the Contractor is required, in terms of clause 2.2.1, to complete the design, including the selection of any specifications for the kinds and standards of the materials, goods and workmanship so far as these are not described or stated in the Employer's Requirements or Contractor's Proposals, in accordance with the Contract Drawings and Contract Bills.

In terms of clause 2.2.2 the Contractor is to comply with the Architect's directions for the integration of the design of the Contractor's Designed Portion with the design of the Works as a whole. This obligation is subject to the provisions of clause 3.10.3, which allows the Contractor, if in his opinion compliance with a direction under clause 2.2.2 or any Architect's instruction would injuriously affect the efficacy of the design of the Contractor's Designed Portion, to give notice in writing to the Architect specifying the injurious effect. In these circumstances, the direction or instruction shall not take effect unless confirmed by the Architect.

The Contractor has an obligation, in complying with clause 2.2 and in terms of clause 2.2.3, to comply with the CDM Regulations. Health and safety matters are considered in Chapter 19.

The Contractor is not responsible for the content of the Employer's Requirements or for verifying the adequacy of any design contained within them, see clause 2.13.2.

Where there is a Contractor's Designed Portion, clause 2.19.1 provides that insofar as its design is comprised in the Contractor's Proposals and in what the Contractor is to complete in accordance with the Employer's Requirements and the contract Conditions, the Contractor has, in respect of any inadequacy in the design, the same liability to the Employer as an Architect or other appropriate professional designer would have who held himself out as competent to take on work for such design.

The Contractor's liability for loss of use, loss of profit or other consequential loss arising from the liability under clause 2.19.1 is, under clause 2.19.2, limited to the amount, if any, stated in the Contract Particulars.

### 5.3.4 Design responsibilities under SBC/DB

Similar provisions to those referred to in section 5.3.3 above apply to SBC/DB. The following features should, however, be noted:

- There is no equivalent to clause 2.3.3 of the SBC.
- Clause 2.11 of the SBC/DB replicates clause 2.13.2 of the SBC, i.e. the Contractor shall not be responsible for the contents of the Employer's Requirements or for verifying the adequacy of any design contained within them.
- Clause 2.12 of the SBC/DB provides that if any inadequacy is found in the Employer's Requirements, then to the extent that such inadequacy is not dealt with in the Contractor's Proposals, the Employer's Requirements shall be altered or modified accordingly and (subject to clause 2.15 in relation to Statutory Requirements), this shall be treated as a Change. If the Contractor becomes aware of any such inadequacy or any discrepancy or

divergence in or between the Employer's Requirements, the Contractor's Proposals, any instruction by the Employer (other than relating to a change), or any of the Contractor's Design Documents issued under clause 2.8, the Contractor shall issue written notice to the Employer who shall then issue instructions. Clause 2.14.1 provides that where the discrepancy or divergence notified by the Contractor is within the Contractor's Proposals, the Contractor shall inform the Employer of their proposed amendment to remove the discrepancy and the Employer shall decide between the discrepant items or may accept the Contractor's proposed amendment, in either case without cost to the Employer. Where the discrepancy is within the Employer's Requirements, the Contractor's Proposals shall prevail without any adjustment to the Contract Sum. Where the Contractor's Proposals do not deal with such a discrepancy, the Contractor shall inform the Employer of his proposed amendment and the Employer's decision, either agreeing the amendment or otherwise determining how the discrepancy is to be dealt with, shall be treated as a Change. Clause 2.15.1 provides that where there is a divergence between the Employer's Requirements or the Contractor's Proposals and a Statutory Requirement, then the Contractor shall propose for the Employer's agreement an amendment for removing that divergence and shall complete the design and construction of the works in accordance with that amendment at his own cost. The exceptions are where the Statutory Requirements change after the Base Date; an amendment to the Contractor's Proposals which is necessary to comply with statutory provisions controlling the development of the site (e.g. planning permission) unless the risk is imposed on the Contractor under the Employer's Requirements; or an amendment is necessary to any part of the Employer's Requirements which the Employer has stated is compliant with Statutory Requirements (see clause 2.1.2). In each of these cases the amendment will be treated as a Change.

- The equivalent limitation of design liabilities to that contained in clause 2.19 of the SBC (where there is a Contractor's Designed Portion) is to be found in clause 2.17 of the SBC/DB. In effect, this excludes the common law 'fitness for purpose' duty of a design and build contractor (see section 5.3.1 above) and replaces it with a liability equivalent to an appropriate professional designer, i.e. one of 'reasonable skill and care'. See also section 14.1.15 below.

The express exclusion of responsibility of the Contractor under the SBC/DB clause 2.11 (and under clause 2.13.2 of the SBC where there is a Contractor's Designed Portion) for the contents of the Employer's Requirements or for verifying the adequacy of any design contained within them is acknowledged by the SBCC Guide to the SBC/DB as being intended to avoid the consequences of the decision in *Co-operative Insurance Society Limited* v. *Henry Boot Scotland Ltd* (2002), see section 5.3.1 above. In that case the Contractor was appointed under the Contractor's Designed Portion Supplement to JCT 80. Due to the absence of a clause equivalent to the SBC/DB clause 2.11, the

Contractor was held responsible for verifying the adequacy of the design in the Employer's Requirements. In practice, however, developers will often wish the Contractor to undertake exactly the type of risk which clause 2.11 is specifically intended to avoid, and for that reason clause 2.11 will often be deleted.

## 5.4 Defective work

### 5.4.1 Common law

The contractor, in addition to the obligations already considered, also remains liable for latent defects for the duration of the prescriptive period. This is on the basis that the latent defect is due to an act, neglect or default of the contractor. The contractor will have no liability if it is not possible to show a link between any breach of duty by the contractor and the loss, injury or damage incurred, if the breach and the damage caused are too remote from each other or if a term of the contract excludes the contractor's liability. The subject of prescription (or time bar) is considered in more detail in section 9.9.

### 5.4.2 The SBC provisions

During the currency of the contract works, the Contractor can, under clause 3.18.1 of the SBC, be instructed to remove from the site any work, materials or goods that are not in accordance with the contract. As an alternative to this, and following consultation with the Contractor and with the agreement of the Employer, the Architect may allow such work, materials or goods to remain. In these circumstances a deduction is made from the Contract Sum under the provisions of clause 3.18.2. It should be noted that this provision does not apply to work, materials or goods which are part of the Contractor's Designed Portion and there is no equivalent clause to 3.18.2 in the SBC/DB. Where, as a consequence of any such instruction being issued in terms of clauses 3.18.1 or 3.18.2, instructions requiring a variation are necessary, the Architect may issue these but no addition is made to the Contract Sum as a result and no extension of time is given under the provisions of clause 3.18.3.

The Architect may also under clause 3.18.4, if work, materials or goods are not in accordance with the contract and having due regard to the related Code of Practice in Schedule Part 4, issue such instructions under clause 3.17, to open up for inspection or to test, as are reasonable to establish to the Architect's reasonable satisfaction the likelihood or extent of any further similar non-compliance. To the extent such instructions are reasonable, whatever the results of the opening up, no addition shall be made to the Contract Sum. However, the opening up may be a Relevant Event under clause

2.29.2.2, entitling the Contractor to an extension of time under clause 2.28, unless the inspection or test shows that the work, materials or goods are not in accordance with the Contract (see clause 3.18.4).

Following practical completion, and if any defects, shrinkages or other faults in the Works appear within the relevant Rectification Period due to materials or workmanship not being in accordance with the contract or any failure of the contractor to comply with his obligations in respect of the Contractor's Designed Portion, these defects, shrinkages or other faults are, in terms of clause 2.38.1 to be specified by the Architect in a schedule of defects which is to be delivered to the contractor as an instruction not later than 14 days after expiry of the Rectification Period.

The Contractor has an obligation, under clause 2.38, and unless the architect otherwise instructs, to make good within a reasonable time after receipt of the schedule of defects the defects, shrinkages or other faults listed in the schedule prepared by the Architect.

The Architect may also, in terms of clause 2.38.2, whenever he considers it necessary, issue instructions requiring any defects, shrinkages or other faults to be made good. No such instruction can be issued after delivery of the schedule of defects under clause 2.38.1 or more than fourteen days after the expiry of the relevant Rectification Period. The Contractor is obliged, unless the Architect otherwise instructs, to comply with such instructions in terms of clause 2.38. Where the Contractor makes good defects, shrinkages or other faults, this is at no cost to the Employer. Where the Architect instructs the Contractor not to make good, an appropriate deduction is made from the Contract Sum in respect of defects, shrinkages or other faults not made good.

Similar provisions to those contained in clause 2.38 of the SBC are contained in clause 2.35 of the SBC/DB and in the latter case the duties of the Architect are undertaken by the Employer or, in practice, the Employer's Agent.


## 5.5  *Progress of the works*

### 5.5.1  Common law

Unless it is specified in the contract that the contractor must complete by a specified date or within a specified time, the contractor is obliged to complete the works within a reasonable time. The reasonableness of the time taken is considered in the light of the circumstances at the time of performance of the contract, see *H & E Taylor* v. *P & W Maclellan* (1891).

The obligation to complete in a reasonable time may also come into play where there are contractual time limits set down but there has been an act or omission of the employer putting the employer in breach of the contract. For example, if the employer failed to give the contractor access to the site timeously the contractor would not be bound by the contractual time limit.

In such circumstances the contractor's obligation is to complete within a reasonable time, see *T & R Duncanson* v. *The Scottish County Investment Co. Ltd* (1915).

Further, if the employer is responsible in any way for the failure to achieve the completion date they are not able to recover any contractual liquidated damages from the contractor for the period of delay for which they were responsible, see *Peak Construction (Liverpool) Ltd* v. *McKinney Foundations Ltd* (1970) and *Percy Bilton Ltd* v. *Greater London Council* (1982).

These rules apply even if the failure by the employer is not due to fault on their part. In a case where there were squatters on a site resulting in the employer being unable to give the contractor possession of the site, the court still held that the employer was in breach which meant the contractor's obligation to complete by the completion date changed to an obligation to complete in a reasonable time, see *Rapid Building Group Ltd* v. *Ealing Family Housing Association Ltd* (1984).

Similarly, if the employer orders extra work beyond that specified in the original contract which, as a consequence, increases the time required to complete the work, in the absence of any provisions in the contract that allow an extension of time, the employer is no longer able to claim any penalties as a result of the late completion, see *Dodd* v. *Churton* (1897). See also section 6.5 below in this regard.

Where the contractor's obligation is to complete within a reasonable time, it is still possible for an employer to claim unliquidated damages (i.e. their actual losses which they would be required to calculate and prove) if the contractor takes longer than the time which would be considered reasonable in the circumstances.

It should be noted that in each of the cases referred to there was no mechanism in the contract to extend the completion date as a result of the matters causing delay. Where there is such a mechanism, this would operate, thereby extending the completion date so that the contractor's obligation would then be to complete by the new completion date rather than within a reasonable time.

### 5.5.2 The SBC provisions

The SBC provides, in clause 2.4, that on the Date of Possession the Contractor shall begin the works, regularly and diligently proceed with them and complete them on or before the Completion Date. This obligation does not sit in isolation. There is a corresponding obligation on the Employer to give the Contractor possession of the site. This is contained within clause 2.4. The Date of Possession is specified in the contract.

In addition to specified commencement and completion dates, the Contractor tends to work to a programme. The Contractor is to provide copies of his master programme to the Architect by virtue of clause 2.9.1.2. This is to be done without charge. If the Architect awards an extension of time under clause 2.28.1 or there is a Pre-agreed Adjustment fixing a revised Completion Date due to the acceptance of a Schedule Part 2 Quotation, the Contractor is to provide, within 14 days, an amendment or revision to the programme to take account of that, see clause 2.9.1.2.

There are consequences if the Contractor fails to meet the Completion Date in the form of liquidated and ascertained damages. These are considered below in Chapter 6. Under clause 2.28.6.1, the Contractor is subject to the overriding obligation to constantly use their best endeavours to prevent delay in the progress of the Works, or any section and to prevent the completion of the Works or Section being delayed or further delayed. Under clause 2.28.6.2, the Contractor is to do all that may reasonably be required to the satisfaction of the Architect to proceed with the Works or Section.

Similar provisions to clauses 2.4 and 2.28 of the SBC are contained in clauses 2.3 and 2.25 of the SBC/DB.

## 5.6 Insurance and indemnity – the SBC provisions

The SBC contains a number of provisions requiring the Contractor to indemnify the Employer in certain circumstances.

Clause 2.21 requires the Contractor to pay all fees or charges (including rates or taxes) legally demandable under any of the Statutory Requirements and indemnify the Employer against any liability resulting from any failure to do so. The Contractor is able to recover this through payment for provisional sums, where applicable, or by addition to the Contract Sum. However, that does not apply to fees or charges which relate solely to the Contractor's Designed Portion, in which event they are deemed to be included in the Contract Sum. The same applies under clause 2.18 of the SBC/DB unless the fees or charges are stated by way of a Provisional Sum in the Employer's Requirements.

Royalties and any other sums payable in respect of the supply and use in the carrying out of the Works of any patented articles, processes or inventions are deemed to be included in the Contract Sum and the Contractor has an obligation in terms of clause 2.22 to indemnify the Employer from and against all claims and proceedings which may be brought or made against the Employer and all damages, costs and expense to which he may be put by reason of the Contractor infringing or having been found to have infringed any patent rights. This is not the case where the Contractor has been instructed to use any patented articles, processes or inventions in which case, under clause 2.23, he is not so liable and any royalties, damages or other monies which the Contractor may be liable to pay shall be added to the Contract Sum. Similar provisions are contained in clauses 2.19 and 2.20 of the SBC/DB.

The Contractor maintains a liability for loss or damage to materials and goods delivered to, placed on or adjacent to the Works and intended for the Works where the Contractor has been paid for them even though, following payment, title in these materials and goods passes to the Employer, all in terms of clause 2.24. The Contractor maintains a similar responsibility for any materials and/or goods purchased prior to their delivery to site under a separate contract for their purchase in terms of clause 4.17. A similar provision to clause 2.24 is contained in clause 2.21 of the SBC/DB.

The Contractor is, in terms of clause 6.1, liable for and obliged to indemnify the Employer against any 'expense, liability, loss, claim or proceedings whatsoever' in respect of personal injury to or the death of any person arising out of or in the course of or caused by the carrying out of the Works. This is except to the extent this is due to any act or neglect of the Employer or any of the Employer's Persons.

In terms of clause 6.2 the Contractor has a similar liability and similar indemnity obligations in respect of any loss, injury or damage to any property to the extent this is due to any negligence, breach of statutory duty, omission or default of the Contractor or of any of the Contractor's Persons. This liability and indemnity does not, in terms of clause 6.3.1, include the Works, work executed and/or Site Materials up to and including whichever is the earlier of the date of issue of the Practical Completion Certificate or the date of termination of the Contractor's employment. There is also an exclusion of this liability and indemnity where Insurance Option C applies where loss or damage to any property required to be insured under that Insurance Option is caused by a Specified Peril. Similar provisions are contained in clauses 6.1, 6.2 and 6.3 of the SBC/DB.

Notwithstanding these indemnity provisions, the Contractor has obligations related to insurance for personal injury and property damage, the Works and, where there is a Contractor's Designed Portion, professional indemnity insurance. The insurance obligations are considered separately in Chapter 14.

## 5.7 Joint Fire Code – the SBC provisions

In terms of the SBC, where the Contract Particulars state that the Joint Fire Code applies, clause 6.14 gives all parties an obligation to comply with it. The Contractor is obliged to ensure compliance by all Contractor's Persons. The Joint Fire Code is defined as being the Joint Code of Practice on the Protection from Fire of Construction Sites and Buildings Undergoing Renovation published by the Construction Confederation and the Fire Protection Association with the support of the Association of British Insurers, the Chief and Assistant Chief Fire Officers' Association and the London Fire Brigade.

If there is a breach of the Joint Fire Code and the insurers under the Joint Names Policy in respect of the Works specify the Remedial Measures they require, clause 6.15.1.1 requires the Contractor, where these Remedial Measures relate to the obligation of the Contractor to carry out and complete the Works, to ensure that they are carried out by such date as the insurers specify.

In terms of clause 6.15.1.2, if the Remedial Measures require a Variation to the Works, the Architect is to issue instructions as necessary to ensure compliance. In an emergency, where compliance with the Remedial Measures requires the Contractor to supply materials or execute work before receipt of such instructions, the Contractor is to supply only such limited work as is reasonably necessary to secure immediate compliance. In these circumstances, the Contractor is required to inform the Architect of the emergency and the steps being taken. Clause 6.15.1.2 provides that save to the extent such emergency work relates to the Contractor's Designed Portion, it is treated as if carried out under an instruction requiring a Variation.

If the Contractor, within seven days of a notice specifying Remedial Measures not requiring an instruction under clause 6.15.1.2 does not begin to carry out or thereafter fails, without reasonable cause, regularly and diligently to proceed with the Remedial Measures, the Employer may employ others to carry these out and the Contractor shall be liable for all additional costs incurred by the Employer, which costs are deducted from the Contract Sum, all in terms of clause 6.15.2.

Under clauses 6.13 to 6.15 of SBC/DB any Remedial Measures required by insurers to achieve compliance with the Joint Fire Code are to be carried out by the Contractor, at their own expense.

## 5.8 *Health and Safety*

There are detailed provisions under statute, at common law and under the SBC in relation to health and safety. These are considered in Chapter 19.

# Chapter 6
# Time

## 6.1 Introduction

For those with a direct interest in a building project, time is an important subject. The employer will be anxious to fix when and over what period of time the works will be carried out so that they can budget and plan ahead. The contractor will be anxious to plan the commencement and carrying out of the works in order to meet their contractual obligations, express or implied, in relation to the period for completion of the works or perhaps sections or phases of them.

A contractor's tender will normally proceed on the basis that certain operations will cost them a particular amount of money to carry out over a certain period of time. Generally, the longer work takes, the more expensive it is to carry out. Tendering at an appropriate level to take account of time-related costs, forward planning and subsequent on-site control are essential elements of a contractor's consideration of time.

In the traditional manner in which building contracts are let in Scotland, namely, where the employer engages consultants to prepare the design and other requirements, the employer should have specified what they want before the tender stage or, at least, before the formation of the contract. This places a heavy onus on the professional team of architects, engineers, services specialists and quantity surveyors. Changes after the formation of the contract should be kept to a minimum because of the effect that these are likely to have on time and cost. In the absence of agreement about the effect of such changes they may give rise to claims and disputes.

## 6.2 Commencement of the works

It is usual for express provision to be made for the date upon which the contractor will be given access to the site for the purpose of carrying out the works. Normally the contract will require the contractor to complete the works either by a specified date, or within a specified period from the agreed date for commencement or the date when access is given to the site. It is very important that the date of commencement of the period for completion is ascertainable and that it is specified what holidays, if any, are to be ignored in computing the period for completion of the works. While these are matters which common sense dictates should be made clear, experience shows that this is not always done.

## 6.3  Time of the essence

The phrase 'time of the essence' is one that is much used but often without much understanding. The need to do something by a specified date or time does not of itself make time of the essence. However, if the contract specifically makes time of the essence, the failure to complete the works by the stipulated date amounts to a material breach of contract that entitles the innocent party to rescind the contract and claim damages. If there is no express stipulation in the contract that time is of the essence, it can be made so by serving a notice fixing a specified time for completion. This, however, must be a reasonable one.

It is unusual for time to be of the essence in building contracts. Usually the failure of the contractor to complete is to be regarded as a breach of contract that will form the basis of a claim for damages for late completion. Even where the phrase is used, the contract must be considered as a whole. In one case the contractual clause was as follows:

> 'Time shall be considered as of the essence of the contract . . . and in case the contractor shall fail in the due performance . . . [the contractor] shall be liable to pay the [employer] . . . liquidated damages.'

In the circumstances it was nevertheless held that time was not of the essence as the contract included other terms, such as an extension of time clause, which were inconsistent with time being of the essence, see *Peak Construction (Liverpool) Ltd* v. *McKinney Foundations Ltd* (1970).

## 6.4  Progress of the works

### 6.4.1  Common law

As discussed in section 6.2, the contractor's obligation is usually to complete by a particular date or within a particular period. In the absence of a relevant express contractual obligation, delay in progress prior to that date or before the end of the period probably does not in itself give the employer any rights, see *Greater London Council* v. *Cleveland Bridge and Engineering Co. Ltd and Another* (1986). In such a case a claim for damages will only arise if there is actual delay in completion. In extreme cases, however, particularly if combined with other failings, it may amount to anticipatory breach of contract, see *Sutcliffe* v. *Chippendale & Edmondson* (1971) and *Carr* v. *J A Berriman Pty Ltd* (1953).

Some commentators suggest that there should be an implied term that the contractor will proceed with reasonable diligence and maintain reasonable progress while others state that to imply such a term would be going too far.

### 6.4.2 The SBC provisions

Clause 2.4 of the SBC expressly requires the Contractor to proceed 'regularly and diligently' with the works. It has been held that proceeding 'regularly and diligently' indicates a sense of activity, of orderly progress and of industry and perseverance probably such as will ensure completion according to the contract, see *London Borough of Hounslow* v. *Twickenham Garden Developments Ltd* (1971) and *West Faulkner Associates* v. *London Borough of Newham* (1994).

Moreover, clause 8.4 of the SBC gives the Employer the right to determine the Contractor's employment if they without reasonable cause wholly or substantially suspend the carrying out of the Works or if they fail to proceed regularly and diligently. Accordingly, if this right is to be exercised, it is important that the Architect is satisfied that there is sufficient and reliable evidence of the Contractor's failure.

## 6.5 *Adjustment of Completion Date and extension of time for completion*

### 6.5.1 General

It is a basic principle applicable in all contracts that one party cannot seek to enforce a contractual obligation of the other party where they have prevented the other from performing that obligation. As Lord Denning put it in *Trollope & Colls Ltd* v. *North West Metropolitan Regional Hospital Board* (1973):

> 'It is well settled that in building contracts . . . where there is a stipulation for work to be done in a limited time, if one party by his conduct – it may be quite legitimate conduct, such as ordering extra work – renders it impossible or impracticable for the other party to do the work within the stipulated time, then the one whose conduct caused the trouble can no longer insist upon strict adherence to the time stated. He cannot claim any penalties or liquidated damages for non-completion in that time . . . The time becomes at large . . . The work done must be done within a reasonable time.'

Given the complex nature of most building contracts, the need to instruct variations and to take account of unforeseen matters, it is almost inevitable that the employer will fall foul of this doctrine. To accommodate such matters, building contracts usually set out an express mechanism by which the original completion date can be changed and specify the circumstances in which an extension of time for completion can be obtained. It is less common to find a contractual term which allows the contractor to make up time by way of some form of acceleration but such provisions do exist, see, for example, clause 3 of the JCT Management Contract.

It is a common but misguided view that extensions of time benefit only the contractor. Clearly, they give the contractor more time to complete the works and reduce or extinguish their liability for liquidated damages. However, were it not for extension of time provisions an employer would not be entitled to claim liquidated damages where they have been the cause of some delay.

Dealing with an employer's default is not usually the sole reason for having extension of time clauses. Most include an entitlement to an extension of time for what might be described as neutral events. These arise through the fault of neither party, for example, war, riots and bad weather. In this sense, such clauses do benefit the contractor by giving them an extension of time for some matters that might otherwise be at their risk.

Indeed the terms of a particular contract may allow an extension in circumstances which some may think go beyond what might be regarded as neutral.

### 6.5.2 Adjustment of the Completion Date under the SBC

The provisions of the SBC contain a significant re-writing of the provisions regarding adjustment of the Completion Date.

Clauses 2.26 to 2.29 contain very complex provisions detailing the circumstances in which the Contractor is entitled to an extension of time. The entitlement to an extension only arises as a result of delay due to specified 'Relevant Events', which are considered below. It is noteworthy that the SBC contains substantially revised Relevant Events. The actual number of Relevant events has decreased but the nature of some of the Relevant Events is more generally expressed as if to give rise to a less prescriptive set of carefully defined Relevant Events. Accordingly, matters which were previously the subject of a particular, specific Relevant Event may be included within a new, more generally expressed, Relevant Event.

### 6.5.3 Relevant Events under the SBC

#### Compliance with Variations

Variations comprise Variations (as defined in clause 5.1) and any other matters or instructions which under the Conditions are to be treated as, or as requiring, a Variation.

**Compliance with certain specified instructions**

There are two categories of Architect's instruction that can entitle the Contractor to an extension of time. Firstly, there are the matters listed in clause 2.29.2.1, which cover a wide range of circumstances where the Architect is obliged to issue instructions under the Contract. Secondly, an instruction requiring the opening up of the Works for inspection or testing may give rise to such an entitlement, unless the inspection or test shows that work, materials or goods are not in accordance with the Contract.

**Deferment by the employer of the giving of possession of the site**

The Employer must give the Contractor the possession of the site anticipated in the contract to allow him to carry out the works. This is of critical importance. If he fails to do so the Employer is in breach of the contract. To address such circumstances, clause 2.5 makes specific provision for the deferment of possession.

**Approximate quantity which is not a reasonably accurate forecast of the quantity of work required**

This relevant event is provided to address any significant understatement in the Contract Bills of a quantity of work required. In such circumstances, the Contractor can be confronted with a requirement to execute far more work than envisaged at the time of entering in to the contract.

**Suspension by the Contractor under clause 4.14**

Assuming the Contractor meets the requirements of the contract in respect of suspension for non-payment (which requirements are considered below in section 10.9.3), and thereafter suspends performance, such a suspension will be a relevant event which will entitle the Contractor to an extension of time.

**Any impediment, prevention or default, whether by act or omission, by the Employer, the Architect, the Quantity Surveyor or any of the Employer's Persons, except to the extent caused or contributed to by any default, whether by act or omission of the Contractor or of any of the Contractor's Persons**

This is a general catch-all provision which replaces previous wording which sought to set out specific acts or omissions for which the Employer was held responsible. Employer's Persons are defined as all persons employed, engaged or authorised by the Employer excluding the Contractor, Contractor's Persons, the Architect, the Quantity Surveyor and any Statutory

Undertaker but including any such third party as is referred to in clause 3.23.

Matters falling within this heading will include, but are not limited to, matters for which previously there was express provision such as:

- delay in receipt of instructions from the Architect;
- delay on the part of persons employed on behalf of the Employer to do other work associated with the Works;
- delay caused by the late supply of materials and goods which the Employer has undertaken to supply;
- failure by the Employer to give access to the site in accordance with the contract; and
- compliance or non-compliance by the Employer with contractual provisions in relation to the CDM Regulations.

### Work by a Statutory Undertaker in pursuance of its statutory obligations or failure to carry out such work

This includes such matters as electricity, gas, water and other services which need to be installed in most, if not all, buildings.

This falls to be contrasted with a quite separate situation where delay to the works is caused by the need to work close to, or in physical contact with, pipes and other apparatus of local authorities or statutory undertakers. These matters will be governed by the terms of the particular contract in question. If there are no express provisions that deal with the Contractor's rights in such a situation, implied terms will need to be relied upon, see *Henry Boot Construction Ltd* v. *Central Lancashire New Town Development Corporation* (1980).

It should be noted that this relevant event applies only to circumstances in which the Statutory Undertaker is independently carrying out work pursuant to its statutory obligations. It will not apply where a statutory undertaker carries out work under contract to the Contractor.

### Exceptionally adverse weather conditions

Bad weather is not, in itself, a good reason for not completing on time. That means that, save where the contract contains provisions which recognise the need for an extension of time due to bad weather, the contractor will be held to have accepted the risk of completing on time notwithstanding bad weather as they are the party best able to deal with it. It is open to the parties to agree where the risk falls.

The SBC has taken a particular route, but the words used require careful consideration. There is a requirement that there is not just exceptionally adverse weather conditions but also delay to the progress of the works as a result.

Proof that the weather has been exceptionally adverse is usually provided by examining local weather records and comparing the actual weather experienced at a particular time of year against that of previous years at that time.

Under JCT 63 conditions it was held to be important to note that the test was whether the weather itself was 'exceptionally inclement' so as to give rise to delay, and not whether the amount of time lost by the inclement weather was exceptional, see *Walter Lawrence and Son Ltd* v. *Commercial Union Properties (UK) Ltd* (1984). Further, any delay due to weather is to be determined at the time the work is carried out, not when it was programmed to be carried out.

**Loss or damage occasioned by any of the Specified Perils**

The Specified Perils are those listed in clause 6.8, namely, fire, lightning, explosion, storm/flood, escape of water from any water tank, apparatus or pipes, earthquake, aircraft and other aerial devices or articles dropped therefrom, riot and civil commotion but excluding the Excepted Risks which are also listed in that clause.

**Civil commotion or the use or threat of terrorism and/or the activities of the relevant authorities dealing with such an event or threat**

A civil commotion appears to be some form of insurrection of the people that is different from a riot or a civil war. The potentially wide-reaching consequences of terrorist activity, whether actual or threatened, are obvious. In recognition of the particular problems that could be occasioned by this, a relevant event dealing with terrorism was first introduced by JCT in July 1993, by way of Amendment 12 to JCT 80.

**Strikes, lock out or local combination of workmen**

Where there is no express provision for such matters in a contract they may be covered by general provisions relating to *force majeure* or special circumstances. The SBC allows the Architect to take into account the possible far-ranging effects of strike action. In other building contracts it may be difficult to know if an extension is to be granted only where the strike relates to on-site work or whether it extends to strikes which have an impact upon the performance of sub-contractors and suppliers. This should be made clear in the contract. Difficulties can sometimes arise, for example, in determining whether the extension should be for strikes or delay due to work to be carried out by statutory undertakers, see *Boskalis Westminster Construction Ltd* v. *Liverpool City Council* (1983). A 'local combination of workmen' is not defined. However, it is thought that it might cover, for example, a go-slow.

### Government intervention

The Contractor may be entitled to an extension of time if, by reason of the United Kingdom Government and/or the Scottish Government exercising a statutory power after the base date which directly affects the execution of the Works.

### *Force majeure*

The term *force majeure* is thought to have been taken from the Code Napoleon. In a contract governed by Scots Law, it does not have any particular technical meaning. *Force majeure* is considered below at section 9.3.2.

### 6.5.4 Requirements for the adjustment of completion date under the SBC

The building contract should set out the procedure which is to be followed when dealing with extensions of time and it is important that those involved in that process adhere to the requirements of the contract. For example, clause 2.27.1 of the SBC provides that if and whenever it becomes reasonably apparent that progress of the Works or any Section is being or is likely to be delayed, the Contractor should forthwith give written notice to the Architect of the material circumstances including the cause or causes of delay and identifying any event which in his opinion is a Relevant Event.

It is important to note that the requirement is to give notice irrespective of whether the Contractor is seeking an extension and irrespective of whether an event is a Relevant Event, provided it becomes reasonably apparent that progress of the Works is being or is likely to be delayed. While a Contractor will always be reluctant to advise the Architect of matters for which they are responsible, for example, defective planning, poor supervision or inefficient working, the logic of this appears to be that, as the Architect is only obliged to grant such extension as is fair and reasonable, it is important that he is aware of all the facts which are relevant in determining what is fair and reasonable.

It is only in respect of Relevant Events that the contract requires the contractor to give, in the notice or as soon as possible thereafter, particulars of the expected effects including an estimate of the extent of any expected delay beyond the Completion Date, see clause 2.27.2. Under clause 2.27.3 the Contractor must forthwith notify the Architect in writing of any material change in the estimated delay or in any other particulars and supply such further information as the Architect may at any time reasonably require.

Provisions like this often give rise to arguments about whether proper and timeous notice by the Contractor is a condition precedent to an award of an extension of time. Architects and Employers often argue that that is the case, but the contractual provisions in each case require careful consideration, see *London Borough of Merton* v. *Stanley Hugh Leach Ltd* (1985). However, where it is expressly stated in the contract that the Contractor shall not be entitled to an extension of time where they have failed to give proper notice under the contract, such a provision will be upheld, see *City Inn Limited* v. *Shepherd Construction* (2003).

A contractor should always consider the terms of an extension of time clause very carefully. Should they give notice of those matters or events that they consider at the time are likely to be non-critical? Should they refrain from giving notice where they believe that they have an adequate float in terms of time to allow them to complete within the required period? Much will depend on the particular wording of the extension of time clause, but it is important to remember that things can change over the course of a contract through no fault of the contractor. In most, if not all, cases it will be prudent to give notice. A failure to give written notice of delay may, in certain circumstances, constitute a breach of contract.

It has been suggested that if the architect, because of a failure on the part of the contractor to give notice, has been unable to avoid or reduce a delay to completion, the contractor should not be awarded an extension greater than that which they would have received had they given notice, see *London Borough of Merton*.

The SBC provides that no extension is to be granted unless the Contractor has constantly used their best endeavours to prevent delay, however caused, and they have done all that may reasonably be required to the satisfaction of the Architect to proceed with the Works. Unfortunately there is little guidance on what is meant by 'best endeavours' and 'all that may reasonably be required' in this context. Some take the view that the Contractor must, if necessary, re-programme, increase resources and work overtime. Others take the view that, strictly, they are not obliged to take steps which would result in them incurring any material additional costs.

### 6.5.5 Fixing a new Completion Date under the SBC

Under the SBC clause 2.28 the Architect must consider if the events notified are Relevant Events and whether, as a result, completion is likely to be delayed beyond the Completion Date. As soon as is reasonably practicable, and in any event within 12 weeks of receiving the required particulars, the Architect must notify the Contractor in writing of his decision in respect of any notice under clause 2.27. This applies whether or not an extension of time is given. In his decision the Architect must state the extension of time he has attributed to each Relevant Event and (in the case of a decision under clause 2.28.4 or 2.28.5) the reduction in the time he has attributed to each Relevant Omission.

Under clause 2.28.4, if work is omitted after an extension has been granted, the Architect may by notice in writing to the Contractor fix an earlier Completion Date.

Although clause 2.28 states that the Architect 'shall' act appropriately within 12 weeks, it is generally regarded that, taken in the context of the other terms of the contract, the timescale is directory only and not mandatory.

After Practical Completion has been achieved, the Architect is obliged to review and reach a final view on the fair and reasonable extension of time to which the Contractor is entitled having regard to any Relevant Events, and that not later than 12 weeks after Practical Completion. He can confirm the Completion Date previously fixed. In fixing a later Completion Date he can review a previous decision and have regard to all Relevant Events, whether notified to him or not. He can only fix a Completion Date earlier than a previously revised Completion Date if that is fair and reasonable taking into account Relevant Omissions. In no circumstances can the Architect fix a date earlier than the original contractual Date for Completion (clause 2.28.6.3) nor is any alteration allowed to the length of any Pre-agreed Adjustment in terms of a Schedule Part 2 Quotation.

Refusal by the Architect to consider an application for extension of time may, in certain circumstances, constitute a breach of contract by the Employer.

### 6.5.6 Calculation of extension of time and proof of entitlement

These matters are the subject of much controversy and a detailed examination of them is beyond the scope of this book. Indeed they appear to have generated a whole industry of consultants who profess an expertise in this area, using critical path analysis, computer technology and other techniques to provide delay analysis which is said to be as accurate as is capable of being achieved. In October 2002 the Society of Construction Law published a Delay Protocol 'to provide guidance to all parties to the construction process when dealing with time/delay matters'. Although it is said that the Protocol 'recognises that transparency of information and methodology is central to both dispute prevention and dispute resolution' the terms of the Protocol have been controversial given the stance it adopts and the divergence of opinion among experts on how delay analysis should be conducted. The particular method used can vary and experts in this field can often disagree as to which method is the correct one to use in the circumstances of the particular case.

### 6.5.7 Contractor's programmes

Under most forms of building contract the contractor's programme is not part of the contract. In the unusual event that the parties have agreed that the contractor's programme does form part of their contract and is binding upon them, it is of considerable significance. In such an event the contractor is obliged to work to that programme and, perhaps more significantly, the employer is obliged to allow the contractor to work to that programme. Conversely, a contractor is not obliged to work to a programme where that has not been made a requirement of the contract, see *Pigott Foundations Ltd v. Shepherd Construction Ltd* (1993).

Contractors are entitled to programme the works in order to complete in a lesser time than that allowed in the contract. That does not alter the obligation of the employer, which is not to impede the contractor in completing the works in the time allowed by the contract, see *Glenlion Construction Ltd v. The Guinness Trust* (1987) and *J F Finnegan Ltd v. Sheffield City Council* (1988).

However, most analyses of delay use the contractor's original programme as part of the process. Whether this can be used as a basis for any proper analysis depends upon whether the original programme was put together properly. Usually the analysis will also involve an 'as built' programme showing the actual start and finish dates for each activity specified on the programme. This allows the actual start and finish dates to be compared with those set out in the contractor's original programme. If the 'as built' programme also highlights the nature and timing of the matters upon which the contractor founds as the source of alleged delay, for example, instructions and variations, suspensions and the like, such an 'as built' programme can give, at the very least, a useful picture of the factual background to the carrying out of the works.

### 6.5.8 Causation

The contractor must prove that a relevant event, and not their own inefficiencies or other matters for which they must accept responsibility under the contract, caused delay. Difficulty is caused by the fact that some contractors do not keep sufficiently detailed records of events and their impact upon the works. Rarely is it the case that there is one clear event that can be shown to be the only cause of delay to the works. If it can, there is usually little scope for real dispute. More usual is the situation where there are different events that are productive of delay some of which are the responsibility of the contractor and others of which are the responsibility of the employer. They may all have an impact upon the works at the same time or they may have an impact upon the works at different times. This makes the calculation of extensions of time a very difficult area. In such circumstances the strict application of certain legal rules relating to causation may not be possible or may give rise to very unsatisfactory results.

Until fairly recently there has been very little authority from the Courts in this area. However, the decision of the Scottish Appeal Court in *John Doyle Construction Ltd v. Laing Management (Scotland) Ltd* (2004) set down general guidance in relation to claims for loss and expense caused by delay and disruption which has had a significant impact far outside Scotland. In that case it was stated that the question of causation must be addressed by 'the application of common sense to the logical principles of causation'.

Given the large number, complex nature and interaction of events on most building sites, it is submitted that the extension of time to which the contractor is entitled will always be very much a matter of opinion.

## 6.6  Partial possession and sectional completion

There may be good reason why the parties to a building contract wish to make provision for partial possession or sectional completion of the works. The employer may need the building desperately. The contractor may wish to be relieved of obligations such as those regarding insurance and site security.

Partial possession refers to the situation where the employer takes possession of part of the works before completion of the whole. If the Contract does not make express provision allowing the employer to take partial possession, he will normally be unable to do so without the consent of the contractor. Clause 2.33 of the SBC makes such provision and alters the Contractor's obligations in respect of liquidated damages (clause 2.37), insurance (clause 2.36) and defects liability (clause 2.35). There is deemed practical completion of the part taken over by the Employer for certain purposes.

Sectional completion refers to the situation where the works are defined in advance in separate sections and a different date is given for the completion of each section. This requires the precise definition of each section, and a date of possession, date or period for completion and liquidated damages for each section. Problems arise where parties do not use a tried and tested standard form. In such circumstances they run the risk that unless great care is taken with, for example, the liquidated damages provisions, they may be inoperable, see, for example, *Taylor Woodrow Holdings Ltd and Another* v. *Barnes & Elliott Ltd* (2004).

## 6.7  Completion of the works

### 6.7.1  Timescale for completion

If no timescale has been specified, the contractor is obliged to complete the works within a reasonable time, see *H & E Taylor* v. *P & W Maclellan* (1891). The implication of a contractual term requiring that the works should be completed within a reasonable time is most common in building operations of small value where more importance is placed on the price and specification of the work than the period within which the work is to be carried out.

Where a completion date has been agreed it may become unenforceable by virtue of some later agreement, or by waiver on the part of the employer, or where the contractor has been prevented from completing on time by acts or omissions of the employer or those for whom he is responsible. In such circumstances, unless a new completion date is agreed or the contract provides a mechanism for an extension of time, time is said to be at large. Contractors like to argue that time is at large in the sense that there is then no date by which the works must be completed. However, that is an erroneous view of what is meant by time at large. In such circumstances the contractor is still obliged to complete the works within a reasonable time.

What is a reasonable time is a question of fact, to be determined in the light of all the surrounding circumstances of each particular case. If time has come to be at large, the employer is unable to recover liquidated damages under the contract because there is no fixed date for completion that can be used in the calculation of the damages. However, it is still possible for the employer to claim unliquidated damages for breach of the contractor's implied obligation to complete within a reasonable time. These matters are discussed in more detail later in this chapter.

### 6.7.2 'Practical completion'

It is perhaps trite to say that the works are complete when the contractor has executed all the work that he has contracted to perform. In building contracts, however, things are not always as simple as they might be.

Completion of the works is an important event. Most building contracts will require completion to the satisfaction of the employer, the architect or some other specified third party. It is the date of completion that is used to determine whether the contractor has completed timeously. Accordingly, where the contractor is in culpable delay it marks the end of the period for which damages for late completion are payable. Given the importance of this, most building contracts require some kind of formal certification that the works are complete.

Whether the works are complete is a matter that is ripe for dispute. If the contractor is in culpable delay and liable to pay damages for late completion, they will be seeking certification of completion as soon as possible. The employer will be more concerned that the works are truly complete.

Clause 2.30 of the SBC provides for certification of 'practical completion'. The term is not defined and what it means has never been properly settled. The use of the word 'practical' has been argued by some to mean something less than full completion. The generally accepted view is that a certificate of practical completion can be issued 'where very minor *de minimis* work had not been carried out' but that 'where there were any patent defects the architect could not have given a certificate of practical completion', see *H W Nevill (Sunblest) Ltd* v. *William Press & Son Ltd* (1981).

Given the importance of the term in the SBC, and in other contracts produced by JCT and SBCC, it is perhaps disappointing that there has been no real attempt made to define precisely what it means. If definition is that difficult or agreement cannot be reached perhaps a different form of words altogether should be considered. If the wording has been left for so long in the belief that it affords some degree of flexibility, is it worth the uncertainty which is thereby created?

## 6.8 Damages for late completion

The failure of the contractor to complete the works on time as required by the contract is a breach of contract. Like any other breach of contract, it gives rise at common law to the possibility of a claim for damages for that breach. The damages are determined after the breach has occurred and require proof of loss by the employer. Such a claim must also meet the requirements of the general law of damages. If the loss is too remote, it will not be recoverable, see *Liesboch Dredger* v. *Edison Steamship* (1933), *Hadley* v. *Baxendale* (1854), and *Victoria Laundry (Windsor) Ltd* v. *Newman Industries Ltd* (1949). The general law of damages is considered below in section 10.4.

It is usually possible for employers to estimate, with a fair degree of certainty, the loss that they will sustain if the contractor does not complete on time. This can be done in a number of ways: for example, by estimating additional financing costs, loss of rental and the like. For an interesting discussion of this area, see *Multiplex Constructions Pty Ltd* v. *Abgarus Pty Ltd* (1992). As a result of this, and the desire of contractors to fix the level of their liability to the employer for damages in the event of late completion, most building contracts are drafted in such a way that the parties fix in advance the damages that will be payable for late completion. If these damages are a genuine pre-estimate of the loss likely to be suffered by the employer, they are called 'liquidated damages'. This subject is considered below in the next section.

What is a genuine pre-estimate of loss in the context of liquidated damages is an issue which has prompted much debate, not least where the project in question is said not to be commercial in nature, see *Clydebank Engineering and Shipbuilding Co. Ltd* v. *Don Jose Ramos Yzquierdo y Castaneda* (1905). That will rarely, if ever, be the case in a building contract.

There is much to be said for the view that, if the contractor does not like the liquidated damages, he should negotiate them down before entering into the contract. It is submitted that the view that liquidated damages provisions, where operable, provide an exhaustive remedy to the employer for late completion is to be preferred to the view, sometimes expressed, that it is not. The contrary view gives insufficient weight to the considerable benefits of the agreed nature of such damages.

## 6.9 *Liquidated damages*

### 6.9.1 General

It is normal in modern building contracts to find a liquidated damages provision to the effect that the contractor will pay or allow the employer a sum for each specified period, for example, per day or per week that the works remain incomplete after the contractual date for completion.

It is less common to find a liquidated damages provision in a sub-contract. A sub-contract may contain a provision putting the sub-contractor on notice that in the event of the main contractor's failure to complete the works timeously the employer may impose liquidated damages upon the contractor. If the sub-contractor is on notice of this, the damages which they may become liable to pay to the main contractor in the event that a breach of contract on their part causes delay to the completion of the main contract may include the amount of liquidated damages payable by the main contractor to the employer as a result of the sub-contractor's breach.

Clauses that specify liquidated and ascertained damages for delay apply where the works are completed in natural course, but not to contract time. They do not apply where the original contractor does not complete the works. They are ineffective if time has become at large since there is no fixed date from which damages can be calculated, see *British Glanzstoff Manufacturing Co. Ltd* v. *General Accident, Fire and Life Assurance Corporation Ltd* (1912).

A valid liquidated damages clause removes the need for proof of actual loss, which may be difficult and costly. It should be recognised that if the clause is valid and applicable, employers are entitled to the agreed liquidated damages even if they have in fact sustained no loss. In circumstances where the liquidated damages clause is inapplicable, the employer must prove the loss which has been caused by the contractor's breach of contract. Sometimes arguments arise about whether the provisions for liquidated damages apply to the particular circumstances or whether damages can still be sought at common law, see *Scottish Coal Company Ltd* v. *Kier Construction Ltd* (2005).

A typical example of a provision for payment of liquidated damages is to be found in clause 2.32 of the SBC. This provides that, subject to the issue of a Non-Completion Certificate under clause 2.32.1 and provided that the Employer has informed the Contractor in writing before the date of the Final Certificate that he may require payment of, or may withhold or deduct liquidated damages, then the Employer may, not later than five days before the final date for payment of the debt due under the Final Certificate, give notice in the terms set out in clause 2.32.2. That clause requires that the notice under clause 2.32.1 shall state that the Employer requires that the Contractor pay or allow the Employer liquidated damages at the rate stated in the Contract Particulars (or at such lesser rate as may be specified in writing by the employer) for the period between the Completion Date and the date of practical completion.

Clause 2.32.2 appears to be linked to the notice requirements in the payment provisions so that the clause 2.32.2 notice could also act as a notice under clause 4.13.4 or 4.15.4 (i.e. a withholding notice required by the payment provisions). Should a single notice be used for both purposes, it will have to satisfy the requirements of both clauses.

The certificate issued under clause 2.32.1.1 is a pre-requisite to the employer's right to deduct liquidated damages under the SBC. Such a certificate may not be issued before the expiry of the period for completion or after the issue of the Final Certificate, see *H Fairweather Ltd* v. *Asden Securities Ltd* (1979). Notwithstanding the issue of such a certificate, liquidated damages may not be payable if the liquidated damages clause does not apply, is invalid or is inoperable. If there is a dispute as to whether the Employer is entitled to deduct liquidated damages from the sum certified the Employer may do so, at his own risk, pending resolution of the dispute.

If a new, later, Completion Date is fixed after a Non-Completion Certificate has been issued under clause 2.32.1.1, the certificate is superseded and a new one needs to be issued if the contractor fails to meet the revised Completion Date. No new notice of deduction is required to be given by the Employer: see clause 2.32.4. The Employer is obliged to repay any liquidated damages already recovered for the period up to the new Completion Date: see clause 2.32.3. If the Contractor should fail to complete by the new Completion Date, the Employer may not deduct liquidated damages unless a new valid Non-Completion Certificate has been issued, see *A Bell & Son (Paddington) Ltd* v. *CBF Residential Care and Housing Association* (1989), *Jarvis Brent Ltd* v. *Rowlinson Construction Ltd* (1990) and *J F Finnegan Ltd* v. *Community Housing Association Ltd* (1995).

If the employers' losses arising from the breach for which liquidated damages have been stipulated are greater than the stipulated amount, they are not entitled to ignore the liquidated damages clause and claim for such losses as they can prove. In effect the clause operates as a limitation of the contractor's liability. Doubt remains as to whether, in the event that the liquidated damages provisions of a contract become inoperable, the employer can recover more by way of unliquidated damages than the amount stated in the contract as liquidated damages.

Occasionally the rate of 'nil' has been inserted as the rate of liquidated damages. Although it has been argued that this simply means that the parties have not agreed the sum payable by way of liquidated damages and that unliquidated damages may still be payable, the better view is probably that it is to be treated as an agreement that no damages are to be paid to the employer for delay, see *Temloc Ltd* v. *Errill Properties Ltd* (1987). It should be noted that the reasoning in *Temloc Ltd* was not followed in *Baese Pty Ltd* v. *R A Bracken Building Pty Ltd* (1989). Although the contract in *Temloc Ltd* was one under JCT 80 conditions, it may have a wider application in other contracts where the terms are similar. It does not assist in determining what the position is where there is a dash (–) inserted in the contract or the rate of damages is left blank.

It has been said that liquidated damages clauses are to be construed *contra proferentem*, (i.e. against the party putting it forward) but this requires detailed consideration of issues such as whether the parties had equal bargaining power to negotiate the contract and whether the contract is in a standard form drawn by a body on which employers, contractors and sub-contractors are represented. In some cases, insofar as the clause has a limiting effect on the contractor's liability for damages for late completion, it may be capable of being challenged by the employer under the Unfair Contract Terms Act 1977.

### 6.9.2 Where liquidated damages provisions are not enforceable

A liquidated damages clause is unenforceable if the amount specified is a penalty. The classic discussion of the differences between a penalty clause and a valid liquidated damages clause is contained in the speech of Lord Dunedin in *Dunlop Pneumatic Tyre Co. Ltd* v. *New Garage & Motor Co. Ltd* (1915) where he said that:

'(1) Though the parties to a contract who used the words "penalty" or "liquidated damages" may *prima facie* be supposed to mean what they say, yet the expression used is not conclusive. The court must find out whether the payment stipulated is in truth a penalty or liquidated damages ... (2) The essence of a penalty is a payment of money stipulated as *in terrorem* of the offending party; the essence of liquidated damages is a genuine covenanted pre-estimate of damage ... (3) The question of whether a sum stipulated is a penalty or liquidated damages is a question of construction to be decided upon the terms and inherent circumstances of each particular contract, judged of as at the time of the making of the contract, not as at the time of the breach ... (4) To assist this task of construction various tests have been suggested which, if applicable to the case under consideration, may prove helpful, or even conclusive. Such are (a) it will be held to be a penalty if the sum stipulated for is extravagant and unconscionable in amount in comparison with the greatest loss that could conceivably be proved to have followed from the breach (b) it will be held to be a penalty if the breach consists only in not paying a sum of money and the money stipulated is a sum greater than the sum which ought to have been paid ... (c) There is a presumption (and no more) that it is a penalty when a simple lump sum is made payable by way of compensation, on the occurrence of one or more or all of the events some of which may occasion serious and others but trifling damage ... On the other hand (d) it is not an obstacle to the sum stipulated being a genuine pre-estimate of damage that the consequences of the breach are such as to make precise pre-estimation almost an impossibility. On the contrary that is just the situation when it is probable that pre-estimated damage was the true bargain between the parties.'

The authority of these rules was reaffirmed by the Judicial Committee of the Privy Council in *Philips Hong Kong Ltd* v. *The Attorney General of Hong Kong* (1993). The rules may appear clear but their application is not always easy. For a more recent discussion of the general rules and their application, see *Alfred McAlpine Capital Projects Ltd* v. *Tilebox* (2005).

Doubt remains in Scots Law about the enforceability of a liquidated damages clause where the works could not have been completed in the time specified, see *Robertson* v. *Driver's Trustees* (1881).

An employer is not entitled to enforce a liquidated damages clause if he has agreed not to enforce the clause or he has waived his right to do so. In the absence of contractual provision to the contrary, payment of the contract price does not constitute waiver of the right to claim liquidated damages, see *Clydebank Engineering and Shipbuilding Co. Ltd* v. *Don Jose Ramos Yzquierdo y Castaneda* (1905).

# Chapter 7
# Certification

## 7.1 Introduction

The use of certificates in building contracts is both common and, it is submitted, essential for the proper administration of the contract. Although certificates fulfil a number of wide-ranging functions, their central use is to provide triggers or mechanisms that regulate the rights and obligations of the parties to a contract during its currency and on completion. In particular, certificates often play an important role in the contractual mechanisms which regulate payment, both interim and final, progress and completion of the works and the rectification of defects in the works. The issue of a certificate is regularly a condition precedent to one of the parties obtaining rights in terms of the building contract.

In order to ascertain whether a building contract has any requirements for the issue of certificates, it is necessary to look at the express terms of the contract. If the express terms of the contract do require certification then the terms have to be carefully considered in order to ascertain what certificates need to be issued, the contractual pre-conditions which must be satisfied before a certificate can be issued, and the rights and obligations which flow from or are extinguished by the issue of a certificate, see *Ata Ul Haq* v. *The City Council of Nairobi* (1962). In the absence of any express terms dealing with certification then the question of certification does not arise. The requirement for certification is not implied by operation of law.

## 7.2 Formal requirements of certificates

As the requirement for the use of certificates has to be expressed in the building contract, similarly the requirements as to the form of a valid certificate can also be stipulated. In the commonly used standard forms of building contract, it is unusual to find the form of certificates specified in detail and even more uncommon for style or specimen certificates to be provided. However, any requirements as to form which are stipulated should be strictly followed, failing which there is a danger that the certificate will be open to challenge and ultimately held to be invalid. See, for example, *B R Cantrell, E P Cantrell* v. *Wright & Fuller Ltd* (2003) in which it was held that a certificate was not a valid certificate in form, substance or intent.

If the contract is silent as to the form a certificate is to take then no particular form is required. If the certifier only has to pronounce himself satisfied in respect of certain matters then the certification may be given orally. Notwithstanding this, it is clearly preferable for certificates to be in writing, if for no other reason than to avoid evidential difficulties in subsequently proving whether certification has or has not been given.

Disputes do regularly arise in the course of building contracts as to whether certification has been given and whether or not a written document amounts to a certificate in terms of the contract. In *Halliday Construction Ltd and Others* v. *Gowrie Housing Association Ltd* (1995) a dispute arose as to whether letters written by the architect to the contractor amounted to non-completion certificates in terms of the contract. The letters simply advised the contractor that the architect had notified the employer that the contract had overrun and that liquidated and ascertained damages might be deducted. The contractor argued that such letters did not constitute certificates as they lacked the necessary form, substance and intent. The court held that the letters did amount to certificates, but only after some considerable hesitation.

In contrast, a letter written by the architect and relied on by the employer to deduct liquidated and ascertained damages was held insufficient to constitute a certificate in the case of *Token Construction Co. Ltd* v. *Charlton Estates Ltd* (1973). The reasoning of the court was that it was unclear and ambiguous whether the architect had intended the letter to constitute a certificate.

In order to avoid such difficulties, when purporting to issue a certificate, the certifier should make it clear that certification is being given. In this connection the use of the word 'certificate' is not essential although it is submitted that its use is prudent, see *Minster Trust Ltd* v. *Traps Tractor Ltd and Others* (1954). See also *H Fairweather Ltd* v. *Asden Securities Ltd* (1979) in which the court attached weight to the fact that a letter relied on as a certificate did not contain the word 'certify'. The use of words such as 'checking', 'approving' and 'satisfies' may not in themselves be sufficient and can give rise to ambiguity.

The certificate should leave the parties in no doubt as to its intention and effect. The rights and obligations which flow from the issue of the certificate should be clear. Where possible a certificate should refer to the relevant clause of the contract under which it is being issued and, insofar as possible, follow the wording contained in the clause.

In the event that a dispute does arise as to whether a document is or is not a certificate, then the use of extrinsic evidence may be permissible. For example, the terms of a covering letter sent with a purported certificate may provide assistance in ascertaining whether a document is truly a certificate. In *H Fairweather Ltd*, the court considered a whole course of correspondence to ascertain whether certain letters were intended to constitute certificates.

Unless otherwise required by the terms of the contract, a certificate does not have to include any reasons in support of the matters decided by or the opinions expressed in the certificate, and a lack of reasons can make the challenge of the certificate by an aggrieved party more difficult. Whether this is a perceived advantage or disadvantage is a matter for the parties to decide and take account of when drafting the contract.

In addition to any requirements regarding the form of certificates, there are other matters that should be borne in mind when preparing and issuing certificates. In particular one should ensure that any express pre-conditions to the issue of a certificate have been complied with. Such pre-conditions may include when the certificate needs to be issued; by what mechanism the certificate should be issued; by whom the certificate should be issued; and to whom the certificate should be issued.

For example, clause 4.15 of the Standard Building Contract (SBC) contains a number of pre-conditions to the issue of a Final Certificate, namely the end of the Rectification Period in respect of the Works or where there are Sections the last such period to expire, the issue of the Certificate of Making Good, and the sending by the Architect to the Contractor of an ascertainment of any loss and expense and a statement of all adjustments to be made to the Contract Sum. In addition, the Final Certificate must be issued no later than two months after whichever of the foregoing is last to occur. Clause 4.15 goes on to stipulate what the Final Certificate should include, being the adjusted Contract Sum; the sum of the amounts already stated as due in Interim Certificates plus the amount of any advance payment; the difference between the two sums expressed as a balance due to the Contractor from the Employer or vice versa; and the basis on which that balance has been calculated.

The SBC also provides, in clause 1.9, that each certificate issued by the Architect shall be issued to the Employer and a copy immediately sent to the Contractor. For a further example, see *G A Group Ltd* v. *Scottish Metropolitan Property plc* (1992) where a certificate of non-completion issued prior to the expiry of the period for completion was held to be invalid. See also *Crestar Ltd* v. *Michael John Carr and Joy Carr* (1987).

It is common for standard forms of building contract to stipulate that the certificate must actually be delivered to the parties to the contract. The requirements for delivery may also be expressed including the method of delivery and the address to which delivery has to be made: for example, to a limited company at its registered office. In the event that the contract does not stipulate that the certificate needs to be delivered to the parties then it is probably implied in any event. See, for example, the comments of Lord Justice Edmund Davies in the case of *Token Construction Co. Ltd* v. *Charlton Estates Ltd* (1973).

Minor errors in complying with any of the formal requirements of a certificate may not result in the certificate being held to be invalid, provided that the substance and effect of the certificate is correct and provided none of the parties to the contract have been misled or prejudiced. Nevertheless, such comfort should not be relied upon and the prudent course is to ensure that the certificate complies entirely with all the contractual requirements. If the certifier issues a certificate which is invalid, it may be open to him to reissue the certificate in a form which is valid provided he is not *functus officio* (disempowered because his role is concluded) and provided he does not alter the substance of the certificate unless the contract permits him to do so, see *Kiu May Construction Co. Ltd* v. *Wai Cheong Co. Ltd and Another* (1983).

## 7.3 *Interim certificates*

One of the most widely used types of certificate found in building contracts is the interim certificate, sometimes known as a progress certificate. Such a certificate is issued during the course of the contract works and is commonly designed to fulfil the dual function of monitoring the progress of the works and at the same time regulating instalment or interim payments to the contractor.

At common law, unless the contract provides otherwise, a contractor has no implied right to interim or instalment payments. This position has been altered in respect of most building contracts by the 1996 Act, see Chapter 8 below for a fuller discussion of this point. Nevertheless, most building contracts do expressly provide for interim or instalment payments to the contractor during the currency of the works.

In the commonly used standard forms of building contract, interim or progress certificates are the mechanism most often used as a means of regulating the timing and amount of such interim or instalment payments. See, for example, clause 4.9 of the SBC which makes provision for the issue of Interim Certificates by the Architect. The dates on which Interim Certificates are to be issued are agreed between the parties at the time of entering into the contract and these details are inserted in the Contract Particulars. If no dates are stated then, in terms of the Contract Particulars, Interim Certificates are to be issued at intervals not exceeding one month up to the date of practical completion of the works, or the date within one month thereafter. It is also provided that the first interim certificate is to be issued within one month of the Date of Possession.

When issued, an interim certificate commonly operates in one of two ways. The interim certificate either certifies the value of work carried out at the date of the certificate and triggers payment of that amount to account of the final contract sum or, alternatively, the Interim Certificate certifies that the works have been completed to a particular stage triggering the release of an agreed instalment payment for that stage.

The SBC recognises both these alternatives. It provides a mechanism in clauses 4.10 and 4.16 for ascertaining the amount to be included in an interim certificate using the former alternative but also stipulates, in the opening lines of clause 4.10, that this is subject to any agreement between the parties as to stage payments.

As a consequence of the fact that interim certificates are issued during the currency of the contract, the valuation of the work carried out, or any assessment of the quality of the work carried out, at the date of the certificate is not an exact science. Accordingly, interim certificates are not normally stipulated to be conclusive in respect of either the amount to be paid to the contractor or to the extent that they provide that the works and materials are of satisfactory quality. In relation to the last point, see *Clark Contracts Ltd* v. *The Burrell Co. (Construction Management) Ltd* (2002). Interim certificates simply have provisional validity, see *Beaufort Developments (NI) Ltd* v. *Gilbert-Ash NI Ltd and Another* (1998). The amount certified in an interim certificate can usually be challenged during the currency of the works. The procedure for challenging interim certificates is considered in more detail below.

In any event, the effect of interim certificates may be superseded by subsequent developments and subsequent interim certificates. In relation to the valuation of the work carried out this can normally be revised at the time of issue of the next interim certificate, see *Scottish Equitable plc* v. *Miller Construction Ltd* (2001). Most standard forms of building contract allow for a revaluation of all work carried out in terms of the contract at the date of issue of an interim certificate and not simply a valuation of the work carried out since the issue of the previous certificate, see, for example, clause 4.16 of the SBC. Confirmation that each interim certificate is intended to be based on a revaluation of all work carried out can be found in *William Verry Ltd* v. *North West London Communal Mikvah* (2004). In this case the Court indicated that each month the works have to be revalued so as to ensure that the total value of work properly executed is ascertained. In addition if work previously valued is discovered to be defective then there will have to be a downward adjustment of the gross value previously certified.

The fact that each interim certificate supersedes its predecessor has important implications with regard to the prescription of claims. It was held in *Scottish Equitable plc* v. *Miller Construction Ltd* (2001) that the whole structure of the contract in question allowed challenges to be made against certificates notwithstanding the fact that a challenge on the same basis could have been made against an earlier certificate. In short, it appears that a failure to challenge one interim certificate in respect of a particular issue does not automatically trigger the start of the prescriptive period in respect of that issue as it also falls to be valued in subsequent interim certificates. Support for such a position is also to be found in the English case of *Henry Boot Construction Ltd* v. *Alstom Combined Cycles Ltd* (2005).

With regard to the quality of work and materials, the issue of an interim certificate does not normally prevent the issue of instructions or directions in relation to remedying defective or unsatisfactory work. Indeed many defects may not be apparent at the time of issue of an interim certificate. Clause 1.11 of the SBC specifically provides that an interim certificate is not conclusive evidence that any work, materials or goods to which it relates are in accordance with the contract. Similarly, clause 3.6 of the SBC stipulates that the Contractor remains wholly responsible for carrying out the Works in accordance with the contract notwithstanding the fact that the value of that work has been included in a certificate for payment.

In many standard forms of building contract, the issue of an interim certificate is a condition precedent to payment of interim amounts to the contractor. In such cases if the contractor does not receive a certificate then it will have no right to payment under the contract. Similarly, an employer is only obliged to pay to a contractor the amount contained in an interim certificate, see *Nicol Homeworld Contracts Ltd* v. *Charles Gray Builders Ltd* (1986), *Costain Building & Civil Engineering Ltd* v. *Scottish Rugby Union plc* (1994) and *Karl Construction Ltd* v. *Palisade Properties plc* (2002). See also the English case of *Lubenham Fidelities and Investments Co. Ltd* v. *South Pembrokeshire DC and Another* (1986).

Until the coming into force of the 1996 Act, if the employer challenged an interim certificate (and provided they could aver a genuine dispute regarding the issue of the certificate) then they could attempt to avoid making payment on the certificate, see *W & J R Watson Ltd* v. *Lothian Health Board* (1986). Employers could also attempt to avoid making payment on an interim certificate if they could rely on their common law rights of retention and set-off, or if there were any contractual rights to make deductions from amounts certified. A fuller discussion of these matters is found below in Chapter 10. The position regarding the withholding of payment is now regulated by section 111 of the 1996 Act and an employer cannot withhold payment without first serving a valid withholding notice, see *Rupert Morgan Building Services (LLC) Ltd* v. *Jervis* (2003).

For many years following upon the decision in *Northern Regional Health Authority* v. *Derek Crouch Construction Co. Ltd* (1984) it was the position that an aggrieved party could only challenge the amount of or the lack of an interim certificate by means of arbitration proceedings and not through the courts. In that case the parties to a building contract conferred on an arbiter the power to open up, review and revise certificates. The English Court of Appeal held that this special power had been expressly conferred on the arbiter, that the courts did not have a similar power and, accordingly, could not open up, review or revise certificates.

The decision in *Northern Regional Health Authority* was followed in England and also in Scotland for 14 years, see *D & J McDougall Ltd* v. *Argyll & Bute DC* (1987) and *Stanley Miller Ltd* v. *Ladhope Developments Ltd* (1988). As a result, great care was required when drafting arbitration clauses to ensure that an arbiter was given sufficiently wide powers to alter certificates. Similarly, great care had to be taken when deleting arbitration clauses, and it became increasingly common for parties to insert provisions in building contracts providing that the courts could open up, review and revise certificates where there was no arbitration clause. Whether such provisions competently gave the courts power to review certificates was never clear.

In 1998, however, the position altered dramatically with the decision of the House of Lords in the case of *Beaufort Developments (NI) Ltd* v. *Gilbert-Ash NI Ltd and Another* (1998) which overruled *Northern Regional Health Authority*. In *Beaufort Developments (NI) Ltd* the court held that merely because an arbitration clause gave an arbiter power to open up, review and revise certificates that did not mean that the courts could not consider the matter. The wording of such an arbitration clause did not confer on an arbiter wider powers than those enjoyed by the courts whose normal powers to enforce contracts were sufficiently wide to achieve the same result. Accordingly, interim certificates do not have binding and conclusive effect before a court and a party to a building contract can sue for payment in the courts of sums not yet certified in an interim certificate.

The reasoning behind the House of Lords' decision was that the parties to the contract had conferred on the arbiter the power to open up, review and revise certificates. This illustrated that interim certificates were not intended to be binding and conclusive at all and accordingly, could not be binding and conclusive before the courts, see also *Robins* v. *Goddard* (1905). The House of Lords did stress that the position would be different in respect of certificates which are expressly stipulated to be binding and conclusive.

Unfortunately, it is not clear from the court's decision in *Beaufort Developments (NI) Ltd* how the contractor's right to raise proceedings against the employer in the absence of a certificate is to be analysed. In *Beaufort Developments (NI) Ltd* the most helpful discussion of available remedies is found in the speech of Lord Hope of Craighead who stated:

> 'On this approach the court will be able to exercise all its ordinary powers to decide the issues of fact and law which may be brought before it and to give effect to the rights and obligations of the parties in the usual way. It will have all the powers which it needs to determine the extent to which, if at all, either party was in breach of the contract and to determine what sums, if any, are due to be paid by one party to the other whether by way of set off or in addition to those sums which have been certified by the architect. It will not be necessary for it to exercise the powers which the parties have conferred upon the architect in order to provide the machinery for working out that contract. This is because the court does not need to make use of the machinery under the contract to provide the parties with the appropriate remedies. The ordinary powers of the court in regard to the examination of the facts and the awarding of sums found due to or by either party are all that is required.'

It was unclear, however, what effect the decision had on the authorities referred to above in which it had already been held that a certificate was a condition precedent to payment of the contractor, see *Nicol Homeworld Contracts Ltd* v. *Charles Gray Builders Ltd* (1986) and *Costain Building & Civil Engineering Ltd* v. *Scottish Rugby Union plc* (1994).

This issue has since been further considered by the English Court of Appeal in the case of *Henry Boot Construction Ltd* v. *Alstom Combined Cycles Ltd* (2005). In that case the court confirmed that certificates were a condition precedent to the contractor's entitlement to payment under the contract in question but that it did not follow that the absence of a certificate was a bar to the right to payment. In particular Lord Justice Dyson stated that:

> 'By "condition precedent" I mean that the right to payment arises when a certificate is issued or ought to be issued, and not earlier. It does not,

however, follow from the fact that a certificate is a condition precedent that the absence of a certificate is a bar to the right to payment. This is because the decision of the engineer in relation to certification is not conclusive of the rights of the parties, unless they have clearly so provided. If the engineer's decision is not binding, it can be reviewed by an arbitrator (if there is an arbitration clause which permits such a review) or by the court. If the arbitrator or the court decides that the engineer ought to have issued a certificate which he refused to issue, or to have included a larger sum in a certificate which he did issue, they can, and ordinarily will, hold that the contractor is entitled to payment as if such certificate had been issued and award or give judgment for the appropriate sum.'

He went on to confirm that he did not consider that the decision in *Beaufort* compelled the conclusion that certificates were not a condition precedent to the right to payment.

The issue was also considered in the Scottish case of *Karl Construction Ltd v. Palisade Properties plc* (2002). In this case Lord Drummond Young held that payment under the standard JCT forms was conditional on the issue of a certificate by the certifier or on the decree of an arbiter or a court on the basis that the decree of an arbiter or court was equivalent to a certificate. He stated that:

'the equivalence of a court decree to an architect or engineer's certificate follows from *Beaufort*, on the basis that a decree of the court can achieve the same result as a decree of an arbiter. In every case, however, until an appropriate certificate or decree has been obtained, the debt due by the employer to the contractor is contingent.'

Consideration also needs to be given to whether an adjudicator has the power to open up, review and revise interim certificates. It is submitted that he must have such a power as the 1996 Act stipulates that a party has the right to refer 'any difference' to an adjudicator for his decision, see s.108(1) to (4) of the 1996 Act. Accordingly, it is arguable that this must imply a right to open up, review and revise interim certificates. If no such right is implied and if the adjudication provisions in a building contract do not allow an adjudicator to open up, review and revise certificates then it is possible that the contract will not meet the requirements of s.108(1) to (4) and the Statutory Scheme for Construction Contracts will apply, see s.108(5). The Scheme specifically provides that an adjudicator may open up, review and revise any decision taken or any certificate given, see Part I of the Schedule to the Scheme for Construction Contracts (Scotland) Regulations 1998, paragraph 20(2)(a).

This potential issue is avoided by clause 9.2 of the SBC which states that if a dispute or difference arises which either party wishes to refer to adjudication then (subject to some minor qualifications) the Scheme will govern the process and, accordingly, an adjudicator has in respect of disputes under that form of contract an express power to open up, review and revise interim certificates. It is submitted that if parties drafting a building contract wish to ensure that their adjudication provisions comply with the requirements of the 1996 Act, and thus avoid any risk of the statutory scheme applying, it is prudent to expressly confer such a power upon the adjudicator.

## 7.4 Final certificates

### 7.4.1 General

A second type of certificate regularly encountered in building contracts is the final certificate. The issue of a final certificate usually signals the end of the contract and can deal with a number of matters, including the final amount payable in terms of the contract which often includes any amount payable for additional or extra work. It can also include, but more normally excludes, any amounts payable in respect of damages for delay or other breaches of contract. It can mean that the contract works have been completed to the satisfaction of the certifier; that additional or extra work has been completed to the satisfaction of the certifier; and that the rectification of patent defects has been carried out to the satisfaction of the certifier.

### 7.4.2 The Final Certificate under the SBC

In order to ascertain the matters that are covered by the Final Certificate, it is necessary to consider the express terms of the contract. It is also necessary to consider the express terms of the contract to ascertain the effect of the issue of the Final Certificate, see *Ata Ul Haq* v. *The City Council of Nairobi* (1962).

Clause 1.10 of the SBC sets out the effect of the Final Certificate. It provides that the Final Certificate shall have effect in any proceedings, whether by adjudication, arbitration or legal proceedings, as conclusive evidence that where and to the extent that any of the particular qualities of any materials or goods or any particular standard of an item of workmanship was described expressly in the Contract Drawings, the Contract Bills, an instruction of the Architect or in any drawing or document issued by the Architect to be for the approval of the Architect, the particular quality or standard was to the reasonable satisfaction of the Architect. The Final Certificate is not conclusive evidence that materials or goods or workmanship comply with any other requirement or term of the contract.

It is conclusive evidence that necessary effect has been given to all the terms of the contract which require that an amount be added to or deducted from the Contract Sum or that an adjustment is to be made to the Contract Sum, save where there has been any accidental inclusion or exclusion of any work, materials, goods or figure in any computation or any arithmetical error in any computation. In such circumstances, the Final Certificate is conclusive evidence as to all other computations.

It is conclusive evidence that all and only such extensions of time, if any, as are due under clause 2.28 have been given.

Finally, it is conclusive evidence that the reimbursement of direct loss and/or expense, if any, to the Contractor pursuant to clause 4.23 is in final settlement of all and any claims which the Contractor has or may have arising out of the occurrence of any of the relevant matters referred to in clause 4.24 whether such claims are for breach of contract, duty of care, statutory duty or otherwise.

The issue of a Final Certificate is unlikely to cover claims in respect of damages for breach of contract, as it is unusual to find such matters within the certifier's remit. The issue of the final certificate can preclude the Employer's ability to deduct liquidated damages. Clause 2.32 of the SBC provides that the Employer may require the Contractor to pay liquidated damages provided they give notice in writing prior to the issue of the Final Certificate. See also *Robert Paterson & Sons Ltd* v. *Household Supplies Co. Ltd* (1974).

The Final Certificate will not have conclusive effect if the certifier has exceeded his jurisdiction or the issue of the certificate is challengeable on other grounds, for example, where the certifier has not acted independently, has acted in bad faith or has acted fraudulently. These issues are more fully considered in section 7.6 below. Clause 1.10 of the SBC specifically provides that the Final Certificate will not be conclusive in the event of fraud. The Final Certificate is conclusive unless and until it is successfully challenged.

### 7.4.3 The final certificate as conclusive evidence

It will be noted that clause 1.10 states on a number of occasions that the Final Certificate has the effect of being 'conclusive evidence' on a matter. In many standard forms of building contract, it is common to find provisions that the final certificate is to some extent conclusive and binding upon the parties. Where a final certificate is stated to be conclusive and binding and has been properly issued then its effect is final in respect of the matters covered by the certificate. Accordingly, the parties to a contract cannot challenge the certificate by adjudication, arbitration or in the courts, or ask the adjudicator, arbiter or courts to review the certificate, simply on the grounds that they are aggrieved by it or disagree with its terms. The Statutory Scheme for Construction Contracts in Scotland stipulates that an adjudicator can open up, review and revise any certificate unless the contract states the certificate is final and conclusive, see Part I of the Schedule to the Scheme for Construction Contracts (Scotland) Regulations 1998, paragraph 20(2)(a).

The certificate is the final expression of the certifier's decision and cannot be interfered with simply on the basis that the certificate is wrong or negligently issued, see, for example, *Rush & Tompkins Ltd* v. *Deaner* (1987) where, due to an error on the part of the certifier, the balance due to the contractor in terms of the final certificate was mistakenly based on sums certified rather than sums certified and paid. It is submitted that the reason for this is that the certifier has been selected from a professional discipline because he possesses and can exercise the requisite skills and knowledge when issuing certificates. It is further submitted that the certifier should have an intimate knowledge of the contract as a result of his involvement, which knowledge would not be available to an independent third party such as an adjudicator, arbiter or court. Accordingly, the certifier is often the person best placed to decide any issues between the parties which fall within his remit.

### 7.4.4 The English and Scottish approaches

The matters in respect of which the final certificate is conclusive and binding differ from contract to contract and it is necessary to consider every contract on its own terms. This may not be an easy exercise particularly if the contract is not clearly drafted. Furthermore, the authorities which exist in this area are often inconsistent.

The English courts have tended to interpret the conclusive effect of final certificates very broadly. In *Crown Estates Commissioners* v. *John Mowlem & Co. Ltd* (1994), the English Court of Appeal considered the then wording of clause 30.9.1.1 of JCT 98. The clause under consideration by the court differs from the wording of clause 1.10.1.1 of the SBC (the current equivalent of clause 30.9.1.1 of JCT 98) in that it provided that the final certificate was to have effect as conclusive evidence that, where the quality of materials or the standard of workmanship were to be to the reasonable satisfaction of the architect, the same were to such satisfaction. The court held that, on a true construction of this clause, all matters of standards and quality of work and materials were for the reasonable opinion of the architect and so were concluded by the issue of a final certificate. Accordingly, if a final certificate was issued and not challenged timeously then all claims for defects arising from the standard or quality of work or materials would be defeated by the conclusive effect of the final certificate. Following this reasoning, claims for latent defects not apparent at the date of issue of the final certificate would also be excluded. Similarly, claims would also be excluded for defects arising from work or materials failing to meet prescribed criteria found, for example, in the bill of quantities or specification. The case of *Colbart Ltd* v. *Kumar* (1992) is a further example of the broad interpretation favoured by the English courts.

It appears that this broad interpretation did not reflect the intention of the Joint Contracts Tribunal when it originally drafted clause 30.9.1.1 of JCT 98. The intention of the Joint Contracts Tribunal was that the final certificate should only be conclusive evidence that the architect was satisfied that certain requirements of the work had been complied with where both the contractor and employer had agreed to abide by the architect's decision in respect of those requirements. It was not intended to have conclusive effect where the contractor had failed to comply with prescribed requirements of the contract documents. Following the decisions in *Colbart Ltd* and *Crown Estates Commissioners*, the Joint Contracts Tribunal revised clause 30.9.1.1 and that revision is carried through to clause 1.10.1.1 of the SBC to try and reflect its original intention. Accordingly, the decisions in *Colbart Ltd* and *Crown Estates Commissioners* may now be of limited application.

In any event, in Scotland the courts appear to have taken a narrower view of the conclusive effect of final certificates. Such a view reflects the original intention of JCT. In *Firholm Builders Ltd* v. *McAuley* (1982) the court considered a clause with wording similar to that considered by the English court in *Crown Estates Commissioners*. The court held, however, that the existence of the final certificate did not necessarily defeat a claim for defective workmanship or materials. The existence of the certificate simply allowed the contractor to rely on it as conclusive evidence that, where materials or workmanship were to be to the architect's reasonable satisfaction, then the final certificate demonstrated that they were to his reasonable satisfaction. It was still open to the employer to argue that the architect should not reasonably have been satisfied.

The decision of the Court of Session in *Belcher Food Products Ltd* v. *Miller & Black and Others* (1998) also appears to support a narrower interpretation of the conclusive effect of final certificates. In *Belcher Food Products Ltd* the court attempted to distinguish *Crown Estates Commissioners* by holding that even where a final certificate was conclusive evidence of the architect's reasonable satisfaction, it did not necessarily follow that it had the further effect of being conclusive evidence that the relevant standard and quality of workmanship or materials had been achieved in a question between the employer and the contractor. In other words, the final certificate would not be conclusive evidence of the standard and quality of workmanship or materials but only conclusive evidence that the architect was satisfied with the standard and quality. It followed that the court could only decide whether the quality and standard of workmanship was satisfactory once it had heard evidence. The final certificate would, however, have strong evidential value in this connection. This was not a distinction which the court had been asked to consider in *Crown Estates Commissioners*. The court in *Belcher Food Products Ltd* further attempted to distinguish *Crown Estates Commissioners* and *Colbart Ltd* on the basis that they both concerned issues which were inherently matters for the subjective opinion of the architect. In contrast, many of the issues in *Belcher Food Products Ltd* related to whether there had been actual compliance with express contractual requirements as to the quality of materials, which could be assessed objectively.

Accordingly, the Scottish courts appear to have taken a slightly different approach to that of the English courts. The authors respectfully suggest that the approach of the Scottish courts is to be preferred. The court in *Belcher Food Products Ltd*, however, clearly felt that *Crown Estates Commissioners* and *Colbart Ltd* were sufficiently authoritative that it was necessary to distinguish them rather than openly disagree with them or refuse to follow them. The result of all this is that it is difficult to draw any general principles from the cases dealing with the conclusive effect of final certificates. Each contract has to be considered on its own terms and against the background of the particular facts which have arisen. The subsequent amendment to the relevant clause is also of significance, the decisions in each of the cases referred to on this point being in relation to the effect of the old, now superseded, wording.

### 7.4.5 Challenging the final certificate

A number of the standard forms of building contract contain provisions providing that final certificates may be challenged by arbitration or other proceedings following their issue. Accordingly an arbiter is usually expressly empowered to open up, review and revise certificates. The SBC does not specifically provide for this but states in clause 9.5 that the arbiter will have the powers set out in the Scottish Arbitration Code 1999 Edition. Unfortunately the Code does not give an arbiter such powers and accordingly, at present, an arbiter appointed under the SBC will not be able to open up, review and revise certificates. It is submitted that it is wise for the drafters of contracts to include such a power.

Following the decision in *Beaufort Developments (NI) Ltd* v. *Gilbert-Ash NI Ltd and Another* (1998), the courts do enjoy such an inherent power without the requirement for an express power to be given to them. Where a Final Certificate can be challenged by arbitration or other proceedings then it should also be challengeable by means of adjudication under the 1996 Act and the Scheme for Construction Contracts expressly provides for this as discussed at paragraph 7.3 in the context of interim certificates.

Clearly such challenges to final certificates are inconsistent with the concept of final certificates having, in some circumstances, binding and conclusive effect.

The means by which this inconsistency is often dealt with in the standard forms of building contract is to provide that a Final Certificate does not have conclusive effect immediately on being issued, rather its conclusive effect is suspended for a stipulated period of time. During this period of time an aggrieved party is given the opportunity to challenge the Final Certificate by raising the appropriate proceedings. At the end of the stipulated period of time, the final certificate will have conclusive effect to the extent that it has not been challenged. In respect that the final certificate is challenged then it will still have conclusive effect subject to any award of the adjudicator, arbiter or court. In this connection see, for example, clause 1.10.3 of the SBC which provides that the final certificate will have conclusive effect 60 days after issue save in relation to any matters in respect of which adjudication, arbitration or other proceedings have been raised. If the challenge to the final certificate is by adjudication then parties are given a further 28 days to raise arbitration or legal proceedings following conclusion of the adjudication in terms of clause 1.10.4. In the English case of *Tracy Bennett* v. *FMK Construction Limited* (2005) the court refused to declare that the final certificate was conclusive despite the fact that an adjudication commenced within the 28-day period was brought to end by the adjudicator and only re-started after the expiry of the 28-day period. It is submitted, however, that the facts of this case were peculiar and in all cases parties should ensure that time limits are strictly adhered to. For the relationship between adjudicator's decisions and final certificates see *Castle Inns (Stirling) Ltd* v. *Clarke Contracts Ltd* (2006).

## 7.5  Other certificates

In addition to interim and final certificates, a number of other types of certificate are commonly found in the standard forms of building contract. These have a wide variety of different functions. The following are some examples.

### 7.5.1  Completion certificates

These certificates are commonly used to record when the works or sections of the works have been substantially or practically completed. This can have important consequences for a number of matters including the start of the rectification, defects liability or maintenance period; the release of retention monies; and the end of the period for which the employer is entitled to deduct liquidated damages. See, for example, clause 2.30 of the SBC which provides for the issue by the Architect of a Practical Completion Certificate which should specify the day on which practical completion of the Works has taken place.

In terms of the Contract Particulars, the date specified in the Practical Completion Certificate signals the beginning of the Rectification Period referred to in clause 2.38 which runs for a period of six months unless the parties have agreed otherwise. It is, however, specifically provided in clause 3.6 of the SBC that the Contractor remains wholly responsible for carrying out the Works in accordance with the contract whether or not a Practical Completion Certificate has been issued.

### 7.5.2  Non-completion certificates

In many standard forms of building contract, as a pre-requisite to the deduction of liquidated damages by the employer, the certifier needs to issue a certificate of non-completion indicating that the works are not substantially or practically complete by the date for completion agreed between the parties or any extended date thereof. The SBC provides for the issue of such a certificate in clause 2.31. Such a certificate is a pre-condition to the deduction of liquidated and ascertained damages using the mechanism set out in clause

2.32, see, for example, *Halliday Construction Ltd and Others* v. *Gowrie Housing Association Ltd* (1995).

### 7.5.3 Partial possession certificates

Often building contracts contain provisions whereby the employer can take possession of part of the works despite the fact that the whole of the works is not yet substantially or practically complete. This often requires the issue by the certifier of a certificate or statement identifying what part or parts of the works is/are being taken into possession by the employer. This can have important consequences for liquidated damages and protection of the works, including the question of which party is responsible for insuring the works. See, for example, clause 2.33 of the SBC which provides for the issue by the Architect of a written statement identifying the part or parts taken into possession and the date when the Employer took possession. The effect of partial possession being taken upon practical completion, defects, insurance and liquidated damages in respect of the relevant part are set out in clauses 2.34 to 2.37.

### 7.5.4 Certificates of making good defects

Such certificates are regularly found in the standard forms of building contract. They are normally issued at the end of the rectification, defects liability or maintenance period when all the defects have been rectified to the satisfaction of the certifier. The issue of such a certificate often triggers the release of any remaining retention and is usually a pre-condition to the issue of a final certificate, see, for example, clause 4.20.3 of the SBC which provides that the Employer need release only half the retention percentage where work has reached practical completion but where no Certificate of Making Good has been issued. Similarly, under clause 4.15.1, the issue of the Certificate of Making Good is a pre-condition to the issue of the Final Certificate. The provision permitting the Certificate of Making Good to be issued is found in clause 2.39. Clause 3.6 nevertheless provides that the issue of a Certificate of Making Good does not relieve the Contractor of his responsibility for carrying out the Works in accordance with the contract.

### 7.5.5 Challenging such certificates

The effect of the foregoing types of certificates and any other certificates which may be provided for in a building contract depends on the express terms of the building contract in question. Such certificates may or may not have conclusive effect although the position under the standard forms of building contract is that they do not normally have conclusive effect and are susceptible to challenge either by way of adjudication, arbitration or court proceedings.

## 7.6 Roles and duties of certifiers

### 7.6.1 Who is the certifier?

In the same way that the certification process requires to be expressly stipulated in a building contract, so should the identity of the certifier. In most standard forms of building contract the certifier is a person with relevant skill and knowledge selected from an appropriate professional discipline, for example, an architect, quantity surveyor or engineer. Rather than naming an individual, it is possible and, indeed, more common to nominate a firm or partnership as the certifier. Naming an individual can give rise to issues of *delectus personae*, considered below in section 9.6. It is also possible to specify the certifier by making reference to the holder of a particular post.

The certifier named in the contract must be the person who issues the relevant certificates. Although he can delegate some of the detailed work, for example, the carrying out of measurements and calculations or the inspection of work, it is the certifier himself who must issue the certificates. He cannot delegate this function. Similarly, if a firm or partnership fulfils the role of certifier, then it must be a partner in the firm who issues the certificate although, again, work of a detailed nature may be delegated to others within the partnership, see *London Borough of Hounslow* v. *Twickenham Garden Developments Ltd* (1970).

In rare cases, contracts sometimes provide that the employer is also the certifier. Such provisions are infrequent in that the contractor is unlikely to agree to them. Furthermore, such provisions are not to be recommended to either party to a contract in that there is an obvious potential for abuse. An employer fulfilling the role of certifier clearly has to act honestly and fairly, failing which his actions will be open to challenge. In addition, the courts are likely to be unsympathetic towards an employer acting as certifier particularly where certification is a pre-condition of payments to the contractor or where decisions require a strong element of subjectivity. The decision of the court in *Scheldebouw BV* v. *St James Homes (Grosvenor Dock) Ltd* (2006) is a good example of the unsympathetic view taken by the courts when the employer assumes the role as certifier.

Where a certifier resigns, dies or becomes incapable of fulfilling the role of certifier then normally the contract will stipulate the procedure for making a new appointment. The SBC, for example, provides in clause 3.5.1 that, in the event of the Architect ceasing to hold that post for the purposes of the contract, then the employer has to nominate a replacement within 21 days. This is subject to the contractors' right of objection within seven days of the nomination. Where the contract is silent then it is submitted that there is, nevertheless, an implied term that the employer has a right to appoint a new certifier, subject to reasonable objections from the contractor. If the employer fails to appoint a new certifier then this may amount to a breach of contract on their part particularly in the event that certification is a pre-condition to rights on the part of the contractor, for example, to payment, see *Croudace Ltd* v. *London Borough of Lambeth* (1986). Similarly, where an employer fails to appoint a new certifier then he may be prohibited from relying on the lack of certification to defend claims by the contractor.

The certifier is normally engaged by the employer and has no direct contractual link with the contractor. The certifier's rights and obligations are set out in his terms and conditions of appointment or implied by law. Usually the certifier is a member of a professional body and his conditions of appointment may be based on standard forms issued by his professional body. As the certifier is normally engaged by the employer then he must act on the instructions of his employer and any acts or omissions on the part of the certifier can amount to a breach of his contract with the employer giving rise to a claim for damages against him. Furthermore, the certifier is normally also acting as the agent of the employer in respect of the building contract and any acts or omissions in this connection can place the employer in breach of contract with the contractor. In this respect, however, a difficult distinction requires to be drawn between the certifier's duties as agent of the employer and his duties as certifier.

### 7.6.2 Jurisdiction of the certifier

The jurisdiction of the certifier is defined by the express terms of the building contract. If the certifier goes beyond his jurisdiction then any certificates issued will be invalid and open to challenge by either party, see, for example, *Hall & Tawse Construction Ltd* v. *Strathclyde Regional Council* (1990) where the certifier made deductions in a certificate which he had no authority to make in terms of the contract. This will apply even to certificates stated to have final and conclusive effect. The certifier also needs to ensure that he has complied with any formal requirements for issuing certificates particularly those which are essential pre-conditions and that he has complied with any time limits set out in the contract.

Once the certifier has completed his functions then his jurisdiction falls and he is *functus officio*, having discharged his function. In many standard forms of building contract this occurs when he issues the final certificate. Thereafter, he is precluded from issuing any further valid certificates, see *H Fairweather Ltd* v. *Asden Securities Ltd* (1979).

The contract can also indicate a number of other events or contingencies which will bring a certifier's jurisdiction to an end. Raising arbitration proceedings, however, will not normally make the certifier *functus officio*, see *GA Group Ltd* v. *Scottish Metropolitan Property plc* (1992). In certain instances the certifier may become disqualified. This can be a difficult area because of the dual function which certifiers are regularly required to fulfil as both agent of the employer and as independent certifier.

### 7.6.3 General duties re certification

As already indicated, the certifier is normally engaged by the employer and acts as his agent in respect of the building contract. Accordingly, he must have regard for his employer's interests and, in respect of many matters, act upon the instructions of his employer. When acting as certifier, however, he is under a duty to act fairly, honestly and independently. See *London Borough of Hounslow* v. *Twickenham Garden Developments Ltd* (1970), *Sutcliffe* v. *Thackrah and Others* (1974) and *Costain Ltd and Others* v. *Bechtel Ltd* (2005).

The comments of Lord Hoffman in the case of *Beaufort Developments (NI) Ltd* v. *Gilbert-Ash NI Ltd and Another* (1998) are instructive in this regard. He stated that:

> 'the architect is the agent of the employer. He is a professional man but can hardly be called independent.'

A certifier must apply the terms of the contract exercising his own skill and judgement, failing which his certificates will be invalid and he will be open to disqualification. He should not be unduly influenced by or act on his client's instructions to the extent that he jeopardises his independence and impartiality, see *Nash Dredging (UK) Ltd* v. *Kestrel Marine Ltd* (1987). Similarly, the parties are under a duty to ensure that they do not interfere with the certifier exercising his certification duties, see *Perini Corporation* v. *Commonwealth of Australia* (1969) and *Nash Dredging Ltd* v. *Kestrel Marine Ltd* (1986). A certifier does not, however, have to apply the strict rules of natural justice and he has a discretion as to how to gather information and whether to allow parties a hearing, see *The North British Railway Company* v. *William Wilson* (1911) and *London Borough of Hounslow* v. *Twickenham Garden Developments Ltd* (1970).

The application of the rules of natural justice was considered further in the English case of *Amec Civil Engineering Ltd* v. *Secretary of State for Transport* (2005). The contract between the parties in that case incorporated the Institution of Civil Engineers Conditions of Contract (Fifth Edition). It was the role of the engineer acting under the dispute provisions in clause 66(1) of that contract which came under review. The court held that the engineer in that role was acting as a certifier and that although he was not obliged to comply with the rules of natural justice applicable to judges he was required to act independently, honestly and fairly. Lord Justice May puts the point simply:

> 'The rules of natural justice are formalised requirements for those who act judicially. Compliance with them is required of judges and arbitrators and those in equivalent position, but not of an engineer giving a decision under

clause 66 of the ICE Conditions . . . Under clause 66, the engineer is required to act independently and honestly.'

In the light of the dual role of a certifier, correspondence or discussion of matters with the employer regarding certification will not necessarily invalidate a certificate nor will the giving of advice by the certifier to the employer. The certifier can consult the employer and the employer's advisers on legal matters that arise out of or in connection with the building contract provided any response is treated solely as advice and not as a direction or instruction. Many certifiers will take independent legal advice and it is submitted that this is the most appropriate course of action as the employer's legal advisers have their own clients' interests at heart and any advice given by them may be tainted or may unduly influence the certifier.

If the certifier does lose his independence then he will become disqualified and any certificates issued by him thereafter will be invalid. Fraud or dishonesty or taking account of unduly influential matters and advice would disqualify a certifier. Similarly, fraudulent misrepresentation on the part of either party to the contract can also invalidate certificates issued in reliance upon such a misrepresentation, see *Gray and Others (The Special Trustees of the London Hospital)* v. *T P Bennett & Son and Others* (1987) and *Ayr Road Trustees* v. *W & T Adams* (1883).

Concealed interests on the part of the certifier can also lead to disqualification. It is implied that certain interests are already known about and accepted by both parties. For example, it is known that the certifier will be paid by the employer for the work carried out by him, is liable to the employer for breach of contract and that, to an extent, he has to look after the employer's interests. Interests in the welfare of either party may, however, disqualify: for example, if the certifier is a shareholder in either of the parties or has a financial interest in the outcome of the certification process. This can lead to particular difficulties where, for example, the certifier has given advice to the employer in respect of the cost of the contract. If the certifier has guaranteed a price to the employer or will receive incentive payments for savings made then this could lead to disqualification. Where, however, the certifier has simply estimated the cost of the job for the employer then it is unlikely that this would amount to an interest sufficient to disqualify.

A certifier may also be disqualified if his dual roles as employer's agent and certifier become incompatible. This may occur where the certifier becomes a witness to fact or a key witness in support of one party's position.

A certifier is not disqualified simply because of an error in judgement or an error in the exercise of his discretion. Where such errors occur then it may be possible for one party to the contract to challenge the certificate by means of adjudication, arbitration or through the courts. There is authority which suggests that there is no obligation on an employer who becomes aware of errors on the part of the certifier to bring them to his attention and ensure that he adequately performs his duties, see *Lubenham Fidelities and*

*Investments Co. Ltd* v. *South Pembrokeshire District Council and Another* (1986). This decision should be contrasted with the decisions in *Perini Corporation* and *Panamena Europea Navigacion Compania Limitada* v. *Frederick Leyland & Co. Ltd* (1947).

Failures by the certifier can place him in breach of contract with his employer and may result in the certifier being liable to the employer in damages, see, for example, *Jameson* v. *Simon* (1899) where the certifier was found liable in damages to his employer for certifying work which did not conform to the contract as a result of failing to exercise reasonable supervision. See also *Sutcliffe* v. *Thackrah and Others* (1974) and *Atwal Enterprises Ltd* v. *Donal Toner Associates* (2006).

Such failures can also place the employer in breach of contract with the contractor although the case of *Karl Construction Ltd* v. *Palisade Properties plc* (2002) suggests that a failure to certify by the certifier will not provide the contractor with a right to damages from the employer but simply the right to arbitrate or sue for payment of any sums that would have been due had a certificate been issued. The certifier himself will generally have no liability to the contractor as there is no direct contractual link between certifier and contractor. The certifier could only be liable to the contractor in circumstances where he has procured the employer to breach his contract with the contractor, see *John Mowlem & Co. plc* v. *Eagle Star Insurance Co. Ltd and Others* (1992), or in delict. A simple under-certification may not generally be sufficient to give rise to delictual liability, see, for example, *Pacific Associates and Others* v. *Baxter* (1988), *Lubenham Fidelities and Investments Co. Ltd*, and *Leon Engineering & Construction Co. Ltd* v. *Ka Duk Investment Co. Ltd* (1989) although a warning is to be found in the case of *William McLaughlan and Another* v. *Keith Edwards* (2004). Although having no direct contractual link with the ultimate purchasers of a house an architect was found to owe the purchasers a duty to take reasonable care in the provision of architectural services in connection with the design and construction of the house and a duty to take reasonable care to ensure that the statements contained in the certificates which he issued were true and accurate. That being so, certifiers should be aware that they may, depending on the particular facts and circumstances, owe duties to those other than their employer.

# Chapter 8
# Payment

## 8.1 Contractual payment

### 8.1.1 Introduction

One of the main obligations owed by the employer under a building contract is to make payment to the contractor for the work carried out by them. The building contract will ordinarily contain express provisions relating to payment and the parties are, subject to the provisions of the 1996 Act, free to agree between them the sum that is to be paid for the works, whether instalment payments are to be made, when payments are to be made, and the mechanism or procedure to facilitate payment.

The commonly used standard forms of building contract contain detailed provisions in respect of payment, see, for example, clause 4 of the Standard Building Contract (SBC).

### 8.1.2 When are payments due?

**Traditional Scots Law position**

In any building contract one of the contractor's prime concerns is the timing of payments for work carried out. Traditionally under Scots Law contractors have no implied right to payment until they have completed all the work they have contracted to carry out, see *Muldoon* v. *Pringle* (1882) and *Readdie* v. *Mailler* (1841). It is a general principle of Scots Law that, in the absence of any provisions in a contract providing for interim or instalment payments, there is no obligation to make payment until the entire contract has been fulfilled. Whether or not this applies to building contracts was considered in the case of *Charles Gray & Son Ltd* v. *Stern* (1953). In this case, the contractor demanded payments to account while building a house, maintaining that it was normal building trade practice to pay contractors for nine-tenths of the work completed. The contract did not expressly provide for interim payments to be made. The court held that the contract was a lump sum contract and that, as the contractors had failed to carry out a material part of the works, they could not sue for payment under the contract.

**Exceptions to the basic principle**

However, whilst it may be the general principle that contractors are not entitled to payment from an employer before they have carried out all their obligations under the contract, there are situations in which the contractor may be entitled to payment notwithstanding the fact that they have failed to complete.

In certain instances, if the work can be said to be 'substantially complete', the contractor may be entitled to payment of the whole Contract Sum, less payment for that part not completed or, alternatively, the cost of remedying any defects in the works. In *Ramsay & Son* v. *Brand* (1898) Lord President Robertson stated that:

> 'A building contract by specification necessarily includes minute particulars, and the law is not so pedantic as to deny action for the contract price on account of any and every omission or deviation. It gives effect to the principle [that if builders choose to depart from the contract they lose their right to sue for the contract price] by deducting from the contract price whatever sum is required to complete the work in exact compliance with the contract.'

Similar authority can be found in the cases of *Speirs Ltd* v. *Petersen* (1924), *Hoenig* v. *Isaacs* (1952) and *Stewart Roofing Co. Ltd* v. *Shanlin* (1958).

Following the case of *Forrest* v. *The Scottish County Investment Company Ltd* (1915), it appears that the contractor's right to payment where there are defects may be stronger in a measurement contract than a lump sum contract, see section 8.1.6 below for a definition of these different types of contract. This approach also receives some support in *Speirs Ltd*.

If, however, the contractor's deviation from the contract is material then he will be prevented from claiming payment under the contract, see *D Ramsay & Son* and also *Dakin & Co. Ltd* v. *Lee* (1916). Unfortunately, it is not always clear whether a deviation is material and this will require to be considered in the light of the facts of each individual case, see, for example, *McMorran* v. *Morrison & Co.* (1906). This can include consideration of the dimension, complexity and value of the contract and consideration of the cost of rectifying the deviation relative to the whole contract price, see *Speirs Ltd*. On the other hand, if the employer has benefited from the work carried out by the contractor then the contractor may still be able to claim compensation under the principle of *quantum lucratus* even where there are material deviations. A fuller discussion of this principle is contained in section 8.5 below.

Where the contractor is prevented from completing the contract works by a matter outwith their control then they may still be able to claim payment for the work carried out. For example, where the employer denies the contractor access to the site to complete the contract works then the contractor will be able to claim payment for the work he has carried out. Similarly, the contractor will be entitled to claim payment for all work executed in accordance with a contract in the situation where the works are destroyed and cannot be completed, see, for example, the cases of *Andrew McIntyre and Company* v. *David Clow and Company* (1875) and *Richardson* v. *County Road Trustees of Dumfriesshire* (1890). This may, however, depend upon which party has assumed the risk of damage to the works during their construction and careful consideration may need to be given to any insurance provisions found in the contract. Insurance is considered in Chapter 14 below.

Finally, and most importantly, the contractor may be entitled to claim payment prior to completing the contract works where the express terms of the building contract specifically provide for the making of instalment or interim payments. In modern construction contracts such provisions are almost always included, as many contractors would be unable to fund the on-going construction costs pending payment upon completion. Procuring external funding would significantly increase construction costs.

### 8.1.3 Payment under the 1996 Act

In respect of building contracts entered into after 1 May 1998, the position in relation to payment altered dramatically following the coming into force of the 1996 Act. The 1996 Act materially improved the rights of a party to be paid under a construction contract as compared to the common law position.

### Sections 109 and 110

Section 109 of the Act deals with payment and provides that a party to a relevant construction contract is entitled to payment by instalments, stage payments or other periodic payments in respect of work carried out under the contract. Where the parties are entitled to interim payments under section 109 then the 1996 Act provides that the parties are free to agree the amounts of such payments and the intervals or circumstances in which they will become due.

Section 110(1) of the 1996 Act stipulates that every construction contract must provide a mechanism for determining what payments become due and when they become due and provide a final date for payment in relation to any sum which becomes due. The parties can, however, agree the interval between the date on which a sum becomes due and the final date for payment.

Section 110(2) stipulates that every construction contract must provide for the giving of notice by a party not later than five days after the date upon which a payment becomes due under the contract, or would have become due if the other party had carried out its obligations under the contract and no set-off or abatement was permitted by reference to any sum claimed to be due under one or more other contracts, specifying the amount (if any) of the payment made or proposed to be made, and the basis upon which that amount was calculated.

**The Scheme for Construction Contracts (Scotland) Regulations 1998**

Should the parties fail to provide for all or any of the matters which are required in terms of section 109 and/or section 110 then the payment provisions found in Part II of the Schedule to the Scheme for Construction Contracts (Scotland) Regulations 1998 will apply to the extent required to cover any matter not otherwise agreed, see *Hills Electrical & Mechanical plc* v. *Dawn Construction Ltd* (2003).

The Schedule deals firstly with 'relevant construction contracts', being any construction contract other than one which specifies that the duration of the work is to be less than 45 days or in respect of which the parties agree that the duration of the work is estimated to be less than 45 days. For the definition of a 'construction contract' for the purposes of the 1996 Act, see section 1.2.2 above.

Paragraph 4 of the Scheme provides that interim payments under a relevant construction contract will become due when the payee has made a claim and seven days have expired following the relevant period. Paragraph 12 provides that the 'relevant period' is as specified in or calculated by reference to the contract, failing which it is a period of 28 days.

Paragraph 5 of the Scheme provides that the final payment under a relevant construction contract, namely the difference between the contract price and the aggregate of any interim payments, will be due when the payee has made a claim and 30 days have expired following completion of the work.

In respect of contracts where the duration of the work is less than 45 days or where the parties agree that the duration of the work is estimated to be less than 45 days then paragraph 6 of the Schedule provides that payment of the contract price shall become due when the payee has made a claim and 30 days have expired following completion of the work. Paragraph 7 provides that any other payment under a construction contract will be due when the payee has made a claim and seven days have expired following the completion of the work to which the payment relates.

Paragraph 8 provides that the final date for any payment under a construction contract will be 17 days from the date when the payment becomes due. Finally, paragraph 9 provides a mechanism for the giving of notice by the paying party in accordance with the requirements of s.110(2) of the 1996 Act, which requires the paying party to specify how a payment is calculated.

### 8.1.4 Payment under the SBC

The payment provisions in the SBC are to be found in clause 4. Clause 4.9 provides for the issuing of interim certificates by the Architect and clause

4.13.1 provides that the final date for payment is 14 days from the date of issue of an Interim Certificate. Failure by the Employer to make payment by this date entitles the Contractor to simple interest on the amount not paid in terms of clause 4.13.6.

The contract leaves it to the parties to agree the intervals at which certificates will be issued and the agreed interval should be inserted in the Contract Particulars. In the absence of such agreement, the Contract Particulars and clause 4.9.2 provide that Interim Certificates are to be issued monthly up to the date of practical completion or the date within one month of practical completion and thereafter as and when further amounts are ascertained, provided at least one month has passed since the issue of the last Interim Certificate.

Clause 4.9.3 of the SBC provides that should the Architect not issue any Interim Certificate then the Contractor is entitled to make an application to the Employer for payment of any sums they consider are due under the contract. This right of application can only be used prior to, and for a period of six months after, the issue of the practical completion certificate and is to be made in accordance with any valuation statement prepared by the Quantity Surveyor under clause 4.12 or, in the absence of such a statement, in accordance with any application submitted by the Contractor to the Quantity Surveyor setting out what they consider to be the amount of their valuation.

For the purposes of clause 4.9.3, the final date for payment is stipulated to be 14 days from the date of receipt of the application by the Employer from the Contractor. The Employer has five days from receipt of the application to give written notice to the Contractor specifying the amount of the payment proposed to be made, the basis on which the amount is calculated and to what the amount relates. That notice or, if no such notice is issued, then the Contractor's application under 4.9.3, is treated as if it were an Interim Certificate.

This mechanism under clause 4.9.3 is designed to provide the Contractor with a means of obtaining payment in a situation where they do not receive an Interim Certificate which would otherwise be a condition precedent to payment. See section 7.3 above for a fuller discussion of this point.

The timing of the final payment to be made to the Contractor under the SBC is also governed by the provisions of clause 4. Clause 4.5 stipulates that, not later than six months after the issue of the Practical Completion Certificate, the Contractor shall provide all documents necessary for the purposes of adjustment of the Contract Sum. The Architect, or, if he instructs, the Quantity Surveyor, then has three months to prepare a statement of all adjustments to be made to the Contract Sum and to ascertain any loss and/or expense due to the Contractor. This statement and ascertainment has to be sent to the Contractor forthwith upon preparation. In terms of clause 4.15, once the statement and ascertainment have been sent to the Contractor under clause 4.5, the Rectification Period has ended and a certificate of making good has been issued, then the Architect shall not later than two months thereafter issue a Final Certificate. The Final Certificate should state the final adjusted Contract Sum and the sum of the amounts already stated as due in Interim Certificates together with any advance payment. The difference between the two is expressed as a balance due to the Contractor by the Employer or *vice versa*. Clause 4.15.4 provides that the final date for payment of this balance is 28 days from the date of issue of the Final Certificate.

### 8.1.5  Pay when paid

Prior to the coming into force of the 1996 Act, the timing of payments under building contracts was often stipulated to be dependent upon the receipt of funds by the paying party from another source. The most common example was for main contractors to make it a condition of a sub-contractor's entitle-ment to payment that the main contractor had in turn received payment from the employer under the main contract, see *Taymech Ltd* v. *Trafalgar House Construction (Regions) Ltd* (1995). Such provisions, commonly known as 'pay when paid' clauses, were outlawed by the 1996 Act, except in very limited circumstances.

Section 113 provides that any provision which makes payment under a construction contract conditional on the payer receiving payment from a third person is ineffective unless that third person is insolvent. Where a payment provision is ineffective then the relevant provisions found in Part II of the Schedule to the Scheme will apply. It may still be open to parties to a building sub-contract to agree to a provision that makes payments to a sub-contractor conditional upon the value of work carried out by the sub-contractor being valued and included in a certificate issued under the main contract although the English case of *Midland Expressway Ltd* v. *Carillion Construction Ltd and Others (No. 2) (2005)* casts some doubt on this.

### 8.1.6  The amount to be paid

The final contract price, or a mechanism for ascertaining the final contract price, is a fundamental and essential part of the contract and should be agreed at the time the parties enter into the contract, see *Uniroyal Ltd* v. *Miller & Co. Ltd* (1985). If no price or mechanism has been agreed then it may be possible for a contractor to obtain payment on the basis of *quantum meruit*. This is discussed in section 8.4 below. The price to be paid by the employer to the contractor for carrying out the contract works may be ascertained by a number of different methods. In many building contracts it may not be possible to calculate the contract price until after completion of the works, see, for example, *Arcos Industries Pty Ltd* v. *The Electricity Commission of New South Wales* (1973).

## Lump sum contracts

In what are commonly known as lump sum contracts the employer and the contractor agree the price for the contract works at the time of entering into the contract. Assuming the contractors complete the contract works then they will be entitled to be paid the agreed price regardless of what the works have actually cost to construct. See, for example, *Mitchell* v. *Magistrates of Dalkeith* (1930). Even in lump sum contracts, however, the price can alter as a result of a number of matters including additions to or omissions from the contract works, events giving rise to loss and expense, and fluctuations in cost.

An error on the part of the contractor in calculating the price will not, however, result in an alteration to the price and the contractor is bound by the price even if the work costs more than they allowed for, see *Seaton Brick and Tile Company Ltd* v. *Mitchell* (1900). A contractor will only be entitled to additional payment if he has a contractual entitlement thereto.

Under the SBC, the Employer and Contractor agree a Contract Sum at the time of entering into the contract and Article 2 provides that the Employer shall pay to the Contractor the Contract Sum or such other sum as shall become payable in accordance with the conditions of contract. Clause 4.2 further provides that the Contract Sum shall not be adjusted other than in accordance with the express provisions of the conditions and, subject to clause 2.14, any error (whether arithmetic or not) in the computation of the Contract Sum shall be deemed to have been accepted by the parties. Clause 2.14.1 provides for the correction of errors in the preparation of the Contract Bills (which may be errors of quantity or description) and such correction is treated as a Variation. The provisions in the conditions governing final adjustment of the Contract Sum are found in clause 4.3. A fuller discussion of the matters which can give rise to adjustment of the Contract Sum is contained below in section 8.2.

## Measurement contracts

In what are commonly known as measurement contracts, no agreed price is ascertainable prior to the carrying out of the works. The price is calculated by measurement of the work actually carried out during the currency of and on completion of the contract and this work is then valued by applying a schedule of rates agreed at the time of entering into the contract. The schedule of rates will often take the form of a bill of quantities. Very basic forms of measurement contracts can be seen in the cases of *Jamieson* v. *McInnes* (1887) and *Wilkie* v. *Hamilton Lodging-House Company Ltd* (1902). Measurement contracts are often used where it is impossible to ascertain the full extent of the contract works at the time of contracting, or where there is insufficient information available to do so. For example, in a contract to construct a road it may not be possible, at the time of contracting, to ascertain the exact ground conditions which the contractor will encounter.

## Reimbursement contracts

A third method often employed to ascertain the price to be paid is that used in what are commonly known as reimbursement contracts. In such contracts contractors are paid for the cost of the work carried out by them, normally with an additional allowance for overheads and profit or, alternatively, a fee for managing the contract. The additional allowance to be paid to the contractor is normally agreed at the time of entering into the contract and is usually a specified sum or, alternatively, an agreed percentage of the total contract price. It is important when drafting reimbursement contracts to ensure that the contractor only recovers costs properly and reasonably incurred in order to avoid extravagance or inefficient working on their part.

## Interim payments

Where the contractor has an entitlement to receive interim payments the contract will normally contain a mechanism for ascertaining the amount of such payments. This often involves the issue of interim certificates, discussed above in section 7.3. Interim payments are payments to account of the final contract sum and normally represent either an agreed instalment payment due on a particular date, or an agreed instalment due at completion of a particular stage of the works (see, for example, *The Government of Newfoundland* v. *The Newfoundland Railway Company and Others* (1888)), or a valuation of the work carried out at a particular date (see, for example, *F R Absalom Ltd* v. *Great Western (London) Garden Village Society Ltd* (1933)).

Interim payments are often subject to review by later payments and on completion of the contract, see, for example, *The Tharsis Sulphur and Copper Company Ltd* v. *McElroy & Sons* (1878) in which Lord Chancellor Cairns stated that 'payments made under [interim certificates] are altogether provisional, and subject to adjustment or readjustment at the end of the contract'. See also *Beaufort Developments (NI) Ltd* v. *Gilbert-Ash NI Ltd and Another* (1998). Thus interim certificates are not usually conclusive as to either the value of work carried out at the date of payment or the quality of work carried out.

It has, however, been suggested that it is for the employer to prove that an interim valuation is inaccurate. In *Johnston* v. *Greenock Corporation* (1951) Lord Sorn stated:

'[T]he proper time for an employer to challenge any item in the contractor's monthly account is at the time he receives it, and when he is checking it with a view to payment. That is the time when the facts are fresh in the contractor's mind and when he can best give explanations, or make the necessary inquiries or investigation into any matter which requires explanation. At that stage the onus is clearly on the contractor to justify and explain every item in his account if called upon to do so. But if the accounts are checked, and all explanations asked for having been satisfactorily given payment is made on them, so that the contractor naturally thinks that the business is over and done with, and then, after the lapse of a year or two, the employer seeks to reopen particular items in the account I think the situation is different . . . [W]here objections can be so infinitely varied in character, it may not be advisable to attempt to lay down any general rule about onus, but it is at least clear that great care must be taken to see that the contractor is not prejudiced by the delay in bringing forward the challenge. Perhaps it would not be going too far to say that, instead of it being for the contractor to justify his charge, it is, at least initially, for the employer to show why the item, which he had already passed and paid for, should not stand.'

## Section 110(1)

Section 110(1) of the 1996 Act stipulates that every construction contract must provide an adequate mechanism for determining what payments become due under the contract. If the contract fails to do so then the relevant provisions of Part II of the Schedule to the Scheme will apply. Paragraph 2(1) provides that the amount of any interim payments shall be the difference between the amount determined in accordance with paragraph 2(2) and the amount determined in accordance with paragraph 2(3).

The amount determined in accordance with paragraph 2(2) is the aggregate of:

- an amount equal to the value of any work performed in accordance with the contract from commencement of the contract to the end of the relevant period;
- where the contract provides for payment for materials, an amount equal to the value of any materials manufactured on site or brought onto the site from commencement of the contract to the end of the relevant period; and
- any other amount which the contract specifies shall be payable from commencement of the contract to the end of the relevant period.

The relevant period is defined in paragraph 12 as the period specified in, or calculated by reference to, the construction contract or (where no period is specified or so calculable) a period of 28 days. The amount determined in accordance with paragraph 2(3) is the aggregate of any sums which have been paid or are due for payment by way of interim payments during the period from commencement of the contract to the end of the relevant period. It is further provided in paragraph 2(4) that the amount of any interim payment shall not exceed the difference between the contract price and the aggregate of the interim payments which have become due.

### Section 110(2)

Section 110(2) of the 1996 Act provides that every construction contract shall provide for the giving of notice by a party not later than five days after the date on which a payment becomes due from them or would have become due if (a) the other party had carried out their obligations under the contract, and (b) no set-off or abatement was permitted. The notice must specify the amount (if any) of the payment made or proposed to be made and the basis upon which that amount was calculated. If a contract does not contain such a provision then paragraph 9 provides a mechanism for the giving of such notice. In practice, however, it appears that there are no consequences for the employer in failing to provide a s.110(2) notice. The failure to provide such a notice does not entitle the contractor to full payment of the amount he has applied for and does not prevent the employer disputing the sum claimed. See, for example, *S L Timber Systems Ltd* v. *Carillion Construction Ltd* (2001) in which Lord Macfadyen stated:

> 'every construction contract will require the giving of the sort of notice contemplated in s.110(2). But there the matter stops. Section 110 makes no provision as to the consequence of failure to give the notice it contemplates. For the purposes of the present case, the important point is that there is no provision that failure to give a s.110(2) notice has any effect on the right of the party who has so failed to dispute the claims of the other party . . . failure to give a s.110(2) notice does not, in any way or to any extent, preclude dispute about the sum claimed.'

The parties to a contract can expressly agree that failure to provide a s.110(2) notice or an equivalent thereto will have a consequence.

### Section 111

Once the employer has issued a s.110(2) notice then he is obliged to pay the amount stated in the notice by the final date for payment subject only to the issue of a notice of intention to withhold payment. Section 111(1) provides that a party to a construction contract cannot withhold payment after the final date for payment unless he has given an effective notice of intention to withhold payment. In order to be effective s.111(2) provides that the notice must specify:

- the amount proposed to be withheld; and
- the ground for withholding;
- if there is more than one ground, each ground and the amount attributable to each ground.

An example of a failure to issue a s.111(2) notice can be found in *Clark Contracts Ltd* v. *The Burrell Co. (Construction Management) Ltd* (2002). In that case an interim certificate was issued by the architect specifying an amount for payment. The court confirmed that the sum specified in the certificate was due under the contract and that if the employer intended to withhold payment because the works did not conform to contract then they required to serve a notice under section 111. This case was distinguished from *S L Timber Systems Ltd* on the basis that in *S L Timber Systems Ltd* there was no s.110(2) notice and importantly no contractual procedure providing for the issue of an interim certificate by the architect. All that existed in that case was an application from S L Timber Systems Ltd. A further example of a failure to give a s.111(2) notice in similar circumstances can be found in the English case of *Rupert Morgan Building Services (LLC) Ltd* v. *Jervis* (2003).

It appears, following the decision of the House of Lords in *Melville Dundas Ltd (in receivership) and Others* v. *George Wimpey UK Ltd and Others* (2007), that no notice of intention to withhold payment will be required to withhold payment following termination of a contract where the contract expressly provides that no further payment requires to be made until after a final accounting has been completed. See Chapter 9 below for a fuller discussion of termination.

The s.111(2) notice must be given not later than the prescribed period before the final date for payment. That prescribed period can be agreed between the parties failing which paragraph 10 of the Scheme prescribes a period of seven days. A combined notice can be given under s.110(2) and section 111.

## The SBC provisions

The SBC contains complex provisions for ascertaining the amount of interim payments. The procedure for ascertaining amounts to be included in Interim Certificates is to be found in clause 4.10. This stipulates that the amount stated as due in an Interim Certificate, subject to any agreement between the parties as to stage payments, shall be the gross valuation of the work carried out by the Contractor pursuant to clause 4.16 less the aggregate of the total amount stated as due in Interim Certificates previously issued, any amount which may be deducted and retained by the Employer by way of retention under clauses 4.18 to 4.20 and the total amount of any advance payment due to be reimbursed to the Employer in terms of the Contract Particulars and clause 4.8. Section 8.6 below contains a fuller discussion of retention. The provisions for ascertaining the gross valuation of the work carried out by the Contractor are to be found in clauses 4.16 and 4.17.

Interim valuations are made by the Quantity Surveyor whenever the Architect considers them necessary for the purpose of ascertaining the amount to be stated as due in an Interim Certificate (clause 4.11). The Contractor can also require the Quantity Surveyor to make an interim valuation by submitting an application under clause 4.12. Such an application must be submitted no later than seven days before the date for issue of an Interim Certificate and should set out what the Contractor considers to be the amount of his gross valuation. To the extent that the Quantity Surveyor disagrees with the gross valuation in the Contractor's application then the Quantity Surveyor shall at the same time as making his valuation submit to the Contractor a statement which identifies the nature of that disagreement.

When the Architect issues an Interim Certificate clause 4.9.1 provides that it should state the amount due to the contractor by the employer; to what the amount relates, and the basis on which the amount has been calculated.

In terms of clause 4.13.3, not later than five days after the date of issue of an Interim Certificate the Employer shall give a written notice to the Contractor which shall, in respect of the amount stated as due in that Interim Certificate, specify the amount of the payment proposed to be made; to what the amount of the payment relates, and the basis upon which that amount is calculated.

Contractors will, accordingly, know how much they are to be paid and how that sum has been arrived at. By the final date for payment the Employer has to pay the Contractor the amount specified in the clause 4.13.3 notice or in the absence of such a notice the amount stated as due in the Interim Certificate, see clause 4.13.5. Should the Employer wish to withhold any of such amount then he is required in terms of clause 4.13.4 to give a written notice specifying the amount proposed to be withheld, the ground or grounds for such withholding and the amount attributable to each ground.

In the absence of an Interim Certificate, the Contractor can still make an application to the Employer for payment under clause 4.9.3. This application should be for an amount in accordance with the statement prepared by the Quantity Surveyor pursuant to clause 4.12 or, in the absence of such a statement, in accordance with the Contractor's application submitted to the Quantity Surveyor.

## 8.2 Adjustment of the contract price

### 8.2.1 Introduction

As indicated above, the final contract price or a mechanism for ascertaining the final contract price should be agreed at the time of entering into the contract. Even where such an agreement has been reached, matters can still arise during the carrying out of the works which will result in either an increase or a decrease in the price. The most common matters which give rise to an adjustment in the price are contractual variations; fluctuations in cost, and claims for direct loss and expense. There are, however, many other matters which can potentially give rise to an adjustment in the price.

Most building contracts provide either expressly or by implication, that the contractor is obliged to carry out, and the employer is obliged to pay for, the work which the parties have agreed will be carried out. Failure by either of the parties will amount to a breach of contract giving rise to the possibility of the contract being brought to an end (as discussed below in Chapter 9) and also to other remedies becoming available to the innocent party (as discussed below in Chapter 10).

If the works cost more than the contractor priced for they are still bound by the price or the mechanism for ascertaining the price which was agreed between the parties, see *Seaton Brick and Tile Company Ltd* v. *Mitchell* (1900). Similarly, the employer is so bound even if the works cost the contractor less than the price agreed or the price ascertained using the agreed mechanism, see *Mitchell* v. *Magistrates of Dalkeith* (1930). In many instances, however, the parties will attempt to claim an increase or a decrease in the contract price as a result of work they claim was added, omitted or varied from the original agreed scope of the works.

If a contractor claims additional payment for work which actually formed part of the original contract works then clearly they will have no entitlement to such additional payment. If claims are made in respect of work which was added, omitted or varied in terms of the express provisions of the contract then there may be an entitlement to an adjustment of the contract price, see section 8.2.2 below. The most difficult situation, however, is where there are no express provisions dealing with such matters.

In such cases, the removal by the employer of any work from the contractor may amount to a breach of contract on the part of the employer unless the work is paid for. If the contractor does not agree to the omission and price reduction then he may have a valid claim against the employer for his loss of profit on the portion of the work which has been omitted.

Similarly, an unauthorised variation by the contractor may amount to a breach of contract on the part of the contractor. Where the deviation is material the contractor may have difficulty claiming payment not only for the cost of the varied work but also for the work he has executed in accordance with the contract, see *Ramsay & Son* v. *Brand* (1898) and the related cases referred to in section 8.1.2 above. Obviously if the contractor can show that the variation was agreed to by the employer then it will not amount to a breach of contract and the contractor will be entitled to be paid for the varied work. It appears that such agreement may be established by words or conduct on the part of the employer or his agent, see *Holland Hannen & Cubitts (Northern) Ltd* v. *Welsh Health Technical Services Organisation and Others* (1981). (Contrast, however, the decision in *Burrell & Son* v. *Russell & Company* (1900).) In a situation where a variation is agreed to by the employer because it assists or is convenient to the contractor then the contractor will not be entitled to any additional payment, see *The Tharsis Sulphur and Copper Company Ltd* v. *McElroy & Sons* (1878).

Where the contractor executes additional work, he will have no entitlement to payment unless he can show that the employer agreed to pay for the work. This is a general principle of Scots Law which does not only apply to building contracts. For example, in *Walter Wright & Co. Ltd* v. *Cowdray* (1973) an electrical contractor was instructed to dry out and test two motors. In addition, the contractor carried out certain repairs to the motors which had not been instructed. The court held that the contractor had no entitlement to payment for the performing of the repairs. See also *Wilson* v. *Wallace and Connell* (1859). In such situations the only means of obtaining payment may be by using the principle of *quantum lucratus* which is discussed below in section 8.5.

It is relatively common in building contracts to find provision for other payments to be made to the contractor in addition to the contract price and sometimes the parties will agree after the contract has been concluded and the works have commenced that additional payments are to be made.

In many of the standard forms of building contract provision is made for the opening up for inspection or testing of work carried out by the contractor. It is usually provided that the contractor will be paid for all such work, unless the opening up discloses that work carried out is not in accordance with the contract, see, for example, clause 3.17 of the SBC. Similar provisions are to be found in ICE contracts, see, for example, *Hall & Tawse Construction Ltd* v. *Strathclyde Regional Council* (1990).

Many of the standard forms of building contracts, for example clause 2.21 of the SBC, provide that the contractor is required to pay any fees or charges in respect of the contract works demandable under any Act of Parliament, byelaw or similar regulation. Under certain contracts, including the SBC, these payments may be reimbursed to the contractor in addition to the contract price. Similarly, clauses 2.22 and 2.23 of the SBC provide that where a Contractor incurs liability by way of royalties, damages or other monies as a result of any infringement or alleged infringement of any patent right arising from compliance with an Architect's instruction then any such liability will be added to the Contract Sum.

Where the employer wishes completion earlier than contracted for, or where the works have been delayed, then the employer may agree a bonus payment to the contractor if they achieve early or timeous completion of the works, see, for example, *Williams* v. *Roffey Bros & Nicholls (Contractors) Ltd* (1990). In such cases, the circumstances in which the payment is to be made should be clearly set out. In particular, it should be made clear whether the payment is truly a bonus in the sense that it is in addition to any other right to payment which the contractor may have in terms of the contract between the parties, for example, direct loss and/or expense. It should also be made clear what is to happen to such payment if the works are delayed by subsequent variations instructed by the employer.

In addition to the contract price the contractor will also be entitled to payment of any value added tax which is applicable. Normally, the agreed contract price is exclusive of value added tax, see, for example, Article 2 and clause 4.6.1 of the SBC. In certain circumstances the contractor may also be entitled to interest on the contract price where the employer has failed to make payments timeously in terms of the contract. Clause 4.13.6 of SBC expressly stipulates that where the Employer fails to pay any amount due to the Contractor by the final date for payment then the Employer shall also pay simple interest to the Contractor at the rate of 5 per cent over the official dealing rate of the Bank of England which is current at the date the payment becomes overdue. See section 10.6 below for a more detailed discussion of interest.

In certain circumstances the employer may be entitled to deduct sums from the contract price before making payment. Where the contractor has delayed completion of the works then the employer may be entitled to deduct liquidated damages, see section 6.9 above. The employer may also have an obligation to deduct tax from payments to the contractor. Employers may also have rights under the contract to make deductions in respect of costs they have incurred. For example, clause 6.4.3 of the SBC provides that if the Contractor fails to take out insurance to cover death or personal injury to third parties then the Employer can take out such insurance and deduct the premiums from any payments otherwise due to the Contractor.

### 8.2.2 Payment for contractual variations

As a result of the magnitude and complexity of most building contracts, there will inevitably arise during the carrying out of the works a need to add, omit or vary some of the work to be executed. For this reason most building contracts, and certainly all the common standard forms of building contract, contain detailed provisions to govern the instruction, execution and payment of variations. See section 4.5 above for a discussion of variations.

A building contract can provide that the contractor will be entitled to no additional payment in respect of such variations. As the contractor is obviously unlikely to agree to such provisions, they are uncommon. It is more normal for provision to be made that the contractor will be entitled to additional payment for variations. Clause 4.16.1.1 and Clause 5.5 of the SBC expressly provide that the Contract Sum should be adjusted by the value of any Variations. Nevertheless, in order to ensure that the contractor is entitled to recover additional payment, it is important that any variations are instructed in accordance with the terms of the contract. If the variations are not so instructed, or if the contractor cannot prove that they were so instructed, then they may have difficulty recovering payment, see, for example, *Robertson* v. *Jarvie* (1907).

In order to try and avoid disputes as to whether variations were or were not instructed, many building contracts provide that all variations should be instructed in writing. In such cases, the contractor may, in the absence of a written instruction, be unable to recover payment under the terms of the contract, see, for example, *Brown* v. *Lord Rollo and Others* (1832) and *Holland Hannen & Cubitts (Northern) Ltd* v. *Welsh Health Technical Services Organisation and Others* (1981). Accordingly, where the contractor is instructed to execute a variation by a mechanism other than that provided for in the contract, the advisable course of action for the contractor is to refuse to carry out the work until the correct procedure has been followed. Otherwise the contractor runs the risk that they will be unable to recover payment.

Disputes often arise as to whether an instruction to the contractor is or is not a variation under the contract. For example, a dispute may arise as to whether the contractor is obliged to execute a particular item of work as part of the original contract works or whether that particular item of work is a variation. In such a case, by refusing to carry out the work because of the absence of an instructed variation, the contractor runs the risk of being in breach of contract if it is ultimately determined that the work did form part of the original contract works. In practice, the contractor often simply carries out the work and makes a claim for payment despite the lack of an appropriate variation order.

Similar difficulties can arise where the contractor is instructed to rectify or alter work which it is alleged is not in accordance with the contract. If the work was in accordance with the contract then the contractor will have incurred the cost of carrying out further work for which they have no appropriate variation order. In such cases the courts have, in certain circumstances, held that the contractor is entitled to payment where a variation order should have been issued, but was improperly withheld, see *Brodie* v. *Corporation of Cardiff* (1919). In other cases the courts have construed instructions not purporting to be variations to be in fact, variations, see *Shanks & McEwan (Contractors) Ltd* v. *Strathclyde Regional Council* (1995).

Where the variation is made for the Contractor's benefit, however, the courts have not been willing to construe instructions as variations entitling the contractor to additional payment, see *The Tharsis Sulphur and Copper Company Ltd* v. *McElroy & Sons* (1878).

### 8.2.3  Payment for variations under the SBC

Where a building contract provides a mechanism to regulate variations to the works, it is common and, it is submitted, prudent for the contract also to contain provisions to govern how any such variations are to be valued. The method of valuation can take a number of different forms and indeed many of the standard forms of building contract contain more than one method of valuation. The relevant provisions in the SBC are to be found in clause 5 which provides a number of possible alternatives for valuation.

In the first place, it is provided that the Employer and Contractor can agree the value of a variation. Unfortunately, this rarely happens in practice as many Variations require immediate compliance leaving little time for agreement of a price in advance between the Contractor and Employer. It is, however, a useful mechanism, particularly in relation to major Variations. In order to try and facilitate the agreement of a price in advance, in terms of clause 5.3.1 the Architect/Contract Administrator when instructing a Variation can stipulate in the instruction that the Contractor is to provide a quotation in accordance with the provisions of Schedule Part 2 and, accordingly, those provisions will regulate the valuation of the Variation unless the Contractor disagrees in writing to the procedure envisaged by the clause within seven days of receipt of the instruction. In terms of Schedule Part 2, the Contractor is required, not later than 21 days from the later of (i) the date of receipt of the instruction, or (ii) the date of receipt by the Contractor of sufficient information to enable the Contractor to quote, to submit a Schedule Part 2 quotation to the Quantity Surveyor. Paragraph 2 of Schedule Part 2 specifies in detail what the quotation should contain. The quotation can then be accepted by the Employer and the acceptance must be confirmed in writing by the Architect. Schedule Part 2 sets out the timescales within which this should happen. Until the quotation is accepted the Variation is not executed by the Contractor. If the quotation is not accepted by the Employer then the Architect should either instruct that the Variation is not to be carried out or that it is to be carried out but valued in accordance with the provisions of the Valuation Rules in clauses 5.6 to 5.10.

The purpose of clause 5.3 and Schedule Part 2 is to deal with Variations which the Employer may require but for which they wish to know the price prior to confirming that the work is to be carried out. Clauses 5.6 to 5.10, on the other hand, provide a mechanism for valuing Variations which the Contractor is contractually bound to carry out when instructed and for which the Employer is contractually bound to pay. Accordingly, clauses 5.6 to 5.10 are used to value all instructed Variations other than those to which clause 5.3 and Schedule Part 2 apply or those where the Employer and Contractor have agreed a price in advance, outwith the Schedule Part 2 procedure.

Clauses 5.6 and 5.7 provide two distinct methods for valuing Variations, namely, 'Measurable Work' and 'Daywork'.

Under clauses 5.6 to 5.10 the Quantity Surveyor must value the Variation in accordance with the valuation rules contained within those clauses depending on the nature of the work to be carried out. Clause 5.6 provides that where the Variation requires the execution of additional or substituted work which can properly be valued by measurement then it shall be valued in accordance with specific rules.

Where the additional or substituted work is of similar character to, is executed under similar conditions as, and does not significantly change the quantity of, work set out in the Contract Bills, then the rates and prices for the work set out in the Contract Bills shall determine the valuation, see clause 5.6.1.1.

Where the additional or substituted work is of similar character to work set out in the Contract Bills but is not executed under similar conditions and/or significantly changes the quantity thereof, then the rates and prices for the work so set out shall be the basis for determining the valuation and the valuation shall include a fair allowance for such difference in conditions and/or quantity, see clause 5.6.1.2.

Where the additional or substituted work is not of similar character to work set out in the contract bills then the work shall be valued at fair rates and prices, see clause 5.6.1.3.

To the extent that the variation relates to the omission of work set out in the contract bills then the rates and prices for such work therein set out shall determine the valuation of the work omitted, see clause 5.6.2.

To the extent that the variation requires the execution of additional or substituted work which cannot properly be valued by measurement then clause 5.7 provides for valuation on a cost/daywork basis.

If the valuation of a variation cannot reasonably be effected using any of the foregoing methods then clause 5.10.1 provides that a fair valuation shall be made.

Regardless of whether the valuation is calculated under the Valuation Rules, agreement between Employer and Contractor or Schedule Part 2, clause 5.5 provides that the valuation will be effected by addition to or deduction from the Contract Sum. In a change from previous JCT and SBCC standard forms of contract, the SBC provides, at clause 5.10.2, that no allowance shall be made under the Valuation Rules for any effect upon the regular progress of the Works or of any part of them or for any other direct loss and/or expense for which the contractor would be reimbursed under any other provision. In those circumstances, the loss and expense provisions in clauses 4.23 to 4.26 should be operated.

This is not the case in relation to Schedule Part 2 quotations and the employer's acceptances of those quotations. Paragraph 2 of Schedule Part 2 provides that the contractor's quotation should contain an amount to be paid in lieu of direct loss and/or expense ascertained under clause 4.23.

As can be seen, the provisions for valuing variations in the SBC are extremely detailed. They have evolved over a number of years. Similar provisions are to be found in a number of the other standard forms of building and engineering contracts, although it is open to the parties at the time of contracting to agree any method they choose for valuing variations. Where the contract does not provide a mechanism then variations will require to be valued on the basis of *quantum meruit*, see section 8.4 below.

### 8.2.4 Fluctuation in cost

In concluding a price for any building contract there is a risk to both the contractor and the employer that the costs involved in constructing the building can fluctuate dramatically due to changes in economic factors entirely outwith the control of either of them. Such economic factors can include inflation, which can affect the price of both labour and materials, and also changes in tax legislation.

The risk to the employer is that costs decrease and they therefore have to pay the contractor far more than the building actually cost to construct. On the other hand, this may not be a substantial risk as the employer will have budgeted for the contract price prior to concluding the contract.

The risk to the contractor is that the costs increase resulting in either a diminution in their profit or, more worryingly, the building costing more to construct than the price contracted for. It is submitted that such an eventuality is not in the interest of either the contractor or the employer as it can result in the contractor having difficulties completing the building and, in extreme cases, may give rise to the contractor trying to cut corners to minimise costs.

Fluctuations in cost are a particularly serious risk where the contract price is substantial or the contract period particularly lengthy. Without any provision in the contract to deal with such fluctuations in cost both parties would be bound by the price agreed. Trying to assess the potential effect of fluctuations can be extremely speculative and, indeed, it could result in buildings becoming more expensive to construct as contractors increase their price to minimise their exposure to cost fluctuations.

In an effort to try and minimise the risk of fluctuation in cost, many of the standard forms of building contract provide a mechanism for adjusting the contract price to take account of increases or decreases in cost during the contract period. Such provisions can be found in clauses 4.21, 4.22 and Schedule Part 7 of the SBC. Schedule Part 7 provides three alternatives for dealing with fluctuations. The parties should choose which alternative is to be employed at the time of entering into the contract and the choice should be inserted in Part 1 of the Contract Particulars.

If no choice is made then Part 1 of the Contract Particulars stipulates that Option A is to apply. It should be noted that, in terms of clause 4.22, the fluctuation in cost provisions do not apply to Variations where a price has been agreed in advance under Schedule Part 2, see section 8.2.3 above.

Of the three options Option A provides for adjustment in the contract price as a result of changes in contributions, levies and taxes, Option B provides for adjustment in the contract price as a result of fluctuations in the cost of labour and materials and as a result of tax changes; and Option C provides for adjustment using a price adjustment formula.

If either party is to rely on the fluctuation provisions then it is important that they fully comply with any pre-requisites contained within the relevant option, see *John Laing Construction Ltd* v. *County and District Properties Ltd* (1982).

## 8.3 Loss and expense

In building contracts, it is not uncommon for the Contractor's progress of the Works to be affected by events that are within the control of the Employer or the Architect. This can significantly increase the cost to the Contractor in carrying out the works. Clauses 4.23 to 4.26 of the SBC contain a mechanism that, in certain circumstances, entitles the Contractor to recover direct loss and/or expense where the regular progress of the works has been materially affected by certain specified relevant matters or where there has been a deferment of giving possession of the site to the Contractor, under clause 2.5.

As soon as the Contractor becomes aware, or should reasonably have become aware, that the regular progress has been affected, they need to make written application to the architect. A list of the relevant matters in respect of which direct loss and/or expense can be claimed is contained in clause 4.24. The matters are:

- Variations (excluding any loss and/or expense relating to an acceptance of a Schedule Part 2 quotation but including any other matters or instructions which under the contract are to be treated as, or requiring a Variation).
- Instructions of the Architect under clause 3.15 (postponement of work) or 3.16 (expenditure of provisional sums).
- Instructions of the Architect for the opening up for inspection or testing of any work, materials or goods under clause 3.17, unless the cost is provided for in the Contract Bills or the inspection shows that the work was not in accordance with the Contract.
- Any discrepancy in or divergence between the Contract Drawings, the Contract Bills and/or the documents referred to in clause 2.15.
- Suspension by the Contractor under clause 4.14 (for failure to pay a sum due under an Interim Certificate) of the performance of his obligations under the contract provided the suspension was not frivolous or vexatious.
- Any impediment, prevention or default, whether by act or omission, by the Employer, the Architect, the Quantity Surveyor or any of the Employer's Persons, except to the extent caused or contributed to by any default, whether by act or omission of the Contractor or of any of the Contractor's Persons.

The number of relevant matters stipulated within the SBC has been greatly reduced from previous JCT and SBCC standard form contracts, although the final relevant matter mentioned above is very much a catch-all matter, consolidating a number of previously discrete relevant matters. In consolidating the relevant matters and including a general relevant matter, there is the potential for an increased number of disputes between Employer and Contractor in relation to the scope of the general relevant matter.

Having received the contractor's written application the Architect has to form an opinion as to whether the regular progress has been or is likely to be materially affected as stated in the application or whether direct loss and/or expense has been or is likely to be incurred due to deferment. He can request from the Contractor such further information as is reasonable to enable him to form such an opinion. Assuming he forms such an opinion, then the Architect from time to time shall ascertain, or shall instruct the Quantity Surveyor to ascertain, the amount of such loss and/or expense which has been or is being incurred by the Contractor. Only the Architect can decide upon the validity of an application, see *John Laing Construction Ltd* v. *County and District Properties Ltd* (1982). Either the Architect or the Quantity Surveyor can request further details as may be reasonably necessary to enable ascertainment of the loss and/or expense due to the Contractor. In terms of clause 4.25, any loss and expense so ascertained is added to the Contract Sum.

Clauses 4.23 to 4.25 are not exhaustive of the Contractor's rights in such circumstances. Clause 4.26 provides that the provisions of clauses 4.23 to 4.25 are without prejudice to any other rights and remedies which the Contractor may possess. It should be noted, however, that under clause 1.10.1.4 a Final Certificate is conclusive evidence that the reimbursement of direct loss and/or expense, if any, to the Contractor pursuant to clause 4.23 is in final settlement of all and any claims which the Contractor has or may have arising out of the occurrence of any of the relevant matters referred to in clause 4.24, whether such claim be for breach of contract, duty of care, statutory duty or otherwise. Accordingly, despite the terms of clause 4.26, the Final Certificate is conclusive as to loss and expense in respect of any of the matters described in clause 4.24, notwithstanding the legal basis upon which payment arising out of such matters was sought.

As one might imagine, the loss and expense provisions to be found in the standard form building contracts have been considered by the courts on numerous occasions. It is not possible to give detailed consideration to all the available case law in this book. However, Scotland does have the benefit of an Inner House decision reviewing the law in this area. In the case of *John Doyle Construction Ltd* v. *Laing Management (Scotland) Ltd* (2004) the court indicated that for a loss and expense claim under a building contract to succeed the contractor is required to prove three matters:

- the existence of one or more events for which the employer is responsible. For example, a relevant matter under clause 4.24 of SBC/Q/Scot 2005;
- the existence of loss and expense suffered by the contractor; and
- a causal link between the event or events and the loss and expense.

This statement is consistent with earlier cases in this area in which it had been held that direct loss and expense was that which flowed naturally in the usual course of things, see, for example, *F G Minter Ltd* v. *Welsh Health Technical Services Organisation* (1980) following *Saint Line Ltd* v. *Richardson Westgarth & Co. Ltd* (1940).

Unfortunately in many building contracts it is not straightforward to establish the causal link between an event and a particular item of loss and expense. Indeed, in many instances loss and expense to the contractor is caused by a number of events which may be the responsibility of the employer, the responsibility of the contractor or the responsibility of neither party. In such instances it may not be possible to identify the causal link between each individual event and the items of loss and expense incurred by the contractor. In such cases attempts have been made by contractors to pursue global claims against employers, where little or no attempt is made to establish any causal link, with varying degrees of success. See, for example, *London Borough of Merton* v. *Stanley Hugh Leach Ltd (1985)* and *Wharf Properties Ltd* v. *Eric Cumine Associates (No.2) (1991)*.

The area of global claims has now been reviewed in *John Doyle Construction Ltd* and guidance produced for the first time by a Scottish court. In delivering the court's opinion Lord Drummond Young indicated that if a contractor can prove that all the events on which he relies are the responsibility of the employer then there is no need to identify any causal link between the individual events and particular items of direct loss and expense. If, however, an event for which the employer is not responsible plays a significant part in the causation of the loss and expense then the claim will fail unless it is possible to separate out the effect of the event for which the employer is not responsible. The court indicated, however, that this was subject to three mitigating considerations as follows:

> 'In the first place, it may be possible to identify a causal link between particular events for which the employer is responsible and individual items of loss . . . In the second place, the question of causation must be treated by the application of common sense to logical principles of causation . . . In this connection, it is frequently possible to say that an item of loss has been caused by a particular event notwithstanding that other events played a part in its occurrence. In such cases, if an event or events for which the employer is responsible can be described as the dominant cause of an item of loss, that will be sufficient to establish liability, notwithstanding the existence of other causes that are to some degree at least concurrent . . . In the third place, even if it cannot be said that events for which the employer is responsible are the dominant cause of the loss, it may be possible to apportion the loss between the causes for which the employer is responsible and other causes. In such cases it is obviously necessary that the event or events for which the employer is responsible should be a material cause of the loss. Provided that condition is met, however, we are of the opinion that apportionment of loss between the different causes is possible in an appropriate case'.

Although *John Doyle Construction Ltd* provides useful guidance in relation to global claims, it should be borne in mind that it does not provide carte blanche to use a global claim and that evidence of the causal links will still be of crucial importance in loss and expense claims. The case concerned the issue of whether a global claim fell to be thrown out at the stage of legal debate and the decision of the court was simply that the claim should be allowed to proceed to a full hearing on the evidence. If, however, evidence could not be produced to satisfy any of the three principles in the foregoing quotation then the claim would still fail in its entirety. Similarly if evidence did satisfy any of the three principles this may still result in only a small proportion of the claim succeeding with the remainder of the claim failing. Accordingly a contractor should still endeavour where possible to prove a causal link between the relevant events and the items of loss and expense. A failure to keep satisfactory records will not be a legitimate excuse for failing to do so.

It should be noted that there is no direct connection between the loss and expense provisions in clauses 4.23 to 4.26 of the SBC and the provisions dealing with extension of time to be found in clauses 2.26 to 2.29. The two sets of clauses have distinct and separate purposes. Support for this proposition can be found in *Methodist Homes Housing Association Ltd* v. *Scott & McIntosh* (1997).

## 8.4 *Quantum meruit*

It is a general principle of Scots Law that the recipient of services in terms of a contract is under an implied obligation to pay for the services. As indicated previously, the final contract price or a mechanism for ascertaining the final contract price should be agreed at the time of entering into a building contract. Similarly it is prudent to agree the basis on which any variations or additions will be priced. In practice, this sometimes does not happen. In such circumstances, the contractor may still be entitled to payment *quantum meruit*, that is, payment of a reasonable sum for the work carried out by them.

In order for a claim for *quantum meruit* to succeed there must be a contract between the parties, see, for example, *Alexander Hall & Son (Builders) Ltd* v. *Strathclyde Regional Council* (1989). There is no scope for a *quantum meruit* claim if the contract between the parties contains an agreed contract price or a mechanism for ascertaining the contract price, see, for example, *Interbild Components Ltd* v. *Fife Regional Council* (1988). As has been indicated previously, however, agreement of the price, or a mechanism for ascertaining the price, is an essential term of any building contract and, in the absence of such agreement, there may be no binding contract between the parties.

In certain circumstances, however, where work has been carried out by agreement and only the price has not been agreed, the courts have been prepared to hold that an implied contract exists between the parties. See, for example, *Avintair Ltd* v. *Ryder Airline Services Ltd* (1994) in which services were performed by one party but no price was agreed. The court held that in those circumstances the law would imply, from the parties' conduct, a contract that a reasonable sum be paid and that the appropriate claim in those circumstances was an implied contract on the principle of *quantum meruit*.

Before the law can imply such a contract, however, it appears that the services must already have been performed by the party seeking payment.

See, for example, *British Bank for Foreign Trade Ltd* v. *Novinex* (1949) in which Lord Denning stated:

> 'In the ordinary way, if there is an arrangement to supply goods at a price "to be agreed", or to perform services on terms "to be agreed", then although, while the matter is still executory, there may be no binding contract, nevertheless, if it is executed on one side, that is, if the one does his part without having come to an agreement as to the price or the terms, then the law will say that there is necessarily implied, from the conduct of the parties, a contract that, in default of agreement, a reasonable sum is to be paid.'

In addition to the contract price, *quantum meruit* can also apply to additional work instructed where no price has been agreed, see *Taylor* v. *Andrews-Weatherfoil Ltd* (1991). If, however, the additional works have not been instructed then the claim will fail, see, for example, *T & R Aitken* v. *Gardiner* (1958). *Quantum meruit* can also apply where a price has been agreed but it becomes inapplicable through the passage of time, see, *Constable Hart & Co. Ltd* v. *Peter Lind & Co. Ltd* (1978) in which a price was agreed which was fixed until a particular date. The contract was delayed through no fault on the part of the sub-contractor and the court held that work carried out after the agreed date was to be paid for at reasonable rates.

In certain circumstances, even where a price has been agreed, it may be possible for a contractor to put forward a claim that they can ignore the contract price and demand payment on the basis of *quantum meruit*. In certain circumstances, it may be possible for the contractor to show that, as a result of breaches of contract on the part of the employer, the contract works have altered so dramatically from those contracted for that the contract price is no longer applicable and a new contract term should be implied that they be paid on the basis of *quantum meruit*, see *Lodder* v. *Slowey* (1904). Before contractors can put forward a claim on the basis of *quantum meruit*, however, it appears that they must rescind the contract in order to make it clear that they no longer consider themselves bound by the original contract price, see *ERDC Construction Ltd* v. *H M Love & Co.* (1995), *Boyd & Forrest* v. *Glasgow & South Western Railway Company* (1915) and *Smellie* v. *Caledonian Railway Company* (1916). In order to allow the contractor to rescind, any breach by the employer will have to be material. In the event that the breach is not material, or should the contractor choose not to rescind, then the contractor's remedies will be limited to payment of the contract price for the work executed together with damages for breach of contract. In *Morrison-Knudsen Co. Inc* v. *British Columbia Hydro & Power Authority* (1978) it was stated that:

> 'It is well established law that a plaintiff's remedies for a defendant's default under a contract between them are limited to those provided in the contract or which may be awarded for breaches of the contract for so

long as the contract remains open and available to the parties. To enable the court to award compensation by *quantum meruit* the Respondents must show that [the contract] has been rescinded or discharged and that mutual obligations thereunder have ceased to exist. While it continues to exist the obligation of [the plaintiff] and the rights of the Respondents are limited by its terms.'

This statement was cited with approval in *ERDC Construction Ltd* in which the court indicated that a party faced with a breach of contract had to elect between affirming the contract and holding the other party to the performance of its obligations or, alternatively, rescinding the contract and suing at once for damages or *quantum meruit* for performance to the date of rescission. The court indicated that the election must be made promptly and communicated to the employer and once made would be binding on the parties and could not be changed. If the contractor simply continues to carry out the contract works then they waive their right to claim payment *quantum meruit*, see *Smellie*.

Another situation in which it may be possible to ignore the contract price and seek payment on the basis of *quantum meruit* is where the nature of the work carried out is altered fundamentally from that which the contractor originally contracted to carry out. As a result, the works may become more difficult and more expensive. In such circumstances it may be open to the contractor to maintain that the original contract has been frustrated by the fundamental alterations and that they are entitled to maintain a claim based on *quantum meruit*, see, for example, *Head Wrightson Aluminium Ltd* v. *Aberdeen Harbour Commissioners* (1958) and *Smail* v. *Potts* (1847).

The alteration to the work may not amount to breach of contract as the employer may, for example, have power to instruct variations in terms of the contract. Similarly, the contractor may suggest variations which are approved by the employer, see *Mercer* v. *Wright* (1953). It appears that if a contractor wishes to claim for payment *quantum meruit*, he may have to advise the employer at the time when the difficulty becomes apparent, see *Mackay* v. *Lord Advocate* (1914). It is submitted that this is correct as it offers the employer an opportunity to choose between proceeding with the contract works on the basis of payment *quantum meruit* or halting the work because of the frustration.

If, however, the works have become more difficult or more expensive because of matters which existed at the time of contracting, but which the contractor did not foresee, then the contract will not be frustrated and the contractor will have no entitlement to payment *quantum meruit*, see *Davis Contractors Ltd* v. *Fareham UDC* (1956).

Where a contractor is entitled to make a claim for payment *quantum meruit* then they are entitled to be paid at ordinary or market rates, or where no such rates are available they are entitled to be paid a reasonable rate, see *Avintair Ltd*. The party seeking payment *quantum meruit* is entitled to lead evidence to prove what would be a reasonable rate in the circumstances, see

*Wilson* v. *Gordon* (1828). It appears that a building contractor can include in their rate elements for work carried out, material supplied, overhead costs and reasonable profit, see *Monk Construction Ltd* v. *Norwich Union Life Assurance Society* (1992). In addition to proving that the rate charged is reasonable, the party claiming payment will also have to prove to the court that the amount of time spent carrying out the work was reasonable, see *Scottish Motor Traction Co.* v. *Murphy* (1949).

## 8.5  *Quantum lucratus*

Disputes sometimes arise in a situation where a person has in good faith carried out works to another's land or property where there is no contract between the parties. In such a situation the party carrying out the work cannot claim payment in terms of the contract or payment *quantum meruit*. There may, however, be an entitlement to payment on a *quantum lucratus* basis, that is, seeking to recover the value of the land or property owner's enrichment, see, for example, *Newton* v. *Newton* (1925). *Quantum lucratus* is a branch of the law of recompense and is an equitable remedy requiring an owner of land to pay for works carried out by another on their land as a result of which they are enriched. *Quantum lucratus* does not apply to the situation where a third party is enriched by work carried out by the owner of land or property to that land or property, see *Edinburgh and District Tramways Company Ltd* v. *Courtenay* (1909). It may, however, apply in the situation where work is carried out to common property, see *Stark's Trustees* v. *Cooper's Trustees* (1900).

Where work is carried out to land or property without the owner's permission or agreement then the owner can insist that the works are removed. If the owner does not do so then the principle of *quantum lucratus* deems him to have accepted the benefit and requires him to pay for that benefit. If, however, the person who has carried out the works has done so in bad faith then he will have no claim based on *quantum lucratus*, see *Barbour* v. *Halliday* (1840) and *Duke of Hamilton* v. *Johnston* (1877).

If works are carried out in terms of a contract between the parties there is no scope for a *quantum lucratus* claim, so long as the contract remains applicable, see *Thomson* v. *Pratt* (1962). It appears that where the contract becomes inapplicable because it has been determined by the employer who retains the benefit of any works already carried out then the contractor may be entitled to a *quantum lucratus* claim, see *Alexander Graham & Co.* v. *United Turkey Red Company Ltd* (1922), *NV Devos Gebroeder* v. *Sunderland Sportswear Ltd* (1990) and *R & J Scott* v. *Gerrard* (1916). A *quantum lucratus* claim cannot be sustained if the contract makes provision for payment on its determination, see, for example, clause 8 of the SBC.

The courts have had difficulty laying down a general definition for *quantum lucratus* and have indicated that each case requires to be looked at on its own particular circumstances, see *Edinburgh and District Tramways Company Ltd,*

*Varney (Scotland) Ltd* v. *Burgh of Lanark* (1976) and *Lawrence Building Co. Ltd* v. *Lanarkshire County Council* (1979). It appears, however, that some essential features must exist in order for a claim to succeed. In both *Varney (Scotland) Ltd* and *Lawrence Building Co. Ltd* it was held that for a claim to succeed the pursuer must have incurred a loss although the cost of carrying out the works will suffice in this respect; the pursuer must not have intended to make a gift to the defenders; and there must be a quantifiable benefit to the defender who is thereby *lucratus*.

Accordingly, if the pursuers carry out the work for their own benefit then they will not be entitled to claim *quantum lucratus*, see *Edinburgh and District Tramways Company Ltd* and *Rankin* v. *Wither* (1886). Some incidental benefit will not, however, bar a claim. It also appears that a claim for *quantum lucratus* cannot succeed where the pursuer has any other legal remedy available, see *Stewart* v. *Stewart* (1878).

In *Varney (Scotland) Ltd* it was stated that:

'Recompense is an equitable doctrine. That being so, it becomes a sort of court of last resort, recourse to which can only be made when no other legal remedy is or has been available. If a legal remedy is available at the time when the action which gave rise to the claim for recompense has to be taken, then normally that legal remedy should be pursued to the exclusion of a claim for recompense.'

Some authorities have indicated that a claim for *quantum lucratus* can only succeed where there has been an error or mistake of fact on the part of the person making the claim, see *Rankin* v. *Wither* (1886), *Buchanan* v. *Stewart* (1874) and *Gray* v. *Johnston* (1928). This can be contrasted, however, with the comments of Lord Justice Clerk Alness in *Gray* who stated that he did not think error was essential in all cases for a claim for *quantum lucratus* to succeed. Similarly in *Varney (Scotland) Ltd* the court indicated that error may found a claim for *quantum lucratus* but that the absence of an error or mistake of fact will not invalidate a claim if the other circumstances justify its imposition.

## 8.6 Contractual retention

In the standard forms of building contract it is common to find a mechanism whereby the employer can deduct an amount from any payment otherwise due to the contractor by way of contractual retention. The purpose of the retention is to allow the employer to retain a proportion of any payment due in respect of work already carried out as security against the risk of any failure by the contractor to complete their obligations under the contract, including the making good of defects. Once the contractor has completed all his obligations in terms of the contract then the retention is released.

Accordingly, the employer can use the retention as a lever to ensure the contractor completes the works or, alternatively, as a fund to pay for completion of the works in the event that the contractor does not fulfil his obligations. This can be particularly important in the event of the contractor's insolvency where, without any retention, the employer might simply be left with an unsecured claim against the contractor for breach of contract, see *Asphaltic Limestone Concrete Co. Ltd and Another* v. *Corporation of the City of Glasgow* (1907).

The standard forms of building and engineering contracts normally contain detailed rules governing both the deduction of contractual retention and its release. Clause 4.10.1 of the SBC provides that the amount stated as due in an Interim Certificate shall be the gross valuation of the work carried out by the Contractor, less any retention which may be deducted and retained by the Employer as provided for in clauses 4.18 to 4.20. Clause 4.20 provides that the retention which the Employer may deduct and retain shall be a percentage of the total amount included in any Interim Certificate. The percentage is stipulated to be 3 per cent unless a different rate is agreed between the parties and inserted in the Contract Particulars.

The retention percentage may be deducted from the amount certified in any Interim Certificate insofar as the amount certified relates to work which has not reached practical completion. Where the work has reached practical completion but no Certificate of Making Good has been issued then the Employer may only deduct half the retention percentage. In practice this operates on the basis that the Employer deducts the whole retention percentage from amounts included in Interim Certificates issued to the Contractor. Half the retention is then released on practical completion of the works with the remaining half being released on the issue of a Certificate of Making Good.

Clause 4.18 of the SBC stipulates that the Employer's interest in the retention is fiduciary as trustee for the Contractor. At the date of each Interim Certificate, the Architect has to prepare or instruct the Quantity Surveyor to prepare a statement specifying the retention deducted in arriving at the amount stated as due in the Interim Certificate and this statement is issued to the Contractor. Thereafter, the Contractor can request the Employer, at the date of payment under each Interim Certificate, to place the retention to be deducted in a separate bank account and certify that this has been so done, see clause 4.18.3. It appears that the Contractor can also make this request at a later date if he has not done so at the date of payment, see *J F Finnegan Ltd* v. *Ford Sellar Morris Developments Ltd* (1991). The Employer is entitled to any interest accruing on the retention while it remains in this separate account.

The objective of clause 4.18.3 is to provide a mechanism whereby the retention deducted by the Employer is to be held in trust on behalf of the Contractor, see *Wates Construction (London) Ltd* v. *Franthom Property Ltd* (1991). This is to afford the Contractor a degree of protection in the event of the insolvency of the Employer. If it is not placed in a separate account then it appears that the Contractor will have no protection, see *Mac-Jordan Construction Ltd*

v. *Brookmount Erostin Ltd* (1991). If the Employer fails to put the money in a separate account then the Contractor's remedy would be an action for specific implement (see section 10.3 below). Unless an interim order can be obtained, given the time it may take to conclude such an action, this remedy may be of little practical assistance. This is particularly so in cases where the Employer disputes that the Contractor is entitled to the retention because the Employer has other claims which he wishes to meet out of the contractual retention: for example, liquidated damages, see *Henry Boot Building Ltd* v. *The Croydon Hotel & Leisure Co. Ltd* (1985) and *GPT Realisations Ltd (in Administrative Receivership and in Liquidation)* v. *Panatown Ltd* (1992). Contrast, however, the decision in *Concorde Construction Co. Ltd* v. *Cogan Co. Ltd* (1984).

Unfortunately, it appears that under Scots Law the terms of clause 4.18.3 are, themselves, insufficient to create a trust without other actions on the part of the Employer, see *Clark Taylor & Co. Ltd* v. *Quality Site Development (Edinburgh) Ltd* (1981) and *Balfour Beatty Ltd* v. *Britannia Life* (1997). Accordingly, in Scotland, under the SBC if an Employer becomes insolvent then, in respect of the payment of retention which has been deducted, the Contractor may find themselves in no better a position than other ordinary creditors. This may differ from the position under English Law, where a trust can be established by less formal means. A detailed examination of the law of creation of trusts is beyond the scope of this book.

A practice has grown up whereby, in order to receive payment of the full amount of interim certificates and the final account, the contractor will often provide the employer with a bond equivalent to the amount which would otherwise have been retained by the employer until full satisfaction of the works by the contractor, including remedying defects. These bonds are either put in place from the commencement of the works or are put in place at the time of practical completion in respect of the remaining half of the retention fund which would otherwise not be payable until after the issue of a Certificate of Making Good. This practice has now been formalised in clause 4.19 of the SBC. The parties can choose to apply clause 4.19 by filling in the Contract Particulars appropriately. The clause sets out the mechanics of operating the retention bond.

# Chapter 9
# Ending a Building Contract

## 9.1 Introduction

Having examined what is required to constitute a building contract in Scotland, and the rights and obligations arising therefrom, it is important to establish when, and in what circumstances, a building contract and the obligations arising from it will be brought to an end. The law of Scotland contains a number of general rules which relate to the extinction of contractual obligations, and these apply equally to the extinction of the obligations under a building contract.

Certain of the methods by which an obligation may be extinguished are of general application rather than being peculiar to building contracts. For example, an obligation may be extinguished by acceptilation, where the creditor discharges his right without payment or performance. An obligation for the payment of money may also be extinguished by confusion, where the same person becomes creditor and debtor in an obligation. This does not apply where there are continuing rights and obligations beyond the payment of money and, thus, were the employer under a building contract to take over the contractor (or vice versa) during the currency of the contract, the doctrine of confusion would not apply. A detailed examination of these doctrines is beyond the scope of this book.

It must be borne in mind that, at any time during the currency of a contract, it is open to parties to enter into an agreement whereby their respective obligations are extinguished. Building contracts habitually contain detailed mechanisms whereby one or other of the parties is, or both of them are, entitled to terminate the employment of the contractor.

In this chapter we will examine certain methods of extinction of obligations that are of particular significance to building contracts. Certain others, such as payment (Chapter 8) and novation (Chapter 12) are dealt with elsewhere in this book.

## 9.2 Frustration and impossibility

Frustration occurs whenever, without fault on the part of either party, intervening circumstances have rendered a contract incapable of being performed, or so altered the conditions that, if there were to be performance, it would, in essence, be performance of a different contract, see *Davis Contractors Ltd*

v. *Fareham UDC* (1956) and *National Carriers Ltd* v. *Panalpina (Northern) Ltd* (1981). In judging whether or not a contract has been frustrated, the contract must be viewed as a whole. The question to be considered is whether the purpose of the contract, as gathered from its terms, has been defeated, see *James B Fraser & Co. Ltd* v. *Denny, Mott & Dickson Ltd* (1945). It follows that if parties had regard to the possibility of a particular event and made provision for it in their contract the occurrence of such an event cannot have the effect of frustrating the contract, see *Cricklewood Property & Investment Trust Ltd* v. *Leighton's Investments Trust Ltd* (1945). If the contract does not contemplate the intervening circumstances, it will be frustrated.

Whether or not a contract has been frustrated will, in each case, be a question of fact to be decided upon the true construction of the terms of the contract, read in the light of the nature of the contract and of the relevant surrounding circumstances when the contract was made, see *Head Wrightson Aluminium Ltd* v. *Aberdeen Harbour Commissioners* (1958).

The propositions relevant to the doctrine of frustration were set out by Lord Justice Bingham (as he then was) in *J Lauritzen AS* v. *Wijsmuller BV* (*'The Super Servant Two'*) (1990):

'Certain propositions, established by the highest authority, are not open to question:

1.  The doctrine of frustration was evolved to mitigate the rigour of the common law's insistence on literal performance of absolute promises ... The object of the doctrine was to give effect to the demands of justice, to achieve a just and reasonable result, to do what is reasonable and fair, as an expedient to escape from injustice where such would result from enforcement of a contract in its literal terms after a significant change in circumstances.

2.  Since the effect of frustration is to kill the contract and discharge the parties from further liability under it, the doctrine is not to be lightly invoked, must be kept within very narrow limits and ought not to be extended.

3.  Frustration brings the contract to an end forthwith, without more and automatically.

4.  The essence of frustration is that it should not be due to the act or election of the party seeking to rely on it ... A frustrating event must be some outside event or extraneous change of situation.

5.  A frustrating event must take place without blame or fault on the side of the party seeking to rely on it.'

In the leading case of *Davis Contractors Ltd*, the House of Lords held that a contract which had been scheduled to take eight months, and was said to be subject to there being adequate supplies of labour available as and when required, but which took 22 months to complete due to unanticipated shortages of labour and materials, had not been frustrated. The qualification as to the availability of adequate supplies of labour was contained in a letter which accompanied the contractor's tender. That letter was held not to form part of the contract and the contractor had to bear the additional costs.

Nevertheless, there may be circumstances where modifications, which necessarily and fundamentally alter the whole design of a project, frustrate the original contract and entitle the contractor to a claim based upon *quantum meruit*. This is considered more fully in section 8.4 above. The absence of intimation by a contractor that he is proceeding upon a *quantum meruit* basis may be an important element in deciding whether there has, in fact, been frustration.

Another example of frustration is where the performance of a contract is dependent upon a certain thing existing and that thing is either destroyed or is so fundamentally altered that the contract cannot be performed. This is known as *rei interitus*. If this occurs prior to the contractor taking possession of the site, then neither party will have a claim against the other. If it occurs when building works are underway, the contractor has a claim for the work carried out and the materials supplied. By the doctrine of accession, property in the building passes to the owner of the ground upon which it is erected and the contractor's entitlement to payment arises under the principle of *res perit domino* (a thing perishes to its owner). A contractor may not be entitled to payment if the work carried out is so defective that the employer would have a defence to an action raised against him. If payments have been made in advance and the contract is subsequently frustrated the payments made can be recovered under the doctrine known as *condictio causa data causa non secuta* (a claim that the consideration has failed of its purpose), see *Cantiere San Rocco, SA* v. *Clyde Shipbuilding and Engineering Co. Ltd* (1923).

Where the contract is frustrated, it is more accurately parties' rights and obligations as to future performance under the contract that are frustrated. In the context of building contracts this distinction is important as even after frustration certain clauses, most notably arbitration clauses, may continue to be enforceable, see *Heyman and Another* v. *Darwins Ltd* (1942). The same position is likely to prevail with adjudication clauses, see *A & D Maintenance and Construction Ltd* v. *Pagehurst Construction Services Ltd* (2000).

## 9.3 Force majeure

### 9.3.1 General

As frustration cannot apply where the parties to a contract have had regard to the possibility of a particular event and made provision for it in their contract, difficulties of interpretation may arise in determining whether frustration has occurred. To address this problem many contracts expressly provide for events that might ordinarily be sufficient to frustrate the contract. Such clauses are known as *force majeure* clauses.

The term *force majeure* is believed to emanate from France and in particular the Code of Napoleon. It has no particular technical meaning in Scotland. The term covers events beyond the control of the party to the contract who seeks to rely upon the clause such as war, epidemics and strikes. It is also said to encompass any direct legislative or administrative interference, see *Lebeaupin* v. *Richard Crispin & Co.* (1920).

By its very nature a *force majeure* clause will have to be read carefully in conjunction with the remaining terms of the contract to establish, precisely, its scope.

### 9.3.2 *Force majeure* under the SBC

By virtue of clause 2.29.13 of the SBC, *force majeure* constitutes a relevant event which may give rise to an extension of time. Civil commotion and the use or threat of terrorism and/or the activities of the relevant authorities in dealing with such events or threat are separate relevant events under clause 2.29.10 although were they not to be specifically provided for they might otherwise, in any event, fall within the ambit of a *force majeure* clause.

Clause 8.11.1.1 of the SBC provides that if, prior to practical completion of the works, *force majeure* causes the carrying out of the whole or substantially the whole of the uncompleted works to be suspended for a continuous period of time specified in the Contract Particulars, either the Employer or the Contractor is entitled to terminate the employment of the Contractor. Termination is considered in section 9.4 below.

## 9.4 Termination

### 9.4.1 Contractual provision

The majority of building contracts contain express provisions regulating the rights of either or both of the parties in defined circumstances to terminate the contract, or bring it to an end. In exercising such rights parties should exercise extreme caution and ensure that the termination procedure laid down in the contract is strictly adhered to, see *Muir Construction Ltd* v. *Hambly Ltd* (1990). Where the contract has already been brought to an end it may not be terminated, see *W Hanson (Harrow) Ltd* v. *Rapid Civil Engineering Ltd and Another* (1987). A party who purportedly operates a termination clause in circumstances where they are not entitled to do so may be treated as having repudiated the contract, see *Architectural Installation Services Ltd* v. *James Gibbons Windows Ltd* (1989), although see also *Lockland Builders Ltd* v. *Richwood* (1995).

By purporting to terminate the contract a party is clearly indicating that they are not going to perform in the future. Unless they are permitted to do that under the contract, such an intention constitutes a repudiation. In such circumstances the other party to the contract is entitled to accept the repudiation, rescind the contract and seek damages. The concepts of repudiation and rescission are considered below at section 9.5. Such a state of affairs may prove welcome to the recipient of the purported termination notice, particularly if that party was finding it difficult to perform in the first place!

Assuming the contract is properly terminated, what is the effect of that termination? The contract as a whole is not terminated. While many of the obligations under the contract, including what might conveniently be termed the principal obligations (e.g. the obligation of the contractor to execute the contract works), will no longer be enforceable, the remaining obligations are fundamentally altered but continue to have effect, see *Mac-Jordan Construction Ltd* v. *Brookmount Erostin Ltd* (1991). Ordinarily a termination clause will also provide for the respective rights and duties of the parties in the event of such a clause being operated. By their nature, those provisions are intended to operate upon the contract being terminated. In each case, it is the employment of the contractor under the contract that is terminated, not the contract itself.

An arbitration clause will continue to be operative, notwithstanding the fact that the contract has been terminated, see *R & J Scott* v. *Gerrard* (1916). The same position is likely to prevail with adjudication clauses, see *A & D Maintenance and Construction Ltd* v. *Pagehurst Construction Services Ltd* (2000). Where the contract contains provisions that deal with an assessment of the sums due to or by either party and an accounting therefore on termination, the courts in Scotland have held that a claim based upon an alleged breach of contract is irrelevant. The correct way to proceed is to claim for payment based upon the contractual provisions, see *Muir Construction Ltd*.

In this section we will examine the termination provisions under the SBC. These termination provisions can conveniently be considered under three headings, namely the circumstances in which there can be termination by the Employer; the circumstances in which there can be termination by the Contractor; and the circumstances in which there can be termination by either party. We shall also consider the general provisions relative to termination.

### 9.4.2 General termination provisions under the SBC

The general termination provisions of the SBC are to be found in clause 8. The clause commences with a provision setting out the meaning of insolvency, for the purposes of these conditions. This provision, clause 8.1, is considered below in section 9.8.2.

Clause 8.2 provides that a notice served under clause 8 is not to be given unreasonably or vexatiously. For a consideration of the phrase 'unreasonably or vexatiously', see *J M Hill & Sons Ltd* v. *London Borough of Camden* (1980) and *John Jarvis Ltd* v. *Rockdale Housing Association Ltd* (1986).

Termination takes effect upon receipt of the relevant notice, see clause 8.2.2. Each notice referred to in clause 8 requires to be given in writing. Unlike many other notices under the SBC (see clause 1.7), notices relevant to termination require to be given by actual, special or recorded delivery, see clause 8.2.3. There is a deeming provision in relation to receipt of notices given by special or recorded delivery post. Failure to comply with the provisions of the contract as to the giving of notice can be fatal, see, for example, *Muir Construction Ltd* v. *Hambly Ltd* (1990). Compare, however, the decision of the House of Lords in *Mannai Investment Co. Ltd* v. *Eagle Star Life Assurance Co. Ltd* (1997).

The relevant provisions of clause 8 are, in terms of clause 8.3.1, stated to be without prejudice to any other rights and remedies available to the Employer and to the Contractor. The other remedies open to the Employer and to the Contractor are considered below in Chapter 10.

It should be borne in mind that irrespective of the grounds of termination, the Contractor's employment may be reinstated at any time and on such terms as the parties agree, see clause 8.3.2.

### 9.4.3 Termination by the Employer under the SBC

Clause 8.4 of the SBC entitles the Employer to terminate the employment of the Contractor if the Contractor continues a 'specified default' for 14 days after receiving from the Architect a notice specifying that default. The 'specified defaults' relied upon must arise before the date of practical completion of the Works and are set out in clause 8.4.1. These are where the Contractor:

- without reasonable cause, wholly or substantially suspends the carrying out of the Works or the design of the Contractor's Designed Portion;
- fails to proceed regularly and diligently with the Works or the design of the Contractor's Designed Portion;
- refuses or neglects to comply with a written notice or instruction from the Architect requiring the removal of any work, materials or goods not in accordance with the contract, where the Works are materially affected by such refusal or neglect;
- fails to comply with the provisions of either clause 3.7 or clause 7.1 (which relate to sub-letting or assignation without written consent); or
- fails to comply with the provisions of clause 3.25 (which requires compliance with the requirements of the Construction (Design and Management) Regulations 2007).

The Employer's right to terminate the contract arises on, or within ten days from, the expiry of the 14-day period. That right is exercised by serving a further notice upon the Contractor, see clause 8.4.2. The termination takes effect on the date of receipt of that further notice.

If the Contractor remedies the specified default, or the Employer elects not to serve the further notice required to terminate, and the Contractor repeats the specified default (whether they have previously repeated it or not), then upon, or within a reasonable time after, such repetition the Employer is entitled to serve notice of termination on the Contractor, see clause 8.4.3. In these circumstances, the specified default need not continue for 14 days; repetition alone is sufficient. A reasonable time need not elapse between the repetition of the specified default and the giving of notice, see *Reinwood Ltd v. L Brown & Sons Ltd* (2007).

Certain insolvency events will also entitle the Employer to terminate. The effect of insolvency is considered below, in section 9.8.

By virtue of clause 8.6 the Employer is entitled to terminate the employment of the Contractor if the Contractor or any person they employ has been involved in any of the corruption-related activities specified in that clause.

The consequences of termination by the Employer are set out in clause 8.7. In those circumstances, the Employer may employ other persons to carry out and complete the Works and/or (where applicable) the design of the Contractor's Designed Portion and to make any good any defects. The Employer may also enter upon and take possession of the site and the Works and, subject to obtaining any necessary third party consents, may use all temporary buildings, plant, tools, equipment and site materials for those purposes.

When required in writing by the Architect so to do (but not before), the Contractor is required to remove or procure the removal from the Works of any temporary buildings, plant, tools, equipment, goods and materials belonging to the Contractor or Contractor's Persons. Where there is a Contractor's Designed Portion, the Contractor is obliged, without charge, to provide to the Employer two copies of all the Contractor's Design Documents then prepared, whether or not previously provided by the Contractor to the Employer. Clause 8.7.2.3 provides that, if required to do so by the Employer (or by the Architect on the Employer's behalf) within 14 days of the date of termination, the Contractor is obliged to assign (so far as assignable and so far as the Contractor may lawfully be required to do so) to the Employer, without charge, the benefit of any agreement for the supply of materials or goods and/or for the execution of any work for the purposes of the contract. The footnote to this clause points out that it may not be effective in cases of the Contractor's insolvency.

Perhaps more significantly in the context of termination by the Employer, by virtue of clause 8.7.3, any other provision of the contract which requires any further payment or release of Retention to the Contractor ceases to apply.

The accounting provision upon termination is to be found in clause 8.7.4. Within a reasonable time after the completion of the Works and the making good of defects, an account requires to be set out in a certificate issued by the Architect or a statement prepared by the Employer. This is to contain the amount of expenses properly incurred by the Employer, including any direct loss and/or damage caused to the Employer and for which the Contractor is liable, whether arising as a result of termination or otherwise, the amount of payments made to the Contractor and the total amount which would have been payable for the Works in accordance with the contract. The difference between the sum of the amount of expenses properly incurred and the amount of payments made to the Contractor, on the one hand, and the total amount which would have been payable for the Works, on the other, is a debt payable by the Contractor to the Employer or, in the rare circumstances of the Works being completed for less money than originally contracted for, by the Employer to the Contractor. Clause 8.8 makes provision in relation to the circumstances where the Employer elects not to complete the Works, within the period of six months from the date of termination of the Contractor's employment.

### 9.4.4 Termination by the Contractor under the SBC

The Contractor's right to terminate their employment is governed by clause 8.9. As with Employer termination, the clause sets out certain specified defaults. In addition, there are also what are termed 'specified suspension events', the occurrence of which can entitle the Contractor to terminate their employment under the contract.

#### Specified defaults

Unlike termination by the Employer, the specified defaults which entitle the Contractor to determine their employment under the contract can arise both before and after practical completion. The specified defaults by the Employer are set out in clause 8.9.1. These are where the Employer:

- does not pay by the final date for payment the amount properly due to the Contractor in respect of any certificate and/or any VAT due thereon;
- interferes with or obstructs the issue of any certificate due under the contract;
- fails to comply with the provisions of clause 7.1 (assigning the contract without the written consent of the Contractor); and
- fails to comply with the Construction (Design and Management) Regulations 2007.

#### Specified suspension events

The specified suspension events, which must arise prior to the date of practical completion, are set out in clause 8.9.2. This provision applies when the carrying out of the whole, or substantially the whole, of the uncompleted Works is suspended for a continuous period of the length specified in the Contract Particulars due to specified events, namely:

- any impediment, prevention or default, whether by act or omission, by the Employer, the Architect, the Quantity Surveyor or any of the Employer's Persons; and/or
- Architect's instructions issued under clause 2.15 (discrepancies in or divergence between contract documents), clause 3.14 (instructions requiring a Variation) or clause 3.15 (postponement of any work to be executed under the contract) unless caused by the negligence or default of the Contractor, or any of the Contractor's Persons.

Once a notice has been given, the ensuing procedure is to all intents and purposes identical to that which operates in the case of Employer termination, the only differences being the necessary modifications made to accommodate specified suspension events. Similarly, the provisions which deal with the repetition of a specified default or of a specified suspension event are virtually identical to those in Employer termination.

The consequences of termination by the Contractor are specified by clause 8.12. Firstly, the other provisions of the contract which require any further payment or any release of Retention to the Contractor shall cease to apply. Upon termination, the Contractor shall with all reasonable dispatch remove or procure the removal from the site of any temporary buildings, plant, tools and equipment which belong to the Contractor or the Contractor's Persons and, unless they have become the property of the Employer, all goods and materials (including Site Materials). Where there is a Contractor's Designed Portion, the Contractor is obliged, without charge, to provide to the Employer two copies of the as-built drawings then prepared.

Where the Contractor's employment is terminated by reason of default by the Employer or the insolvency of the Employer, the Contractor shall as soon as reasonably practicable prepare an account or, not later than two months after the date of termination, provide the Employer with all documents necessary for the Employer to prepare the account, which the Employer shall do with reasonable dispatch (and in any event within three months of receipt of such documents).

The account, which is prepared in accordance with clause 8.12.3, sets out the total value of the work properly executed at the date of termination; any sums ascertained in respect of direct loss and/or expense (whether ascertained before or after the date of termination); the reasonable costs of removal of any temporary buildings, plant, tools and equipment; the cost of materials or goods (including Site Materials) properly ordered for the Works for which the Contractor then has paid or is legally bound to pay; and any direct loss and/or damage caused to the Contractor by the termination.

After taking into account amounts previously paid to the Contractor, the Employer is required to pay to the Contractor the amount properly due in respect of the account within 28 days of its submission by the Employer to the Contractor (or vice versa), without deduction of any Retention. Payment by the Employer for any such materials and goods as are referred to in the account shall be subject to such materials and goods thereupon becoming the property of the Employer.

Certain insolvency events entitle the Contractor to terminate. These are considered below at section 9.8.

### 9.4.5 Termination by either party under the SBC

Clause 8.11 of the SBC provides for certain circumstances which will entitle either the Employer or the Contractor to terminate the employment of the Contractor. Each of the specified circumstances must arise before the date of practical completion and must cause the carrying out of the whole or substantially the whole of the uncompleted Works to be suspended for the relevant continuous period of time set out in the Contract Particulars. The events, provided for by clause 8.11.1, are:

- *force majeure;*
- loss or damage to the Works occasioned by any of the Specified Perils set out in clause 6.8;
- civil commotion (which has been defined as a stage between riot and war, see *Levy* v. *Assicurazioni Generali* (1940) or the threat of terrorism and/or the activities of the relevant authorities in dealing with such event or threat);
- Architect's instructions under clause 2.15, 3.14 or 3.15 issued as a result of the negligence or default of any Statutory Undertaker;
- the exercise by the United Kingdom Government of any statutory power which directly affects the execution of the Works.

Upon the occurrence of one or more of the aforementioned events, and once the period specified in the Contract Particulars has expired, either party may give notice to the other to the effect that unless the suspension ceases within seven days after receipt of that notice the employment of the Contractor may be terminated. This is done by way of further notice, see clause 8.11.

The Contractor is not entitled to give notice where the loss or damage to the Works occasioned by one or more of the specified perils is caused by negligence or default on their part or on the part of any of the Contractor's Persons. The consequences of termination under this clause are identical to those where the Contractor terminated, see clause 8.12 and see section 9.4.3 above.

## 9.5 *Repudiation and rescission*

Notwithstanding the absence in a contract of detailed termination provisions, circumstances may arise whereby a party is freed from future performance. The concepts of repudiation and rescission are inextricably linked. Rescission is considered in more detail below at section 10.2. In certain circumstances a material breach of contract by one party may entitle the other party, the 'innocent party', to terminate the contract. Such a material breach of contract is referred to as a repudiation and gives the innocent party a choice. They can accept the repudiation and rescind the contract or, alternatively, they may elect to ignore the repudiation and continue with the performance of the contract. This option exists because, as stated by Lord Keith in the case of *Woodar Investment Development Ltd* v. *Wimpey Construction UK Ltd* (1980), the doctrine of repudiation exists for the benefit of the innocent party. However, whether in certain circumstances the option is restricted is considered below in section 10.2.

If the repudiation is accepted the acceptance should be communicated to the party in breach. The method by which communication is made would appear to be immaterial, see *Monklands DC* v. *Ravenstone Securities* (1980).

The remedy that is open to an innocent party who elects to rescind, namely damages, is considered below at section 10.4. Should the innocent party elect to ignore the repudiation they may well be barred from relying upon the material breach at a later date.

It is particularly difficult to generalise as to what conduct is, and what conduct is not, a repudiation. Not every material breach will constitute a repudiation, see *Blyth* v. *Scottish Liberal Club* (1982) approved in *Tehrani* v. *Argyll and Clyde Health Board (No.2)* (1989). Should one party refuse to perform their obligations under the contract that is likely to constitute a repudiation. Should an employer prevent a contractor from carrying out the contract works, for example by engaging another contractor to carry out all or part of those works, that too is likely to constitute a repudiation, see *Sweatfield Ltd* v. *Hathaway Roofing Ltd* (1997).

In Scotland, the precise effect of the acceptance of a repudiation and resultant rescission of the contract has been examined by the Inner House of the Court of Session in the case of *Lloyds Bank plc* v. *Bamberger* (1993) which provides a clear and succinct exposition of the position under Scots Law where a contract has been rescinded.

In *Lloyds Bank plc* Lord Ross stated that, following rescission, both parties are freed from future performance of their primary obligations under the contract. Nevertheless parties continue to be bound by the primary obligations which are extant at the time of rescission. The contract does not come to an end. The innocent party is entitled to sue the party in default for damages for breach of contract. Ancillary clauses which the parties intended would survive rescission, such as arbitration clauses, may be enforced after rescission. Apart from such ancillary clauses, the contract may also contain clauses which affect damages due for breach of contract, such as a liquidated damages clause. The language of the contract may be such as to demonstrate that the parties intended such clauses to be enforceable after rescission.

Rescission should be distinguished from contractual termination, considered above in section 9.4. In the latter, the employment of the contractor is terminated, in certain instances upon the occurrence of events that are not the fault of either party. Contractual termination clauses seek to bring some degree of certainty to the circumstances in which the parties' contract comes to end prematurely.

## 9.6 Death and illness

The effect of the death or incapacity of a party to a building contract will primarily depend upon whether or not the contract involves an element of *delectus personae*. A contract that involves *delectus personae* means that one party to the contract entered into it in reliance upon certain qualities possessed by the other. Where such qualities are a necessary element of the contract, the death or incapacity of the party who is bound to perform clearly prevents the contract being performed and, thus, brings it to an end. For examples of this, see the cases of *Hoey v. McEwan & Auld and Others* (1867) and *Smith v. Riddell* (1886). The existence of *delectus personae* in a contract has a direct bearing upon whether or not that contract is capable of being assigned. This is considered below in Chapter 12.

The delegation of building work (through the use of sub-contractors) is an everyday occurrence and, therefore, in the absence of special circumstances or an express contractual provision to the contrary, *delectus personae* will not apply and the obligation to perform will pass to the personal representatives of the deceased party. It will be for the representatives to secure alternative contractors to carry out the works, or to complete them themselves.

As a building contract is ordinarily divisible (unlike a contract for a painting or a sculpture), it would appear that remuneration can be claimed by a deceased party's representatives for work partially carried out up to the date of death. The valuation of that work may be problematic, particularly if the contract does not have a mechanism for valuation, and may require equitable adjustment.

Illness and incapacity need to be treated in a like manner, although the position is, perhaps not surprisingly, not as clear cut as in the case of death. The effect of illness or incapacity is one of degree and will depend upon the whole circumstances, most notably the likely duration of the illness or incapacity in relation to the length of the contract. Even where illness is not sufficient to bring the contract to an end, it has been enough to entitle the employer to rescind the contract, see *Manson v. Downie* (1885), and to constitute a breach of contract, see *McEwan v. Malcolm* (1867).

Since the vast majority of contractors are now limited companies, the problems occasioned by death and illness are unlikely to arise on a regular basis. However, it should be noted that *delectus personae* may arise in employer/contractor relationships that do not involve individuals, as demonstrated by the case of *Scottish Homes v. Inverclyde DC* (1997). The issue may also arise in the case of architects or engineers appointed under a construction contract or in the case of an adjudicator named in a construction contract, see *Amec Capital Projects Ltd* v. *Whitefriars City Estates Ltd* (2004).

## 9.7 *Illegality*

While a detailed examination of the concept of illegality is beyond the scope of this work, it does merit some consideration.

In general terms, an illegal contract is one which the law will not enforce. However, there is a distinction between illegal contracts and those that are associated with an unenforceable transaction. Perhaps the best example that can be given to illustrate the latter is gambling. Whilst gambling is not illegal, the Scottish courts will not entertain actions to determine wagers. This is the case for reasons of public policy, not illegality. This long-standing principle was confirmed in *Ferguson* v. *Littlewoods Pools Ltd* (1997).

What precisely constitutes an illegal contract is open to question. A number of vague and differing concepts such as 'moral turpitude' and 'subversive of the interests of the State' have been used, see *Jamieson* v. *Watt's Trustee* (1950). The matter is far from clear, as is demonstrated by the decision in *Cuthbertson* v. *Lowes* (1870) in which it was held that a contract which contravened a statute was not necessarily illegal.

Whether or not either party questions the legality of the contract the court will have regard to it, see *F W Trevalion & Co.* v. *J J Blanche & Co.* (1919). Where a contract is held to be illegal the court will not interfere as between the rights of the parties to the contract. This is consistent with the general principle that the courts will not assist the party who is in breach of a statute, albeit that the corollary of this is that the other party to the contract is entitled to keep the advantage gained by them. This may be regarded as unfortunate where the parties were equally aware of the illegal nature of the transaction.

If the contract is not itself illegal, but has a connection with some other illegal transaction, the contract is said to be tainted with illegality. If one of the parties was unaware of the illegality, they will be entitled to enforce their rights under the contract. However, should they fail to resile from the contract, after becoming aware of the illegality, they may be held to have acquiesced. As a consequence, they may not be entitled to enforce their rights under the contract.

Where only part of a contract is illegal, that part may be capable of being severed from the remainder of the contract. In a building contract which contains the power to instruct variations it may well be possible to instruct a variation to remove the 'offending' part of the contract. The question of severance is a complex one upon which there is little Scottish authority, although the English authorities on this subject are likely to be regarded as highly persuasive. Whether or not an illegal provision is capable of being severed will depend upon the nature of the illegality.

The contract may be valid, but the works executed under it illegal. For example, in *Townsend (Builders) Ltd* v. *Cinema News and Property Management*

*Ltd* (1959) the works as built, but not as specified, contravened a byelaw. In the rather special circumstances of that case the contractor was held to be entitled to recover payment, although it would appear that but for those special circumstances the contractor would not have succeeded.

If a contractor carries out work in the absence of necessary consents they take the risk that the work is illegal and they may be unable to recover payment for that work, see *Designers and Decorators (Scotland) Ltd* v. *Ellis* (1957). The contract will often expressly oblige the contractor to give statutory notices and comply with statutory requirements, and may also provide for the circumstances in which there is a change in the statutory requirements. For example, clause 2.1 of the SBC makes such provision.

## 9.8 Insolvency

### 9.8.1 General

Insolvency, in itself, does not affect a contract, but has potentially far-reaching implications that merit some examination within the confines of this work.

The insolvent party may be unable to implement their obligations under the contract, which would entitle the other party to withhold performance of their obligations under the contract, see *Arnott and Others* v. *Forbes* (1881). In a case of personal insolvency (known as bankruptcy) the party contracting with the insolvent debtor can compel the debtor's representative (known as a permanent trustee) to make his position clear in relation to the contract. Section 42 of the Bankruptcy (Scotland) Act 1985 provides that the permanent trustee is deemed to have refused to adopt the contract unless he responds within 28 days from the receipt by him of a request in writing from any party to a contract entered into by the debtor, or within such longer period of that receipt as the court on application by the permanent trustee may allow, to adopt or refuse to adopt the contract.

### 9.8.2 Insolvency under the SBC

#### Meaning of insolvency

The SBC defines a party as insolvent in the circumstances set out in clause 8.1. Those circumstances are if a party

- enters into an arrangement, compromise or composition in satisfaction of their debts (excluding a scheme of arrangement as a solvent company for the purposes of amalgamation or reconstruction); or
- without a declaration of solvency, passes a resolution or makes a determination that they be wound up; or

- has a winding-up order or bankruptcy order made against them; or
- has appointed to them an administrator or administrative receiver; or
- is the subject of any analogous arrangement, event or proceedings in any other jurisdiction; or
- finds themselves in a situation whereby, in the case of a partnership, each partner is the subject of an individual arrangement or any other event or proceedings of the types referred to above.

### Insolvency of the Contractor

Clause 8.5 makes provision in respect of the insolvency of the Contractor. If the Contractor is Insolvent, the Employer may at any time by notice to the contractor terminate the Contractor's employment under the contract.

The Contractor is obliged to immediately inform the Employer in writing if they make any proposal, give notice of any meeting or become the subject of any proceedings or appointment relating to any of the matters referred to in the definition of Insolvency, above. As from the date the Contractor becomes Insolvent, whether or not the Employer has given such notice of termination, the provisions of the contract requiring further payment or any release of Retention cease to apply; the Contractor's obligations to carry out and complete the Works and the design of the Contractor's Designed Portion are suspended; and the Employer may take reasonable measures to ensure that the site, the Works and Site Materials are adequately protected and that such Site Materials are retained on site. The Contractor is obliged to allow and not to hinder or delay the taking of those measures.

### Insolvency of the Employer

Clause 8.10 makes provision in respect of the Insolvency of the Employer. If the Employer is Insolvent, the Contractor may by notice to the Employer terminate the Contractor's Employment under the contract.

The Employer is obliged to immediately inform the Contractor in writing if they make any proposal, give notice of any meeting or become the subject of any proceedings or appointment relating to any of the matters referred to in the definition of Insolvency above. As from the date the Employer becomes Insolvent, the Contractor's obligations to carry out and complete the Works and the design of the Contractor's Designed Portion are suspended.

## 9.9 Prescription

### 9.9.1 General

Prescription is the establishment or definition of a right or the extinction of an obligation through the lapse of time. The former is termed positive prescription, the latter negative prescription. Positive prescription applies to interests in land, servitudes and public rights of way. It has no relevance to building contracts and will not be considered further in this book.

Prescription falls to be contrasted with limitation. Limitation does not affect the subsistence of rights and obligations. It is a doctrine that denies certain rights of action after the passage of a certain lapse of time, see *Macdonald* v. *North of Scotland Bank* (1942). Limitation periods may be statutory or conventional. Conventional limitation is where the parties set out in their contract that a particular obligation will be extinguished by the lapse of a stipulated time period without a claim being made.

Such a provision can appear in construction contracts. Clause 15(6) of the Federation of Civil Engineering Contractors Form of Sub-Contract (the 'Blue Form') provides that the contractor has no liability to the sub-contractor for any matter or thing arising out of or in connection with the sub-contract or the execution of the sub-contract works unless the sub-contractor has made a written claim in respect of that matter or thing to the contractor before the engineer issues the maintenance certificate in respect of the main contract works. See *Loudonhill Contracts Ltd* v. *John Mowlem Construction Ltd* (2001).

The law in relation to both prescription and limitation is to be found in the Prescription and Limitation (Scotland) Act 1973 (which we will refer to in this chapter as 'the 1973 Act'). Whilst a detailed examination of this subject is beyond the scope of this work, we shall consider those aspects of it which are most pertinent to building contracts, namely short negative prescription and long negative prescription.

Under the 1973 Act the party under the relevant obligation is known as 'the debtor' and the party to whom the obligation is owed is known as 'the creditor'. In relation to the short negative and the long negative prescriptive periods, the general rule is that the burden of proof in establishing whether or not an obligation has prescribed rests with the party alleging the affirmative. For example, if the assertion is that the obligation had subsisted for the prescriptive period it would be for the party so affirming to prove, see *Strathclyde Regional Council* v. *W A Fairhurst & Partners* (1997).

### 9.9.2 Short negative prescription

The short negative prescriptive period of five years is the one most familiar to those in the construction industry. Section 6(1) of the 1973 Act provides that if, after the 'appropriate date', an obligation which is set out in Schedule 1 to the 1973 Act has subsisted for five years (a) without any relevant claim having been made in relation to it; and (b) without the subsistence of the obligation having been relevantly acknowledged, then as from the expiration of the five year period the obligation in question is extinguished.

A number of technical expressions are used in s.6(1). As we will see below, many of these are equally relevant to long negative prescription. We shall examine each of these expressions in turn.

### 9.9.3 The appropriate date

The short negative prescriptive period commences upon what is termed the 'appropriate date'. This date varies from obligation to obligation. Schedule 2 to the 1973 Act sets out various obligations and the appropriate date relative to each of them. None of the Schedule 2 obligations are particularly relevant to building contracts. With the exception of obligations of the kind specified in Schedule 2, the appropriate date in relation to an obligation is the date upon which that obligation became enforceable.

Section 11 of the 1973 Act defines when certain types of obligation become enforceable. For example, an obligation to make reparation for loss, injury or damage caused by an act, neglect or default is regarded as having become enforceable on the date when the loss, injury or damage occurred or was discovered.

There must be an act, neglect or default and resultant loss, injury or damage. The obligation to make reparation does not arise, and thus does not become enforceable, until the loss, injury or damage occurs, see *Watson* v. *Fram Reinforced Concrete Co. (Scotland) Ltd* (1960), *Dunlop* v. *McGowans* (1979) and *Strathclyde Regional Council* v. *W A Fairhurst & Partners* (1997).

The loss, injury or damage must arise from the act, neglect or default. For example, in *Sinclair* v. *MacDougall Estates Ltd* (1994) it was held that the defenders' act, neglect or default founded upon by the pursuers was not a breach of the general duty to construct in accordance with the contract, but was constituted by certain specified failures on the defenders' part to design and construct the building in a workmanlike manner in terms of the contract. The minor breaches of the contract which had caused damage discovered at earlier stages (in 1972 or 1977) were not sufficient to constitute *injuria* in relation to major and different failures to design and construct the building properly which had resulted in the damage discovered in 1988. The loss, injury or damage sustained in 1988 did not arise from the act, neglect or default discovered in 1972 or 1977 and the case was held not to be time barred.

A number of the relevant cases on this subject arise from building contracts and these usefully illustrate the position. In *George Porteous (Arts) Ltd* v. *Dollar Rae Ltd* (1979) contractors were refused planning permission and the work executed by them had to be demolished. In that case it was held that the prescriptive period ran from the date of service of the enforcement notice, that being the date upon which the pursuers suffered loss. In *Scott Lithgow Ltd* v. *Secretary of State for Defence* (1989) the prescriptive period was held to have commenced as from the date when the materials in question were found to have been defective.

In *Scottish Equitable plc* v. *Miller Construction Ltd* (2001), the Respondents sought payment of sums in respect of direct loss and expense that they maintained ought to have been included in an interim certificate issued by the architect on 18 June 1992. That was the last interim certificate issued under the parties' contract. No final certificate was issued. The events upon which the claim was based all took place prior to practical completion being certified on 6 August 1990. A notice to concur in the appointment of an arbiter was issued on 7 May 1996, that being the relevant date for the purposes of prescription. The appellants argued unsuccessfully that the rights founded upon by the respondents had prescribed. The Inner House held that time only began to run on the loss and expense claim from the date of issue of the relevant interim certificate, namely, 18 June 1992.

Section 11(2) of the 1973 Act provides that where, as a result of a continuing act, neglect or default, loss has occurred prior to the act, neglect or default ceasing, the loss is deemed to have occurred on the date when the act ceased.

Where the creditor is not aware, and could not with reasonable diligence have become aware that loss, injury or damage has occurred, the prescriptive period does not commence until the date on which the innocent party first became, or could with reasonable diligence have become so aware, see s.11(3). This provision has particular relevance in the case of latent defects; the five-year period will commence from the date of discoverability of the defect, subject to the long-stop of the 20-year-long negative prescriptive period, which is considered below at section 9.9.7.

### 9.9.4 Schedule 1 obligations

The types of obligations that are affected by the short negative prescriptive period are defined in Schedule 1 to the 1973 Act. Unlike long negative prescription, short negative prescription applies only to a limited number of obligations. Of these, certain are particularly relevant to building contracts. These are set out in paragraph 1 of Schedule 1 and are any obligation

- based on unjustified enrichment (including restitution, repetition or recompense);
- arising from liability to make reparation; and
- arising from, or by reason of any breach of, a contract or promise, not being an obligation falling within any other provision of paragraph 1.

An obligation arising under a contract will include an obligation to refer disputes under an engineering contract to the contract engineer, see *Douglas Milne Ltd* v. *Borders Regional Council* (1990). The same will apply in the case of an arbitration clause. A performance bond has been held to be a cautionary obligation subject to the short negative prescriptive period, see *City of Glasgow DC* v. *Excess Insurance Co. Ltd* (1986). The appropriate date in such a case is the date of issue of an architect's certificate ascertaining the extent of the damages due for default, see *McPhail* v. *Cunninghame DC* (1985) and *City of Glasgow DC* v. *Excess Insurance Co. Ltd (No.2)* (1990).

### 9.9.5 Relevant claims

An obligation affected by short negative prescription will be extinguished if it has subsisted for a continuous period of five years without either of two events occurring, namely, the making of a relevant claim or a relevant acknowledgement.

If a relevant claim is made, the prescriptive period is said to have been interrupted and a new five-year period commences as from the date of interruption, see s.9 of the 1973 Act.

A 'relevant claim' is one made by or on behalf of the creditor in an obligation for implement or part implement of the obligation in 'appropriate proceedings' or in certain insolvency related circumstances. An examination of the latter is beyond the scope of this work. 'Appropriate proceedings' means court proceedings in Scotland; an arbitration in Scotland; or an arbitration outside Scotland in which an award would be enforceable in Scotland.

The date of the relevant claim is the date of service of court proceedings, except in relation to Court of Session proceedings which do not subsequently call. If Court of Session proceedings do not call, a relevant claim is not made. In the case of an arbitration, the date of the relevant claim is the date when the claim is made in the arbitration or the preliminary notice is served, whichever is the earlier. If no preliminary notice is served the relevant claim in an arbitration will be made on the date when the claim is actually made. To be a relevant claim the preliminary notice must state the nature of the claim, see *Douglas Milne Ltd* v. *Borders Regional Council* (1990).

### 9.9.6 Relevant acknowledgements

Section 10 of the 1973 Act defines a 'relevant acknowledgement'. The subsistence of an obligation is regarded as having been relevantly acknowledged if, and only if, either of two defined conditions is satisfied. Firstly, there must have been such performance by or on behalf of the debtor towards implement of the obligation as clearly indicates that the obligation still subsists. Secondly, and alternatively, there has to have been made by or on behalf of the debtor to the creditor or his agent an unequivocal written admission clearly acknowledging that the obligation still subsists. As with a relevant claim, if a relevant acknowledgement is made the prescriptive period is interrupted and a new five-year period commences as from the date of interruption.

### 9.9.7 Long negative prescription

In Scotland, the long negative prescriptive period is 20 years. Section 7(1) of the 1973 Act provides that if, after the date when an obligation became enforceable, the obligation has subsisted for a continuous period of 20 years without either a relevant claim or a relevant acknowledgement, then as from the expiration of the 20-year period the obligation is extinguished. Long negative prescription does not apply to obligations arising under s.22A of the 1973 Act (liability under the Consumer Protection Act 1987 for a defect in a product) or specified in Schedule 3 to the 1973 Act (imprescriptible rights and obligations) or to obligations under Schedule 1 of the 1973 Act to which the short negative prescriptive period applies.

Other than the length of the period the main difference between the short negative and long negative prescriptive periods is the point in time at which they commence. As we have seen, the former commences as from the appropriate date. The latter commences as from the date upon which the obligation in question became enforceable.

The practical consequence of this in the context of building contracts is significant. The concept of 'discoverability' of a latent defect (which applies to the five-year period) does not apply to the 20-year period, and thus an obligation arising from a latent defect will, in the absence of a valid interruption of the prescriptive period, prescribe 20 years after the date upon which the obligation became enforceable which is, broadly, when there has been both an act, neglect or default and loss, injury or damage arising therefrom. Thus a latent defect that is discovered 19 years after the obligation in question became enforceable will prescribe 20 years after the date upon which the obligation became enforceable, i.e. in these circumstances only one year after the discovery. A defect that is discovered less than 15 years after it became enforceable will prescribe five years after it is discovered.

It should be noted that, in long negative prescription, there is no equivalent provision to s.11(3) of the 1973 Act. Accordingly, even if the creditor was not aware, and could not with reasonable diligence have been aware, that loss, injury or damage had been caused, the long negative prescriptive period continues to run. Discoverability is not an issue in long negative prescription.

As with short negative prescription, the long negative prescriptive period can be interrupted by the making of a relevant claim or by a relevant acknowledgement. In this regard, the provisions set out in sections 9.9.5 and 9.9.6 above apply equally to long negative prescription.

# Chapter 10
# Remedies

## 10.1 Introduction

Disputes arise under building contracts as with any other type of contract. While the resolution of such disputes is considered in Chapters 15, 16 and 17, in this chapter we will consider certain of the remedies that are open to parties where a dispute arises.

Whilst certain of the remedies are, perhaps, peculiar to building contracts, the ordinary remedies that are open to the parties to any form of commercial contract are available. The remedies that are most commonly associated with building contracts are to be found within the provisions of the standard form contracts, such as the SBC. Certain of these remedies, such as liquidated and ascertained damages and extensions of time (Chapter 6), and termination (Chapter 9) have been considered previously. However, certain others are considered in this chapter. Separately, we will consider the general common law remedies open to parties, certain of which are quite independent of those arising under the terms of a specific contract.

Ordinarily, the general common law remedies and the remedies provided for in a specific contract will exist at the same time, see *Gilbert Ash (Northern) Ltd v. Modern Engineering (Bristol) Ltd* (1974). A party's common law rights can only be taken away by clear, unequivocal words, see *Redpath Dorman Long Ltd v. Cummins Engine Co. Ltd* (1981). The extent to which that is achieved will depend upon the terms of the contract in question. See, for instance, the Scottish case of *Eurocopy Rentals Ltd v. McCann Fordyce* (1994) in which it was held that the contractual termination provision was the exclusive method of termination.

There are both advantages and disadvantages associated with each of the types of remedy. For example, a liquidated damages provision of the nature contained in clause 2.32 of the SBC is of advantage to the employer in that they are not required to prove the actual loss they have sustained as a result of the contractor failing to complete the works on time. The downside of clauses such as this is that the employer must adhere strictly to the provisions of the clause to entitle them to deduct liquidated damages.

## 10.2 Rescission

The concepts of repudiation and rescission are considered in Chapter 9. In certain circumstances a material breach of contract by one party may be such as to entitle the other party (the 'innocent party') to terminate the contract. If the breach constitutes a repudiation of the contract, the innocent party has a choice. They can either accept the repudiation and rescind the contract or, alternatively, they may elect to ignore the repudiation and continue with the performance of the contract. The extent to which there is a right to continue with performance may, however, be limited.

The remedy open to the innocent party is to rescind the contract. Where a contract has been rescinded, both parties are freed from future performance of their primary obligations thereunder. Parties continue to be bound by the primary obligations that were extant at the time of rescission. The contract does not come to an end. The innocent party is entitled to sue the party in default for damages for breach of contract. Ancillary clauses which the parties intended would survive rescission, such as arbitration clauses, may be enforced after rescission. Apart from such ancillary clauses, the contract may also contain clauses which affect the amount of damages due for breach of contract, such as a liquidated damages clause. The language of the contract may be such as to demonstrate that the parties intended such clauses to be enforceable after rescission, see *Lloyds Bank plc* v. *Bamberger* (1994).

It is well established law that the innocent party's remedies for the other party's breach of contract are limited to those provided for in the contract, and for those breaches committed while the contract subsisted. However, where the contract has been rescinded and the mutual obligations thereunder have ceased to exist, the court has the power to award compensation on the basis of *quantum meruit*, see *Morrison-Knudsen Co. Inc* v. *British Columbia Hydro and Power Authority* (1991), approved by the Inner House of the Court of Session in *ERDC Construction Ltd* v. *H M Love & Co.* (1995). The subject of payment *quantum meruit* is considered above in section 8.4.

The ordinary position in contract is that the innocent party is entitled to ignore the repudiation and continue with the performance of the contract. This is supported by the decision of the House of Lords in *White & Carter (Councils) Ltd* v. *McGregor* (1962) and, in the case of building contracts, by the decision of the Inner House of the Court of Session in *ERDC Construction Ltd*. The courts have, however, recognised that there may be limitations upon the right of the innocent party to insist upon performance. In *White & Carter (Councils) Ltd*, Lord Reid made it clear that:

> 'had it been necessary for the defender to do or accept anything before the contract could be completed by the pursuers, the pursuers could not and the court would not have compelled the defender to act, the contract would not have been completed, and the pursuers' only remedy would have been damages.'

It must be noted that in *White & Carter (Councils) Ltd* the pursuers did not require any co-operation, either active or passive, on the part of the defender. Building contracts patently cannot be performed without co-operation between employer and contractor. The courts in England have made it clear that they will not enforce an agreement for two people to live peaceably under the same roof, see *Thompson* v. *Park* (1944). They have also expressed the opinion that a repudiatory breach cannot be ignored where it can be shown that the innocent party has no legitimate interest in performing the contract, provided that damages would be an adequate remedy and keeping the contract alive would be unreasonable, see *Ocean Marine Navigation Ltd* v. *Koch Carbon Inc ('The Dynamic')* (2003). The rationale behind this is identical to that identified by Lord Reid in *White & Carter (Councils) Ltd.* A multitude of practical problems would arise if the courts compelled performance.

In these circumstances, the authors respectfully suggest that the *obiter* comments of Lord Reid in *White & Carter (Councils) Ltd* should generally apply in relation to building contracts and the innocent party's right to insist upon performance is limited. Support for this proposition is to be found in the case of *London Borough of Hounslow* v. *Twickenham Garden Developments Ltd* (1970). In essence, the innocent party may be forced to accept a repudiation and rescind the contract, see *Decro-Wall International SA* v. *Practitioners in Marketing Ltd* (1971) and *Ocean Marine Navigation Ltd.* The nature of building contracts is such that the option to ignore an employer's repudiation may not be one that is open to a contractor.

## 10.3 Specific implement

When parties enter into a contract, they each undertake certain obligations. In Scotland, it is presumed that contractual obligations will be enforced by the courts, unless there are considerations which make implement impossible or unjust, see *Stewart* v. *Kennedy* (1890) and *Beardmore* v. *Barry* (1928). The remedy open to the innocent party to compel performance of contractual obligations by the party in breach is known as specific implement.

As with rescission, the innocent party, in most circumstances, has a choice. Either they can insist upon their entitlement under the contract, or they can seek damages for the breach, see *Holman & Co.* v. *Union Electric Co.* (1913). Damages are considered below in section 10.4. It will, however, always be at the discretion of the court as to whether the remedy of specific implement or that of damages is the appropriate one, see *Graham* v. *Magistrates and Police Commissioners of Kirkcaldy* (1881). Specific implement is not an appropriate remedy in every case. It is not available in respect of the enforcement of a party's monetary obligations under a contract, see *White & Carter (Councils) Ltd* v. *McGregor* (1962). It is also an inappropriate remedy where performance would require the party in breach to become a partner in a commercial undertaking, see *Pert* v. *Bruce* (1937). It is an inappropriate remedy where performance is impossible, see *McArthur* v. *Lawson* (1877). There are a number of other instances in which specific implement has been held to be inappropriate. A more detailed examination of these is beyond the scope of this book.

The issue of specific implement in the context of building contracts is a difficult one. It raises similar issues to those that arise in relation to rescission. In *London Borough of Hounslow* v. *Twickenham Garden Developments Ltd* (1970) it was argued on behalf of the borough that the contract (which incorporated the RIBA conditions) was not specifically enforceable. Whilst a decision on this point was not necessary to resolve the case, Lord Megarry (as he then was) stated that he could not see why the contract should not be held to be specifically enforceable. In contrast to rescission, whether or not specific implement is an appropriate remedy in relation to a particular contractual obligation will depend upon whether the party in breach is required to do, allow or accept something. Such co-operation may be essential in relation to certain obligations, but unnecessary in respect of others.

In the context of building contracts, the authors respectfully submit that where co-operation by the party in breach is required, specific implement is not an appropriate remedy. Such an approach is consistent with the comments of Lord Reid, and indeed the dissenting opinion of Lord Morton of Henryton, in *White & Carter (Councils) Ltd*. The innocent party must have an interest to insist upon specific implement of the obligation. If the court is not satisfied that they have such an interest their claim will be for damages, see *Clea Shipping Corp* v. *Bulk Oil International Ltd* (1984). The reality is that, in the majority of cases, the innocent party in a building contract may have no legitimate interest in performing the contract, rather than claiming damages. In such cases, it has been suggested that the innocent party can, in one sense, be said to be forced to claim damages. To insist upon any other remedy would be of little value, see *Decro-Wall International SA* v. *Practitioners in Marketing Ltd* (1971) and *Ocean Marine Navigation Ltd* v. *Koch Carbon Inc (The Dynamic)* (2003). As stated by Lord Justice Sachs in *Decro-Wall International SA*, 'in such cases it is the range of remedies that is limited, not the right to elect'.

In Scotland, the remedy of specific implement is available both in the Court of Session and in the Sheriff Court. By virtue of s.47(2) of the Court of Session Act 1988, interim orders for specific implement can competently be granted, see *Scottish Power Generation Ltd* v. *British Energy Generation (UK) Ltd* (2002), *Va Tech Wabag UK Ltd* v. *Morgan Est (Scotland) Ltd* (2002) and *Purac Ltd* v. *Byzak Ltd* (2005). These cases are considered below in section 15.2.3. No equivalent remedy is available in the Sheriff Court.

## 10.4 Damages for breach of contract

### 10.4.1 General

Perhaps the most commonly used legal remedy is that of damages. Damages are expressed in monetary terms. The purpose of damages for breach of contract is to place the innocent party in the position they would have been in had the breach not occurred. Damages may also be recoverable where no contract exists but one party owes the other a duty of care and is in breach of that duty. In those circumstances damages will be recoverable under the law of delict rather than for breach of contract. Delictual claims are considered below in section 10.10.

The law of damages is a vast and complex subject and a detailed examination is beyond the scope of this work.

It is open to the parties to a contract to decide in advance what damages, if any, will be payable in the event of a breach by one, or any, of them. In essence, it is open to parties to exclude or limit liability. This is a common occurrence in building contracts, for example, clause 2.32 of the SBC, which provides for the payment of liquidated and ascertained damages for non-completion. Under clause 2.17.3 of the SBC/DB the parties may elect to limit the Contractor's liability for loss of use, loss of profit or other consequential loss arising from an inadequacy in design. It should also be borne in mind that claims for damages are subject to the law of prescription.

### 10.4.2 Causation, foreseeability and remoteness

The loss which the pursuer is entitled to recover is that which has been caused by the defender's breach, see *Bourhill* v. *Young* (1942). The pursuer must establish not only that there has been a breach of contract and they have suffered loss, but also that there is a causal connection between the breach and the losses sought to be recovered, and that such losses are not too remote. In complex building contract disputes, there can be a multitude of losses and breaches of contract which can make it extremely difficult to link a specific loss to a specific breach. This has often resulted in the presentation of what is termed a 'global claim'. It is competent, in certain circumstances, to present a claim in this manner, see *John Doyle Construction Ltd* v. *Laing Management (Scotland) Ltd* (2004).

Only losses that were foreseeable as being the likely consequences of a breach at the time the contract was entered into are recoverable. If the losses were not foreseeable at that time, they are too remote and cannot be recovered.

These issues were considered in the case of *Hadley* v. *Baxendale* (1854). This case laid down the rules that apply in assessing the measure of damages in a breach of contract case. In delivering the judgment of the court, Baron Alderson stated:

> 'Where two parties have made a contract which one of them has broken, the damages which the other party ought to receive in respect of such breach of contract should be such as may fairly and reasonably be considered either arising naturally, i.e., according to the usual course of things, from such breach of contract itself, or such as may reasonably be supposed

to have been in the contemplation of both parties, at the time they made the contract, as the probable result of the breach of it.'

That part of the judgment of the court has been widely repeated and relied upon since 1854. In the context of building contracts, however, the following part of the judgment is also significant. Baron Alderson went on to state:

'[I]f the special circumstances under which the contract was actually made were communicated by the [pursuers] to the [defenders], and thus known to both parties, the damages resulting from the breach of such a contract, which they would reasonably contemplate, would be the amount of injury which would ordinarily follow from a breach of contract under these special circumstances so known and communicated. But on the other hand, if these special circumstances were wholly unknown to the party breaking the contract, he, at the most, could only be supposed to have had in his contemplation the amount of injury which would arise generally . . . from such a breach of contract.'

An example of such special circumstances is to be found in *Balfour Beatty Construction (Scotland) Ltd* v. *Scottish Power plc* (1994). In that case the pursuers were engaged in the building of a roadway and associated structures, including an aqueduct. They contracted with the defenders' predecessors for the supply of electricity to operate a concrete batching plant. The construction of the aqueduct required a continuous pour operation. In the course of the construction of the aqueduct, the batching plant stopped working. It was established that the electricity supply had been interrupted and that the interruption was a breach of contract by the defenders' predecessors. The pursuers claimed the cost of demolishing and rebuilding a substantial part of their works, this having been rendered necessary by the interruption of the electricity supply and the consequent interruption of the required continuous pour. It was established that the defenders' predecessors had not known of the need for a continuous pour. The Lord Ordinary concluded that the need to rebuild part of the works as a result of the interruption of the continuous pour had not been within the defenders' reasonable contemplation and the action failed. Ultimately, the House of Lords upheld the decision of the Lord Ordinary. Had the special circumstances, namely, the need for a continuous pour, been known to the defenders, it is likely that the pursuers would have succeeded.

### 10.4.3 Damages recoverable and mitigation

The law of Scotland is clear in respect of the method of assessment of damages, assuming the necessary pre-requisites considered above at section 10.4.2 have been met. As was stated by Lord Pearson in *The Govan Rope & Sail Co. Ltd* v. *Andrew Weir & Co.* (1897):

'[I]t appears to me that the criterion of damage now adopted by the pursuers is in accordance with the principle which governs the whole law on the subject, namely, that the party observing the contract is to be put as nearly as possible in the same position as he would have been if the contract had been performed.'

As damages is a monetary remedy, the party suffering the loss can only be put in the position it would have been in, but for the breach, insofar as a payment of money to them allows.

Building contracts will often confer on the contractor a right to an increase in the contract sum for direct loss and/or expense incurred by the contractor on the occurrence of certain events, e.g. failure or delay in issuing instructions or information, which otherwise would be treated as damages for breach of contract. Although the nature of the claim in such cases is conceptually different insofar as it is a claim for payment under the contract rather than a claim for damages, the calculation of the direct loss and/or expense is likely to be little different from a claim for damages for breach of contract, see clauses 4.23 to 4.26 of the SBC.

If the contract is rescinded by the contractor due to a material breach by the employer, the contractor is likely to be entitled to recover by way of damages the profit he would have made had the contract been completed in the ordinary course. If the works had been partially carried out, the contractor retains the right to payment for the value of such works. The rescission of a contract in consequence of a repudiation does not affect accrued rights to payment under the contract, unless the contract provides that it was to do so, see *Hyundai Heavy Industries Co. Ltd* v. *Papadopoulos* (1980).

In the event of a breach of contract by the contractor, again the contract may provide the remedy in certain circumstances, see, for example, the liquidated and ascertained damages provisions in respect of non-completion under clause 2.32 of the SBC. If the contractor does not complete the contract works the employer's loss will be the additional cost of completing the works, if any. If the works are completed at no additional cost there will be no loss. It should, however, be noted that there is authority in Scotland to the effect that where a breach of contract is established the pursuer is entitled to nominal damages, even if no loss can be demonstrated. This comes from the opinion of the Lord President in *Webster & Co.* v. *The Cramond Iron Co.* (1875) in which he stated that:

'[Where the] contract and the breach of it are established . . . that leads of necessity to an award of damages. It is impossible to say that a contract can be broken even in respect of time without the party being entitled to claim damages – at the lowest, nominal damages.'

Another common breach of contract by the contractor is the existence of defects in the works executed or that the works executed do not conform to the requirements of the parties' contract. Assuming the contract contains no specific mechanism under which the contractor is obliged to remedy defects, such as clauses 2.38 and 2.39 of the SBC, and the contractor will not do so voluntarily, the measure of the employers' loss can, ordinarily, be assessed in one of two ways. The first is the cost of the necessary repairs. The second is the difference in value between the building in the condition contracted for and the building in its actual condition, i.e. with the defective work, see *GUS Property Management Ltd* v. *Littlewoods Mail Order Stores Ltd* (1982).

A pursuer can, ordinarily, proceed on the basis of either measure. These are not the only available measures of loss and a court is not confined to making an award based on one of these measures, see *Ruxley Electronics and Construction Ltd* v. *Forsyth* (1995). It may be prudent, where possible, to proceed on the basis of both measures as alternatives. The proper measure of damages may be determined by checking one measure against the other, see *Prudential Assurance Co. Ltd* v. *James Grant & Co. (West) Ltd* (1982).

The law in relation to this matter was clarified in England in the case of *Ruxley Electronics and Construction Ltd* (1995). The House of Lords held that in assessing damages for breach of contract for defective building works, should the court decide that the cost of reinstatement would be out of all proportion to the benefit to be obtained to the innocent party by reinstatement, the innocent party's claim would be restricted to the difference in value between the building in the condition contracted for and the building in its actual condition. Whether or not the innocent party actually intends to reinstate will be relevant in determining if it is reasonable to insist upon reinstatement.

The position in Scotland was more recently clarified in *McLaren Murdoch & Hamilton Ltd* v. *Abercromby Motor Group Ltd* (2002). Lord Drummond Young generally accepted the principles set out in *Ruxley* that ordinarily a party is entitled to claim the cost of making works conform to contract. He also set out exceptions to that rule. The first, as with *Ruxley*, is where the cost involved is manifestly disproportionate to any benefit that will be obtained from it. The second exception is where the other party leads evidence to show a significant disproportion between cost and benefit. In the latter situation the court considered that the balance between cost and benefit should not be weighed too finely.

It should be borne in mind that certain contracts have detailed mechanisms for assessing the sum due by one party to the other on termination, see, for example, clause 8 of the SBC. In part, at least, this deals with damages arising out of the termination. Termination is considered above in Chapter 9.

Finally, it must always be borne in mind that only such losses as are consequent on the breach may be recovered. An example of this can be seen in the case of *British Westinghouse Electrical & Manufacturing Co. Ltd* v. *Underground Electric Railways Co. of London Ltd* (1912).

## 10.5 Finance charges

It has long been judicially recognised that, in the ordinary course of things, when contractors require capital to finance a contract they either borrow the capital and pay for the privilege, or use their own capital and, as a consequence, lose the interest which they would otherwise have earned. See, for example, *F G Minter Ltd* v. *Welsh Health Technical Services Organisation* (1980). Similarly, it has been judicially recognised that, in the construction industry, delay in payment to contractors might naturally result in them being short of working capital, thus causing them to incur finance charges. See, for example, *Ogilvie Builders Ltd* v. *City of Glasgow District Council* (1995). Whether or not such finance charges are recoverable by contractors has been the subject of considerable judicial discussion over the years but it is now well settled, both in Scotland and England, that finance charges are recoverable in certain defined circumstances.

Firstly, finance charges are recoverable as direct loss and/or expense under clauses 4.23 to 4.26 of the SBC, but only if the requirements of that clause are satisfied. See *Ogilvie Builders Ltd*, following *F G Minter Ltd* and *Rees & Kirby Ltd* v. *Swansea City Council* (1985). Clauses 4.23 to 4.26 of the SBC are considered above in Chapter 8.

Secondly, finance charges are recoverable as damages in a case based on breach of contract. The words 'direct loss and/or expense' are to be given the same meaning in a case of breach of contract as they would be given in a case for payment under contract, see *Ogilvie Builders Ltd*. Recovery by way of a claim based upon breach of contract (at least until the decision in *Ogilvie Builders Ltd*) proved more problematic in Scotland, with claims being unsuccessfully advanced in cases such as *Chanthall Investments Ltd* v. *F G Minter Ltd* (1975). It was stressed in that case, however, that, in each case where this issue arises, it is a question of fact and the particular circumstances as to whether or not the loss in question was within the contemplation of the parties. This approach was approved by the Inner House of the Court of Session in *Margrie Holdings Ltd* v. *City of Edinburgh District Council* (1994). This approaches recovery by way of the second branch of the rule in *Hadley* v. *Baxendale* (1854), which is considered above in section 10.4.2. That part of the rule permits the recovery of such losses as may reasonably have been supposed to have been in the contemplation of both parties, at the time the contract was entered into, as the probable result of a breach of it. This falls to be contrasted with the first branch of the rule, namely, that where two parties have entered into a contract and there has been a breach of contract by one of the parties, the damages to which the innocent party is entitled should be such as may fairly and reasonably be considered as arising naturally from the breach.

In *Ogilvie Builders Ltd*, Lord Abernethy stated that he did not read any of the Scottish cases cited to him as indicating any general proposition that claims for finance charges, if recoverable at all, could only be recoverable under the second branch of the rule in *Hadley* v. *Baxendale*. He held that that a claim for finance charges under the first branch was relevant as a matter of law. In Scotland, claims advanced under the second branch of the rule have been held to be relevant as a matter of law, see *Caledonian Property Group Ltd* v. *Queensferry Property Group Ltd* (1992). What *Ogilvie Builders Ltd* recognised was the commercial reality that extra finance charges could arise 'naturally' from a breach of contract in the construction industry.

## 10.6 Interest

### 10.6.1 Common law

Late payment of sums admittedly due is commonplace in the construction industry. One way in which this can be addressed is by way of interest. The general rule in Scotland is that, unless a contract provides otherwise, interest will only be awarded from a date prior to the serving of a writ if the money has been wrongfully withheld. That has been the position in Scotland for some considerable time and was enunciated by Lord Atkin in *Kolbin & Sons* v. *Kinnear & Co.* (1931). His Lordship stated that:

> '[I]t seems to be established that, by Scots Law, a pursuer may recover interest by way of damages where he is deprived of an interest-bearing security or a profit-producing chattel, but otherwise, speaking generally, he will only recover interest, apart from contract, by virtue of a principal sum having been wrongfully withheld and not paid on the day where it ought to have been paid.'

The observations of Lord Atkin were accepted in *F W Green & Co.* v. *Brown & Gracie Ltd* (1960) as setting out the broad principle. Whilst a number of cases have dealt with the issue of interest, none of them has ever precisely said what is meant by 'wrongfully withheld'. Various views have been expressed as to its meaning, including failure to pay following the issuing of a certificate, 'negligent' under-certification and client interference in the certification process. The law of Scotland in relation to the entitlement to interest was commented upon by the Inner House of the Court of Session in *Elliott* v. *Combustion Engineering Ltd* (1998).

Whilst a decision of the Inner House of the Court of Session on this topic is welcome, it must be said that the opinion of the court in *Elliott* does not, in reality, answer many of the questions that have been posed in this field over the years. The difficulty with the decision is that, perhaps understandably, 'wrongful withholding' is not directly defined. The court's conclusion was that modern authority indicated that, in general, interest would run on contractual debts from judicial demand (that is service of a writ), and that while there might be qualifications or exceptions to the general rule, the circumstances of *Elliott* did not fall within any such qualification or exception.

Unfortunately, the extent of the qualifications or exceptions to the general rule is not fully set out in *Elliott*. It must, however, be recognised that this was not necessary to resolve the problem then before the court. In relation to the decision in *Elliott*, it is also pertinent to observe that it flowed from an arbitration in which the power of the arbiter was to award interest if the claimant was entitled to it. That is, as the court observed, if the claimant had a right to it by the application to the circumstances of the relevant law. In *Elliott*, the arbiter did not have a power to award interest from such date and at such rates as he saw fit. Such a power in relation to interest is found in clause 9.5 of the SBC, which incorporates article 16.5 of the Scottish Arbitration Code 1999 ('the Code'). Such a clause is necessary as, at common law, an arbiter in Scotland does not have power to award interest from a date prior to that of his award. For so long as arbitration remains a forum for the resolution of construction disputes and the Scots common law is unamended by legislation, the incorporation of provisions such as article 16.5 of the Code will, in fact, go a long way to removing the uncertainty that remains after the decision in *Elliott*.

### 10.6.2 The Late Payment of Commercial Debts (Interest) Act 1998

It is interesting to note that the Court of Session in *Elliott* stated that it was a matter of concern that in modern commercial contexts the law did not, in general, allow for interest to run on debts from a date earlier than judicial demand (that is the date of service of a writ) and that reform of the law on interest on debts was a matter for government. At or about the time of the decision in *Elliott*, this was a subject upon which the government had been consulting and that process resulted in the enactment of the Late Payment of Commercial Debts (Interest) Act 1998, which came into force on 1 November 1998.

The Late Payment of Commercial Debts (Interest) Act 1998 ('the 1998 Act') was introduced with a view to encouraging purchasers to pay on time and to compensate suppliers where late payment persisted. The right to claim interest is to compensate suppliers for not being able to make use of the money owed to them and to cover the cost of increased borrowing resulting from late payment. The 1998 Act provides suppliers with a statutory right to interest on late payments. The rate of interest currently prescribed is 8 per cent over the base rate of the Bank of England. The 1998 Act operates by implying a term into contracts to which it applies to the extent that any qualifying debt carries interest at the prescribed rate. A 'qualifying debt' is simply one where an obligation to make payment of the contract price arises under a contract to which the 1998 Act applies, namely, a contract for the supply of goods and/or services where both the purchaser and supplier are acting in the course of a business. The interest to which the supplier is entitled is simple interest.

All businesses and United Kingdom Public Authorities have the right to claim interest at the statutory rate against all other businesses and United Kingdom Public Authorities. A 'United Kingdom Public Authority' is defined at length in the commencement order for the 1998 Act but, in general, it means any emanation of the State.

A supplier is free to decide whether or not to claim interest. The statutory right is not compulsory. The right to claim interest arises when a payment is late. A payment is late when it is not made by the 'relevant day'. The relevant day is the date agreed for payment or, in the event that no such date has been agreed, the last day of the period of 30 days beginning with the later of the day of the supply/performance or the date of notice to the purchaser of the amount of the debt – in practice, the invoice date.

Different rules exist where the contract requires advance payment. These are dealt with in s.11 of the 1998 Act. The principle is that the 1998 Act does not give a right to claim interest unless and until at least some of the goods have been delivered or part of the service performed. In essence, the section 11 provisions allow for the right to claim interest 30 days after delivery/performance.

Once the payment is late, interest runs at the prescribed rate from the day after the relevant day until the principal sum is extinguished by payment. Unless the supplier accepts a payment on other terms, any payment received goes first to extinguish or reduce the accrued interest. A claim for interest is made by the supplier informing the purchaser, once the payment is late, that they are claiming interest. Notification can be in any fashion but it would appear prudent to make such a claim in writing. A claim for interest need not be made immediately. The ordinary rules of prescription will apply. These are considered below in Chapter 9.

It is, of course, common to find standard terms and conditions providing for interest to run on late payment. In recognition of that, the 1998 Act provides that, where arrangements have already been made, the statutory right to interest will not apply. To prevent purchasers abusing their right to agree arrangements with a supplier, any contractual remedy must be what is termed a 'substantial remedy'. This term is defined by s.9 of the 1998 Act. A remedy for late payment is 'substantial' if it is sufficient to compensate the supplier for the cost of late payment or to deter late payment, and it is fair and reasonable to allow the remedy to oust or vary the statutory interest that would otherwise apply.

In determining whether or not a remedy satisfies the fair and reasonable test, regard is to be had to the benefits of commercial certainty; the relative strength of bargaining power between the parties; whether the term was imposed by one party to the detriment of the other; and whether the supplier received an inducement for agreeing to the term. If the contractual remedy is not a substantial remedy, it is void.

The scope of the 1998 Act was extended by the introduction of the Late Payment of Commercial Debts (Scotland) Regulations 2002 ('the 2002 Regulations').

The 2002 Regulations introduce a right to a fixed sum by way of compensation for the costs suffered by suppliers arising from late payment. This fixed sum is based on the size of the debt. The 2002 Regulations also provide that a representative body may bring proceedings on behalf of small and medium sized enterprises in the Court of Session where standard terms used by the purchaser include a term varying or excluding the statutory interest in relation to contracts to which the 1998 Act applies. 'Small and medium sized enterprises' and 'representative body' are defined in the Regulations.

### 10.6.3 Interest under the SBC

The entitlement to interest in respect of Interim Certificates is dealt with by clause 4.13.6 of the SBC. If the Employer fails properly to pay the amount, or any part thereof, due to the Contractor under the conditions by the final date for its payment, the Employer is obliged to pay to the Contractor, in addition to the amount not properly paid, simple interest thereon for the period until such payment is made. Payment of such simple interest is treated as a debt due to the Contractor by the Employer.

The rate of interest payable is 5 per cent over the base rate of the Bank of England current at the date the payment by the Employer became overdue. This rate should be contrasted with the statutory rate provided for by the 1998 Act. It is conceivable that it could be argued that it is not a substantial remedy in the context of s.9 of the 1998 Act.

Clause 4.15.6 makes similar provisions in respect of sums due under a Final Certificate, whether those sums are due to the Employer or the Contractor. In each case, any payment of simple interest under the clause in question shall not, in any circumstances, be construed as a waiver by either party of their right to proper payment of the principal amount due.

### 10.6.4 Interest on damages

In terms of the Interest on Damages (Scotland) Act 1958, as amended by the Interest on Damages (Scotland) Act 1971, where a court grants a decree for payment by any party of a sum of money as damages, the court's order may include provision for payment by that party of interest on the whole or any part of the amount of damages for the whole, or any part, of any period between the date when the right of action arose and the date of the court's order. The court also has a discretion as to the rate or rates at which such interest is to be paid. The mere fact that a right of action arose on a particular date prior to decree does not, of itself, justify an award of interest from that date, see *James Buchanan & Co. Ltd* v. *Stewart Cameron (Drymen) Ltd* (1973).

In *MacRae* v. *Reed and Malik Ltd* (1961) the Inner House of the Court of Session stated that the discretion conferred upon the court by the 1958 Act must be exercised on a selective and discriminating basis and that the exercise of that discretion was open to review on the question as to whether the circumstances of the case warranted the course taken. They also held that interest from a date earlier than the date of decree could be allowed only on damages awarded for loss suffered before the date of decree and where such loss could be definitely ascertained.

## 10.7 Interdict

Where it can be demonstrated by a party that a legal wrong is continuing or that they are reasonably apprehensive that such a wrong will be committed, they are entitled to seek interdict against the wrong, see *Hay's Trustees* v. *Young* (1877). If the wrong has been completed, and it cannot be contended that there is a likelihood of it recurring, interdict will not be granted, see *Earl of Crawford* v. *Paton* (1911).

Both permanent and interim interdict can be granted in either the Court of Session or the Sheriff Court. In practice, few actions in which interdict is sought proceed beyond the interim interdict stage. The grant or refusal of interim interdict is often determinative of the issue between the parties.

Assuming the pursuer can satisfy the court that they have title and interest to bring the action and that they are confronted by, or threatened with, a wrong on the part of the defender, interim interdict will still only be granted if the balance of convenience favours the pursuer. To meet this test, the pursuer must demonstrate a cogent need for interim interdict, see *Deane* v. *Lothian Regional Council* (1986).

Although a detailed examination of the law of interdict is beyond the scope of this book, in the context of building contracts its availability as a remedy should not be overlooked. The remedy is available should there be a continuing, or reasonably anticipated, breach of contract.

## 10.8 Withholding payment

### 10.8.1 General

Having examined the issue of payment in Chapter 8, it is appropriate to consider the remedies that are open to a party under a building contract who is, on the face of it, obliged to make payment, but has reasons for not doing so. In Scotland, there exist two distinct and separate remedies, namely, retention and compensation. These are frequently confused. The term 'set-off' is often used in place of compensation. It is also to be found in the 1996 Act, see s.110(2)(b). Here, we will consider retention and compensation in the context of payment obligations. It should, however, be noted that retention applies not only to obligations to pay but also to all other obligations incumbent upon a party under a contract. The wider application of retention is considered below in section 10.9.1. Finally, we will consider the statutory right of withholding payment as contained within s.111 of the 1996 Act.

### 10.8.2 Retention

The principle of retention is, perhaps, best illustrated by the opinion of Lord Shand in *Macbride* v. *Hamilton* (1875) in which he stated:

'[I]n cases of mutual contract a party in defence is entitled to plead and maintain claims in reduction or extinction of a sum due under his obligation where such claims arise from the failure of the pursuer to fulfil his part of the contract.'

For retention to operate, both claims must arise from the one contract. Retention, when considered in the context of withholding payment, should not be confused with compensation. Retention is, in effect, a form of security, whereas compensation extinguishes a debt, in whole or in part.

Retention has long since been a favoured remedy in building contract disputes, see, for example, *Johnston* v. *Robertson* (1861). In that case, the employers were entitled to plead in defence a claim for liquidated damages for non-completion against the contractors' claim for the balance of the contract price and payment for extra works.

In Scotland, there was at one time authority which suggested that the general rule in respect of retention may not apply to the case of a building contract which contained provision for payment by instalments, it being doubted whether the employer had any right to withhold payment of an instalment by virtue of a claim against the contractor, see *Field & Allan* v. *Gordon* (1872). That position has, however, been accepted to be incorrect. Unless it is shown in clear and unequivocal words that the parties had agreed in the contract that the common law right of retention was to be excluded, that right would be available in respect of breaches of contract, see *Redpath Dorman Long Ltd* v. *Cummins Engine Co. Ltd* (1981). Retention is considered further in section 10.9.1.

### 10.8.3 Compensation

The essence of compensation is that sums are due at the same time by parties to each other. Where each party owes the other a sum of money, compensation can operate to extinguish, or partly extinguish, the debts. Certain prerequisites must be satisfied. Firstly, the debts must be due at the same time. A debt that is due at a future date cannot be set against one that is presently due, see *Paul & Thain* v. *Royal Bank* (1869). Secondly, each debt must be what is termed 'liquid'. A liquid debt is one that is for a readily ascertainable amount and is not disputed. A claim for damages is not a liquid debt, see *National Exchange Co.* v. *Drew* (1855). There must also be what is termed *concursus debiti et crediti*, which is that each party must owe money and be owed money in the same capacity. An example of this is the case of *Stuart* v. *Stuart* (1869) in which it was held that the defender, as an individual, could not plead in compensation certain alleged counterclaims competent to him as his father's executor.

In Scotland, there has been legislation governing compensation for over 400 years, see the Compensation Act 1592.

### 10.8.4 Withholding payment under the 1996 Act

In construction contracts governed by the 1996 Act (see Chapter 1) the circumstances in which payment under the contract may be withheld are clearly defined. A party to a construction contract may not withhold payment after the final date for payment of a sum due under the contract unless they have given an effective notice of intention to withhold payment.

To be effective, such a notice must specify the amount proposed to be withheld and the ground for withholding payment. If there is more than one ground, each ground and the amount to be withheld in relation to it must be specified. That notice must be given not later than the prescribed period before the final date for payment. Parties are free to agree what that prescribed period is to be, but if they do not, the Scheme for Construction Contracts applies.

Paragraph 10 of Part II of the Schedule to the Scheme provides that any notice of intention to withhold payment shall be given not later than seven days before the final date for payment under the contract. The notice of intention to withhold payment can form part of the notice that is required under s.110(2) of the 1996 Act, being the notice which specifies the amount of the payment made or proposed to be made, and the basis upon which that amount is calculated.

An effective notice in terms of s.111 is required to be in writing and is required to be sent in response to an application for payment. It is not sufficient to refer to an earlier communication which states that payment would be withheld, whether or not it was subsequently confirmed in an oral communication, see *Strathmore Building Services* v. *Greig* (2000). Nor is it possible to withhold against sums found due under an adjudicator's decision. Any notice purporting to do so will be invalid, see *Construction Centre Group* v. *Highland Council* (2002).

There does remain an obligation on the party seeking payment to prove that the sum claimed is in fact due, see *S L Timber Systems Ltd* v. *Carillion Construction Ltd* (2001). That obligation will, however, be satisfied where a certificate is issued in accordance with the contract identifying a sum being due for payment, see *Clark Contracts Ltd* v. *The Burrell Co. (Construction Management) Ltd* (2003) and *Rupert Morgan Building Services* v. *David and Harriet Jervis* (2004).

### 10.8.5 Withholding under the SBC

Clause 4.13.4 of the SBC contains provisions consistent with the 1996 Act regarding the giving of a notice of withholding in relation to a sum which is due under an Interim Certificate. Not later than five days before the final date for payment of an amount due under an Interim Certificate, the Employer may give a written notice to the Contractor which specifies any amount proposed to be withheld and/or deducted from the due amount. The notice must also specify the ground or grounds for such withholding and/or deduction and the amount of withholding and/or deduction attributable to each ground. A similar provision exists in relation to final certificates under the SBC, namely, clause 4.15.4.

## 10.9  Suspending performance

### 10.9.1  General

The principle of retention, considered above in section 10.8.2 in the context of withholding payment, has a wider application. That wider application emanates from what is known as the mutuality principle. It is perhaps best shown in the opinion of Lord Benholme in the building contract case of *Johnston* v. *Robertson* (1861). Lord Benholme stated that:

> 'One party to a mutual contract, in which there are mutual stipulations, cannot insist on having his claim under the contract satisfied unless he is prepared to satisfy the corresponding and contemporaneous claim of the other party to the contract.'

Accordingly, where the common law right of retention is open to a party, such as a contractor, they are entitled to suspend performance when confronted by an employer who refuses to pay. It should be noted that it is possible to contract out of the common law right of retention, see *Redpath Dorman Long Ltd* v. *Cummins Engine Co. Ltd* (1981). That can only be achieved by the use of clear and unequivocal words in the parties' contract.

### 10.9.2  Suspension of performance under the 1996 Act

The 1996 Act provides a right to suspend performance for non-payment where a sum due under a construction contract is not paid in full by the final date for payment and no effective notice to withhold payment has been given. In those circumstances, the person to whom the sum is due is entitled to suspend performance of their obligations under the contract to the party by whom payment ought to have been made. This right is without prejudice to any other right or remedy open to the party entitled to payment. This would allow them to raise separate proceedings for payment, should they so wish. The right to suspend performance does not deprive the entitled party of any other rights competent to them. The right to suspend performance under the 1996 Act only arises in the event of non-payment.

The right may not be exercised without first giving to the party in default at least seven days' notice of intention to suspend performance. The notice must state the ground or grounds upon which it is intended to suspend performance. The contract can stipulate that a period in excess of seven days' notice of intention to suspend performance must be given. In practice, employers under a main contract (and main contractors in a sub-contract) will insist upon a greater period of notice. The right to suspend performance ceases when the party in default makes payment in full of the amount due. Any period of suspension of performance is disregarded in computing the time taken by the party to complete the works. Not only does this apply to the party exercising the right to suspend, but also to any affected third party.

### 10.9.3 Suspension under the SBC

The Contractor's statutory right of suspension is provided for by clause 4.14 of the SBC. A written notice of intention to suspend must be given to the Employer, with a copy to the Architect. If the failure to pay continues for seven days after that notice is given, the Contractor may suspend performance of their obligations under the contract to the Employer until payment in full occurs. A suspension under clause 4.14 is not a default by the Contractor under clause 8.4.1, nor is it a failure to proceed regularly and diligently with the Works, another contractor default, under clause 8.4.2.

By virtue of clause 2.29.5 of the SBC, a delay arising from a suspension by the Contractor of the performance of their obligations under the contract pursuant to clause 4.14 is a relevant event which may entitle the Contractor to an extension of time, see Chapter 6 above. Further, such a suspension is also a matter materially affecting the regular progress of the Works under clause 4.24.3 which may entitle the Contractor to recover direct loss and/or expense, considered above in Chapter 8.

## 10.10 Delictual claims

### 10.10.1 General

One party can owe a duty to another in the absence of a contractual relationship. In the context of building contracts, for example, a sub-contractor owes certain duties to the employer, see *British Telecommunications plc* v. *James Thomson & Sons (Engineers) Ltd* (1999).

Liability in delict in construction projects is most likely to arise under the law of negligence or the law of nuisance, although claims may also arise in relation to breach of statutory duty.

### 10.10.2 Losses recoverable

Broadly speaking, in order to establish a claim in negligence the pursuer must show that:

- the defender owed the pursuer a duty of care in respect of the type of loss in question;
- this duty was breached;
- the breach of duty caused the pursuer's loss; and
- the loss is not too remote.

It should be noted that the precise rules on remoteness of damage differ between claims based on breach of contract and those based on delict, see *Koufos* v. *C Czarnikow Ltd* (1967). In delict, the losses recoverable are those reasonably foreseeable to the defender at the time of the negligent act, see *Allan* v. *Barclay* (1864). In breach of contract cases, on the other hand, the losses recoverable are those foreseeable at the time the contract is entered into, see section 10.4.2 above. The reasoning behind this distinction is that in a contract there is the opportunity for one party to obtain protection against a particular type of potential loss by directing the other party's attention to it before the contract is made. In cases arising out of delict there is no such opportunity.

### 10.10.3 Economic loss

As a general rule, the losses claimed in delict must not be too remote. This means that damages for personal injury, death and loss of or physical damage to property (and economic loss flowing from such loss of or physical damage to property) arising from a breach of duty would normally be recoverable. However, the right to recover economic loss in the absence of physical damage is a particularly problematic area. A detailed examination of the issue is beyond the scope of this book, but the following is a brief overview.

A convenient starting point, which illustrates the type of situation in which matters of this nature arise, is the decision of the House of Lords in the Scottish case of *Junior Books Ltd* v. *The Veitchi Co. Ltd* (1982). In this case the pursuers owned a factory. They entered into a contract with builders for, amongst other things, the laying of flooring in the factory's production area. The builders sub-contracted this work to the defenders, who were specialist flooring contractors. The pursuers subsequently raised an action against the defenders, seeking damages for loss allegedly sustained as a result of their negligent workmanship. This loss included the cost of replacing the floor surface, allegedly defectively laid; storing goods and moving machinery during the period of replacement; paying wages to employees unable to work during this period; and fixed overheads which would produce no return during this time.

The pursuers also claimed for loss of profit sustained by the temporary closure of the business. They argued that the defenders, as specialists, knew what products were required; were alone responsible for the composition and construction of the flooring; must have known that the pursuers had relied upon their skill and experience; and must be taken to have known that if they did the work negligently, the pursuers would suffer economic loss in requiring to expend money to remedy the resulting defects. The pursuers did not argue that actual or prospective danger to persons or property arose from the state of the flooring. If they had done so there would have been a duty of care under the principles laid down by *Donoghue* v. *Stevenson* (1932).

The defenders argued that the case was irrelevant in law. They contended that the law did not make them liable in delict for the cost of replacing the floor or for economic or financial loss consequent upon that replacement. They argued that while they were under a duty of care to prevent harm being done to property or persons by their faulty work (in accordance with *Donoghue*), they had no duty of care to avoid such faults being present in the work itself. They argued that for the court to hold otherwise would extend the duty of care owed by manufacturers and others far beyond the limits to which the courts had previously extended them; and that a manufacturer's duty not to make a defective product set a standard of care which was much less easily ascertained than that for a duty not to make a dangerous product.

The Inner House of the Court of Session and the House of Lords rejected that argument. They held that there was sufficient proximity between the parties so as to give rise to the relevant duty of care relied on by the pursuers. Further, they held that there were no considerations in this particular case to negate, restrict or limit that duty of care. Pure economic loss was the sort of loss which the defenders, standing in the relationship to the pursuers which they did, ought reasonably to have anticipated as likely to occur if their workmanship was faulty.

The law in England in relation to economic loss now rests with the decision of the House of Lords in *Murphy* v. *Brentwood District Council* (1991), in which it was held that the defendants, who had negligently approved plans that contained erroneous calculations submitted by the builders constructing the plaintiff's house, owed no duty of care to the plaintiffs. The consequence of the plans being incorrect was that the plaintiff, upon selling the house, was unable to obtain the full market value. In this case it was clear, according to the court, that there was no proximity between the plaintiff and the defendants. In essence it could not be said that the defendants had assumed any responsibility to the plaintiff in respect of the plans which they approved.

Further policy considerations are evident in their lordships' decision, namely the 'floodgates' argument and the fear that had a duty been imposed the court would have introduced a transmissible warranty of quality into property transactions which was a legislative matter for Parliament. A further consequence of the decision in *Murphy* was the restriction of *Junior Books Ltd* to its own special facts, mirroring the court's reluctance in previous cases, such as *D & F Estates Ltd* v. *Church Commissioners for England* (1989), to apply the decision in *Junior Books Ltd*.

It was held in *Murphy*, which was also followed in the subsequent case of *Department of the Environment* v. *Thomas Bates & Son* (1990), that foreseeability of harm based on *Donoghue* principles will not of itself generally be sufficient to impose a duty of care for economic loss. Rather, the courts now have to determine whether there was sufficient proximity between the parties to justify the imposition of a duty of care and also whether it is fair, just and reasonable to impose a duty, see *Caparo Industries plc* v. *Dickman* (1990). It is not, however, necessary to demonstrate that the imposition of a duty of care is 'fair, just and reasonable' where it is established that there is an assumption of responsibility by one party combined with reliance by the other, see *Henderson* v. *Merrett Syndicates Ltd* (1995). The tests set out in *Caparo* and *Henderson* have been followed by the Scottish courts, see, for example, *The Governor and Company of the Bank of Scotland* v. *Fuller Peiser* (2002) and *Royal Bank of Scotland plc* v. *Bannerman Johnstone MacLay* (2005).

The law in England in relation to economic loss was reviewed by the House of Lords in *White and Another* v. *Jones and Others* (1995). Whilst the case addresses the issue of whether a solicitor, who negligently drew up a will, owed a duty of care to disappointed prospective beneficiaries, it is submitted that the principles enunciated by the court are of general application. The court expounded the view that proximity was to be assessed by considering whether it could be said that the party causing the loss assumed responsibility in whatever form to the party suffering that loss. The court also reaffirmed their commitment to allowing recovery by analogous extension only. That is, the court will look to determine whether recovery has been permitted in similar situations before allowing recovery in the case under consideration. The court in *White and Another* reiterated their opposition to any carte blanche extension of the law in relation to economic loss. In essence the law will only be allowed to develop by increment rather than by quantum leap.

Notwithstanding the above, it must be borne in mind that *Junior Books Ltd*, being a House of Lords decision in a Scottish case, is still binding upon Scottish courts. It has not been overruled by any of the subsequent House of Lords decisions in English cases. Instead, its applicability has been stated to be confined only to the very limited circumstances which pertained to the facts of that case. However, there have been several decisions of the Scottish courts which have at least indicated that, while the House of Lords decisions in *Murphy* and *D & F Estates Ltd* will be of very high persuasive authority to a Scottish court, it is perhaps rather premature to assume that such cases will be followed unquestioningly by Scottish courts or that, as some commentators would suggest, *Junior Books Ltd* is dead and buried, see *Parkhead Housing Association Ltd* v. *Phoenix Preservation Ltd* (1990) and *Scott Lithgow Ltd* v. *GEC Electrical Projects Ltd* (1992).

To conclude this brief overview of economic loss, it is perhaps worth considering one of the major policy restrictions often cited as the principle reason for imposing restrictions on the recovery of economic loss, namely the 'floodgates' argument. The floodgates argument should not be misunderstood as being a reflection of the courts' unwillingness to countenance a multitude of claims against one party. Rather the floodgates argument is the courts' unwillingness to allow liability in an indeterminate amount for an indeterminate time to an indeterminate class. The courts' formulation of the test of proximity will, inevitably, filter out those claims where liability is indeterminate.

# Chapter 11
# Sub-contractors and Suppliers

## 11.1 Introduction

On any large construction project it is not uncommon for the majority of the works to be performed by sub-contractors. Indeed it is not unheard of for all the works to be sub-contracted by the main contractor. In turn many sub-contractors will themselves engage sub-sub-contractors. Shortly prior to the publication of this Second Edition, the SBCC issued its Standard Building Sub-Contract, including a separate version with Contractor's Design. The principles regarding the formation of a building contract, considered in Chapter 3, apply equally to sub-contracts. Similarly, many of the issues considered in Chapters 4 and 5 will apply in a sub-contract situation. This chapter will deal with the types of sub-contractor and the relationship between employer, main contractor and sub-contractor, and finally will outline some of the issues which frequently arise in practice.

## 11.2 Nominated and domestic sub-contractors

Until very recently, under the umbrella of the JCT forms of main contract, sub-contractors were typically either domestic or nominated. A nominated sub-contractor would submit his quotation to the architect or quantity surveyor and in turn be nominated on behalf of the employer if successful. A domestic sub-contractor is usually invited by the main contractor to tender competitively. Historically main contractors have always exhibited a preference for domestic sub-contracts. The SBCC published the Sub-Contract DOM/A/Scot as the standard form for domestic sub-contracts in Scotland where the main contract was governed by JCT 98.

Although JCT and SBCC have issued a new suite of sub-contracts, for the next few years we will continue to see the use of the DOM/A/Scot and we will also continue to see references to nominated sub-contractors. For that reason it is still necessary and appropriate to examine the distinction between the two forms of sub-contractor. Under the Standard Building Contract (SBC) and other contracts forming the latest JCT/SBCC suite, however, there exists no reference to either nominated or named sub-contractors.

What are the important differences between nominated and domestic sub-contracts? In the first place, an important difference exists between the respective payment provisions. Under clause 35.13.1.1 of JCT 98 the architect was obliged to identify that portion of the sum due under any Interim Certificate which related to work carried out by Nominated Sub-Contractors. Thereafter, the Architect was required to inform each Nominated Sub-Contractor of the amount of any interim or final payment allocated to their work. Prior to any further certification in favour of the Contractor, the Contractor was obliged to provide the Architect with reasonable proof of payment to the Nominated Sub-Contractor. No equivalent provisions existed under JCT 98 in respect of payments to domestic sub-contractors.

In certain circumstances, it has been held possible for an aggrieved sub-contractor to recover damages from the employer in respect of a failure to observe this provision which resulted in loss to the sub-contractor, see *Pointer Ltd* v. *Inverclyde DC* (1990). Prior to the implementation of s.113 of the 1996 Act, which outlaws certain forms of 'pay when paid' clauses, domestic sub-contractors had little scope for identifying, with any degree of precision, what sums, if any, had been paid by an employer to a main contractor in respect of the sub-contract works. Even with the assistance of the recovery of documents through the courts, the position could often remain blurred, particularly when a large proportion of the main contract works had been carried out by the main contractor rather than by sub-contractors.

The second important difference between nominated and domestic sub-contracts was the ability of the Nominated Sub-Contractor under JCT 98 to secure payment direct from the Employer. In the absence of an express term in the main contract enabling an employer to pay a sub-contractor direct, the employer should not do so as his obligation to pay the main contractor for the sub-contract works is not satisfied by making payment to the sub-contractor.

Any direct payment provision should not only confer a right on the employer to make a direct payment to a sub-contractor in certain defined circumstances, but must also allow the employer to deduct an equivalent amount from sums otherwise due to the main contractor. Clause 35.13.5 of JCT 98 provided that where the Contractor had failed to provide reasonable proof of payment to a Nominated Sub-Contractor of the amount included in an Interim Certificate, the Architect should issue a certificate to that effect stating the amount in respect of which the Contractor had failed to provide proof; the amount of any future payment otherwise due to the Contractor was reduced by the amount due to Nominated Sub-Contractors which the Contractor had failed to pay; and the Employer made payment of the relevant amounts direct to the Nominated Sub-Contractors concerned. The obligation on the part of the Employer to make direct payment only arose if the Employer had entered into the direct agreement, NSC/W/Scot, with the Nominated Sub-Contractor.

No direct payment could be made if, at the date when the deduction and payment to the Nominated Sub-Contractor would otherwise be made, the Contractor had become bankrupt, had become 'apparently insolvent' or had had a winding-up order made. This left open the question whether the direct payment provisions could be operated upon the appointment of an administrator or receiver to the Contractor.

JCT 98 did allow direct payment to domestic sub-contractors in certain circumstances. Clause 27.5.2.2 (as amended by the Scottish Supplement) provided that in the event of determination of the main contractor's employment, and except where the determination occurred due to an insolvency event of the type specified in clause 27.3.2 (bankruptcy, winding up, receivership, etc. of the Contractor), the Employer was entitled to make direct payments to sub-contractors and suppliers (whether nominated or not). It should be noted that, in contrast to the mechanism contained in clause 35.13, the employer had a discretion, not an obligation, under clause 27.5.2.2 to make a direct payment. An equivalent provision does not appear in the SBC.

Nomination had the advantage to employers of allowing them to specify who actually performed the relevant sub-contract works. This might be important in the case of specialist sub-contract works.

Given that much, if not all, of the work performed by Nominated Sub-Contractors was of a specialist nature, what was the liability of the Contractor to the Employer in the event of default by the Nominated Sub-Contractor? Where there was delay on the part of the Nominated Sub-Contractor (or nominated supplier), which the main contractor had taken reasonable steps to reduce, clause 25.4.7 of JCT 98 provided that this was a relevant event for the purposes of the Contractor securing an extension of time.

Clause 35.21 of JCT 98 provided that the Contractor had no liability to the Employer in four specified situations:

- for the design of any Nominated Sub-Contract works insofar as they were designed by the Nominated Sub-Contractor;
- for the selection of the kinds of materials and goods which had been selected by the Nominated Sub-Contractor;
- for the satisfaction of any performance specification or requirement insofar as that was included in the nominated sub-contract works;
- for the provision of information by the Nominated Sub-Contractor in reasonable time in order that the Architect could comply with the relevant provisions of the main contract.

Mention should also be made of 'named' sub-contractors. Clause 3.8 of the SBC provides that, in certain circumstances, work must be carried out by one of a number of persons named in a list which is either in or annexed to the Contract Bills. The work in question will have been priced by the main contractor, and the selection of the person to carry out the work is at the sole discretion of the main contractor. This procedure has the benefit for the employer that certain specialist work will be carried out by suitably experienced sub-contractors, whilst not involving the employer with the complications that can be associated with nomination.

Difficulties have arisen, and will continue to arise, where, for commercial considerations, employers agree to pay sub-contractors direct. An illustration of the issues that can arise is the Extra Division decision of *Brican Fabrications Ltd* v. *Merchant City Developments Ltd* (2003). In this case, Merchant City, as Employer, agreed to pay Brican direct (as sub-contractor) on account of what turned out to be the latter's well grounded concerns as to the solvency of the main contractor. The sub-contract entered into between the main contractor and Brican provided that the main contractor assented to the direct payment arrangement between Merchant City and Brican. The main contractor thereafter went into liquidation and the parties to the action could not agree whether Merchant City had agreed to pay Brican direct or whether the agreement was that Merchant City would deduct from sums due to the main contractor that portion which the main contractor owed to Brican and pay it direct to Brican, as agent of the main contractor. The Extra Division preferred the former.

## 11.3 *Privity of contract*

### 11.3.1 General

Ordinarily there is no direct contractual relationship between the employer and the sub-contractor, and the individual contracts which make up the contractual chain between sub-contractor and employer are (subject to collateral warranties and to the circumstances described in section 11.3.2 below) enforceable only by the parties to such contracts. This principle is known as privity of contract.

The law would, however, in certain circumstances, permit an employer to sue a supplier direct, should the supplier have given certain assurances or warranties as to, for example, the fitness for purpose of the supplier's product, notwithstanding the fact that the contract for the sale of the product was with the contractor appointed by the employer, see *Shanklin Pier Ltd* v. *Detel Products Ltd* (1951) and *British Workman's and General Assurance Co.* v. *Wilkinson* (1900).

Another exception is where appropriate rights are assigned by a main contractor to a sub-contractor, see *Constant* v. *Kincaid & Co.* (1902). Assignation is considered below in Chapter 12. In the absence of a direct contractual relationship, or an assignation of rights, neither employer nor sub-contractor can sue the other under contract. A practical example of this is that, in the absence of the former direct agreement, NSC/W/Scot, an employer and nominated sub-contractor would not be able to enforce any rights against the other, for example, direct payments (see above).

It should be noted that (if so provided for in the Contract Particulars) clause 7F of the SBC specifically requires any sub-contractor to give a collateral warranty in favour of the Employer. Clause 7E makes similar provision in relation to collateral warranties from a sub-contractor to purchasers, tenants and/or funders.

### 11.3.2 *Jus quaesitum tertio*

The above statement on privity of contract is, however, qualified where a *jus quaesitum tertio* has been created by the contract. The creation of such a right will give a third party (the *'tertius'*) a right to sue under the contract, notwithstanding that he is not a party to it. In order to create the right, the contract must expressly, or by implication, confer a benefit on the *tertius* or a class of persons of which the *tertius* is a member. Unless an intention on the part of the contracting parties to create a *jus quaesitum tertio* in favour of a third party is expressed or can be inferred from the terms of the contract, no such right will be created. See *Scott Lithgow Ltd* v. *GEC Electrical Projects Ltd* (1992) and *Strathford East Kilbride Ltd* v. *HLM Design Ltd* (1997). In relation to third party rights under the SBC, see section 13.5 below.

In England the Courts for a period permitted companies within the same Group to pursue losses in contract notwithstanding the fact that the losses in question were sustained by another connected company. This approach was accepted where the entity sustaining the loss had no direct course of action against the wrongdoer. This was to avoid a 'legal black hole' preventing the loss being recoverable. In *Clark Contracts Ltd* v. *The Burrell Co. (Construction Management) Ltd* (2002) the court held that the existence of the *jus quaesitum tertio* in favour of another group company of the defenders did create a direct course of action, and as such the English authorities could not be relied upon by the defenders in support of a counterclaim for damages in respect of losses allegedly sustained by the defenders' sister company. Lord Drummond Young, in *McLaren Murdoch & Hamilton Ltd* v. *The Abercromby Motor Group Ltd* (2003), stated that the *jus quaesitum tertio* is of limited utility. His Lordship took the view that the decision of the House of Lords in *Alfred McAlpine Construction Ltd* v. *Panatown Ltd (No.1)* (2001), albeit an English case, was wholly consistent with the principles of Scots law and that Scots law should adopt the general rule in that case as described by Lord Clyde. See also section 12.3 below for a more detailed analysis.

### 11.3.3 Delict

Prior to certain case law in the late 1980s, and in particular, *D & F Estates Ltd* v. *Church Commissioners for England* (1989) and *Murphy* v. *Brentwood DC* (1991), it had been understood that an employer could sue a sub-contractor direct under delict and recover economic loss, see *Junior Books Ltd* v. *The Veitchi Co. Ltd* (1982). Collateral warranties emerged as a result of *D & F Estates Ltd* and *Murphy*. (See also section 13.2 below.) Market forces dictated that any perceived vacuum in the law of negligence be filled by the law of contract. Developers, owners and funders of large commercial developments need the ability to sue professional team members and/or specialist sub-contractors.

This branch of the law of negligence has nevertheless continued to develop in both Scotland and England. In *White and Another* v. *Jones and Others* (1995) the House of Lords in an English appeal decided by a majority that a solicitor owed a duty of care to beneficiaries under a will which had been negligently drawn up. In the Scottish case of *Scott Lithgow Ltd* Lord Clyde allowed to proceed to proof a case in which an employer sued a domestic sub-contractor for recovery of economic loss stemming from allegedly defective wiring. He held that nomination was not a necessary factor before a duty of care could arise but it was an important element where it did exist. Where it does exist it obviously serves to point towards the degree of proximity which is required for the employer to succeed. For a further discussion on the law of delict, see section 10.10 above.

It must be fair, just and reasonable for a duty of care to exist. This issue was addressed by the House of Lords in the Scottish case of *British Telecommunications plc* v. *James Thomson & Sons (Engineers) Ltd* (1999). In that case the employer sued a sub-contractor in delict in respect of losses sustained as a consequence of a fire breaking out in the employer's premises for which the employer held the sub-contractor responsible. The sub-contractor had been engaged by the main contractor on the same terms and conditions of contract as those ruling between the employer and the main contractor. The insurance provisions in the main contract made it clear that damage caused in the way suggested by the employer was to be covered by an insurance policy which the employer was bound to take out. In short, the damage in question was one of the specified perils under the main contract. As such it was contended by the sub-contractor that it would not be fair, just or reasonable to impose a duty on them to avoid such damage. Their Lordships, however, attached significant weight to the fact that the insurance arrangements in the main contract afforded any nominated sub-contractor the benefit of a waiver by the relevant insurers of any right of subrogation which they may have against the nominated sub-contractor but no such provision existed for the benefit of domestic sub-contractors. As such the unanimous decision of the court was that it would be fair, just and reasonable to impose a duty of care on the domestic sub-contractors to the employer. See more recently *European and International Investments* v. *McLaren* (2001) and *Tartan American Machinery Corp* v. *Swan & Co.* (2004).

## 11.4 Relationship between main and sub-contracts

It is common for main contractors to attempt to incorporate by reference the terms of the main contract into the sub-contract. This practice of wholesale incorporation is not to be encouraged and frequently leads to disputes between the parties. The degree of incorporation can vary. Many main contractors attempt to incorporate their own programme into the sub-contract, see *Scottish Power plc* v. *Kvaerner Construction (Regions) Ltd* (1998).

The effect of incorporation of main contract terms was considered in *Babcock Rosyth Defence Ltd* v. *Grootcon (UK) Ltd* (1998). In this case the sub-contractor raised an action against the main contractor. The main contract incorporated a modified form of the ICE Conditions of Contract (Fifth Edition). The issue for the court was whether or not clause 66, the arbitration clause, formed part of the sub-contract. The main contractor maintained that the ICE Fifth Edition was incorporated into the sub-contract, subject to the express qualifications made and to its adaptation for practical effectiveness in the sub-contractual relationship. To that extent the main contractor's submissions did not go as far as those made in *Parklea Ltd* v. *W & J R Watson Ltd* (1988). In the latter case the court rejected the contention that the whole provisions of the main contract were to be incorporated *mutatis mutandis* into the sub-contract. In *Babcock Rosyth Defence Ltd* the defenders acknowledged that certain of the main contract provisions would have no place in the sub-contract. The judge, Lord Hamilton, stated:

> 'When parties make reference to a set of conditions designed primarily for use in another contract but do not expressly adapt those conditions to meet the circumstances of their own relationship, it is often difficult to determine with confidence the contractual effect. Where, on the one hand, the circumstances demonstrate a plain common intention to incorporate terms, albeit expressed in language designed primarily for another purpose, the court will, where it is possible to do so without substantially rewriting the parties' bargain, give effect to the parties' plain common intention by incorporating terms subject to appropriate linguistic adaptation . . . Where, on the other hand, the common intention is not plain or there are major difficulties about linguistic adaptation, the result will be otherwise. Even in cases where incorporation subject to linguistic adaptation is possible and appropriate, there may yet remain a question as to the extent to which conditions are so incorporated.'

Lord Hamilton held that the parties had plainly intended that the ICE Fifth Edition should apply to some extent, albeit with appropriate linguistic adaptation. He was not satisfied, however, that it was sufficiently clear that the parties intended to incorporate the arbitration clause into the sub-contract. To avoid ambiguity, therefore, parties should make it clear which particular main contract provisions are to be incorporated into the sub-contract and to what extent.

Similar difficulties were encountered by the Pursuers in *Watson Building Services* v. *Harrison* (2001) when they unsuccessfully contended that the adjudication provisions of the main contract had been incorporated by reference into their sub-contract with the Defenders.

## 11.5 *Main contractor's discount*

It is common for sub-contracts to allow the main contractor a discount on the price of the sub-contract works. Unless the parties to a sub-contract make an express provision which connects the main contractor's ability to deduct discount with prompt payment, the courts are likely to view the discount as being no more than a reduction in the sub-contract price, see *Team Services plc* v. *Kier Management and Design Ltd* (1993).

## 11.6 Suppliers

Contracts of supply or sale are regulated by the Sale of Goods Act 1979, as amended by the Sale and Supply of Goods and Services Act 1994. In terms of s.14 of the 1979 Act as amended by s.1(1) of the 1994 Act, there is an implied term that the goods supplied under a contract of supply or sale are of 'satisfactory quality'. The quality of goods is deemed to include their state and condition and, in appropriate cases, their fitness for all the purposes for which goods of the kind in question are commonly supplied, their appearance and finish, their freedom from minor defects, their safety and their durability.

## 11.7 Retention of title clauses

Suppliers' terms and conditions commonly include a retention of title clause. The object of such a clause is to protect the supplier against the insolvency of its customer by delaying the passing of ownership of the goods in question to the customer until payment has been made. Otherwise, the ownership of the goods will normally transfer upon delivery, by virtue of s.17 of the Sale of Goods Act 1979.

Section 19 of the Sale of Goods Act 1979 permits a seller to retain ownership of goods, notwithstanding delivery to the purchaser, in the event that the parties to the contract expressly provide that change of ownership is to be conditional. The most obvious condition will, of course, be as to payment of the price. Section 19 is a restatement of the position at common law and under the Sale of Goods Act 1893. The period between the mid-1970s and 1990 saw considerable litigation on the subject of retention of title clauses, starting with *Aluminium Industrie Vaassen BV* v. *Romalpa Aluminium Ltd* (1976) and ending with *Armour* v. *Thyssen Edelstahlwerke AG* (1990). In the latter case, the House of Lords held that 'all sums' retention of title clauses were effective in Scotland, as had been the case in England for some time. Prior to the decision by the House of Lords, the Scottish courts had restricted the applicability of retention of title clauses to the extent that they reserved title to the seller of goods in the event that the purchase price for those goods had not been paid. The courts had refused to give effect to retention of title clauses which purported to reserve title to the seller until all sums due by the purchaser to the seller, including sums due in respect of other goods, had been paid.

A retention of title clause will not protect the unpaid supplier in the event of the contract of sale being governed by s.25(1) of the Sale of Goods Act 1979, that is where a third party has purchased the relevant goods in good faith and without notice of the retention of title clause. Section 25(1) provides that:

'Where a person having bought or agreed to buy goods obtains, with the consent of the seller, possession of the goods or the documents of title to the goods, the delivery or transfer by that person, or by a mercantile agent acting for him, of the goods or documents of title, under any sale, pledge, or other disposition thereof, to any person receiving the same in good faith and without notice of any lien or other right of the original seller in respect of the goods, has the same effect as if the person making the delivery or transfer were a mercantile agent in possession of the goods or documents of title with the consent of the owner.'

The application of s.25 is illustrated by the case of *Archivent Sales and Developments Ltd* v. *Strathclyde Regional Council* (1985). In that case the supplier delivered goods to site and payment was made by the employer to the main contractor. The main contractor failed, in turn, to make payment to the supplier, who sought to recover the goods from the employer on the basis of the retention of title clause in its contract with the contractor. The supplier's claim to ownership failed because the existence of the supplier's retention of title clause in the contract of sale to the main contractor had not been brought to the employer's attention.

There are a number of other practical difficulties in enforcing a retention of title clauses, not least of which is that the clause cannot be founded upon in a question with the building owner where the materials have been incorporated into the structure, provided that there is no element of bad faith on the part of the building owner, see *Archivent Sales and Developments Ltd*. This arises from the principle of Scots law that all buildings and fixtures pass into the ownership of the party who has title to the ground upon which they are erected, see *Brand's Trustees* v. *Brand's Trustees* (1876). Whether an article attached to a structure (as distinct from remaining moveable property) becomes, by virtue of the principle of accession, a fixture and thus part of the structure is a matter of fact to be determined by the circumstances of the case, see *Scottish Discount Co. Ltd* v. *Blin* (1986).

On a further practical level, the seller will need to identify their goods and, if necessary, distinguish them from other similar goods. A seller of identifiable items bearing serial or batch numbers is likely to enjoy greater success in enforcing a retention of title clause than a supplier of sand or bricks. In the latter situation (in the absence of an 'all sums' retention of title clause) even if the seller can identify the bricks they supplied, that will not be enough unless they can connect particular quantities of unfixed brick with particular unpaid invoices.

## 11.8 Supply of goods by sub-contractors

A distinction falls to be drawn between materials supplied by a supplier and those supplied under a sub-contract, see *Thos Graham & Sons* v. *Glenrothes Development Corporation* (1986). As seen above, title to goods or materials supplied by a supplier will normally pass to the contractor upon delivery to site, unless title has been retained by the supplier under a retention of title clause. In contrast, in the case of a sub-contract, i.e. a contract for the supply of goods and services, the common law applies and ownership passes when the goods or materials are fixed to the structure, see *Stirling County Council v. Official Liquidator of John Frame Ltd* (1951).

The conceptual difference between goods or materials supplied under a contract of sale and those supplied under a contract for the supply of goods and services is further illustrated by the way in which the SBC deals with the purchase of off-site materials. Clause 4.17 of the SBC provides that if the Architect is of the opinion that it is expedient to do so the Employer may enter into a separate contract for the purchase from the Contractor or any Sub-Contractor of any materials or goods prior to their delivery to site. If such a contract is entered into the materials or goods cease to form part of the contract and the Contract Sum is adjusted accordingly. Such a provision is particularly useful in the case of major equipment which is being manu-factured by a specialist supplier in his premises and which needs to be paid for prior to delivery to site. This has the result of characterising the transac-tion as a contract of sale, which is subject to the Sale of Goods Act 1979, which allows ownership to pass prior to delivery.

Clause 4.17 of the SBC falls to be contrasted with the corresponding clause in JCT 05 which allows the amount stated as due in an interim certificate to include the value of 'listed items' before their delivery to site, provided that the Contractor demonstrates that after payment, such listed items will become the property of the Employer. For the reasons stated above, under Scots law it would not be possible to demonstrate that ownership had effec-tively transferred in such circumstances, and hence the difference in approach under the SBC.

In terms of clause 2.15.2 of the Standard Building Sub-Contract Conditions for use in Scotland, where the value of unfixed materials or goods which have been delivered to or placed on or adjacent to the works has been included in any Interim Certificate issued under main contract, and the amount properly due by the Employer to the Contractor has been dis-charged, then such materials or goods become the property of the Employer, and the Sub-Contractor agrees that they cannot deny that such materials or goods are and have become the property of the Employer. Should the Con-tractor pay the Sub-Contractor for any such materials or goods prior to the Employer having first discharged his obligation to pay the Contractor for same, then clause 2.15.3 of the Standard Building Sub-Contract provides that the materials or goods become the property of the Contractor. These provisions meet the terms of clause 3.9.2 of the SBC which sets out certain mandatory provisions which must be contained in any sub-contract let under the SBC.

# Chapter 12
# Assignation, Delegation and Novation

## 12.1 Introduction

This chapter considers three separate methods of transferring rights and obligations, namely, assignation, delegation and novation.

Assignation is a method of transfer of moveable property. In modern building projects, the employer's heritable interest in the project may be transferred by sale or lease. To provide the purchaser or lessee with an interest in the building contract, it is possible to assign that interest. In the standard forms of building and engineering contract, specific, detailed provisions are made in respect of assignation. The specific provisions of the SBC in this regard are considered below in section 12.5.

All contracts contain both rights and obligations. In England, it is trite law that the obligations under a contract, or the burden, cannot be assigned without the consent of the party entitled to enforce those obligations, see *Linden Gardens Trust Ltd* v. *Lenesta Sludge Disposals Ltd and Others* (1994). The position in Scotland is different to that in England. It is a matter of some controversy in Scotland as to whether the contract as a whole is capable of being assigned. In Scotland, it would appear that obligations, as well as rights, under a contract are capable of being assigned, provided that they do not involve an element of *delectus personae* (a specific choice of natural or legal person). *Delectus personae* is considered below in section 12.4. The distinction is an important one. Whilst certain rights and obligations may involve elements of *delectus personae*, and thus not be assignable without consent, certain others may not and so may be assigned. An express provision in a building contract that prohibits assignation, or only permits assignation with consent, will override the common law. In those circumstances, *delectus personae* is of no relevance.

## 12.2 Common law

In the absence of any express provision of the contract governing assignation, the common law will apply.

No particular wording is required to constitute an assignation under Scots law as long as it effects a transfer, see *Carter* v. *McIntosh* (1862). The general principle is that, to be effective, an assignation of a right must be intimated to the person against whom the right may be enforced. For example, where a contractor assigns his right to receive payment of retention monies, the assignee, that is, the party in whose favour the assignation is granted, must intimate such assignation to the employer. Failure to intimate assignation may prevent rights being transferred, see *Laurence McIntosh Ltd* v. *Balfour Beatty Group Ltd* (2006), where the resulting relationship was analysed in terms of *ad hoc* agency and meant there was no title to sue. In the event of competing assignations, these rank in priority of date of intimation, not date of execution.

The assignee under a contract is entitled to no greater benefit than the assignor. This is often expressed by way of the Latin maxim *assignatus utitur jure auctoris*, which means that the assignee can never be in a better position than the assignor. Thus any defences available to the debtor in respect of the claim by the assignor will also be available against a claim by the assignee. For example, it is a complete defence to demonstrate that a debt was settled before the right to sue for that debt was assigned. An example of this arose in *Smiths Gore* v. *Reilly* (2001), where it was held that an 'empty vessel' had been assigned which could not ground a meaningful claim.

## 12.3  *Effect of assignation upon claims*

Questions often arise in the construction industry as to the effect of an assignation upon claims. This has been considered by the House of Lords in the Scottish case of *GUS Property Management Ltd* v. *Littlewoods Mail Order Stores Ltd* (1982) and in the English cases of *Linden Gardens Trust Ltd* v. *Lenesta Sludge Disposals Ltd* (1994), *Darlington BC* v. *Wiltshier Northern Ltd* (1995) and *Alfred McAlpine Construction Ltd* v. *Panatown Ltd (No.1)* (2001).

*GUS Property Management Ltd* concerned the assignee's right to claim losses arising from a delict where that right has been validly assigned. A building in Glasgow, owned by a company named Rest Property Co. Ltd, was damaged in the course of building operations being carried out on a neighbouring property. Rest transferred the property to a related company, namely GUS, for its full book value ignoring the cost of repairing the damage. GUS carried out repairs to the property and Rest then assigned to GUS all claims competent to them arising out of the building operations. GUS raised an action for damages against the neighbouring proprietors and those involved in the building operations. The defenders argued that because the property had been transferred for its full book value, the assignor had not sustained any loss at all, and thus the assignee could not recover damages for any such loss. The House of Lords, overruling the Court of Session, held that such a defence was not sustainable and refused to allow the claim to fall into some kind of legal 'black hole'. Rest would have been able to sue for damages at the time of the assignation, following the general rule in *Gordon* v. *Davidson* (1864) that the owner of a property damaged as a result of a delict does not lose the right to sue on parting with that property. The fact that the transfer price had been fixed for internal accounting purposes did not affect the true loss suffered by Rest, and Rest had assigned its right to sue for that loss to GUS.

Whilst *GUS Property Management Ltd* is a case dealing with a delictual claim, it is submitted that the principles set out in it are equally applicable to claims under contract. Although the decision was based on a specific set of circumstances, it appears that the court would reject a defence to a claim by an assignee on the ground that no loss has been suffered because the assignor (i.e. the original developer) sold for full value. Such 'no loss' arguments have been resisted by both the Scottish and English courts, see *McLaren Murdoch & Hamilton Ltd* v. *The Abercromby Motor Group Ltd* (2003) and *Darlington BC* respectively. This seems to be the case whether the transaction is between related companies, as in *GUS Property Management Ltd*, or at arm's length, as in *Technotrade Ltd* v. *Larkstore Ltd* (2006).

The appeal in *Linden Gardens Trust Ltd* was heard by the House of Lords with the appeal in *St Martin's Property Corporation Ltd* v. *Sir Robert McAlpine & Sons Ltd* (1994). Both cases concerned an exception to the rule that a contracting party may only recover its own losses under the contract.

In each case the contract was subject to the JCT 63 conditions. Clause 17 of JCT 63 (as with clause 7.1 of the SBC) prohibited assignation of the contract by the Employer without the Contractor's written consent. The House of Lords held that, on a true construction of the contracts, the wording of clause 17 prohibited assignation by the Employer, without the Contractor's consent, of the benefit of the contract and the assignation of any cause of action. On the facts this meant there had been no valid assignation in either case. However, it was held that the original Employer was entitled to recover from the Contractor the loss sustained by the purchaser. As the contract was expressly not assignable without the Contractor's consent, the House of Lords deemed that the Employer and the Contractor should be treated as having contracted on the basis that the Employer would be entitled to enforce his contractual rights against the Contractor for the benefit of third parties who would suffer from defective performance.

The exception established by *Linden Gardens Trust Ltd* was revisited in *Alfred McAlpine Construction*. Panatown employed McAlpine to build an office block and car park on a site owned by Unex Investment Properties Ltd, a member of the same group as Panatown. McAlpine granted a duty of care deed to Unex. When Panatown's claim for substantial damages reached the House of Lords, it was held by majority that the exception did not apply because of the existence of the duty of care deed, which gave Unex a direct contractual claim against McAlpine. The Court of Appeal emphasised that the direct route must be taken if one exists when the matter came back before it in *Alfred McAlpine Construction Ltd* v. *Panatown Ltd (No.2)* (2001).

The decision in *Alfred McAlpine Ltd* was considered in the Outer House in *McLaren Murdoch & Hamilton Ltd* v. *The Abercromby Motor Group Ltd* (2003) and its result was adjudged to be 'wholly consistent with the principles of Scots law'. The view was taken that the exception should be conferred as a matter of general legal policy, rather than based on any considerations of the intent of the parties, and *jus quaesitum tertio* was ruled out as a general solution as this would require the contracting parties to set out to benefit a third party, and identify that third party, at the time of making the contract. However, it was acknowledged that the primary remedy for breach of contract in Scots law remains implement, whereas in England it is damages.

## 12.4 Delectus personae

A contract which involves *delectus personae* is one where a party to the contract has entered into it in reliance upon certain qualities possessed by the other. In such circumstances, the contract cannot be performed by a third party and, consequently, the obligation to perform cannot be assigned without consent, see *Anderson* v. *Hamilton & Co.* (1875). Authorities in relation to delegation (see section 12.6) may assist in identifying whether or not a contract contains an element of *delectus personae*.

If the contract does not place reliance upon a special skill of one of the parties, or is for the provision of an item of a certain standard specified in the contract, no element of *delectus personae* exists, see *Cole* v. *Handasyde & Co.* (1909). Even if the contract involves *delectus personae*, and is thus not assignable, certain rights arising out of that contract may be assignable. For example, an accrued right to payment of a sum of money under the contract may be assigned, notwithstanding that the contract itself cannot, see *International Fibre Syndicate Ltd* v. *Dawson* (1901).

## 12.5 Assignation under the SBC

The assignation provisions of the SBC are to be found in clauses 7.1 and 7.2. Clause 7.1 provides that neither the Employer nor the Contractor may assign the contract or any rights thereunder without the written consent of the other. If the Contract Particulars state that clause 7.2 applies, that clause entitles the Employer to assign certain rights after practical completion. Where clause 7.2 does apply, then if the Employer alienates by sale or lease, or otherwise disposes of his interest in the contract works, they may at any time after the issue of the certificate of practical completion assign to the party acquiring his interest in the Works, his right, title and interest to bring proceedings, in his name as Employer, to enforce any of the rights of the Employer arising under or by reason of breach of the contract.

This provision recognises the practice that certain Employers will transfer their interest in property once practical completion has been certified. Should it apply, however, the provisions of clause 7.2 are of limited use. It is only the Employer's right, title and interest to bring proceedings which may be assigned, and there may be occasions where the employer wishes to assign prior to the practical completion. The wording is a little odd, given that an assignation of rights under the building contract would, *ipso facto*, confer the right to raise proceedings to enforce such rights, and the proceedings would normally be brought in the name of the assignee. There appear to be no reported cases applying the provisions of clause 7.2 (or its predecessor, clause 19.1 of JCT 98).

## 12.6 Delegation

The delegation of building work, through the use of sub-contractors, is commonplace within the construction industry. Although delegation raises similar issues to assignation, the two concepts should not be confused. In the case of assignation, it is the assignee who is bound, as opposed to the original contracting party. With delegation, the original contracting party remains bound, albeit that performance of the contractual obligations is carried out by another party. Delegation has the effect of adding another link to the contractual chain.

As with assignation, the existence or otherwise of *delectus personae* will determine whether or not the obligation of performance can be delegated. The work content of the contract will assist in determining whether or not delegation is competent. Work which consists chiefly of manual labour has been held to contain no element of *delectus personae*, see *Asphaltic Limestone Concrete Co. Ltd and Another* v. *Corporation of the City of Glasgow* (1907). However, it has been recognised that the execution of repair work on and in residential properties is of a character which might well be the subject of *delectus personae*, see *Scottish Homes* v. *Inverclyde DC* (1997).

The question of *delectus personae* in building contracts generally was considered in *Karl Construction Ltd* v. *Palisade Properties plc* (2002) in which the court stated that:

'In general, it is clear that a building contract involving complex work will be personal to the contracting parties. That applies particularly if detailed administrative or management work is called for, or if elements of design are involved.'

The SBC contemplates delegation. Clause 3.7 permits the sub-letting of any part of the Works, subject to the written consent of the Architect. Such consent is not to be unreasonably delayed or withheld. The underlying principle of responsibility resting with the original contracting party is reflected in clause 3.7.1, which states that the Contractor will remain wholly responsible for carrying out and completing the Works, notwithstanding the subletting of any part of them.

## 12.7 Novation

Novation is, broadly, the substitution of a new party for an existing party to a contract, with the result that the new party assumes the rights and obligations under the contract. Novation requires the consent of all of the parties to the original contract. That consent need not be express and can be inferred from the conduct of the parties, see *McIntosh & Son* v. *Ainslie* (1872). Strictly speaking, novation has the effect of simultaneously extinguishing the old obligation and creating a new obligation. The effect of this must be carefully considered by the parties before proceeding with novation. For example, claims for breach of the original contract may be extinguished by novation, see *Hawthorns & Co. Ltd* v. *Whimster & Company* (1917).

Novation is very commonly used in the context of design and build contracts, where the design consultants are initially engaged by the employer for the purposes of the pre-contract design but the appointments are then novated to the contractor at the same time as the design and build contract is entered into. The potential problems with novation in such circumstances are illustrated in *Blyth & Blyth Ltd* v. *Carillion Construction Ltd* (2002).

Blyth & Blyth provided consulting engineering services to their employer, and after some months this was formalised by a deed of appointment, which expressly provided that the agreement covered the period from when services were first provided. Under that deed, the employer instructed Blyth & Blyth to enter into a tripartite novation agreement, the effect of which was to add Carillion, the main contractor, as a party. When Blyth & Blyth raised an action for payment of fees, Carillion counterclaimed for losses arising from alleged breaches of duty, some of which related to the period before the novation agreement was executed. In spite of the retrospective nature of the deed of appointment, it was held that the novation agreement should be construed as an agreement under which Blyth & Blyth were to provide future services to Carillion. Thus Carillion were not entitled to recover losses relating to the period before novation.

Novation may also be of relevance where the contractor becomes insolvent. One of the options open to the employer, and the insolvency practitioner responsible for the affairs of the contractor, is the novation of the original contract to a substitute contractor, whether on the same terms as the existing contract or on varied terms. In construction insolvency, a true novation, that is where the substitute contractor steps into the position of the original contractor and the contract continues as if the substitute contractor had been the original contractor, is most unlikely. Considerations such as liability for defects and the potential liability for liquidated and ascertained damages will militate against true novation. In most cases, therefore, the transaction will be a conditional novation, in terms of which the substitute contractor takes on only certain limited obligations, for example, the obligation to complete, and does not assume responsibility for antecedent breaches.

# Chapter 13
# Rights for Third Parties

## 13.1 General

There may be a range of parties that have a commercial or financial interest in the design and construction of a building, both during the design and construction process and following completion of the development. Although the identity of those having an involvement in a particular project will depend on the nature and use of the building being constructed, those having an interest will often include developers, funders, purchasers and tenants. Not all of those persons will be a party to, and therefore be in a position to rely upon, the building contract and other construction agreements entered into in connection with the development. For those reasons, parties with an interest in the development, and who are not party to the principal construction agreements, will need to consider how best to protect their respective interests.

The decision of the House of Lords in *Murphy* v. *Brentwood DC* (1991) reinforced the need for rights to be created in favour of such third parties. For a further discussion of *Murphy* and related cases, see section 11.3.3 above.

This chapter provides a practical overview of three ways in which rights in connection with a building contract can be created for the benefit of third parties having an interest in the building, namely, collateral warranties; third party rights schedule; and assignation.

## 13.2 Collateral Warranties

### 13.2.1 Introduction

A practice had arisen in the early 1980s of requiring contractors, sub-contractors and construction professionals to acknowledge, by contractual means, duties of care to parties with whom they had otherwise no contractual relationship', for example, tenants, funders and subsequent owners. The perceived inadequacies and uncertainties of a remedy based upon delict led to the practice of creating, by means of a collateral warranty, a contractual nexus, which would otherwise be absent. The purpose of a collateral warranty is to impose, by contract, duties and obligations on the part of the contractor, sub-contractor or consultant in favour of a third party who is not the original building owner or employer but who may nevertheless suffer loss in the event of a construction or design defect.

Collateral warranties essentially deal with the apportionment of risk. Negotiation of the terms of collateral warranties has become widespread, with the need to satisfy the conflicting interests of the beneficiary and the grantor. Bodies within the construction industry, including the Scottish Building Contract Committee, have made various attempts to satisfy these conflicting interests without the need for protracted negotiation by producing standardised forms of collateral warranty.

The use of collateral warranties in the construction industry has continued and there is now included in the Standard Building Contract (SBC) an option for the contractor to provide collateral warranties, see Contract Particulars Part 2 and clause 7.

Despite the number of collateral warranties being granted in the construction industry, there are relatively few reported cases involving collateral warranties, see *Hill Samuel Bank Ltd* v. *Frederick Brand Partnership* (1994) and *Glasgow Airport Ltd* v. *Kirkman & Bradford* (2007).

### 13.2.2 Interests in obtaining warranties

The reasons why parties involved in a construction project require collateral warranties vary depending upon the nature of their interest in the project.

### Developer

In a typical commercial development, the developer of the project will intend either to realise their investment at, or shortly after, completion of the project by disposal to a third party purchaser, or to grant a leasehold interest to one or more tenants. In either case the marketability of the development will demand that collateral warranties from the contractor and the consultants are available to the purchaser and/or tenants.

### Funder

Whilst the funder will normally be protected by a heritable security over the development, they will wish to preserve a right of recourse against any party whose actions may diminish the value of that security. In addition, the funder will wish to have the option of ensuring that the development is completed (and the value of the security therefore maximised) in the event of the developer becoming insolvent prior to completion. This is achieved by exercising 'step-in rights', see section 13.3.6 below.

From a funder's perspective, a collateral warranty from the quantity surveyor or other consultant administering payment is also important. Interim valuations under the building contract will normally be carried out by the quantity surveyor or other consultant on behalf of the developer and will, ordinarily, be reflected in payments to the contractor. In turn, drawdowns from the funder's loan to the developer will typically reflect the amount of such valuations and payments, hence the need for the funder to secure some degree of comfort in relation to the actions of the quantity surveyor.

### Purchaser/tenant

Since the decision in *Murphy* it is clear that, except in very specialised circumstances, a purchaser or tenant will have no claim in delict against a contractor or consultant with whom the purchaser or tenant has no contract. Hence the need for purchasers and tenants to protect themselves against the manifestation of latent defects caused by faulty design or construction. The principle of *caveat emptor* (buyer beware) applying in contracts for the sale of heritable property prohibits any recourse against a seller, and the obligations undertaken by tenants under a typical commercial full repairing lease will require them to make good all damage to the leased property howsoever caused (notwithstanding that it may be due to a latent defect) without recourse to the landlord. The case of *Royal Insurance (UK) Ltd* v. *Amec Construction Scotland Ltd and Others* (2005), an action raised pursuant to a collateral warranty, demonstrates the potential commercial significance to a tenant of the rights under a collateral warranty.

### Sub-contractors

Collateral warranties from domestic sub-contractors in favour of interested third parties may be regarded as 'belt and braces'. In other words, primary liability will lie with the main contractor under their collateral warranty and additional warranties from sub-contractors will need to be enforced only in the event that recovery cannot be made from the main contractor, notwithstanding that liability is established. However, a sub-contractor's collateral warranty may also fulfil an important purpose of ensuring, by means of step-in rights to the employer, that the sub-contractor remains committed to price and to performance in the event of termination of the main contract.

### Design consultants

It is common practice for external professional consultants engaged by or novated to a design and build contractor to be required to give collateral warranties to the usual third party beneficiaries (i.e. purchaser, funder and tenants). This is in addition to the warranties to be granted to those parties by the contractor. This again may be regarded as a belt-and-braces approach, but with perhaps some justification in this instance, given the risk of the contractor becoming insolvent and the availability of professional indemnity insurance (in most cases) to back up claims made under such warranties. Where a design consultant appointment is novated to the contractor, it is also important to the employer to procure a collateral warranty in its favour from the consultant to cover both pre-novation and post-novation design, particularly if pre-novation design responsibility is not fully assumed by the contractor. For other potential pitfalls arising from the novation of consultants' appointments, see section 12.7 above.

## 13.3 Typical clauses

The following are examples of typical clauses found in collateral warranties. However, these are by no means exhaustive and the drafting of provisions intended to have the same effect may differ considerably from one warranty to another.

### 13.3.1 Standard of care

'The [Contractor/Sub-Contractor] warrants that it has exercised and will continue to exercise the reasonable skill, care and diligence to be expected of a suitably qualified and competent [Contractor/Sub-Contractor] experienced in projects of a similar size, scope and complexity to the Development in the performance of its services to the Employer under the [Building Contract/Sub-Contract].'

From the point of view of the grantor, it is important that the standard against which its responsibilities will be measured for the purposes of the collateral warranty is no higher than the standard of the primary or underlying contract.

### 13.3.2 Prohibited materials

'The [Contractor/Sub-Contractor] undertakes that it has not used and will not use materials in the Works other than in accordance with the guidelines contained within the edition of "Good Practice in Selection of Construction Materials" (Ove Arup & Partners) current as at the date of the Building Contract.'

Until fairly recently, the practice for many years had been to specify a list of materials not to be used, or specified for use, in the development. These lists were often prepared with little thought and lawyers were criticised (often with justification) for drafting collateral warranties containing lists of prohibited materials without any regard for the nature of the project or the particular properties of a prohibited material. A blanket prohibition may not be appropriate for a particular material, depending on the nature of the project and the intended use of the material. The matter was brought to a head when a manufacturer of calcium silicate bricks successfully obtained an interim interdict against a local authority preventing it from including calcium silicate bricks in the list of deleterious materials in its collateral warranties. It is now common practice to use a more general clause.

Parties should be clear as to whether the grantor is warranting that the materials have not been used during the construction of the development, or whether it is warranting only that they have used reasonable skill, care and diligence to ensure that they have not been used, or have not been specified for use as the case may be. It should also be borne in mind that references to 'good building practice' are potentially subjective and, in terms of scope, very wide.

Knowledge of the unsuitable nature of the material is usually stated to be tested at the time of either specification or use of the material in question. There is some danger in a contractor or sub-contractor accepting the time of use as the relevant benchmark, given that the material may have been capable of being used legitimately or its unsuitable properties may not have been known at the time of specification, and yet the contractor/sub-contractor will be in breach of the warranty if that state of affairs changes prior to the use of the material in the development.

### 13.3.3 Limitations on proceedings

'No action or proceedings for any breach of this Agreement shall be commenced against the [Contractor/Sub-Contractor] after the expiry of [12] years from the later of the date of termination of the Building Contract or the date of practical completion of the Development or the last section of the Development (where the Development is being completed in sections) as certified under the Building Contract.'

A clause of this type is particularly important where the grantor does not enter into the collateral warranty until after practical completion. Failure to include such a clause could potentially leave the grantor owing contractual duties to a third party of longer duration than those owed to the client under the primary contract as, in the absence of such a provision, the prescriptive period may not then commence until the date of execution of the collateral warranty, notwithstanding that the design or construction failure giving rise to breach of the warranty occurred prior to the execution of the warranty.

It is sometimes otherwise difficult to see a rational justification for imposing a limitation period in a collateral warranty which reduces the grantor's period of exposure to claims (at least in the case of latent defects) to a period usually significantly less than the statutory prescriptive period (see Chapter 9). The period of 12 years is often chosen for no apparent reason other than its familiarity under English law. Ultimately it is a commercial matter. The grantor will argue that, as the beneficiary is being granted rights beyond those otherwise available to it at law, there is sound commercial sense for the grantor to place limitations on the period during which such rights may be exercised. Pragmatic considerations may also apply. For instance, a funder may consider it unnecessary to require a limitation period longer than the period for repayment of the loan. Clauses of this type fail to be construed strictly, see *Port Jackson Stevedoring Ltd* v. *Salmond & Spraggon (Australia) Pty Ltd ('The New York Star')* (1980).

### 13.3.4 Net contribution

'The liability of the Consultant for costs under this Agreement shall be limited to that proportion of the Beneficiary's losses which it would be just and equitable to require the Consultant to pay having regard to the extent of the Consultant's responsibility for the same and on the basis that [list names of other Consultants] shall be deemed to have provided contractual undertakings on terms no less onerous than this Clause [ ] to the Beneficiary in respect of the performance of their services in connection with the Development and shall be deemed to have paid to the Beneficiary such proportion which it would be just and equitable for them to pay having regard to the extent of their responsibility.'

The above is commonly known as a 'net contribution' clause and is intended to alleviate what are regarded (at least in the eyes of grantors and their insurers) as the harsh consequences of joint and several liability. This arises where damage to the beneficiary is caused as a result of a breach of duty by more than one party. If each breach of duty has materially contributed to the same damage to the beneficiary, the beneficiary is entitled to recover the losses arising from such damage from any or all of the parties in breach. Thus one sub-contractor may (in the absence of a net contribution clause) be pursued for the whole of the loss, notwithstanding that other consultants or contractors may have contributed to that loss.

The clause creates the fiction that all the relevant parties are deemed to have granted collateral warranties (whether, in reality, they have or not) to the beneficiary. To the extent that they have a responsibility, they are deemed to have already paid their fair share of the recoverable loss or damage suffered by the beneficiary. The relevant grantor is then left liable only for its share of the loss on the basis that the other grantors are deemed to have paid their contribution. Care needs to be taken when agreeing the terms of a net contribution clause in a consultant collateral warranty in the context of a design and build contract, that the design and build contractor is not named as one of the parties 'deemed' to have provided similar undertakings and paid the relevant proportion according to its responsibility. Since the design and build contractor's responsibility is for the whole of the design, its 'deemed' payment will be for the whole of the claim and so the consultant who has the benefit of such a net contribution clause could unintentionally end up escaping all liability as a consequence.

This clause is intended to reflect the principles of section 3 of the Law Reform (Miscellaneous Provisions) (Scotland) Act 1940 which gives the court the power to apportion damages against joint wrongdoers, and the clause may, on the face of it, seem equitable. However, unlike the 1940 Act, the clause places on the beneficiary the onus of obtaining similar warranties from the other parties 'on terms no less onerous' and also the risk that recovery may not in fact be made from one of the relevant parties, notwithstanding that liability of the other parties is calculated on the basis that it is deemed to be so made.

There have been some concerns expressed regarding evidence that may be admitted by the courts and the potential of a decree being granted against an unrepresented party. Many professional indemnity insurers will insist upon the inclusion of a net contribution clause in collateral warranties before extending cover to liabilities arising out of them and these clauses are probably now regarded as standard in collateral warranties. There are also attempts to extend such clauses to appointments, which are normally met with resistance. This form of clause remains untested by the courts.

### 13.3.5 Equivalent rights of defence

> 'The [Contractor/Sub-Contractor] shall be entitled in any action or proceedings by the Beneficiary to rely on any limitation in the [Building Contract/Sub-Contract] and to raise the equivalent rights in defence of liability as it would have against the Employer under the [Building Contract/Sub-Contract], had the Beneficiary been named as Employer under the [Building Contract/Sub-Contract].'

The intention of this clause is to ensure that liability under the collateral warranty is co-extensive with that under the primary contract. For example, the contractor or sub-contractor would be able to raise in defence of liability any rights of retention, set-off or counterclaim that it has against the employer under the building contract. However, in the drafting of this type of clause (which may be worded in a number of different ways) care must be taken to ensure that it does not confer a 'no loss' right of defence on the grantor.

### 13.3.6 Step-in rights

The rights contained in this clause allow the beneficiary to step into the shoes of the employer in certain pre-defined situations, typically insolvency events or where the grantor seeks to exercise its right to determine the principal contract.

Step-in provisions will normally appear in a funder's collateral warranty, although in some situations they may also be appropriate in a purchaser's collateral warranty and (in the case of sub-contractors) in an employer's collateral warranty. Step-in allows the beneficiary to step into the shoes of the employer under the primary contract by way of novation. Novation is considered above in Chapter 12. It is generally activated where the beneficiary wishes to prevent the grantor from terminating the primary contract or otherwise wishes to ensure completion of the project following default by the developer or (in the case of sub-contractor collateral warranties) default by the contractor.

The beneficiary will normally be obliged to assume all the outstanding and future obligations of the employer, for example, payment of outstanding and future fees. The beneficiary has the right, but not the obligation, to step-in and therefore there will generally be a specified time within which they may receive all of the relevant information to allow them to reach an informed view as to whether they wish to exercise their right or not. Grantors will wish to keep this period to a minimum as they are otherwise prevented from terminating during this period, even although they may not be getting paid.

Collateral warranties containing step-in provisions will normally be tripartite, with the employer, beneficiary and grantor being signatories. The reason for the employer being a party is that it acknowledges that the grantor will not be in breach of its obligations to the employer by reason of the grantor complying with its obligations to the beneficiary in respect of step-in.

### 13.3.7 Assignation/obligation to enter into further warranties

A beneficiary will normally require that a collateral warranty in its favour is capable of being assigned without the beneficiary having to obtain the prior consent of the grantor. In the ordinary course of events, the grantor, to limit their exposure, will attempt to limit the number of occasions upon which the collateral warranty may be assigned. Where relevant both grantor and beneficiary should check the provisions of the grantor's professional indemnity insurance cover when considering the number of assignations as most insurers will wish to restrict the permitted number of assignations, especially where the collateral warranty contains few restrictions on liability.

For the reasons described in section 13.6 below, an assignation of a collateral warranty may be of limited value and a second purchaser or tenant would normally prefer a new warranty in its favour.

### 13.3.8 Professional indemnity insurance

'The [Contractor/Sub-Contractor] shall maintain professional indemnity insurance in an amount of not less than [ ] for every occurrence or series of occurrences arising out of any one event with insurers of substance and repute in the UK Insurance Market until [12] years from the date of Practical Completion under the Building Contract, provided always that such insurance is available to the [Contractor/Sub-Contractor] at commercially reasonable rates. The [Contractor/Sub-Contractor] shall immediately inform the Beneficiary if such insurance ceases to be available at commercially reasonable rates in order that the [Contractor/Sub-Contractor] and the Beneficiary can discuss the means of best protecting the respective positions of the Beneficiary and the [Contractor/Sub-Contractor] in the absence of such insurance. As and when it is reasonably requested to do so by the Beneficiary, the [Contractor/Sub-Contractor] shall produce for inspection documentary evidence that its professional indemnity insurance is being maintained.'

The well advised grantor will, where it maintains professional indemnity insurance in respect of its obligations in terms of the collateral warranty, refer any collateral warranty it proposes to enter into to its professional indemnity insurers for comment. Where the grantor has responsibility for design, it will normally be required to maintain professional indemnity insurance for a number of years after practical completion. For the same reasons as mentioned in section 13.3.3 above, a period of 12 years would seem to be the norm. Further qualifications to this obligation include the requirement for insurance to be available at commercially reasonable rates and on reasonable terms and conditions.

It is worth noting that there are few, if any, insurers prepared to underwrite any form of absolute risk. Professional indemnity insurance traditionally covers the 'legal liability' of the insured, i.e. in the case of a professional, the exercise of reasonable skill and care. Any voluntary assumption of a greater duty by the insured in contract is generally covered by way of an extension to the policy. This can either be a general endorsement within certain parameters, or require 'approval' of each contract by the insurer.

### 13.3.9 Intellectual property licence

Most collateral warranties will contain a non-exclusive licence by the grantor in favour of the beneficiary in respect of the use of intellectual property rights in the design documentation prepared relative to the development. This may be particularly important, for example, to a purchaser who wishes to construct an extension to the property consistent with the existing design.

### 13.3.10 No greater duties or liabilities

In *Safeway Stores Ltd* v. *Interserve Project Services Ltd* (2005) a collateral warranty clause in the following terms was considered:

'The Contractor shall owe no duty or have no liability under this deed which [is] greater or of longer duration than that which it owes to the Developer under the Building Contract.'

Not surprisingly it was decided that this clause permitted the contractor to set off against claims made against it under the collateral warranty sums that were owed to it under the primary building contract.

### 13.3.11 Limitations

A grantor often wishes to restrict, either in *quantum* or nature, the losses for which it may be liable under the collateral warranty. For example, it is common, particularly in the standard forms of warranties (and is often demanded by professional indemnity insurers) that the grantor's liability be restricted to the reasonable cost of repair, renewal or reinstatement of the development, to the extent attributable to the grantor's breach. Any liability, for example, for loss of use would therefore be excluded. However, to successfully restrict the grantor's liability, any such limitation must be clearly expressed, see *Glasgow Airport Ltd* v. *Kirkman & Bradford* (2007).

## 13.4 Effects of the 1996 Act on collateral warranties

Are collateral warranties agreements for the carrying out of construction operations in terms of s.104(1)(a) of the Housing Grants, Construction and Regeneration Act 1996?

Conflicting views have been expressed on the answer to this question. The authors respectfully suggest they are not agreements for the carrying out of construction operations. If collateral warranties do indeed fall within the ambit of s.104(1)(a), disputes under warranties would, in the absence of express adjudication provisions, fall to be determined by adjudication under the statutory scheme. Given that adjudication under the 1996 Act was brought in to facilitate prompt payment in the construction industry and that collateral warranties do not typically include payment obligations, it has not become standard practice for collateral warranties to include express dispute resolution clauses that mirror the underlying contract.

## 13.5 Third party rights schedule

### 13.5.1 Introduction

A third party rights schedule is a schedule forming part of a primary contract, such as a building contract, which sets out a series of rights which can, in the circumstances set out in the primary contract, be conferred on third party beneficiaries without the need for a separate contract to be entered into with the third party beneficiary. In a construction context the rights in a third party rights schedule will typically be very similar to the rights that are contained in a collateral warranty.

In England, the Contracts (Rights of Third Parties) Act 1999 (which does not apply in Scotland) provides a legal basis for the use of third party rights schedules as an alternative to collateral warranties. Although, under the common law doctrine of *jus quaesitum tertio* it has always been legally possible in Scotland (unlike in England) for the parties to a contract to confer rights in favour of third parties, provided certain criteria are fulfilled, it was not until third party rights schedules were adopted in England that they were considered for use in Scotland.

The SBC provides for third party rights pursuant to clauses 7A and 7B and Part 5 of the Schedule, as an alternative to the provision under clause 7C of collateral warranties from the Contractor to purchasers, tenants and/or funders. The parties in whose favour such rights are to be granted require to be set out in the Contract Particulars. The Contract Particulars further provide that, if in relation to an identified person it is not stated whether third party rights or collateral warranties will apply, then the former will apply. Compared to collateral warranties the use of third party rights schedules is a recent innovation and it remains to be seen whether in time these will replace collateral warranties as the medium of choice for providing rights in favour of third parties.

### 13.5.2  Creation of the rights

To create third party rights in Scots law under the *jus quaesitum tertio*, the parties to the contract need to show an intention to create such rights in favour of a particular person or class of persons and to make those rights irrevocable. See also the cases cited in section 11.3.2.

### 13.5.3  Advantages

There are a number of perceived advantages to using third party rights schedules.

From the beneficiary's perspective probably the most compelling benefit is that where third party rights are properly conferred on a beneficiary the parties to the primary contract will (in the absence of an express right to do so) be unable to change the primary contract so as to interfere with the third party rights. In the absence of express terms in a collateral warranty prohibiting them from doing so, it would be open to the parties to the primary contract to adjust it in such a way as may affect the rights being granted under the collateral warranty.

Third party rights schedules could reduce the requirement to prepare and complete large numbers of collateral warranties in major projects. Instead the grantor would agree to one third party rights schedule which will contain many of the general collateral warranty clauses outlined above.

Third party rights can be prepared at the same time as the main contract and the beneficiary can be identified as a specific legal entity or as a class of persons (e.g. tenants). This means that third party rights can be made available for beneficiaries that have not yet been identified or that are not in existence at the time the building contract is entered into.

## 13.6 *Assignation*

It is not unusual for developers to offer to assign to a purchaser or tenant their rights against the contractor and/or consultants responsible for constructing and designing the development (and express provision is made for this in clause 7.2 of the SBC). However, assignation is arguably an unsatisfactory substitute for a collateral warranty or third party rights schedule. This is because the principle *assignatus utitur jure auctoris* applies to assignation, i.e. the assignee stands in the shoes of the assignor, can acquire no better rights than the assignor, and is subject to any defence available against the assignor. Although judicial decisions of both the English and Scottish courts suggest that claims in such circumstances would not be allowed to fall into a legal 'black hole' (see section 12.3 above), these are arguably based more on considerations of policy rather than legal principle.

# Chapter 14
# Insurance, Guarantees and Bonds

## 14.1 Insurance – general principles

### 14.1.1 Introduction

Construction insurance is a specialised and complex subject, a comprehensive exploration of which is beyond the scope of this chapter. This chapter deals only with the essentials of the subject, primarily in the context of the Standard Building Contract (SBC) insurance provisions. However, most standard form building contracts contain insurance provisions which are broadly similar.

In the majority of building contracts the contractor undertakes to indemnify the employer for loss and liabilities arising from death of or injury to persons and loss of or damage to property, and the contractor will be obliged to maintain employer's liability and public liability insurance to cover the risk of such loss or liability occurring.

Such types of insurance fall within the category of 'liability' insurance. In other words, the insurance will cover the liability which the insured party has to a third party as a result of the insured event.

Most construction contracts will also expressly deal with the other common category of insurance, namely, property insurance. In the context of construction contracts this type of insurance will cover the contract works, site materials, plant and equipment. The obligation to take out and maintain such insurance may be dealt with in differing ways. Thus, while in most cases insurance will be in the joint names of employer and contractor, some contracts may provide that the obligation to take out such insurance is that of the employer, while others may impose that obligation on the contractor.

It should also be borne in mind that the characteristics of certain types of contract may demand more extensive insurance requirements. For example, insurance may need to be taken out for certain contracts (but not others) relating to business interruption, fortuitous pollution, marine claims and/or professional indemnity. At the same time, not all risks are insurable (or at least not under conventional policies). An obvious example of this is a construction defect not involving a design error. While this may be insurable under a specialist latent defects policy (see section 14.4 below), it will not be covered by a standard property insurance policy or a professional indemnity policy.

### 14.1.2 Definition of insurance

Broadly speaking, a contract of insurance is a contract whereby, for a consideration (normally involving payment of a premium), the insured obtains a benefit (usually payment of money) upon the happening of a certain event in respect of which there is uncertainty as to either whether it will happen or when it will happen. Finally, the insurance must be 'against something', see *Prudential Insurance Co.* v. *IRC* (1904).

### 14.1.3 Legal characteristics of insurance

The requirement that insurance must be 'against something' is generally taken to mean that the insured must have an 'insurable interest'. This means that the insured must have a pecuniary interest in the subject matter of the insurance so that upon the occurrence of the insured event the insured has, as a result, either himself suffered a loss or incurred a legal liability.

The other fundamental principle to which all insurance contracts are subject is that of *uberrimae fidei*, or utmost good faith. This principle requires each party to make a full disclosure of all material facts which may influence the other party in deciding to enter into the contract. A failure to disclose such material facts may render the policy void, which in practical terms would allow the insurer to refuse to meet a claim. This would apply even in the absence of fraudulent intent.

### 14.1.4 Subrogation

The principle of subrogation is common to all insurance contracts which involve the insurer indemnifying the insured in respect of a loss or a liability. Subrogation means that the insurer is entitled to exercise any remedy which may have been exercisable by the insured in respect of the insured event. In practice, it means that the insurer can pursue a claim (in the name of the insured) against a third party who may be responsible, either wholly or partly, for the insured loss. Such a right is subject to the insurer having made payment in respect of the insured's claim and to subrogation rights not having been excluded by any express contractual term. It should be noted that subrogation rights are not available against a party who is a joint insured under a joint names insurance policy, see *Petrofina (UK) Ltd and Others* v. *Magnaload Ltd and Others* (1983). An example of this is the Joint Names Policy to be effected under Options A–C of the SBC, considered below in section 14.2.4.

### 14.1.5 Indemnities and insurance

It is important to recognise the distinction between indemnity and insurance. A building contract will normally contain provisions in terms of which the contractor will undertake to indemnify the employer against the occurrence of certain events. The contract will also impose obligations on either or both of the parties relative to the insurance of risks. There is a crossover between these indemnity and insurance obligations, insofar as insurance may be required to be taken out against the risks covered by certain indemnities, but the obligations are not necessarily co-extensive. Risks covered by a particular indemnity may not necessarily be insurable. This is a matter which it is prudent for the party giving the indemnity to check. Further, the parties may agree that a certain risk be covered by insurance and that neither party should have liability, notwithstanding fault.

Clauses 6.1 and 6.2 of the SBC broadly impose an obligation on the Contractor to indemnify the Employer against two matters: firstly, against death and personal injury arising out of the carrying out of the Works, except to the extent that the death or injury is due to the act or neglect of the Employer or any of the Employer's Persons; and secondly, against property damage (other than damage to the Works) arising out of the carrying out of the Works and to the extent that the damage is due to any default of the Contractor or any of the Contractor's Persons.

It should be noted that the Contractor's liability for property damage arises to the extent due to his negligence and/or default whereas his liability for death or personal injury is not so limited. In either case, loss or damage arising from the act or neglect of the Employer, or those for whom he is responsible will be excluded and so should normally be insured separately.

## 14.2 Insurance under the SBC

### 14.2.1 Introduction

The SBC imposes (or, in some cases, gives an option to impose) obligations to take out and maintain insurance covering the following risks:

- personal injury and death (see section 14.2.2 below);
- damage to property (other than the Works) arising from the Contractor's default (again, see section 14.2.2);
- 'non-negligent' damage to property (other than the works) (see section 14.2.3);
- damage to the Works (see section 14.2.4).

Insurance against the risk of loss of liquidated and ascertained damages (formerly an option pursuant to clause 22D of JCT 98) is no longer to be found within the SBC, largely due to the limited scope of cover which has been available and low level of use. Excepted Risks are excluded from the obligation to insure (see section 14.2.9 below).

There are certain types of insurance cover not provided for by the SBC, for example, latent defects insurance (see section 14.4 below). A well-advised party to a construction contract will consider whether any such (and other) risks should be covered by insurance.

### 14.2.2 Insurance against injuries to persons or damage to property

Under clause 6.4 of the SBC, the obligation to insure against the death of, or injury to, any person or loss of, or damage to, any property arising out of or in consequence of the execution of the Works is imposed on the Contractor. This reflects the indemnity given by the Contractor under clauses 6.1 and 6.2 for such injury, damage or loss (see section 14.1.5 above). The cover is usually contained in two separate policies, namely a public liability policy and an employer's liability policy.

Insurance relating to personal injury or death of an employee of the Contractor must comply with the Employers' Liability (Compulsory Insurance) Act 1969 which specifies a statutory minimum level of cover, currently £5 million, see regulation 3(1) of the Employers' Liability (Compulsory Insurance) Regulations 1998.

Insurance cover in respect of the death of, or injury to, other persons and loss of, or damage to, property will be effected under a public liability policy. The minimum amount of public liability cover in respect of any one occurrence should be stated in the Contract Particulars. The insurance must remain in force until practical completion.

### 14.2.3 Clause 6.5.1 insurance

There is a further option open to the Employer under clause 6.5.1 of the SBC. This insurance need only be taken out by the Contractor if the Contract Particulars so specify and it covers the potential liability of the Employer to third parties which would not normally be met by the Contractor's public liability insurance nor covered by their indemnity under clause 6.2.

This insurance relates to damage to property, other than the Works, and to Site Materials, caused by certain specified risks, namely collapse; subsidence; heave; vibration; weakening or removal of support, or lowering of ground water arising out of, or in the course of carrying out, the Works. This cover is most commonly required when there is neighbouring property susceptible to damage by any of these risks.

Under clause 6.5.1 fault does not need to be established, but there are a number of exceptions which reduce considerably the scope of this insurance cover, namely:

- injury or damage for which the Contractor is liable under clause 6.2 (which should be insured under clause 6.4.1).
- injury or damage attributable to errors or omissions in the designing of the works (which, where there is a Contractor's Designed Portion, should be covered by professional indemnity insurance under clause 6.11);

- injury or damage which can reasonably be foreseen to be inevitable, having regard to the nature of the work to be executed or the manner of its execution;
- injury or damage which is the responsibility of the Employer to insure where Insurance Option C (insurance of existing structures) applies;
- injury or damage arising from war risks or the Excepted Risks (see section 14.2.9 below);
- injury or damage directly or indirectly caused by or arising out of pollution or contamination during the period of insurance, save in respect of a sudden identifiable, unintended and unexpected incident; and
- injury or damage which results in costs or expenses being incurred by the Employer or any other sums being payable by the Employer in respect of the damages for breach of contract, save to the extent which they would have attached in the absence of any contract.

### 14.2.4 Insurance of the Works

The SBC provides three options ('Insurance Options') for insuring the Works. A choice must be made in the Contract Particulars. However, certain provisions apply regardless of which option is selected.

The contract calls for a Joint Names Policy for All Risks Insurance. Both terms are defined in clause 6.8. Where the policy is in joint names both the Contractor and the Employer are named as an insured and either may make a claim under the policy in its own name. The insurer has no right of subrogation against either party (see section 14.1.4 above).

The All Risks Insurance which either the Contractor or Employer, as the case may be, is obliged to take out should provide cover against any physical loss or damage to work executed and Site Materials, but excluding the costs necessary to repair, replace or rectify:

- property which is defective due to wear and tear, obsolescence, deterioration, rust or mildew;
- any work executed or any Site Materials lost or damaged as a result of its own defect in design, etc; and
- loss or damage caused by or arising from the consequences of war, invasion, rebellion, nationalisation, etc., disappearance or shortage (if such disappearance or shortage is only revealed when an inventory is made or is not traceable to an identifiable event), or an Excepted Risk.

### 14.2.5 All risks insurance by the Contractor

If Option A of the SBC is selected, the Contractor must take out and maintain a Joint Names Policy for All Risks Insurance for the full reinstatement value of the Works plus a percentage, if any, to cover professional fees as stated in the Contract Particulars. Under the SBC, this Joint Names Policy must be maintained up to the date of issue of the certificate of practical completion or the date of termination of the employment of the Contractor, whichever is the earlier. Where the contract is silent as to the duration of the obligation on the Contractor to maintain the Joint Names Policy, the obligation will cease on practical completion, notwithstanding the Contractor's continuing defects liability obligations, see *TWF Printers Ltd* v. *Interserve Project Services Ltd* (2006).

An alternative open to the Contractor, and which is widely used in the industry, is to use an existing annual policy which complies with the obligations in Schedule Part 3 (Insurance Options). However, the policy must still be a Joint Names Policy and the Contractor must provide documentary evidence that the policy is being maintained and, when so required, supply for inspection the policy itself and the premium receipts.

### 14.2.6  All Risks Insurance by the Employer

The second option, contained in Option B, is for the Employer to take out the Joint Names Policy for All Risks Insurance on the same terms and for the same period as described above. There is a corresponding provision to that contained in Option A, entitling the Contractor to take out the Joint Names Policy if the Employer fails to do so.

### 14.2.7  Existing structures

The third option, Option C, applies where the contract is for alteration or extension to existing structures owned by the Employer or for which they are responsible. In this case the Employer takes out and maintains the Joint Names Policy for All Risks Insurance for the Works themselves (as per Option B) but must also maintain a Joint Names Policy for existing structures to cover the cost of reinstatement, repair or replacement of loss or damage due to one or more of the Specified Perils. If the Employer fails to take out either of these two insurances the Contractor is entitled to do so and recover the cost of the premiums. The Specified Perils are defined as fire, lightning, explosion, storm, tempest, flood, bursting or overflowing of water tanks, apparatus or pipes, earthquake, aircraft and other aerial devices or articles dropped therefrom, riot and civil commotion, but excluding Excepted Risks.

Option C, and its interaction with the Contractor's obligations to indemnify the Employer against property damage to the extent that it is due to default of the Contractor, has produced some interesting results. The equivalent to Option C under JCT 63 stated that existing structures and the contents thereof were at the sole risk of the Employer. In the Scottish appeal of *Scottish*

*Special Housing Association* v. *Wimpey Construction UK Ltd* (1986) the House of Lords held that the effect of this wording was that the Employer was bound to insure the property against the risk of damage by all of the Specified Perils, including fire, and that the liability for risk of such damage rested with the Employer, notwithstanding that the fire was caused by the negligence of the Contractor.

The SBC does not expressly state that the existing structures are to be at the Employer's sole risk as regards the Specified Perils, however, clause 6.2 (which follows clause 20.2 of JCT 98) states that where insurance Option C applies, the Contractor's obligation thereunder to indemnify the Employer against damage to property excludes loss or damage to any insured property caused by a Specified Peril. The effect is that the Employer continues to bear the whole risk of damage to the existing structure caused by the Specified Perils notwithstanding the Contractor's negligence.

In the House of Lords decision in *British Telecommunications plc* v. *James Thomson & Sons (Engineers) Ltd* (1999) it was held that domestic sub-contractors may be under a duty of care to the Employer to prevent damage to existing structures. In that case the duty was implied as subrogation rights for nominated sub-contractors were removed, whereas they were preserved for domestic sub-contractors. In *Kruger Tissue (Industries) Ltd* v. *Frank Galliers Ltd* (1998), it was held that a negligent contractor could be liable for consequential losses suffered by an Employer notwithstanding that the damage occurred to an existing structure covered by a Joint Names Policy. This was on the basis that consequential losses were not included in the losses where the Employer is required to insure under what is now Option C.

Whilst at one time it may not have been clear whether the Employer had a right of indemnity against a negligent Contractor where insurance has been effected under Option C, it does now appear clear that the Employer has no obligation to indemnify the contractor against claims by third parties against the Contractor, in respect of this same damage, see *Aberdeen Harbour Board* v. *Heating Enterprises (Aberdeen) Ltd* (1990).

### 14.2.8  Claims

The consequences of loss of or damage to the works under the SBC vary according to which insurance Option has been selected.

If the Contractor has taken out insurance under Option A the Contractor must give notice of the loss or damage to the Architect or to the Employer and, following any inspection by the insurers, the Contractor must restore the damaged work and repair or replace any lost or damaged Site Materials. The contractor must authorise the insurers to pay any monies to the Employer, who then passes them on to the Contractor by way of interim certificates.

No other sums are payable to the Contractor by virtue of the loss or damage (this would appear to exclude a claim for loss and expense under clauses 4.19 to 4.22), although an extension of time may be granted if the loss or damage was occasioned by any of the Specified Perils (see clause 2.26.8).

Where the All Risks Insurance has been taken out by the Employer under Option B there is a similar procedure for the Contractor to give notice, but any restoration, replacement or repair work is to be treated as a Variation and valued accordingly. In this case, any shortfall between the insurance proceeds and the cost will be made up by the employer. Under Option A, in contrast, the contractor will only receive such monies as the insurers pay out.

Where loss or damage affects work being carried out to existing structures which have been insured by the employer, there is an option under the SBC for either party to terminate the employment of the contractor if it is just and equitable so to do. Any dispute on this point is to be referred for resolution by adjudication, arbitration or the court. If no notice of termination is served, or where the adjudicator, arbiter or court decides that it was not just and equitable to terminate the contractor's employment, then the contractor must restore, replace or repair the loss or damage, such work being treated as a variation. There is little authority on what is meant by 'just and equitable' but it would appear to include commercial viability of the project from either party's perspective.

### 14.2.9 Excepted Risks

The provisions of clauses 6.1, 6.2 and 6.4.1 of the SBC are each subject to clause 6.6 which excludes from the Contractor's liability personal injury to or the death of any person or any damage, loss or injury caused to the Works or Site Materials, work executed, the site or any other property by the effect of an Excepted Risk. These are defined in the SBC as ionising radiations or contamination by radioactivity from any nuclear fuel or from any nuclear waste from the combustion of nuclear fuel, radioactive, toxic, explosive or other hazardous properties of any explosive nuclear assembly or nuclear component thereof, and pressure waves caused by aircraft or other aerial devices travelling at sonic or supersonic speeds.

## 14.3 *Professional indemnity insurance*

Consideration of the terms and conditions of appointment of construction professionals is outside the scope of this book. However, with the continuing demand for design and build packages, professional indemnity or design liability insurance for contractors has become an integral part of the building contract structure in terms of spreading risk.

Under a design and build contract the contractor assumes responsibility for both design and construction of the project and, in the absence of in-house designers, will sub-contract design to one or more professional firms of architects, structural engineers, services engineers or the like. Nonetheless, the employer's contract remains with the contractor alone, albeit a prudent employer would also seek collateral warranties from each member of the design team.

In the event of a defect in design the employer's primary claim will lie against the contractor and it is for this reason that the contractor would be well advised (if not obliged under the contract) to maintain professional indemnity insurance to cover any such claim. The contractor or his insurers may have a right of recovery against the design consultants and/or their professional indemnity insurers. It should be tied to any limitation of actions period.

An obligation on the Contractor to take out and maintain professional indemnity insurance is contained within clause 6.11 of the SBC.

It is worth noting the extent of the Contractor's liability under clause 2.19.1 of the SBC, where there is a Contractor's Designed Portion, is 'the like liability to the Employer . . . as would an architect or as the case may be other appropriate professional designer holding himself out as competent to take on work for such design'. The comparable obligation in the SBC/DB is to be found in clause 2.17.1.

This design warranty therefore equates the duty of the contractor to that of a professional designer, namely the duty to exercise reasonable skill and care. This removes any term, which may otherwise be implied, that the design is fit for the purpose for which it is required. Most insurers are not prepared to cover such a fitness for purpose warranty given by a design professional, and similarly are not prepared to cover such a warranty from a contractor with design responsibility.

Professional indemnity policies are usually issued on a 'claims made' basis. This means that any claim will be dealt with under the policy in force during the year in which the claim is made. For that reason it is prudent for the contractor to maintain professional indemnity insurance long after completion of a project. Clause 6.11 of SBC (and of the SBC/DB) provides that such insurance should be maintained for the period stated in the contract particulars. For most projects this will be a period of 10 or 12 years.

The amount of professional indemnity insurance cover should ideally be sufficient to cover any loss likely to result from a defect in design. Parties should, however, be aware that this is a continuing annual obligation. Notwithstanding the usual qualifications relating to availability of cover and the terms of renewal, parties should take care when agreeing the level of cover, bearing in mind the potentially volatile nature of the insurance market.

It is of course possible to limit the potential liability of the contractor and indeed clause 2.19.2 of the SBC (and clause 2.17.3 of the SBC/DB) permits the parties to insert a ceiling of liability for loss of use, loss of profit or other consequential loss arising in respect of the liability of the Contractor for inadequacies in design.

## 14.4 Latent defects insurance

This is a separate type of policy which the employer himself can take out to cover physical damage to the works regardless of who is legally at fault. The policy will normally run from practical completion of the works for ten years (it is otherwise known as 'decennial insurance'), and covers major physical damage or inherent defects in the structure which threaten its stability. The defect must be inherent, (i.e. existing from the outset) but not discovered until after completion of the building.

As such a policy is intended to cover major damage, regardless of who is responsible, premiums tend to be high and this may explain why latent defects insurance is not currently widely used in the UK. Further, such policies do tend to contain exclusions which have not found favour in the UK. Also, from the contractor's perspective, unless such a policy contains a waiver of subrogation (available at additional cost) it is of little benefit to them. Such insurance does, of course, have the advantage that, in the event of a design fault becoming apparent, it is not necessary for the employer to prove breach of contract and/or negligence on the part of the contractor and/or design consultant. Although consequential loss extensions are available at additional cost, it should be noted that these policies will normally only cover physical damage to the building. Therefore a claim for negligent design, for example, on account of a building having a smaller net internal area than that set out in the employer's requirements, would have to be dealt with by a claim in the usual way against the contractor or designer who produced the drawings.

## 14.5 Guarantees

### 14.5.1 Introduction

It is common in construction contracts for the employer to require a guarantee of the contractor's obligations to be given by a third party. The third party may guarantee to carry out and complete the construction works and/or pay to the employer the damages they incur due to the contractor's breach of contract. Guarantees of the contractor's obligations will usually take the form of a parent company guarantee or a bond granted by a surety or bank.

Less common in the Scottish construction market is a guarantee in favour of the contractor of the employer's obligations. Such a guarantee may be granted by an employer's holding company to guarantee that payment will be made to the contractor.

The third party providing the guarantee will usually levy a charge against the party it is guaranteeing as well as requiring a counter-indemnity for any payment it makes under the guarantee.

The requirement for any guarantee depends on the circumstances of each transaction, the creditworthiness of the contracting parties and balancing the additional cost of the guarantee against the risk of not having third party backing.

The need to provide a guarantee will usually be specified in tender documents and in turn made a condition of the construction contract. It may be that delivery of the guarantee in a pre-agreed form is a suspensive condition to the building contract coming into effect or to the first payment being made. Alternatively, non-delivery of the guarantee or a substantial change in the financial value of the guarantor may be included as a material breach entitling the other party to terminate the contract.

### 14.5.2 Nature of guarantees

In broad terms, a contract of guarantee is an undertaking by a person to secure the performance of the obligations of a party under a contract. A guarantee may (subject to the law of prescription) be unlimited as to time and amount.

A bond may, except in certain circumstances where it is construed as an on-demand bond (see section 14.6.3 below), be regarded as a form of guarantee, see *City of Glasgow District Council* v. *Excess Insurance Company Ltd* (1986).

Despite the frequent use of guarantees, few of the institutions responsible for promoting standard forms of construction contract have published standard forms of guarantee (other than for performance bonds) so it is left to the parties to devise their own wording.

### 14.5.3 Cautionary and principal obligations

A distinction may need to be drawn between a guarantee which is an independent obligation and one which is truly a 'cautionary obligation' and thus accessory to the principal obligation. The distinction can be important as, in the absence of express wording, variation of the principal contract may discharge a cautionary obligation. It is a question of fact whether the obligation is one of caution or a principal obligation, although clear wording should remove any doubt.

If the obligation is truly one of caution, it must be given the narrowest construction which the words will reasonably bear, see *Harmer* v. *Gibb* (1911). The cautioner's liability can never exceed that of the principal debtor and on payment of the debt a cautioner is entitled to recover from the principal debtor all sums which they have paid to the creditor. They are also entitled to demand from the creditor an assignation of the debt, any security held for it, and any diligence done upon it, so as to enable them to enforce their right of relief against the principal debtor.

Under section 6 of the Prescription and Limitation (Scotland) Act 1973 the prescriptive period applicable to cautionary obligations is five years. The creditor should also have regard to any provision in the guarantee which provides for service of a demand on the guarantor.

Under section 8 of the Mercantile Law Amendment (Scotland) Act 1856, unless stated expressly to the contrary, there is no need for the creditor to pursue a remedy against the principal debtor before suing the cautioner (as was previously the position under common law).

In *De Montfort Insurance Co. plc* v. *Lafferty* (1997), which related to a performance bond, it was held that a guarantor was not released from their obligations as a result of novation of the original building contract, the effect of which was to substitute the original employer with another party.

### 14.5.4 Parent company guarantees

In response to a tender request to provide a guarantee, contractors will often offer a parent company guarantee instead of a conditional bond. However, although such guarantees and bonds are based on the same legal principles, they offer distinct remedies and should be considered by the employer as separate elements of the contractor's overall performance security package.

There is no industry style of parent company guarantee but typically the trigger for calling on the guarantee will be the default or insolvency of the contractor. The parent company or holding company may undertake to physically perform the contractor's obligations and/or pay such damages to the employer as arise from the contractor's default. As with a conditional bond, a parent company guarantee will often contain a specific limitation on the level of the guarantor's liability and the duration of the guarantee although an employer may expect such limitations to be equivalent to the contractor's liability under the construction contract and to endure for the same period as the contractor's liability under the construction contract.

## 14.6 Bonds

### 14.6.1 Introduction

A bond is usually provided up to a maximum sum of money which will become payable in certain circumstances should one of the parties to a contract default. Normally, a performance bond will subsist only in respect of claims made prior to an end-date, typically either the date of practical completion or of making good defects. Thus, it will not normally, as a parent company guarantee often will, cover the cost of making good latent defects.

## 14.6.2 Performance bonds

These are the most commonly used types of bond in the construction industry. The main purpose of a performance bond is to enable the employer to secure completion of the works for which they have contracted without incurring additional costs arising due to the non-performance, default or insolvency of the contractor. What the grantor of the bond undertakes to perform will depend on the wording of the bond, e.g. its performance obligations may be to pay a sum equivalent to the loss or damage suffered by the employer, to pay the costs of employing another contractor to complete the works, or to pay a specified sum.

Performance bonds fall into two general categories, namely on demand bonds and conditional bonds.

## 14.6.3 On demand bonds

Unlike a guarantee, an on demand bond constitutes a primary obligation not dependent on first establishing the liability of a third party, i.e. (in most cases) the contractor. An on demand bond is payable upon the creditor's demand without any requirement to prove default or the amount of damages. The bondsman is then obliged to pay up to the level of the demand, subject to any monetary limit to the bond itself and subject to the demand complying with the terms of the bond.

In the absence of fraud, a court will not normally prevent enforcement of an on demand bond, see *Edward Owen Engineering Ltd* v. *Barclays Bank International Ltd* (1978). The party challenging the demand must be able to show that the only realistic inference from the facts is that the demand was fraudulent and that the bondsman was aware of the fraud. In most cases the bondsman will be prepared to pay upon demand, without challenge, because it, in turn, has obtained a counter-indemnity from the contractor.

It will be apparent that such bonds are open to abuse and are becoming less and less common, harder to agree and very expensive (if available at all). They are used more in international contracts where a dispute over the conditionality of a bond (see section 14.6.4 below) is likely to be very difficult to resolve.

The question also arises as to the consequences where a bond is improperly called. It is suggested that the employer should account to the contractor for the proceeds of the bond where the employer has not in fact suffered a loss in respect of the matter for which the bond was allegedly called.

In *The Royal Bank of Scotland Ltd* v. *Dinwoodie* (1982) the bondsman paid out monies pursuant to a performance bond. The bond was supported by a counter-indemnity from individual guarantors who argued that the bank was wrong to make payment under the performance bond. On the wording of the bond, which guaranteed 'the damages sustained by the employer' by the contractor's default, it was held by the Court of Session that the surety bank was obliged to be satisfied, at the very least, that damages had been sustained by the employer and also as to the quantification of those damages.

### 14.6.4 Conditional or default bonds

Unlike an on demand bond, a conditional bond will normally provide that it can only be called upon the occurrence of certain events relative to the contractor's obligations under the principal construction contract. If there is no liability under the principal contract there will be no liability under the bond.

A conditional bond is payable upon the creditor's demand, which will usually require to be accompanied by evidence that the condition entitling a call on the bond has been triggered. The creditor may also be required to provide evidence that the amount claimed reflects the actual amount of damages it has suffered.

The triggers for calling the bond should be clearly set out in the bond. These may include, for example, the employer establishing that the contractor is in breach of contract and the extent of the damages arising therefrom, the insolvency of the contractor or upon presentation of an arbiter's award or court decree or possibly the decision of an adjudicator pursuant to the 1996 Act.

### 14.6.5 ABI model form bond

There are a number of standard forms of bond and one of the most commonly used is the model form of the Association of British Insurers (ABI). This was published in 1995 (and revised in 2004) primarily in response to the English Court of Appeal decision in *Trafalgar House Construction (Regions) Ltd* v. *General Surety and Guarantee Co. Ltd* (1994), in which a form of bond then in common use (described by the Court of Appeal as 'archaic') was treated effectively as an on demand bond, despite earlier assumptions to the contrary. This decision was later overruled by the House of Lords, which followed *inter alia* the decision of *City of Glasgow District Council* v. *Excess Insurance Co. Ltd* (1986) that a performance bond in similar terms was a cautionary obligation.

The ABI bond provides that the guarantor will 'satisfy and discharge the damages sustained by the employer as established and ascertained pursuant to and in accordance with the provisions of or by reference to the contract'. Thus the employer's entitlement is linked expressly to the contract itself. If, as with most standard forms, the contract contains a mechanism for ascertainment of loss and damages following breach by the contractor, then this mechanism must be followed before any money is payable under the bond. However, the wording of the bond does not go so far as to state that the employer has to establish the amount of his loss, if necessary by going to court or to arbitration, and it therefore leaves some uncertainty as to exactly at what stage and in what circumstances the bond can be called.

The ABI bond expressly limits liability as to time and money. The expiry date for making a call on the bond is a matter for negotiation but typically the date will be stated as the date of practical completion of the works or the issue of the certificate of completion of making good.

The bond contains a prohibition on assignation by the employer without the prior written consent of the guarantor and the contractor. In practice this can lead to difficulties where, as in *De Montfort Insurance Co. plc* v. *Lafferty* (1997), there is a change in the employer, either due to novation or because a funder has stepped into the building contract on the employer's default. This particular difficulty can be overcome by inserting additional wording stating that the bond will be assignable to any successor to the employer under the contract.

The ABI bond also makes clear that the bond operates as a guarantee, i.e. it is ancillary to the principal contract. Therefore if there is no liability or limited liability under the principal contract, liability under the bond will be similarly excluded or limited. In order to avoid the potential difficulties associated with cautionary obligations, referred to above, it is made clear that the guarantor shall not be discharged or released by any alteration of any of the terms, conditions and provisions of the principal contract.

One of the most likely situations in which an employer would wish to call on a bond is the insolvency of the contractor. This will of course depend upon the wording of the bond but in *Perar BV* v. *General Surety and Guarantee Co. Ltd* (1994) the English Court of Appeal held that insolvency and consequent termination of the contractor's employment was not a breach of contract which could trigger the bond. Although a termination event, insolvency was not itself a breach of the contract and the right to call for payment of the bond would not arise until, for example, the contractor had failed to make payment of any sums consequently due to the employer.

The ABI bond does not provide that the contractor's insolvency would allow the employer to demand payment of the bond amount. This difficulty is often addressed by the insertion of additional wording to specify that insolvency will be treated as a breach of contract by the contractor and establishing a method of determining what level of damages is payable to the employer.

### 14.6.6 Retention bonds

Such bonds are becoming more commonplace as an alternative to the employer making a cash retention from the contract sum. The bond, backed up by a bank or insurance company, will secure the level of retention until the contractual date for release. If the contractor fails to honour its obligations to remedy defects, the employer can call upon the bondsman to pay the requisite sum up to the maximum amount of the bond. A form of Retention Bond is to be found in Part 2 of Schedule Part 6 to the SBC.

### 14.6.7 Advance payment bonds

Clause 4.8 of the SBC provides that, if so stated in the Contract Particulars, an advance payment may be made by the Employer to the Contractor which shall be reimbursed on the terms set out in the Contractor Particulars. Although this provision is not often used it may be of value in cases where the Contractor requires to expend significant amounts of money, e.g. for pre-ordering specialist materials, at the commencement of the contract. In such circumstances, the Employer may obtain security for reimbursement of the advance payment by means of an advance payment bond, a form of which is contained in Part 1 of Schedule Part 6 to the SBC.

# Chapter 15
# Dispute Resolution

## 15.1 Introduction

Disputes frequently arise under construction contracts. In this chapter, we will consider certain of the available methods by which disputes can be resolved. Two methods of dispute resolution are, however, so significant that they merit chapters in their own right. In Scotland, the majority of construction industry disputes were, traditionally, resolved by arbitration. That arose from the commonplace insertion of arbitration clauses into construction contracts, and the right of a party to such a contract to insist upon arbitration in such circumstances. Arbitration is considered in Chapter 17. Nevertheless, the Scottish courts frequently become involved in construction contract disputes, with many cases that are ultimately resolved by arbitration having started off in the courts, whether in the Court of Session or the Sheriff Court.

The 1996 Act introduced a statutory right to adjudication. Adjudication was not a creation of the 1996 Act; it had been available in Scotland in relation to certain disputes arising under the DOM/1/Scot and DOM/2/Scot forms of sub-contract and the With Contractor's Design versions of the Scottish Building Contract (SBC). Adjudication is considered in Chapter 16.

## 15.2 Litigation

### 15.2.1 Introduction

Prior to the advent of adjudication, as we now understand it, in the absence of an arbitration agreement, or where parties have waived the arbitration agreement, the courts in Scotland traditionally resolved building contract disputes. While the number of disputes reaching the courts has dropped following the introduction of adjudication, the courts are, on the whole, becoming the preferred forum of final determination due to the perceived cumbersome nature of arbitration in Scotland.

The SBC has, as a default provision, legal proceedings as the means of dispute resolution unless arbitration is specifically contracted for. Articles 8 and 9 of the SBC contain provisions related to arbitration and court proceedings. If the parties wish to resolve disputes by arbitration, then the Contract

Particulars require to be completed to state that article 8 and clauses 9.3 to 9.8 of the Conditions apply and the words 'do not apply' which appear in the Contract Particulars need to be deleted.

If court action is proceeded with, the action can be raised either in the Sheriff Court, which is the local court for each area, or the Court of Session, which is based in Edinburgh. Typically, small to medium sized claims are pursued in the Sheriff Court whilst larger value or more complex claims are pursued in the Court of Session. In which Sheriff Court the action can be pursued depends upon the rules of jurisdiction. For example, the Sheriff Court local to the defender's place of business, or that of the pursuer's business address where the sums sued for are to be paid, are two possible grounds of jurisdiction. The Civil Jurisdiction and Judgments Act 1982 sets out the various grounds of jurisdiction. Parties may agree in the building contract which courts have jurisdiction. A detailed consideration of the law relative to jurisdiction is beyond the scope of this book.

Claims with a monetary value of up to £1,500 must be pursued in the Sheriff Court. This figure is set to rise to £5,000 in January 2008. Above this figure, the Court of Session and the Sheriff Court have concurrent jurisdiction in respect of monetary claims.

Within the Court of Session, a choice needs to be made by the pursuer as to whether to initiate proceedings in the Commercial Court or under the ordinary procedure. The court rules provide for a more flexible procedure to be adopted by the Commercial Court.

### 15.2.2 The procedure

The rules of procedure of the Sheriff Court are set out in the Sheriff Courts (Scotland) Act 1907, the First Schedule of which contains the Ordinary Cause Rules 1993. The rules of procedure of the Court of Session are set out in the Act of Sederunt (Rules of the Court of Session 1994) 1994 Schedule 2, which contains the Rules of the Court of Session 1994. Both of these are amended from time to time.

A detailed examination of court procedure is beyond the scope of this book, however, certain important features of Court of Session and Sheriff Court actions are considered below.

### The initiating writ or summons

An action for payment in the Court of Session, whether a commercial action or under ordinary procedure, is initiated by a summons. An ordinary cause in the Sheriff Court is initiated by an initial writ. In each case, these set out details of the remedy sought by the pursuer, the relevant facts and circumstances and the legal basis of the claim.

**Sheriff Court**

In the Sheriff Court a defender, ordinarily, has 21 days from service upon him of an initial writ to defend the action. The 21-day period can be shortened with the permission of the Sheriff. A defender defends the action by lodging a notice of intention to defend. If the defender does not lodge a notice of intention to defend within that period, the pursuer may seek a decree.

If a notice of intention to Defend is lodged, the defender must lodge defences 14 days after the 21-day period of notice has expired. If the defender also has a claim against the pursuer in certain defined circumstances, a counterclaim setting this out may be lodged and dealt with at the same time as the principal action. There then follows a fixed period in which each party expands on their pleadings (the initial writ, defences and any counterclaim and answers to it) to respond to the other side's case and focus the issues between them. This is known as the period of adjustment. After the period of adjustment, the court will hear both parties at an Options Hearing to determine further procedure.

Further procedure may take the form of a debate, which is a hearing to deal with legal issues. These could include arguments that one party's case is not specific or detailed enough to give the other party fair notice of the party's position or arguments that even if one party proved everything it offered to prove, it would still have no legal entitlement to the remedy sought. The debate may resolve the whole action or it may lead to refinement of a party's case. A proof or a proof before answer may be ordered after, or instead of, a debate. The purpose of a proof is to try the factual issues of the case by hearing evidence from witnesses. Where legal arguments have been reserved and are to be heard at the conclusion of the evidence, the hearing is known as a proof before answer.

Incidental applications for matters such as the recovery of documents or interim decree are made by way of written application to the court known as a motion.

If a commercial action is raised in the Sheriff Court, the initial steps are the same as with an ordinary action. However, the defender only has seven days after the expiry of the period of notice in which to lodge defences. Thereafter, a Case Management Conference is arranged for no sooner than 14 days and no later than 28 days after the expiry of the period of notice. The sheriff has power in commercial actions to make whatever orders he thinks fit for the progress of the case. The sheriff's purpose is to secure the expeditious resolution of the action. The sheriff will remain proactive throughout the duration of the case.

**The Court of Session**

The ordinary procedure of the Court of Session is broadly similar to that of the Sheriff Court. Once the 21-day period of notice has expired, the pursuer in the action requires to formally lodge the Summons with the Court of Session for calling. This is a procedural step as opposed to a hearing of the case in court. Once the action calls, which means it appears in the rolls of court, the timetable for the action starts running. The party proposing to defend an action must enter appearance within three days of the action calling. This involves attending at the court office and formally notifying them that the action is being defended. The period for lodging defences is seven days from the date of calling.

Once defences are lodged, the pursuer is required, within 14 days, to lodge an open record, a document which comprises the summons and defences. Once this is lodged, the court fixes a start date for the period of adjustment which then runs for eight weeks. The adjustment period can be extended by the court, on application by one of the parties to the action. At the end of the adjustment period, parties can opt to go to Debate, known in the Court of Session as a procedure roll hearing, a proof or a proof before answer.

The Commercial Court of the Court of Session has a somewhat more flexible procedure. There is no automatic right to adjustment of pleadings. The procedure and progress in the case is under the direct control of the commercial judge who is proactive in his handling of the case. A case will normally be dealt with by the same judge throughout. The case first calls in front of this judge for a preliminary hearing within 14 days of the expiry of the period for lodging of defences. Thereafter, there will follow a series of hearings designed around the requirements of the case. A proof, proof before answer, debate or some alternative procedure may follow. Incidental applications are made by written motion.

It is important to be aware of the Court of Session Practice Note No. 6 of 2004 regarding commercial actions, introduced in November 2004. This includes directions as to the pre-action stage. It sets out the aim of having the matters in dispute discussed and focused in pre-action correspondence between the solicitors for both parties. It is stated in the Practice Note that the commercial action procedure works best where issues have been investigated and ventilated before the action is raised. The Practice Note directs that the pursuer should fully set out, in correspondence to the defender, the nature of the claim and the factual and legal background on which it proceeds, supply all documents relied upon and disclose any expert's report commissioned, prior to raising a commercial action. The defender is expected to provide a considered and reasoned reply and to disclose any document or expert report on which they rely. It is suggested by the Practice Note that parties may wish to consider whether all or some of the dispute may be amenable to some form of alternative dispute resolution. A failure to comply with the Practice Note may result in awards of expenses against the non-compliant party.

The Practice Direction reflects a stated desire to reserve the Commercial Court for cases in which there is a real dispute between the parties which requires to be resolved by judicial decision rather than by other means, and to enable an early ventilation of the issues in dispute. While it is a shadow of the English Civil Procedure Pre-Action protocols it reflects the same desire to make litigation in the courts the final step in the resolution of claims as opposed to the first.

### 15.2.3  Protective measures

The right to seek protective measures to secure the claim or the subject matter of the dispute, pending the outcome of proceedings, may be exercised at the outset of Sheriff Court or Court of Session proceedings, or at a later date by application to the court. In this section we consider the principal protective measures available in Scotland. It should be noted that certain of these can only be sought in the Court of Session.

#### Arrestment and inhibition

The principal protective measures are the rights to arrest or inhibit pending the outcome of the action, known as arrestment and inhibition on the dependence.

Arrestment is a means of attaching money or other moveable property of the defender in the hands of a third party. So, for example, a pursuer in an action might attach any funds at credit in the defender's bank account by placing an arrestment in the hands of the bank. That freezes the money in that account and prevents the bank from releasing it to the defender. Warrant to arrest can be granted in either the Court of Session or the Sheriff Court.

Inhibition is similar but attaches heritable property of the defender preventing the defender from selling it. Warrant to inhibit can only be granted by the Court of Session. Accordingly, a pursuer who wishes to inhibit upon the dependence of a Sheriff Court action is required to make a separate application to the Court of Session.

While previously these protective measures were granted as of right, a series of cases involving Article 1 of the First Protocol to the European Convention on Human Rights radically altered the regime, see *Karl Construction Ltd* v. *Palisade Properties plc* (2002), *Advocate General for Scotland* v. *Taylor* (2004), *Barry D Trentham Ltd* v. *Lawfield Investments Ltd* (2002), *Fab-Tek Engineering Ltd* v. *Carillion Construction Ltd* (2002), *Gillespie* v. *Toondale Ltd* (2005) and *F G Hawkes (Western) Ltd* v. *Szipt Ltd* (2007).

In *Karl Construction Ltd*, it was considered that an inhibition was an exorbitant remedy where there was no court hearing to test the case or the need for there to be an inhibition. The court rules which allowed this to be granted automatically, without any consideration by a judge, were not compliant with the Human Rights Act 1998. It was held that a warrant to inhibit should only be granted where a judge was satisfied there was a *prima facie* case (a relevant and persuasive case on the face of the facts as set out) and a genuine need for the use of the inhibition, such as substantial risk of insolvency or inability of the defender to pay. This could be evidenced by a refusal to make payment where there was no obvious defence to the claim.

In *Advocate General for Scotland* it was held that the applicant for a warrant to arrest or inhibit need only establish a *prima facie* case on the merits of the action. They do not require to demonstrate a need for the diligence although it would assist the judge being asked to grant the warrant if they did. It is also necessary to show that the diligence sought is proportionate to the claim.

In *Barry D Trentham Ltd*, it was held that the burden of justifying the use of inhibition was on the pursuer. Its use will be justified where the pursuer can establish a significant risk of the defender's insolvency, either in the sense of an excess of liabilities over assets or simply an inability to pay debts as they fall due. In deciding whether or not there is a risk of insolvency, the court looks at the defender's present financial situation but also at future events, insofar as they can be predicted with any accuracy. If there is considerable doubt about whether the pursuer's claim will succeed, it may not be reasonable to grant security in respect of it. The effect of a defence on a *prima facie* case was also considered in *Barry D Trentham Ltd*. The existence of a defence could cast doubt on the pursuer's prospects of success, in which case security may not be justified. The *prima facie* case test was meant to be a substantial hurdle for the pursuer to surmount akin to the good arguable case test used in England in relation to Mareva injunctions. The existence of an apparently substantial defence meant the court should scrutinise the claim and defence to determine whether inhibition was appropriate.

In *Gillespie* the court again considered the test to be applied by the court when a party applied for an inhibition to be recalled. The test in *Barry D Trentham Ltd* was approved, with the Inner House recognising that the serious interference caused to a party's property rights by granting the security justifies the application of a high test. At the stage of an application for recall, the court should consider the pleadings as a whole (i.e. the summons or initial writ and the defences) as well as oral submissions made in support of or opposition to the application for recall to allow a decision to be made on the whole circumstances of the case. The pursuer's case needs to be cogent and convincing and the pursuer must demonstrate good cause for the remedy he seeks.

*Fab-Tek Engineering Ltd* dealt with arrestment and it was confirmed that the same criteria as for inhibitions applied in relation to arrestments.

In *F G Hawkes (Western) Ltd*, further guidance was given on what constituted a *prima facie* case. It was argued there that arrestments should be recalled on the basis that there were substantial lines of defence available. This was not accepted by the court. There is no principle that the existence of a positive defence prevents the granting of diligence. However, it was recognised that the greater the apparent strength of a defence, the more difficult it may be to find that a *prima facie* case exists. It will always be a matter of fact and degree but a claimant's case will be scrutinised with extra care where a positive defence was stated.

It is now necessary to apply for both a warrant to arrest and a warrant to inhibit on the dependence of an action. The latter can only be sought in the Court of Session. The application must be considered by the court. A hearing may be required by the court in certain cases, but a summons or initial writ which sets out a *prima facie* case and a full explanation as to why the warrant is required will lessen the chance of a hearing being required.

### Interim possession of property

Another protective measure available in certain circumstances in the Court of Session is provided by s.47(2) of the Court of Session Act 1988. This allows the court to make orders regarding the interim possession of property which is the subject of a court action. It is a powerful remedy in that the court may be asked to make an interim order at a very early stage of an action, without having to wait for written pleadings to be finalised or evidence to be heard. The decision is made on the basis only of the written cases and legal argument. This is because the decision is only interim and it is open to the court, at the end of the process, to reverse the interim order.

An ultimately unsuccessful attempt to use the remedy was made in *Scottish Power Generation Ltd* v. *British Energy Generation (UK) Ltd and Another* (2002). In that case, the pursuer sought to have sums of money, said to have been overpaid, placed by the defenders into a designated account to be held in trust in order to protect the funds from the claims of the first defender's creditors. The Inner House, on appeal, confirmed the basis on which the court should exercise its discretion to grant an interim order. Quoting Lord President Hope (as he then was) in *Mackenzie's Trustees* v. *Highland Regional Council* (1995), the Inner House held that the question must depend on the balance of convenience, namely the nature and degree of the harm likely to be suffered on either side by the grant or refusal of the interim order. Regard should also be had to the relative strength of the cases put forward by each party as one of the factors to be considered in determining where the balance of convenience lies. Following *Church Commissioners for England* v. *Abbey National plc* (1994), the Inner House confirmed that in order to justify an interim order, the person seeking it must establish a *prima facie* case that an obligation exists, that there is a continuing or threatened breach of that obligation and that the balance of convenience favours the making of the order sought.

The s.47(2) remedy was successfully used in *VA Tech Wabag UK Ltd* v. *Morgan Est (Scotland) Ltd* (2002). The test applied by the court was whether a valid legal case had been made out and consideration of the balance of convenience. In relation to balance of convenience, the court considered the relative strengths of the parties' cases and the maintenance of the *status quo*. The judge was prepared to treat the *status quo* as being the making of payments under the construction contract as they fell due. An exception to this may be if there are serious doubts about the solvency of the party to whom payments were to be made, although that consideration was not relevant in this particular case.

In *Purac Ltd* v. *Byzak Ltd* (2005), the court considered a s.47(2) application on the basis of three tests, namely, whether the pursuers had set out a *prima facie* case; whether the balance of convenience favoured the making of the order; and the need to maintain the integrity of the parties' contractual arrangements (or what had been referred to in *Va Tech Wabag UK Ltd* as maintaining the contractual *status quo*).

In this case, the application failed on the third test because the defenders argued there was a right of retention in any contract where there were mutual obligations between the parties. This allows one party to withhold performance until the other performs its obligations. The contractual arrangements between the parties required the right of retention to prevail over any obligation to pay. This case therefore restricted the circumstances in which it will be possible to obtain an order.

## Recovery of documents

Under the Administration of Justice (Scotland) Act 1972, section 1, an order may be sought from the court for the inspection, photographing, preservation, custody and detention of documents and other property where the documents or property appear to be relevant to any question which might arise in a court action which is likely to be brought. The order may also cover the production and recovery of the documents or property, taking of samples or carrying out experiments. Applications for such an order are sometimes referred to as 'dawn raids', as they tend to be used where there is a fear that documents or property will be destroyed and so are sought at short notice and, often, without the person in possession being given any prior notice.

The test for granting a section 1 application was confirmed in *Pearson* v. *Educational Institute of Scotland* (1997), namely that proceedings are likely to be brought and, in relation to those proceedings, that the person making the application has a *prima facie*, intelligible and stateable case.

The procedure for making an application under the 1972 Act is to apply by petition to the Court of Session. The petition requires to set out a list of the documents or other property which the applicant, known as the petitioner, wishes to be subject to the order, the address of the premises where these are likely to be and the facts on which the petitioner relies in believing that if the order is not granted, the listed documents would cease to become available. The petition is accompanied by an affidavit (a sworn witness statement) from the petitioner which supports the statements made in the petition. The petitioner also requires to give an undertaking to the court that they (1) will comply with any court order for payment of compensation if recovery of the listed items causes loss; (2) will commence a court action within a reasonable time; and (3) will not use any information obtained for any purpose other than the court action they intend to raise.

It is possible, with the court's agreement, for an application to be heard outwith the presence of the party holding the documents or property. Most applications under this procedure are dealt with in this way. In *The British Phonographic Industry Ltd* v. *Cohen, Cohen, Kelly, Cohen & Cohen Ltd* (1983) it was held that an application can be granted outwith the presence of that party if the documents are essential to the petitioner's case and are at risk of destruction or concealment. If the respondent has lodged a caveat (see below), a section 1 order can be granted without the respondent having the opportunity of being heard.

There are separate provisions in the court rules related to recovery of evidence in court actions which have already been raised. This is known as a commission and diligence for recovery of documents and is the equivalent in Scotland of the English process of discovery, albeit the former is more restricted in scope. Prior to a proof or proof before answer being allowed, the only documents that may be recovered are those required to allow a party to make more specific what is already included in their case or to allow specific replies to the other side's case, see *Moore* v. *Greater Glasgow Health Board* (1978).

An application for recovery of documents under this procedure would be accompanied by a specification of documents which is a list of the documents, property or information which the party wishes to recover.

### Suspension and interdict

Suspension is used to stop unlawful conduct taking place. It would most commonly be used in the context of suspension of a court decree where, for some reason, it has been invalidly obtained. It is often used in conjunction with the remedy of reduction where the decree would be reduced or set aside. Suspension can deal only with past actions and prevents them taking effect.

Interdict is the Scottish equivalent of an injunction in England. Its purpose is to prevent a party from carrying out an activity where their doing so would be unlawful or would infringe the rights of another party. It can also be used where there is a wish to maintain the *status quo* until a decision is made in a case. Interdict prevents a future action from taking place. It can only be used where action is threatened or where there is a reasonable apprehension that that action will be taken. It does not require the defender to do anything but prevents them from doing so thereby maintaining the *status quo*. See also section 10.7 above.

Both suspension and interdict can be obtained on an interim basis at the outset of a case with the final decision on permanent suspension and interdict being taken at the conclusion of the matter.

### Reinstatement of possession or specific relief

Where a party who is respondent in an action has done something which the court could have prohibited by interdict, there is provision in section 46 of the Court of Session Act 1988 to allow the court to order that respondent to take a positive action in order to reinstate the pursuer or petitioner in the action to the position he would have been in had the interdict been obtained. This can include an order to reinstate possession or the granting of specific relief.

**Caveats**

Caveats are a form of early warning procedure. They are documents lodged with the court to allow the party lodging them to be given notice of applications for orders being made where, in the absence of a caveat, those orders could be granted without any notice being given.

Caveats can be lodged to give notice only of certain orders, as specified in the court rules. These include interim interdict, orders for sequestration (bankruptcy) of an individual, orders for winding up or appointment of an administrator to a company and other interim orders.

It is not possible, by lodging a caveat, to gain notice of arrestment or inhibitions being sought.

### 15.2.4 Appeals

In the Sheriff Court parties have, in certain defined circumstances, a right of appeal to the Sheriff Principal or to the Court of Session. Leave (or permission) to appeal is necessary in certain circumstances. A further appeal from the Sheriff Principal to the Court of Session may also be competent. The appeals procedure in the Sheriff Court is regulated by the Sheriff Courts (Scotland) Act 1907 as amended by the Sheriff Courts (Scotland) Act 1971.

The appeal function of the Court of Session is exercised by the Inner House. If an appeal is taken from a Court of Session judge's decision, it is known as a Reclaiming Motion. As with the Sheriff Court, leave to appeal may be required in certain circumstances.

Finally, an appeal from the Inner House of the Court of Session to the House of Lords may be competent. The appeals procedure in the Court of Session, including the method by which an appeal to the House of Lords can be taken, is regulated by the Rules of the Court of Session 1994 and the Court of Session Act 1988.

## 15.3 Mediation

### 15.3.1 Introduction

Only a very small percentage of building contract cases proceed to a decision in arbitration or litigation. The vast majority of cases settle in the run up to the full hearing or proof. Settlement is often the result of negotiations at client or lawyer level. A more formal process of negotiating a case to settlement has developed, known as Alternative Dispute Resolution or ADR. Mediation is one important form of ADR. It can be initiated as an alternative to litigation or arbitration or it may be conducted in parallel with the litigation or arbitration.

The aim of mediation is to achieve a negotiated settlement in an economic and effective manner. As the process is consensual, a reference to mediation is non-binding unless the parties choose it to be binding. Parties may withdraw at any time until they have formalised the terms of any settlement reached.

The mediator is a third party 'neutral' who conducts or facilitates the process. His role is to mediate between the two or more parties to the dispute to facilitate settlement. This often involves a form of shuttle diplomacy with the mediator putting the parties' positions to each other, only bringing them together once common ground has been found. A number of organisations have trained mediators available for appointment.

One of the advantages of mediation, apart from speed and being relatively inexpensive, is that the settlement can cover any number of matters. It is not constrained by the issues in dispute, in the way that litigation and arbitration are, or by availability of legal remedies. It may be that what a party requires is an explanation or apology, to continue a business relationship, to regulate a relationship going forward or other remedy not available in the courts but in the power of the other party to provide. Creative solutions can be found and it is entirely within the control of parties what package can be put together which then results in a settlement.

The timing of a successful mediation is all important. If a reference is sought too early, the issues may not be sufficiently well prepared or focused to form a background for discussion; too late and the parties may have become entrenched in their positions. A will to resolve the matter through the process is necessary before progress can be made.

Mediation can be initiated at any time by either of the parties inviting the other to accede to the process, or by having one of the mediation bodies open up dialogue. Parties may be represented by lawyers through the process, but that is not essential. Normally, the costs of the whole process are shared equally by the parties.

### 15.3.2 Mediation and the SBC

A significant new provision in the SBC is Article 9.1 which provides that the parties may by agreement seek to resolve any dispute or difference arising under the contract through mediation. This would be implied in any event since parties can agree to mediate any dispute at any time. However, adding reference to it is useful in directing parties to consider this as a potential way of resolving disputes.

### 15.3.3 The approach of the courts

Mediation is developing in Scotland. The Scottish courts have become more favourably disposed towards mediation although they have not yet embraced mediation in the way courts in other jurisdictions have. In the Court of Session, the Commercial Court Practice Note No. 6 of 2004 encourages parties to consider ADR before an action is raised. In the Sheriff Court, there are a number of mediation initiatives, including a provision in the commercial action rules that a sheriff may make an order for the use of ADR.

The courts are becoming increasingly aware of the benefits of mediation. In the case of *Candleberry Ltd.* v. *West End Home Owners Association and Others* (2006) Lord Nimmo Smith observed:

'we hope that we have said enough to reinforce our observations in court, that this is a dispute which ought to be resolved. It cannot be in the interests of the neighbourhood that it be prolonged, and we would encourage a resolution by compromise, perhaps with the assistance of a mediator.'

This is a clear indication of the promotion of mediation by the Scottish courts, which will continue to develop. There have been a number of endorsements of mediation in the English courts.

In *Dunnett* v. *Railtrack plc* (2002), Lord Justice Brooke said.

'Skilled mediators are now able to achieve results satisfactory to both parties in many cases which are quite beyond the power of lawyers and courts to achieve.'

In *Cowl and Others* v. *Plymouth City Council* (2002), Lord Woolf CJ said:

'insufficient attention is paid to the paramount importance of avoiding litigation whenever this is possible . . . both sides must by now be acutely conscious of the contribution alternative dispute resolution can make to resolving disputes in a manner which both meets the needs of the parties and the public and saves time, expense and stress.'

In *Reed Executive plc* v. *Reed Business Information Ltd* (2004), Lord Justice Jacob said:

'a good and tough mediator can bring about a sense of commercial reality to both sides which their own lawyers, however good, may not be able to achieve.'

In *Halsey* v. *The Milton Keynes General NHS Trust* (2004), Lord Justice Dyson said:

'But it is also right to point out that mediation often succeeds where previous attempts to settle have failed.'

The Government has also endorsed mediation. In March 2001, the Chancellor of the Exchequer announced an 'ADR Pledge' in which all government departments and agencies made commitments including that ADR would be considered and used in all suitable cases, where accepted by the other party. A number of government initiatives have followed since the pledge was made.

The position in England merits some consideration, simply because direction by the courts for parties to go to mediation is, in all probability, inevitable in Scotland. Under the English Civil Procedure Rules, there is an overriding objective requiring the court to actively manage cases which includes encouraging the use of ADR procedures to prompt an earlier settlement.

The courts have tended to stop short of compelling parties to mediate as it is considered this would amount to an unacceptable obstruction on their right of access to the court, which would be contrary to the European Convention on Human Rights. Further, it is recognised that ADR procedures work best when parties voluntarily take part in them and that compelling people to do so would not be effective. The Pre-Action Protocol for Construction and Engineering Disputes which came into force on 6 April 2007 expressly recognises that no party can or should be forced to mediate or enter into any form of alternative dispute resolution.

Despite this, however, in the case of *Shirayama Shokusan Co. Ltd* v. *Danovo Ltd (No.1)* (2004) the judge granted an order for mediation which had been applied for by the defendant but opposed by the claimant. The court considered that, under the Civil Procedure Rules, it had jurisdiction to direct ADR between the parties even if one party is unwilling. It was also considered that in the circumstances of this case, an attempt at mediation was worthwhile. The parties were likely to need to work together in future years and a number of the disputes between them appeared to be in relation to small points where it was considered mediation could be beneficial. They also had a shared commercial interest.

Where parties have contracted to mediate, the courts have been willing to enforce the contractual commitment. In *Cable & Wireless plc* v. *IBM United Kingdom Ltd* (2002), the parties' contract contained a mediation clause. It provided that if disputes arose, they should be resolved through negotiation and that, if that was not successful, an attempt should be made in good faith to resolve the dispute through ADR as recommended to the parties by CEDR.

Cable & Wireless objected to the Court action being put on hold while a mediation took place but the judge found against them for two reasons. Firstly, the contract obliged the parties to participate in an ADR procedure and this was an obligation sufficiently certain to allow a court to ascertain whether it had been complied with. Secondly, it would be contrary to public policy to decline to enforce references in contracts to ADR. It was said that strong cause would have to be shown before a court could justify declining to enforce such an agreement. It would not be sufficient that an issue of construction of a long-term contract (as in this case) was involved. The judge, Mr Justice Colman, stated that parties entering into an ADR agreement should recognise that:

> 'mediation as a tool for dispute resolution is not designed to achieve solutions which reflect the precise legal rights and obligations of the parties, but rather solutions which are mutually commercially acceptable at the time of the mediation.'

Despite the lack of compulsion, there have been a number of cases in England in which the courts have considered whether a party ought to be penalised in costs for failure to mediate. The general principle, as established by the Court of Appeal in *Cowl and Others* and in *Dunnett* is that a party who refuses to go to mediation without good and sufficient reasons may be penalised for that refusal, particularly, in respect of costs. In *Cowl and Others*, Lord Woolf said:

> 'Today sufficient should be known about ADR to make the failure to adopt it, in particular when public money is involved, indefensible.'

Mr Justice Lightman in *Hurst v. Leeming* (2003) endorsed this fully stating:

> 'Mediation is not in law compulsory . . . But alternative dispute resolution is at the heart of today's civil justice system, and any unjustified failure to give proper attention to the opportunities afforded by mediation, and in particular in any case where mediation affords a realistic prospect of resolution of a dispute, there must be anticipated as a real possibility that adverse consequences may be attracted.'

*Hurst* was a professional negligence action. The action was found to have no merit and was dismissed by the court. The normal situation in such circumstances would be that Leeming would be entitled to his costs. Hurst argued that Leeming should not be entitled to costs because both before and after the action commenced, Hurst had proposed mediation but Leeming had refused. The court held that the fact that substantial costs had already been incurred would not be good reason to refuse to mediate – this was simply a factor to take into account in the mediation process. Neither was it a good reason to refuse to mediate that the action was one of professional negligence or that one party believed it has a watertight case. Where details had been provided refuting the other party's case, this would be a relevant consideration but would not, in itself, be sufficient to justify refusing to mediate.

The judge considered the critical factor to be whether, viewed objectively, a mediation has any real prospect of success. If it does not, a party may refuse to mediate. However, the word of warning was that if that ground was relied on and the court disagreed, the cost penalty could follow. The court stated that:

> 'the mediation process itself can and often does bring about a more sensible and more conciliatory attitude on the part of the parties than might otherwise be expected to prevail before the mediation, and may produce a recognition of the strengths and weaknesses by each party of his own case and of that of his opponent, and a willingness to accept the give and take essential to a successful mediation. What appears to be incapable of mediation before the mediation process begins often proves capable of satisfactory resolution later.'

On the particular facts of this case, it was found that the refusal to mediate was justifiable. However, that was said to be exceptional.

In *Halsey* the court gave further guidance as to how the question of whether a defendant had acted unreasonably in refusing ADR should be answered. The starting point was to say that regard should be had to all the circumstances of the particular case. Among the relevant matters to take into account are:

- the nature of the dispute;
- the merits of the case;
- the extent to which other settlement methods have been attempted;
- whether the costs of the ADR would be disproportionately high;
- whether any delay in setting up and attending the mediation would have been prejudicial; and
- whether the ADR had a reasonable prospect of success.

None of these, on its own, would be decisive and this is not an exhaustive list of factors. The factors set out in *Halsey* are now accepted as the standard test in considering whether a party has acted unreasonably in refusing to mediate. The case of *P4 Ltd* v. *Unite Integrated Solutions plc* (2006), for example, considered the question with reference to those factors.

The English courts have been involved in other issues regarding mediation including, importantly, that of the use of documents prepared for the purposes of mediation in subsequent legal proceedings.

In *Aird* v. *Prime Meridian Ltd* (2007), the parties were involved in a court action which was stayed (put on hold) to allow a mediation to take place. Prior to that, the court had ordered the parties' expert architects to meet on a without prejudice basis and put together a joint statement setting out areas of agreement and disagreement between them with a view to this being used in the mediation. They did so. The parties, in the mediation agreement, agreed to 'keep confidential all information, whether oral or written or otherwise produced for or at the mediation.' The joint statement was then used in the mediation. The mediation which followed did not result in a settlement. The court action recommenced and the defendants wished to use the joint statement. The claimants objected on the basis that the statement was privileged, having been prepared for the purpose of, and to be used in, the mediation. The Court of Appeal decided that the joint statement was not privileged. It was ordered by the court and required to assist the court to exercise its case and trial management functions.

The fact that the court had made the order to assist a contemplated mediation did not alter the status and interpretation of the court's order.

It was a question of fact whether the document produced was for the mediation alone or was produced to comply with the court order. As the experts in this case had removed the words 'without prejudice' from the final, signed version of the statement, the court took the view that the document was a joint statement prepared to comply with the court order. It was not privileged and could be referred to in the court proceedings.

This particular case turned on a specific rule within the English Civil Procedure Rules. However, it does highlight the need to be clear as to the basis on which experts are instructed and documents prepared and to take care as to the content of documents. If a document is prepared solely for a mediation and not for future use, it should state this on the face of the document to avoid any dubiety later.

### 15.3.4 Settlement agreements

In the event that a settlement is achieved in the course of a mediation, it is normal practice to record the terms of settlement in a formal written agreement which is then signed by parties before bringing the mediation to an end.

It is important to ensure that the settlement agreement deals with all matters in dispute between the parties and sets out fully the terms of settlement agreed. It should deal with matters such as payment of VAT, tax, interest, legal costs and the disposal of any proceedings underway in court, arbitration or any other forum. It should cover the mechanisms to implement the settlement, including who is to do what, by when and what is to happen if a party fails or delays in taking action required or a dispute develops as to the terms of settlement. It would often include provisions covering confidentiality of the terms of settlement and sometimes of the existence or content of the dispute.

Mediation services often provide a *pro forma* agreement covering the standard clauses. It is then for parties and their solicitors to prepare and negotiate the remainder of the agreement during the mediation.

## 15.4 Expert determination

Expert determination is a method of dispute resolution which is available either where parties include a provision to this effect in their contract or if they subsequently agree to use it. It is included in some of the standard forms of contract. An example is the Institution of Chemical Engineers' Model Forms of Contract where there is provision for disputes in relation to certain matters to be referred to an expert, the identity of whom is to be agreed between parties to the contract (failing which appointed by a specified appointing body). The Institution of Chemical Engineers has published 'Rules for Expert Determination' which detail how the determination is to be conducted. The expert's remit is, in terms of those contracts, to decide all disputes referred to him and the parties agree to be bound by and to comply with decisions made. Provisions for expert determination are also often found in bespoke forms of contract.

The procedure (unless this is set down in the contract or in procedural rules such as in the Institution of Chemical Engineers' Rules referred to above) is flexible. The expert's remit requires to be set down by the party referring the dispute.

The identity of the expert is a matter for the parties. They can agree to a named individual (or a list of individuals) in the contract or else agree to apply to an appropriate professional body for the appointment of an expert. Normally the expert would be someone skilled in a discipline relevant to the subject matter of the contract or the dispute between the parties.

There is a distinction between judicial decisions and the decisions of experts, see *Bernhard Schulte GmbH & Co. KG* v. *Nile Holdings Ltd* (2004). Judicial decisions are made on the basis of submissions and evidence presented. Expert decisions are made (unless the contract provides otherwise) on the basis of the expert's own investigations, opinions and conclusions, regardless of what is submitted by the parties. An expert determination (as opposed to a judicial determination) is not limited by the submissions made or the evidence put forward by the parties unless the contract and the terms of reference state that this is the case. It is this distinction which is being made when phrases such as 'acting as an expert and not as an arbitrator' are used.

Perhaps surprisingly, it has been found that there is no requirement for the rules of natural justice or due process to be followed in an expert determination for the decision in that process to be valid and binding. However, a decision made due to actual bias (not just a perception of bias) on the part of the expert would be capable of being set aside.

The courts have established ground rules as to how an expert determination should be conducted. In *Toepfer* v. *Continental Grain Co.* (1974) it was said:

'When parties enter into a contract on terms that the certificate of some independent person is to be binding as between them, it is important that the court should not lightly relieve one of them from being bound by a certificate which was honestly obtained and not vitiated by fraud or fundamental mistake on the part of the certifier.'

In *Jones and Others* v. *Sherwood Computer Services plc* (1992) it was said the principal ground for challenge would be that an expert had materially departed from his instructions, so that the determination is not a determination made in accordance with the terms of the contract. Material is said to be anything other than trivial or *de minimis*, meaning that it is so minor as not to make any possible difference to either party. In such cases, the determination would not be binding on the parties.

In *Nikko Hotels (UK) Ltd* v. *MEPC plc* (1991), it was said that unless the terms of the contract provided otherwise, an expert determination cannot be challenged on the ground the expert made a mistake, as long as the expert answered the question which was put to him and had not otherwise departed from his instructions.

In *Veba Oil Supply & Trading GmbH* v. *Petrograde Inc* (2002) the principle was stated (following Lord Denning in *Campbell* v. *Edwards* (1976)) that:

'if an expert makes a mistake whilst carrying out his instructions, the parties are nevertheless bound by it for the very good reason that they have agreed to be bound by it. Where, however, the expert departs from his instructions, the position is very different: in those circumstances the parties have not agreed to be bound.'

It was said that once a material departure from instructions is established, the court is not concerned with the effect of that on the result. The departure itself is sufficient to render the decision non-binding. The case set out the test for establishing whether an expert has materially departed from his instructions. It was said that any departure would be material unless it could truly be characterised as trivial or *de minimis*. In considering what parties would have regarded as being material, the court will take into account the subject matter and express terms of the contract and all the relevant circumstances.

Decisions of experts can be subject to scrutiny by the courts in certain circumstances, see *Bernhard Schulte GmbH & Co. KG*. In that case there were claims that the reference to the expert had been made outwith the timescales allowed for in the contract, that the expert acted outwith his mandate, that the expert conducted the reference unfairly and that the expert, without regard for the agreed procedure, made findings without giving one of the parties adequate opportunity to make submissions to him and did not properly take into account the submissions they did make.

The court recognised that there was a distinction between the expert making a mistake in carrying out his functions on one hand (which was said to be part of the risk run by parties in agreeing to be bound by the expert's decision) and failures to carry out his instructions on the other (which would mean the expert's determination had not been made under the contract and would therefore not be binding due to the failure to adhere to the contract requirements and failure to carry out the functions required of him). It was also noted that where the contract provides for the decision of an expert to be final and binding, it binds the parties as long as there is no fraud, collusion, bias or material departure by the expert from his instructions.

The courts again indicated a willingness to become involved in the regulation of expert determination in *Halifax Life Ltd* v. *The Equitable Life Assurance Society* (2007). In this case, the contract between the parties provided for certain disputes to be dealt with by a binding expert determination. A dispute arose and the parties agreed the expert's terms of reference. These included provisions that his decision would be binding, save for manifest error, and that he would provide a reasoned decision. Halifax were dissatisfied with the expert's decision and sought a declaration from the court that the determination was not binding. This was on the basis that the expert had 'materially departed from the agreed terms of reference by failing to provide any adequate reasons for his decision'. It was also said the determination contained a manifest error.

In relation to the question of manifest error, the court observed that:

'If a decision is issued in a dispute where it is binding 'save for manifest error' a party wishing to challenge the decision may face insuperable difficulties if the expert is not obliged to give reasons and fails to set out the reasons for his decision.'

This has previously been defined in *Veba Oil Supply & Trading GmbH* v. *Petrotrade Inc* (2002) to mean oversights and blunders so obvious and obviously capable of affecting the determination as to admit of no difference of opinion. In relation to the provision of reasons for a decision, Mr Justice Cresswell drew on a number of cases related to other forms of tribunal. In *English* v. *Emery Reimbold & Strick* (2002) it was said:

'We would put this matter at its simplest by saying that justice will not be done if it is not apparent to the parties why one has won and the other has lost.'

In *South Buckinghamshire DC* v. *Porter (No.2)* (2004), Lord Brown of Eaton-under-Heywood stated:

'The reasons for a decision must be intelligible and they must be adequate. They must enable the reader to understand why the matter was decided as it was and what conclusions were reached on the "principal important controversial issues", disclosing how any issue of law or fact was resolved. Reasons can be briefly stated, the degree of particularity required depending entirely on the nature of the issues falling for decision.'

The issues of error and provision of reasons were linked. Where the parties provided for a decision to be subject to review in cases of manifest error, it was essential the decision contained reasons sufficient to explain why, on each head of claim, one party won and the other lost. In the absence of this, it would not be possible to tell whether or not an error had been made.

The expert held private meetings with each party. That in itself was not criticised but it was said that if an expert proceeded in this manner, it was essential that he set out in his decision what information and evidence he had taken into account from the private meetings, and how that information influenced him in reaching his decision. The requirement to give reasons was said to mean the reasons should explain what the expert's conclusions were on the heads of claim and give adequate reasons in the circumstances. The court considered it had power to direct the expert to state further reasons to allow them to properly consider the overriding issue of whether his decision was binding on the parties.

In cases of fraud or collusion by the expert, the determination would not be binding, irrespective of whether this affected the result, see *Veba Oil Supply & Trading GmbH* and *Campbell*. The expert does not have immunity if he has acted negligently and it would be open to the party who sustained a loss due to such negligence to pursue a claim against the expert for loss suffered. In this respect the position of the expert is different from that of arbiters and adjudicators.

The advantages of expert determination are that it is private, it can be cost-effective and speedy and the decision is made by a person skilled in the relevant area. The disadvantages are the lack of control which may be exercised by the courts in a situation where an expert is making a final and binding decision given the unavailability of any appeal and the very restricted grounds for challenge available.

## 15.5  Early neutral evaluation

Early neutral evaluation is a process whereby parties may present their cases to an independent third party who will then give their preliminary views of the likely ultimate outcome of the case or of particular aspects of it. The evaluation of the case is non-binding but may assist parties in any negotiations or avoid unnecessary other forms of procedure. Parties agree the matters to be submitted to the process and the material to be presented to the evaluator. It is possible for this to be dealt with on the basis of only written submissions and documents or to include a hearing with oral submissions. This would be a matter either for agreement by the parties or for the evaluator to direct.

This is a process which is offered by the English courts and there is provision in their court rules for a judge to act as the evaluator. The rules provide that in what are considered to be appropriate cases, and with the agreement of all parties, the court will provide a without prejudice, non-binding evaluation of a dispute or particular issue. The judge who conducts the evaluation is then not involved any further in the case and if the case proceeds following the evaluation it is dealt with by a different judge.

The advantages of the procedure are that at an early stage, and before significant costs are incurred, parties can be given an indication of where matters might ultimately end up, thereby facilitating negotiations and resolution. Should the view be negative for one party, it allows them to make an early decision on whether or not to proceed further and, potentially, to obtain the further evidence which is required to avoid the predicted outcome. The procedure is confidential. The disadvantage, if one party receives a negative appraisal of their prospects, is that that party has effectively 'shown its hand' and others will be aware that there exists a poor view on prospects, which could make a negotiated settlement on good terms more difficult to achieve.

## 15.6 Dispute boards

The purpose of dispute boards is either to prevent disputes occurring or to achieve resolution of disputes quickly whilst work proceeds and to prevent escalation of disputes to the extent that relationships break down completely. The members of the board are appointed at the beginning of the project and remain in place until completion. These boards can have a roving role whereby they visit the site and the parties on a regular basis and either identify possible future areas of dispute or deal with any matters which have arisen. Alternatively, they can be brought in as and when disputes arise. These boards tend to be used particularly on larger and long-running contracts.

Members of the boards are chosen for their skills and experience in both dispute resolution procedures and also the technical issues involved in the particular contract. They should also be independent of the parties. If the board are involved in visiting sites on a regular basis then not only do they become aware of disputes at an early stage but also, if disputes do arise, they are able to gain an understanding of the issues very quickly given their knowledge of the project.

Dispute boards in the formal sense first came into being in the United States in the 1960s and 1970s. It is understood that the procedure was first used on the Boundary Dam project in Washington in the 1960s. It is a procedure which, since then, has extended internationally. In 1981, the World Bank suggested a board be appointed for the El Cajon Dam and Hydro project in Honduras and, in 1990, it produced a modified FIDIC contract incorporating a Dispute Review Board procedure. In 1995 the World Bank made their use mandatory for certain projects over US$50 million, which increased its use further. The procedure was used on the 'Big Dig' tunnel project in Boston – a US$14 billion and 14-year-long contract. In the UK, it was used on the Channel Tunnel and Docklands Light Railway projects and, most recently, the Olympic Delivery Authority has indicated an intention to appoint a Dispute Resolution Board to oversee all contracts for the 2012 Olympics.

Provisions regarding dispute boards are to be found in certain standard form contracts. For example, from 1995, the FIDIC Orange Book contract (and later the Red and Yellow Books) introduced the concept of a Dispute Adjudication Board to which claims would be submitted for consideration and which would issue decisions to parties to the contract which would be binding unless a contrary decision was subsequently made in arbitration proceedings. The International Chamber of Commerce produced a set of Dispute Board Rules in 2004 and the Institution of Civil Engineers (ICE) produced a Dispute Resolution Board Procedure in 2005.

Provision for a dispute board tends to be built into contracts prior to the commencement of works. A board of a specified number of named individuals (often three) is put in place. They are agreed by the parties and tend to be made up of people with relevant technical and contractual experience.

They are used in a number of different ways. The function of a Dispute Review Board (DRB) is to make a recommendation to the parties with which the parties may comply on a voluntary basis, although they may not be required to do so. A Dispute Adjudication Board (DAB) issues decisions which may be binding on the parties, on an interim basis, if the contract so provides. A Combined Dispute Board (CDB) is a combination of both DRBs and DABs and can either issue a recommendation or make a decision, depending on what the parties request in the particular situation.

There tend to be time limits built into the procedure within which the board is required to make its decision or recommendation The aim is for this to be done quickly. The decision or recommendation is often binding only on an interim basis and the dispute can ultimately be taken to court or arbitration, should the parties so desire. However, like adjudication, it is often a quick decision, even if it is rough and ready, that is required in order to allow parties to move on and there may then be little appetite for later arbitration or court proceedings.

A similar sort of procedure, without the formal rules, is often built into bespoke contracts. Sometimes there can be a number of boards or panels set up, containing individuals at a number of levels within the management structure of the parties to the contract. The idea of this is that if those at, say, quantity surveyor level are unable to resolve a dispute, it is then referred to senior manager or director level then, ultimately, to the managing directors/chief executives of the parties. This can take the heat out of a situation where it may be personalities rather than real issues that are getting in the way of resolution. In some contracts, these boards or panels are the first port of call when any dispute arises. The dispute is referred to the board so that the board can attempt to reach a resolution, generally within a short and specified period of time. This would be dealt with while the project was on-going and would allow the works to continue. Normally if resolution is not achieved, the dispute is referred to a more formal form of dispute resolution procedure.

# Chapter 16
# Adjudication

## 16.1 Introduction

While it was appreciated that Part II of the Housing Grants, Construction and Regeneration Act 1996 ('the 1996 Act') would have a very significant impact upon dispute resolution in the construction industry, when the first edition of this book was published, there had been very little experience of the operation of the 1996 Act in practice. In the first edition, only two pages of text were devoted to adjudication. Such has been the impact of adjudication that there have been hundreds of decisions from the courts and numerous books written on the subject.

The 1996 Act came into force on 1 May 1998. It was, arguably, the most significant piece of legislation to affect the construction industry for decades. The legislation sought to address certain long-standing problems within the industry, as set out by Sir Michael Latham in his 1994 Report 'Constructing the Team', namely serious payment problems affecting many in the construction industry, particularly smaller firms; and the problem of the costs and delays in resolving construction disputes. Adjudication and payment are, by their nature, inextricably linked. Payment is considered above in Chapter 8.

As far as adjudication itself is concerned, the aim of the 1996 Act was to offer a quick means of resolving disputes. The 1996 Act introduced a right to adjudication as a means of dispute resolution for construction contracts as those contracts are defined by the 1996 Act. This is considered above in Chapter 1.

## 16.2 The scope of Part II of the 1996 Act

To properly appreciate the scope of Part II of the 1996 Act requires an understanding of sections 104 to 107. These sections are discussed in Chapter 1.

Section 108 enshrines the right to refer a dispute to adjudication. It provides that:

(1)   A party to a construction contract has the right to refer a dispute arising under the contract for adjudication under a procedure complying with this section.

For this purpose 'dispute' includes any difference.

(2) The contract shall –

    (a) enable a party to give notice at any time of his intention to refer a dispute to adjudication;

    (b) provide a timetable with the object of securing the appointment of the adjudicator and referral of the dispute to him within 7 days of such notice;

    (c) require the adjudicator to reach a decision within 28 days of referral or such longer period as is agreed by the parties after the dispute has been referred;

    (d) allow the adjudicator to extend the period of 28 days by up to 14 days, with the consent of the party by whom the dispute was referred;

    (e) impose a duty on the adjudicator to act impartially; and

    (f) enable the adjudicator to take the initiative in ascertaining the facts and the law.

(3) The contract shall provide that the decision of the adjudicator is binding until the dispute is finally determined by legal proceedings, by arbitration (if the contract provides for arbitration or the parties otherwise agree to arbitration) or by agreement.

The parties may agree to accept the decision of the adjudicator as finally determining the dispute.

(4) The contract shall also provide that the adjudicator is not liable for anything done or omitted in the discharge or purported discharge of his functions as adjudicator unless the act or omission is in bad faith, and that any employee or agent of the adjudicator is similarly protected from liability.

(5) If the contract does not comply with the requirements of subsections (1) to (4), the adjudication provisions of the Scheme for Construction Contracts apply.

For Scotland, the Scheme may include provision conferring powers on courts in relation to adjudication and provision relating to the enforcement of the adjudicator's decision.

The 1996 Act gives a party to a construction contract the right to refer a dispute arising under the contract to adjudication under a procedure complying with section 108. While the 1996 Act allows parties to agree their own adjudication provisions, care is required not to fall foul of s.108(5). It is to be noted that if any bespoke adjudication provisions in the contract do not comply with the requirements of s.108(1) to (4), all of the Scheme will apply. The Scheme will not just apply to the extent that the bespoke provisions do not meet the requirements of the 1996 Act. Accordingly, when considering adjudication, it is always important to determine whether any bespoke adjudication provisions apply because they comply with the requirements of the 1996 Act, or whether the Scheme applies (even if the latter only arises because the bespoke provisions do not apply, by virtue of s.108(5)).

It is perhaps noteworthy that, despite the concluding words of section 108, the Scottish Scheme did not confer any new powers on the courts.

## 16.3 *The Notice of Adjudication*

The 1996 Act and Scheme require a written notice to start the adjudication procedure which must be sent to every other party to the contract. It would be difficult to overemphasise the importance of this notice and the need for its terms to be considered with great care.

The notice has four basic purposes:

- it informs the other parties to the contract that there is a dispute and the nature of the dispute, but it cannot create the dispute;
- it informs the adjudicator (when appointed) of the dispute;
- it provides information to allow the appointing body to select an appropriate person to act as adjudicator; and
- it defines the jurisdiction of the adjudicator.

The nature and brief description of the dispute should be fairly general to avoid restricting the issues unduly.

In *K & D Contractors* v. *Midas Homes Ltd* (2002), His Honour Judge Lloyd said that in considering the validity of the Notice of Adjudication, the essential questions will include whether a dispute has arisen. 'A dispute is not lightly to be inferred.' Paragraph 1(3) of the Scheme requires the dispute to be defined. In this case, the Notice of Adjudication dated 3 May took the form of a letter from the Referring Party's solicitors to the Respondents' solicitors. Within the letter, reference was made to letters to the Respondents dated 11 and 13 April. The 3 May letter said that as no payments had been forthcoming from the Respondents in respect of either of the attached letters 'a dispute now exists between our client and your client and this dispute will be referred to adjudication'. The Judge refused to enforce the adjudicator's decision. He highlighted the fact that as at 3 May there were a number of issues in dispute: valuation of the sub-contract account, whether the Respondents had properly determined the sub-contract, and damages for loss of profit in respect of the wrongful determination. The Respondents wrote to the Referring Party's solicitors and stated that they had absolutely no idea 'from the notice which of the numerous items were in fact being referred to the adjudicator'. This request for clarity was ignored.

Although it is possible to give a Notice of Adjudication by reference to other correspondence, the Scheme requires the dispute to be defined. A degree of precision is required. The issue of whether a dispute has arisen between the parties is considered further below in section 16.10.2.

The courts have construed strictly the requirement that notice can be given at any time, see, for example, *John Mowlem & Co. plc* v. *Hydra-Tight Ltd (2000)* in which His Honour Judge Toulmin decided that a clause in a standard ICE contract which provided a mechanism called a Notification of Dissatisfaction (which delayed a referral to adjudication for four weeks during which time the parties had the opportunity to meet and resolve their differences) contravened the entitlement contained in the 1996 Act to adjudicate at any time. This case has had an impact upon other ICE standard forms which provide for a Notice of Dissatisfaction procedure as a pre-condition for a dispute to arise. It is generally believed that, whatever good intention lay behind the Notice of Dissatisfaction provisions in ICE conditions, they resulted in the adjudication provisions being not 1996 Act compliant.

## 16.4 *Appointment of the adjudicator*

Whilst almost anyone could act as an adjudicator, as no qualifications are required, it is an extremely important appointment. Parties should try to get the right person for the job.

If there is no agreement as to who should act as adjudicator, nor is there a specified nominating body in the contract, the adjudicator will be chosen by an Adjudicator Nominating Body. The Scheme definition of an Adjudicator Nominating Body is somewhat circular. The early drafts of the Scheme listed 16 organisations that were to be the only approved Adjudicator Nominating Bodies, but this was dropped because every future amendment to the list would require a further statutory instrument. Different disputes require different skills and the wider the choice of adjudicator, the better chance of the right person being selected.

If application is made to an Adjudicator Nominating Body, then they must communicate the selection of an adjudicator to the Referring Party within five days of receiving a request to do so, see paragraph 5(1) of the Scheme.

It is advisable to find out the prospective adjudicator's terms and conditions (including fees) for acting, but this should not delay the start of the adjudication.

If no adjudicator is named, but an Adjudicator Nominating Body is, then application must be made to that body for the nomination of an adjudicator. Most nominating bodies require payment of a fee before they will act, as well as completion of an application form.

Once the nomination has been made, the Referring Party should contact the person nominated and request confirmation that the person is willing to act, as the person requested to act as adjudicator must indicate within two days of receiving the request whether or not he is willing to act, failing which a party can apply to the Adjudicator Nominating Body to select a different person to act as adjudicator.

The terms of paragraph 10 of the Scheme should be noted. It provides:

'Where any party to the dispute objects to the appointment of a particular person as adjudicator, that objection shall not invalidate the adjudicator's appointment nor any decision he may reach in accordance with paragraph 20.'

Therefore whilst an objection to the appointment must be made as soon as the appointment is made, it will not invalidate the appointment.

## 16.5  The referral notice

'Referral notice' is arguably a misnomer, as it is a full submission with supporting documentation, rather than a 'notice'. It should include details of the contract (including the parties) the background to the dispute, the relevant facts of the dispute plus supporting documents, the contractual basis of the claim, comment on what the other side's position appears to be and should set out the redress the Referring Party wishes the adjudicator to grant. This should mirror the redress set out in the Notice of Adjudication.

## 16.6  Conduct of the adjudication

### 16.6.1  The adjudicator's powers

Paragraph 13 of the Scheme sets out the wide-ranging powers of the adjudicator. It provides:

'The adjudicator may take the initiative in ascertaining the facts and the law necessary to determine the dispute, and shall decide on the procedure to be followed in the adjudication. In particular, he may –

(a) request any party to the contract to supply him with such documents as he may reasonably require including, if he so directs, any written statement from any party to the contract supporting or supplementing the referral notice and any other documents given under paragraph 7(2);

(b) decide the language or languages to be used in the adjudication and whether a translation of any document is to be provided and, if so, by whom;

(c) meet and question any of the parties to the contract and their representatives;

(d) subject to obtaining any necessary consent from a third party or parties, make such site visits and inspections as he considers appropriate, whether accompanied by the parties or not;

(e) subject to obtaining any necessary consent from a third party or parties, carry out any tests or experiments;

(f) obtain and consider such representations and submissions as he requires, and, provided he has notified the parties of his intention, appoint experts, assessors or legal advisers;

(g) give directions as to the timetable for the adjudication, any deadlines, or limits as to the length of written documents or oral representations to be complied with; and

(h) issue other directions relating to the conduct of the adjudication.'

The Scheme gives the adjudicator the necessary express powers to enable them to ascertain the facts and the law. Whether and to what extent an adjudicator should do so is a matter of some controversy among adjudicators, given the difficulties to which it can lead in the relatively short period normally available to conclude the adjudication. However, where the adjudicator makes use of the power conferred on him, he must only take the initiative to the extent that it is necessary on the submissions he has received.

### 16.6.2 Time limit for decision

Paragraph 19 sets out the deadlines imposed upon the adjudicator. It provides: –

'(1) The adjudicator shall reach his decision not later than –

(a) twenty eight days after the date of the referral notice mentioned in paragraph 7(1);

(b) forty two days after the date of the referral notice if the referring party so consents; or

(c) such period exceeding twenty eight days after the referral notice as the parties to the dispute may, after the giving of that notice, agree.

(2) Where the adjudicator fails, for any reason, to reach his decision in accordance with sub-paragraph (1) –

(a) any of the parties to the dispute may serve a fresh notice under paragraph 1 and shall request an adjudicator to act in accordance with paragraphs 2 to 7; and

(b) if requested by the new adjudicator and insofar as it is reasonably practicable, the parties shall supply him with copies of all documents which they had made available to the previous adjudicator.

(3)   As soon as possible after he has reached a decision, the adjudicator
      shall deliver a copy of that decision to each of the parties to the
      contract.'

A very strict time limit is imposed by the Scheme. There is no leeway and if
a decision is not reached within the requisite timescale, it will be invalid.

The leading case from the Inner House is *Ritchie Brothers (PWC) Ltd* v.
*David Philp (Commercials) Ltd* (2005). David Philp was the employer and
Ritchie Brothers were the main contractor under a building contract. Disputes arose between the parties which were referred to an adjudicator. An
undated Referral Notice was issued to an adjudicator by Ritchie Brothers on
18 September. The 28-day period therefore expired on 16 October. However,
due to delays with the postal service, the adjudicator did not receive the
Referral Notice until 23 September.

On 21 October David Philp's solicitors wrote to the adjudicator indicating
that the adjudicator had no power to issue a decision after 16 October, and
that any decision reached after that date by the adjudicator would be a
nullity. By letter, also dated 21 October, the adjudicator wrote to both parties
requesting an extension of the period for reaching his decision until at least
23 October. Subsequently, on 23 October, the adjudicator wrote to the parties
indicating that he had reached a decision and this decision was intimated to
the parties on 27 October.

In the Outer House, Lord Eassie held that the adjudicator's failure to reach
a decision within the 28-day period did not bring the adjudicator's jurisdiction to an end. He expressed the view that the provisions of paragraph 19
of the Scheme were directory rather than mandatory. He was satisfied that
this provision illustrated Parliament's intention that, once initiated, the
process of adjudication should be completed. Neither party had served a
fresh adjudication notice. Lord Eassie held that the decision should be
enforced. David Philp appealed.

Ritchie Brothers' primary submission was that, notwithstanding the statutory time limit, the adjudicator's jurisdiction only came to an end when a
party to the dispute served a fresh Notice of Adjudication. In the alternative,
relying on the reasoning of Lord Wheatley in *St Andrews Bay Development
Ltd* v. *HBG Management Ltd* (2003), they argued that a failure to reach a decision within the time limit was a technical error which was not serious
enough to invalidate the adjudicator's decision.

David Philp argued that the adjudicator's jurisdiction expired at the end
of the 28-day period. In circumstances where the adjudicator is unable to
reach a decision within 28 days, he can avoid losing his jurisdiction by
requesting and obtaining an extension within the 28 days.

The appeal was allowed. In the leading opinion, the Lord Justice Clerk
held that the statutory time limit set out in the Scheme is mandatory and the
adjudicator's decision was null and unenforceable. Paragraph 19 of the
Scheme provides that the adjudicator 'shall reach his decision' not later than
28 days after the Referral Notice (subject to possibilities of extension agreed

by the parties). Applying the natural meaning to the words in paragraph 19 of the Scheme provides a clear time limit. This provides certainty as to the extent of the adjudicator's jurisdiction. If Parliament had a contrary intention then this could have been expressed in plain terms.

The Lord Justice Clerk also rejected Ritchie Brothers' alternative submission that a failure to reach a decision within the 28-day time limit was not a fundamental error. The Lord Justice Clerk specifically rejected the reasoning in *St Andrews Bay Development Ltd* on that particular point. That decision did not provide any hard and fast criterion by which a court could determine for how long after the time limit a failure to reach a decision can be considered to be merely a technical failure, or in what circumstances the jurisdiction of the adjudicator could be said to come to an end.

Following a number of Scottish and English decisions which did not provide clear guidance on the law in this area, this decision finally provides Appeal Court guidance in Scotland that the 28-day time limit is mandatory in Scheme adjudications. The decision sends a clear message to adjudicators that their decision must be reached within the 28-day period. If this is not possible, then they must request and obtain an extension prior to the expiry of the period for reaching the decision. If they fail to obtain such an extension, their decision will be invalid. This line of reasoning has been followed in the English Technology and Construction Court case of *Epping Electrical Co. Ltd* v. *Briggs & Forrester (Plumbing Services) Ltd* (2007).

While *Ritchie Brothers (PWC) Ltd* deals with the situation where a decision is not reached within the requisite time period, it does not deal expressly with the situation where the decision is reached timeously but it is not then immediately communicated to the parties. Some have argued that as the statutory requirements only refer to reaching a decision, not communicating it to the parties, some short delay in communicating it to the parties is permissible without such delay affecting the validity of the decision. Lord Wheatley in *St Andrews Bay Development Ltd*, in comments not expressly criticised by the Appeal Court, was firmly of the view that the obligation to reach a decision must include a contemporaneous duty to communicate the decision to the interested parties. Not to require such an interpretation of the obligation to reach a decision would render the whole purpose of the legislation meaningless. This is very much in line with the need for certainty stressed in *Ritchie Brothers (PWC) Ltd*. While it may still be arguable that a decision reached timeously but communicated a very short period thereafter may be valid, the position in law is unclear and it is submitted that the better and safer course is to ensure that the decision is not only reached but also communicated to the parties within the relevant timescale.

### 16.6.3  More than one dispute

Paragraph 8(1) of the Scheme provides that an adjudicator can deal with more than one dispute arising at the same time if all parties to the disputes agree.

It is important to distinguish between on the one hand, different disputes and on the other, different aspects of a single dispute. This has greatly exercised the minds of judges in England. For example, in *David McLean Housing Contractors Ltd* v. *Swansea Housing Association Ltd* (2003) His Honour Judge Lloyd considered when a dispute is more than one dispute. His starting point was paragraph 8(1) of the (English) Scheme which precludes the reference of more than one dispute to adjudication. In the event the Referring Party wishes to refer more than one dispute, then the consent of the other party is required. In this case, consent was not given by the Respondents.

His Honour Judge Lloyd stated that one had to consider the Notice of Adjudication in its context. When this was examined it was plain that the real dispute was what payment ought to have been made as a result of Application 19. This contained various elements which were set out in the Notice of Adjudication. The Notice was valid in referring the dispute about the payment to be made and could not be decided without considering each element. The Judge applied what he called a 'benevolent interpretation' and said that the Notice did not refer more than one dispute. It referred one dispute namely 'How much should I be paid or how much should I have been paid on Application 19?'

It is considered that in Scotland this approach is one which is consistent with the wording of the Scheme ('The adjudicator shall decide the matters in dispute and may make a decision on different aspects of the dispute at different times '). This wording is not used in the English and Welsh Scheme. A Notice that refers more than one dispute is invalid. The appointment of an adjudicator in consequence of it is similarly invalid, unless the other party has nonetheless clearly and knowingly accepted the Notice or the appointment so that there exists consent for the purpose of paragraph 8 of the Scheme.

Paragraph 8(2) of the Scheme provides that the adjudicator may, with the consent of all parties to those contracts, adjudicate at the same time on related disputes under different contracts. While multi-party adjudication is possible if consent is obtained, it is relatively rare, perhaps because of the 1996 Act timetable, the reluctance of some parties to agree to it, or because of the difficulty in ensuring that contracts are clearly 'back to back'.

### 16.6.4 Resignation of the adjudicator

Paragraph 9 of the Scheme provides that an adjudicator may resign at any time by giving written notice to the parties. An adjudicator must resign where 'the dispute is the same or substantially the same as one which has previously been referred to adjudication, and a decision has been taken in that adjudication'. There have been various cases regarding whether a dispute is the 'same or substantially the same' as a previous dispute and these are considered at section 16.10.2 below.

## 16.7  The decision

### 16.7.1  Reasoned decision

Paragraph 22 of the Scheme states that the adjudicator must provide reasons for his decision if requested to do so by one of the parties to the dispute.

The Scheme does not specify the timescale within which a party must ask for reasons or the period within which the adjudicator needs to produce his reasons.

Practical considerations suggest that a party should ask for reasons before the decision is issued in order that the adjudicator knows that reasons are required and in order that he produces them with or shortly after the decision. The reasons for the decision can be vitally important in considering whether there are grounds for challenging an adjudicator's decision or resisting its enforcement. It is important that reasons are produced with, or very quickly after, the decision.

### 16.7.2  Compliance with the adjudicator's decision

Paragraph 21 of the Scheme provides:

'In the absence of any directions by the adjudicator relating to the time for performance of his decision, the parties shall be required to comply with any decision of the adjudicator immediately on delivery of the decision to the parties in accordance with paragraph 19(3)'.

This is a default provision should the adjudicator fail to specify a timetable for compliance with the decision.

### 16.7.3  Effect of the decision

Paragraph 23 of the Scheme deals with the effects of the decision. Sub-paragraph 2 provides:

'The decision of the adjudicator shall be binding on the parties, and they shall comply with it, until the dispute is finally determined by legal proceedings, by arbitration (if the contract provides for arbitration or the parties otherwise agree to arbitration) or by agreement between the parties.'

The adjudicator's decision is a temporary decision which is put into effect and must be complied with by the parties until the dispute is finally resolved as indicated by arbitration, litigation or agreement.

The adjudicator may, if he thinks fit, order any of the parties to comply peremptorily with his decision or any part of it. In England, failure to comply with a peremptory order permits the courts to enforce the decision under section 42 of the Arbitration Act 1996. However, this provision does not apply in Scotland.

### 16.7.4 Registration of the decision

The Scheme provides that a party or the adjudicator can, if they so wish, register the adjudicator's decision for execution in the Books of Council and Session. On request, the other party must consent to such registration by subscribing the decision before a witness.

On the face of it, this provision is better than its English counterpart which requires the enforcing party to go to court in order to enforce the adjudicator's decision. Once a decision has been registered in this way it does not require a court decree to confirm that the aggrieved party is entitled to enforce a decision. However, for some, this paragraph does not go far enough. The non-complying party is required to sign the decision before a witness to record his consent to registration. If the other party refuses to sign the award, the enforcing party will need to go to court. In practice, however, this route to enforcement is seldom, if ever, used.

## 16.8  Adjudicator's fees and costs/expenses of the parties

Paragraph 25 of the Scheme provides:

'(1)  The adjudicator shall be entitled to the payment of such reasonable amount as he may determine by way of fees and expenses incurred by him and the parties shall be jointly and severally liable to pay that amount to the adjudicator.

(2)  Without prejudice to the right of the adjudicator to effect recovery from any party in accordance with sub-paragraph (1), the adjudicator may by direction determine the apportionment between the parties of liability for his fees and expenses.'

Paragraph 25(1) effectively means that if one party refuses to pay their share of the fees and expenses, the adjudicator can claim the whole amount from the other. Disagreement with the adjudicator's decision is not of itself a reason for non-payment.

In *Stubbs Rich Architects* v. *W H Tolley & Son Ltd* (2001) the Judge applied the criteria of a reasonably competent solicitor when assessing adjudicator's fees, i.e. how long it would take a solicitor to read the files and write his decision. On appeal, his decision was reversed as he was not comparing like with like; if comparative evidence was relevant it should not have been a solicitor, rather an expert architect/adjudicator, and the court should be reluctant to substitute its own views of what constitutes reasonable hours. With reference to s.108(4) of the 1996 Act, the judge held that the adjudicator's fees may be challenged if, and only if, the adjudicator has acted in bad faith. The RICS Guidance Notes for Surveyors acting as adjudicators forbid adjudicators holding on to their decisions until their fees are paid unless they have the agreement of the parties.

There is no express provision in the statutory framework allowing an adjudicator to include in his decision an award in relation to the costs or expenses which the parties have themselves incurred in relation to the adjudication. There is conflicting authority in England on this point.

In *John Cothliff Ltd* v. *Allen Build (North West) Ltd* (1999) the claimants entered into a contract with the defendants to carry out building works. A dispute arose but the contract did not contain an express provision for adjudication. The Scheme provisions applied. The adjudicator made an award in favour of the claimants. The claimants had also asked for the adjudicator to determine the payment of their costs of adjudication. The adjudicator decided that the provisions of the Scheme gave him power to do this and he awarded the claimants 70 per cent of the costs of the adjudication. The defendants refused to comply with the costs element of the adjudicator's decision. The claimants sought summary judgment in court.

His Honour Judge Evans decided, controversially, that the adjudicator had power to award costs, at least where, as in this case, costs had been expressly sought in the application placed before the adjudicator and when he had allowed representation. In particular, he relied on paragraph 13(h) of the Scheme which provides that the adjudicator can issue other directions relating to the conduct of the adjudication and read this in the light of paragraph 16 which allows for representation. He said that the intention was to give the adjudicator very wide control of the procedures to be adopted. He also considered that it would be appropriate to imply a term into the contract to give the adjudicator the power to award costs, although the reasoning behind this is questionable.

In *Northern Developments (Cumbria) Ltd* v. *J & J Nichol* (2000) His Honour Judge Bowsher said that nowhere in the Scheme is the adjudicator given power to order one party to the adjudication to pay the costs of the other. However, the parties were free to add their own terms provided that they did not detract from the requirements of the 1996 Act and the Scheme. Each party was represented in this case and asked the adjudicator in writing for their own costs, and neither submitted that the adjudicator did not have the power to order costs. Accordingly, the judge considered that there was an implied agreement between parties to give the adjudicator jurisdiction to deal with the parties' costs.

It is widely considered that, in the absence of express agreement to the contrary, an adjudicator does not have power to order one party to pay the legal and other costs of the other party. Accordingly, the reasoning in *John Cothliff Ltd* has been the subject of some criticism.

In *Bridgeway Construction Ltd* v. *Tolent Construction Ltd* (2000) the parties entered into a construction contract which provided that each party should bear its own costs and expenses in adjudication. Clauses in the contract were varied so as to provide that the party serving the Notice of Adjudication should bear not only the fees and expenses of the adjudicator but the costs and expenses of both parties to the adjudication.

Bridgeway started adjudication proceedings and an award was made in its favour. The adjudicator refused to order Bridgeway its costs, declaring that Bridgeway was bound by the provisions of the contract. Tolent paid the sum ordered less its own legal costs and expenses. Bridgeway challenged the validity of the contract provision that they should pay Tolent's costs of the adjudication on the basis that the provisions in question inhibited the parties from pursuing their lawful remedies.

His Honour Judge Mackay decided that the provision which stated that the party instituting the adjudication should have to bear the costs and expenses of the adjudicator and the responding party was not void. The contract had been freely negotiated and the disputed provision related solely to costs which are not covered by the 1996 Act.

Whilst, in theory, parties are free to contract as they like, in practice, commercial considerations are such that a party may end up accepting more onerous terms and conditions than might otherwise be the case. These compliant adjudication provisions must discourage a party from exercising its right to refer disputes to adjudication.

Contrast this position with, for example, *R G Carter Ltd* v. *Edmund Nuttall Ltd* (2002) where the Judge held that a contractual requirement that parties should attempt to resolve their dispute by mediation prior to commencing adjudication proceedings undermined the right of either party to refer the dispute to adjudication 'at any time' as required by section 108 of the 1996 Act.

Notwithstanding these cases, it is considered that the better view is that an adjudicator does not have the power to deal with the costs and expenses of the parties. The manner of the drafting of the statutory framework indicates that Parliament did not intend that the adjudicator should deal with the costs and expenses of the parties, and if it had intended that to be the case, an express provision would have been made. In arbitration or litigation costs can become of crucial importance, sometimes prolonging the dispute by making it harder to settle. A similar situation in adjudication is not desirable as it is not supposed to be akin to arbitration or litigation.

## 16.9  Liability of the adjudicator

Paragraph 26 of the Scheme provides that an:

'adjudicator shall not be liable for anything done or omitted in the discharge or purported discharge of his functions as adjudicator unless the act or omission is in bad faith, and any employee or agent of the adjudicator shall be similarly protected from liability'.

This protects the adjudicator from being sued by the parties unless he acts in bad faith.

## 16.10 Enforcement proceedings

### 16.10.1 Introduction

Generally, it is considered that the courts have taken a robust, purposive attitude to the enforcement of adjudicators' decisions, and will generally enforce any decision made by an adjudicator with jurisdiction to make that decision.

In Scotland, the method of enforcement is to raise court proceedings (an action for payment) and the practice has been to raise proceedings in the Commercial Court of the Court of Session. The court can be asked to shorten the period of notice which is otherwise 21 days. This can then be followed by a motion to the court for summary decree at the earliest opportunity if there is no defence to the action, or a part of it, disclosed in the defences. If a defence is stated, an early legal debate is normally sought unless there are issues of fact which need to be resolved. In the latter case some form of proof at which evidence is led will be required. However, even if the payment action is successful at first instance, the decision can be appealed (without leave) which can delay enforcement considerably. Early disposal of an appeal should normally be sought if one is acting for a Referring Party.

A petition for Judicial Review would be an appropriate procedure where a party wants to review a decision of an adjudicator, see for example, *Karl Construction (Scotland) Ltd* v. *Sweeney Civil Engineering (Scotland) Ltd* (2002).

### 16.10.2 Jurisdictional challenges

Probably the most regularly stated defence to enforcement proceedings is a challenge on jurisdictional grounds. An adjudicator's jurisdiction is derived from his appointment by the agreement of the parties. The adjudicator will only have jurisdiction to determine a dispute referred to him arising out of a construction contract in writing as defined in the 1996 Act. If any requirement is absent, his decision is a nullity and not binding on the parties. In fact, many cases contain some sort of jurisdictional challenge. Below we examine some of the most common jurisdictional challenges raised in adjudication proceedings. The starting point is the early case of *Macob Civil*

*Engineering Ltd* v. *Morrison Construction Ltd* (1999). Mr Justice Dyson (as he then was) said:

> 'If his decision is wrong, whether because he errs on facts or the law, or because in reaching his decision he made a procedural error which invalidates his decision, it is still a decision on the issue. Different considerations may well apply if he purports to decide a dispute which was not referred to him at all.'

In *Macob Civil Engineering Ltd* it was alleged that the adjudicator had committed a procedural error in that he had decided that the mechanism for payment in the contract was not 1996 Act compliant. He found that the Scheme provisions on payment applied. It was also argued that as the arbitration clause included referral of disputes regarding an adjudicator's decision, enforcement of the adjudicator's award should be postponed pending the outcome of the arbitration.

Mr Justice Dyson rejected both arguments and held that despite the attack 'an adjudicator's decision which appears on the face to have been properly issued will be binding and enforceable in the court whether or not the merits or the validity of the decision are challenged'. To adopt any other approach would be 'to drive a coach and horses through the Scheme'.

Matters have progressed significantly since Mr Justice Dyson wrote the words quoted above and they must now be treated with care. The courts have since made it clear that they will uphold proper jurisdictional challenges. Accordingly, a decision which is not valid because of lack of jurisdiction or breach of the rules of natural justice will not be enforced. Examples of commonly made jurisdictional challenges are set out below.

### No construction contract between the parties

Chapter 1 considered the definition of 'construction contract' for the purposes of the 1996 Act. In *Project Consultancy Group* v. *Trustees of the Gray Trust* (1999) it was argued in defence of enforcement proceedings that the contract in question was not a 'construction contract' within the meaning of the 1996 Act as it had either (1) been entered into pre-1 May 1998 or (2) had never been entered into at all. Complicated evidence had been led before the adjudicator as to what had and had not been agreed between the parties. The adjudicator determined firstly that it was a construction contract and then made a monetary award.

Mr Justice Dyson distinguished this case from *Macob Civil Engineering Ltd* on the basis that a different test might require to be applied where the adjudicator purports to decide a dispute not referred to him at all, that is when he was determining his own jurisdiction. It was suggested that such an approach would enable every responding party to raise spurious jurisdictional issues, but the judge considered these fears were exaggerated. Others may disagree. In this case it was found that there was sufficient doubt as to whether there had been offer and acceptance and therefore a contract. If there was no contract, the adjudicator could not have jurisdiction. The judge declined to award summary judgment to enforce the decision.

The question whether the adjudicator has the necessary jurisdiction is not itself a dispute arising under a construction contract. An adjudicator has no power to decide his own jurisdiction.

### Matter not referred to adjudicator/failure to exhaust referral

An adjudicator should exercise what jurisdiction he has and reach a decision on any matter properly referred to him, see *Ballast plc* v. *The Burrell Company (Construction Management) Ltd (2003)*. An adjudicator cannot decide a matter which has not been referred to him. He must decide all the matters referred to him, see *S L Timber Systems Ltd* v. *Carillon Construction Ltd* (2002).

In *F W Cook Ltd* v. *Shimizu (UK) Ltd* (2000) four items in the final account were referred to adjudication, but no request for payment was actually set out in the Referral Notice. The adjudicator attempted to assess a monetary value on each of the four items, and Cook tried to enforce the decision. The judge took a different view and said that Cook had sought to achieve a decision on the specific items with the hope that other items in the final account might be negotiated. The adjudicator had not made any decision on payment and would have exceeded his jurisdiction if he had done so. Summary judgment was refused.

### No dispute

*Sindall Ltd* v. *Solland and Others* (2002) considered the issue of whether a dispute had arisen. Solland determined Sindall's employment in December 2000 on the grounds of failure to proceed regularly and diligently with renovation works at a property in Mayfair, a notice of default having been served. The adjudicator appointed to determine the extension of time issue decided that Sindall was entitled to an extension of time to October 2000 in respect of events to August 2000. In January 2001 Sindall sought a further award of extension of time. The contract administrator requested further information which Sindall provided with a letter stating that a formal response was required within seven days. Adjudication proceedings were commenced with Sindall seeking:

- A declaration that the determination was wrongful.
- A declaration that it was entitled to an extension of time to the date of determination.

The adjudicator found in favour of Sindall on both points and enforcement proceedings were raised. Solland argued that the adjudicator had acted without jurisdiction, as at the date of service of the adjudication notice there was in fact no dispute between the parties regarding the extension of time question.

His Honour Judge Lloyd decided that no dispute had arisen on the basis of Sindall's letter enclosing further information in support of the claim for an extension of time requesting a response within seven days. The contract administrator should have been given sufficient time to make up his mind before the inference could be drawn that the absence of a substantive reply meant that there was a dispute. However, the adjudicator had jurisdiction in relation to the dispute because the dispute before him concerned the determination issue. As an integral part of this was the time within which the works should have been completed, it involved considering the extension of time claim.

Again, the judge favoured a wide interpretation of 'dispute' to encompass all matters that are contentious between the parties at the relevant time. Specifically, the judge said that the courts should endeavour to adopt a pragmatic approach to adjudication as opposed to a legalistic approach.

In 2003 two cases appeared to indicate a shift in the attitude of the courts to the definition of dispute for the purposes of adjudication, which had until that point appeared to be different from the definition of dispute for the purposes of arbitration.

Firstly, in the case of *Beck Peppiatt Ltd* v. *Norwest Holst Construction Ltd* (2003), the judge quoted with approval the words of His Honour Judge Lloyd in *Sindall Ltd*:

'For there to be dispute for the purposes of exercising the statutory right to adjudication it must be clear that a point has emerged from the process of discussion or negotiation that has ended and that there is something which needs to be decided.'

However, the judge decided that he did not see any conflict between this approach and the approach of the Court of Appeal in *Halki Shipping Corp* v. *Sopex Oils Ltd ('The Halki')* (1998) where it was said that there is a dispute once money is claimed unless and until the defendants admit that the sum is due and payable.

In *Orange EBS Ltd* v. *ABB Ltd* (2003) the judge applied the tests set out in *Beck Peppiatt Ltd*. Part of the dispute related to the final account. Orange submitted a final account on 2 December 2002, but served a notice of adjudication on 6 January 2003. Orange's contract had been terminated in July 2002, but it had taken no further steps between July and December. ABB instructed an investigator to consider the final account and suggested that they would be able to respond by 20 January and if no agreement had been reached within seven days thereafter ABB indicated that they would be willing to submit to adjudication.

ABB said that there could be no dispute because the contractual machinery under DOM/1 in relation to the time given for ABB to consider the final account had not run its course before the Notice of Adjudication was served. Orange said that the effect of repudiation was to bring the sub-contract to an end and thus the contractual mechanism for payment of sums due fell away. Applying the *Halki* test the fact that ABB had not admitted the claim or paid meant that a dispute had arisen. Applying the *Sindall Ltd* test was more difficult. Notwithstanding the Christmas industry shutdown and the fact that ABB had made what they thought was a reasonable alternative suggestion in relation to the timetable, the judge concluded that by 6 January sufficient time had elapsed for ABB to have both evaluated the claim and to have concluded any discussions and/or negotiations with Orange.

From the point of view of a Referring Party this approach has much to commend it at a time when there had been a growing trend for potential respondents to adjudication to either try to put off the fateful day of adjudication or to set up a possible jurisdictional challenge that there was not a dispute at the time of the adjudication notice. This trend was evidenced by no positive rejection of a party's case or claim but merely asking for more information or for an allegedly reasonable time to consider it. It is always a matter of fact and degree when a dispute can be said to have arisen following the submission of a claim.

In *R G Carter Ltd* v. *Edmund Nuttall Ltd* (2002), His Honour Judge Seymour refused to enforce the decision of an adjudicator since the adjudicator had no jurisdiction. When Nuttall commenced adjudication proceedings, the notice included a claim for an extension of time based on a claim document prepared in May 2001. When the Referral Notice was served, it included a delay analysis prepared by an expert on behalf of Nuttall, which made a claim for an identical extension of time, however, the justification for the extension was different to that put forward in the May claim.

The judge was required to decide whether the dispute which had been adjudicated upon and in respect of which a decision was given, was the dispute which was the subject of the Notice of Adjudication.

The judge rejected the submission that the dispute should be identified by reference, at least principally, to what was being claimed. Nuttall suggested that it was enough that the extension of time sought was always the same and it was irrelevant that the facts and arguments relied upon in the expert report were significantly different from the facts and arguments relied upon in the previous claim. The judge considered that for there to be a dispute there must have been an opportunity for the protagonists each to consider the position adopted by the other and to formulate arguments of a reasoned kind. He felt that some form of rejection of a party's claim was required. The judge said that 'a party can refine its arguments and abandon points not thought to be meritorious' but it cannot 'abandon wholesale facts previously advanced'. Such wholesale abandonment would prevent a party from asserting that the 'claim' or 'dispute' remained the same.

In *Fastrack Contractors Ltd* v. *Morrison Construction Ltd and Another* (2000) Morrison were the main contractors for the construction of a new leisure arena. Fastrack were the brickwork sub-contractors. The case concerned second adjudication proceedings (the first concerned interim application 12). The Notice of Adjudication provided:

> 'the disputes to be referred to are the issues as to the [Claimant's] rights to payment . . . under the following headings/descriptions: measured work; scaffold variations; other variations; dayworks; storm damage; prolongation costs, and loss and expense arising from delay and disruption caused to the sub-contact works by the [Defendants'] breaches of contract; a fair and reasonable extension of time for completion of the sub-contract works; loss of profit as a result of repudiation; additional overheads; such other sums as the Adjudicator deems appropriate'.

The Notice of Adjudication sought payment of approximately £483,000. The Referral Notice claimed approximately £479,000.

Morrison argued that the only dispute in existence at the time the Notice of Adjudication was served was in relation to application 13 and there were significant differences between the sums claimed in that application for measured works, variations, scaffolding, preliminaries, disruption and damages.

The adjudicator decided the issues were materially the same as application 13 so there was a pre-existing dispute, and he awarded payment of approximately £120,000.

Morrison defended enforcement proceedings. His Honour Judge Thornton decided 'the dispute' was whatever claims, heads of claim, issues, contentions or causes of action were in dispute at the moment that the Referring Party first intimated an adjudication reference. All the issues in the Notice of Adjudication had been referred by Fastrack to Morrison, had been rejected by Morrison and had therefore ripened into disputes by the time the Notice of Adjudication was served.

### The same or substantially the same dispute

In *Skanska Construction (UK) Ltd* v. *The ERDC Group Ltd and Another* (2003), Skanska sought to have an adjudication suspended by challenging the adjudicator's jurisdiction to hear the dispute. The adjudication was the second one brought by ERDC against Skanska, and Skanska claimed it centred on a dispute, which was 'the same or substantially the same' as the first dispute. Accordingly, Skanska said that it could not be adjudicated upon and invited the adjudicator to step down. He refused.

The first adjudication had arisen over an interim application, whereas the second concerned ERDC's final account submission. Skanska argued that both disputes concerned the quantification of the loss and expense element of ERDC's claim. ERDC argued that it was quite different to the interim valuation dispute, albeit that it did concern similar claims and sums. Since the first adjudication, significant further information and documentation had come to light and been exchanged. The second adjudication centred on different sub-contract clauses and would proceed upon a different basis.

The adjudicator and the judge agreed with ERDC's arguments. Skanska's petition was refused. The judge stated that in the second adjudication a different stage in the contract had been reached; different contractual provisions applied; considerably more information might be available by the date of issue of the final account; and different considerations and perspectives might apply.

As we have seen, there are numerous possible challenges to jurisdiction such as:

- no contract between the parties;
- no dispute on the matters referred;
- the contract is not a construction contract;
- failure by the Referring Party to fulfil conditions precedent.

As a matter of practice, the appropriate approach is for the adjudicator to enquire into his jurisdiction and insofar as he finds it to be the case that he has jurisdiction he should continue with the adjudication unless and until the court orders otherwise. In the event that the adjudicator considers that he does not have jurisdiction, he should resign.

### Error in adjudicator's decision

In the case of *Bouygues (UK) Ltd* v. *Dahl-Jensen (UK) Ltd* (2000) the adjudicator dealt with cross adjudications. Dahl-Jensen issued a Notice to Adjudicate claiming sums for additional work and the cost of delay and disruption.

Bouygues issued a Notice to Adjudicate claiming repayment of sums they claimed they had overpaid to Dahl-Jensen, liquidated damages for delayed completion and damages for costs incurred as a result of the determination. This claim was treated effectively as a counterclaim to Dahl-Jensen's claim.

The adjudicator considered both claims. In carrying out his calculations, the adjudicator took a gross sum which included 5 per cent retention and deducted it from sums paid which were net of retention. The effect of this was to release retention before it was due to be released. The practical effect was that instead of finding the sum of £141,254 was due to Bouygues, the adjudicator awarded the sum of £207,700 to Dahl-Jensen.

Bouygues went to court to set aside the adjudicator's decision and to substitute it with an award in their favour. Neither party had made any submissions on the issue of retention. Dahl-Jensen argued that if there was a mistake, it was in the adjudicator's calculations, and not a mistake in his decision to deal with a dispute that was outside his jurisdiction.

The court decided that the adjudicator plainly made a mistake. However, he did not purport to determine that Dahl-Jensen were entitled to the release of the retention. Rather, his mistake was an arithmetical one with which the court could not interfere. Effectively, the adjudicator had answered the right question, but in the wrong way.

The judge concluded:

'the court should bear in mind that the speedy nature of the adjudication process means that mistakes will inevitably occur, and, in my view, it should guard against characterising a mistaken answer to an issue that lies within the scope of the reference as an excess of jurisdiction.'

In *Bloor Construction UK Ltd* v. *Bowmer Kirkland (London) Ltd* (2000) a mistake had been made by the adjudicator in his decision which was dated 9 February, and sent to the parties on 11 February. He had not taken into account in his calculations payments made to date by the main contractor. The adjudicator then realised his mistake, wrote to the parties on 11 February along with a corrected decision, still dated 9 February.

Bloor sought summary judgment. His Honour Judge Toulmin reached a practical decision that, in the absence of a specific agreement to the contrary, there will be an implied term that an adjudicator can correct, clarify or remove an error or accidental omission, provided that it is done within a reasonable time, and causes no prejudice to the other party. However, that decision appears to proceed at least in part, by way of analogy with the power given to an arbitrator in England and Wales to correct arbitration awards, see section 57 of the Arbitration Act 1996. That provision does not apply to Scotland. Accordingly, it still remains an open question in Scotland as to whether an adjudicator has power to correct an error in his decision. A court may be attracted by the idea of implying such a term in order to avoid the delay and expense that would be occasioned by having to have a new adjudication, see *C & B Scene Concept Design Ltd* v. *Isobars Ltd* (2002). However, this is an area where some express legislative provision would be welcome in Scotland.

The leading case from the Scottish Appeal Court *Gillies Ramsay Diamond* v. *PJW Enterprises Ltd* (2004) concerned the appeal against the decision of Lady Paton in the judicial review of a decision by an adjudicator.

In this case the court found that although the adjudicator had not applied his mind to the proper legal test that required to be met before it was proper to make a finding of professional negligence, the court, with some reluctance, held that the decision had to be enforced.

The Inner House affirmed Lady Paton's decision and made a number of important observations on adjudication:

- Adjudication is not a form of arbitration as had been suggested in some decisions by a single judge. The Scottish adjudicator is not subject to the common law limitations on the powers of an arbiter. An adjudicator has power to award damages for loss arising from breach of contract, including professional negligence. The 1996 Act and the Scheme properly construed confer on an adjudicator the power to award damages. The reference in s.108(1) to 'a dispute under the contract' must comprehend a dispute on a claim that there has been a breach of the contract.

- An adjudication award, although provisional, creates a liability that is immediately enforceable and should not be viewed as an interim award. So long as it is undisturbed, it has the effect of a decree.
- The court has jurisdiction to review a decision of an adjudicator that proceeds on an erroneous exercise of jurisdiction such as where an adjudicator has exceeded his jurisdiction or has exercised it fraudulently or in breach of natural justice.
- As long as the adjudicator asks himself the right question, the decision is not reviewable on the ground that he has answered it incorrectly. If an adjudicator provides inadequate reasons for his decision, as long as they are not so unintelligible that it is impossible for the reader to make sense of them, the court will not review that adjudicator's decision.
- It should be assumed that the adjudicator has taken into account all relevant information placed before him unless his decision and his reasons suggest otherwise.

### 16.10.3 Natural justice

The statutory requirement for adjudicators to act impartially is set out at paragraph 12 of the Scheme which provides:

'The adjudicator shall –

(a) act impartially in carrying out his duties and shall do so in accordance with any relevant terms of the contract and shall reach his decision in accordance with the applicable law in relation to the contract; and
(b) avoid incurring unnecessary expense.'

Whilst the Scheme is silent on the procedure to be adopted by the adjudicator, and there is no requirement for the Respondent to submit anything, to fulfil the requirement to act impartially, in practice, the adjudicator will ask for a response to the Referral Notice.

There is now a considerable body of case law which attaches critical importance to the need for adjudicators to act impartially and in accordance with basic rules of natural justice and fairness. However, the courts have recognized that any alleged breach of such rules has to be viewed in the context of the nature of adjudication and its tight timescales.

In *Discain Project Services Ltd* v. *Opecprime Development Ltd* (2000) His Honour Judge Bowsher declined to enforce an adjudicator's award where the adjudicator had failed to consult with one party upon submissions which had been made by the other party. The judge stated that he found it 'distasteful' and could not bring himself to enforce an adjudication decision which had been arrived at in that way.

The power of an adjudicator to use his initiative in investigating the facts and the law must be read in conjunction with the duty to act impartially. If an adjudicator procures any information from whichever source and certainly if it might have a bearing on his decision, both parties should be informed of this so that they are given an opportunity to comment on it. Despite the pressure of time on adjudicators, with the result that it may be almost impossible to give parties the opportunity to be heard on every possible topic within the time available, it would be prudent for an adjudicator to record what information has been obtained and to pass it on to the parties in sufficient time to enable them to comment before he reaches his decision. Some adjudicators interpret this as a prohibition on private meetings or conversations with one party only. It is certainly the safer course to adopt.

In *Woods Hardwick Ltd* v. *Chiltern Air-Conditioning Ltd* (2001), Woods Hardwick were engaged to provide architectural services at a development. Disputes arose between the parties and Woods Hardwick claimed for unpaid fees and additional work. They commenced adjudication proceedings. After two site meetings the adjudicator consulted Woods Hardwick's representatives, two of Chiltern's sub-contractors, the local authority's litigation department and RIBA's legal helpline. He did not inform Chiltern either that he had obtained information from those sources or of its content. Chiltern was not given an opportunity to comment upon the information obtained. The adjudicator issued his decision dismissing Chiltern's defence and awarding Woods Hardwick most of the sums claimed.

Woods Hardwick sought to enforce the decision and submitted a detailed witness statement from the adjudicator which indicated that he had taken an adverse view of Chiltern's performance and of the representatives who appeared at the meetings.

The judge dismissed the proceedings on the basis that the adjudicator acted in a manner which could be easily perceived as partial in approaching one side without informing the other, in seeking additional information from third parties and in then making adverse findings against the party left in ignorance. This was compounded by the adjudicator's voluntary provision of a particular type of witness statement. The adjudicator's witness statement effectively confirmed in the judge's mind the lack of impartiality of the adjudicator.

The case of *Balfour Beatty Construction Ltd* v. *The Mayor and Burgess of the London Borough of Lambeth* (2002) concerned a late completion dispute.

The adjudicator adopted a 'collapsed as-built' method of analysis which had not been advanced by the parties but did not present his analysis to the parties for their comment. His Honour Judge Lloyd held that the adjudicator should have invited comments on whether the as-built programme he had drawn up was a suitable basis from which to derive a retrospective critical path. He should have informed parties of the methodology that he intended to adopt, or sought observations from them as to the manner in which it or any other methodology might reasonably and properly be used in the circumstances to establish or test Balfour's case.

The adjudicator should not have used his powers to make good fundamental deficiencies in the material presented by one party without first giving the other party a proper opportunity of dealing with that intention and the results.

Lambeth was entitled to have the dispute decided on the material provided by Balfour Beatty, either originally or in answer to the adjudicator's requests, not on a basis devised by the adjudicator. The judge said that if an adjudicator uses his powers to find out more about the facts or to form the opinion that a different principle should be applied, he should tell the parties what he has found, and the potential implications of those findings. Constructing, or reconstructing, a party's case for it without confronting the other party is such a potentially serious breach of the requirements of both impartiality and fairness that the decision was invalid, so the enforcement application was dismissed. This case illustrates that whilst an adjudicator can take an inquisitorial approach to ascertaining the facts, the adjudicator must act with care and even-handedly.

In the leading Scottish case in this area, *Costain Ltd* v. *Strathclyde Builders Ltd* (2004), the Court of Session has given helpful guidance on the practical application to adjudication of the principles of natural justice.

Costain raised enforcement proceedings against Strathclyde Builders, seeking payment of sums found due by an adjudicator, which were various amounts deducted as liquidated and ascertained damages. Summary decree was sought by Costain.

The adjudicator had sought and was granted an extension to the deadline for reaching his decision as he wished to discuss one point in particular with his legal adviser. Neither the terms nor the result of his discussions with the legal adviser were made known to either party.

Strathclyde Builders argued that the advice given was material to which the adjudicator would probably have attributed significance in reaching his decision. Consequently, his failure to disclose the substance of the advice, and invite comments, prior to reaching his decision was a breach of the principles of natural justice.

The judge refused to grant summary judgment. He decided that it was not clear whether the one particular matter which the adjudicator indicated he intended to discuss with his legal adviser was adequately covered by the parties' submissions. It was immaterial that no actual prejudice was demonstrated, the mere possibility of prejudice was sufficient. The judge stated that if confidence in the system of adjudication was to be maintained it was important that adjudicators' decisions should be free from any suspicion of unfairness. It was not an answer to say that an adjudicator's decision could be re-opened at the end of the contract by arbitration or litigation. Basic standards of fairness should be applied to adjudicators and vigorously enforced.

It is quite common for adjudicators to seek legal or other specialist advice. The position is now clear. If matters are raised, parties must be given the opportunity to comment. Even if new matters are not raised, parties should still be informed of the content of the discussions. Failing which, a breach of natural justice may be held to be established and the courts will not enforce the adjudicator's decision.

## 16.11 Proceedings following adjudication

It is important to know what matters have been referred to and decided upon by an adjudicator, where there are time bar provisions in relation to proceeding with litigation or arbitration for a final decision, see *Castle Inns (Stirling) Ltd* v. *Clark Contracts Ltd* (2007).

In cases where proceedings are raised to finally determine matters it will not ordinarily be competent to seek recovery in those proceedings of the fees and outlays of the adjudicator where it is contended that the adjudicator was in error, see *Castle Inns (Stirling) Ltd* v. *Clark Contracts Ltd* (2006). However, it should be noted that that case does not deal with the situation where the decision of the adjudicator is reduced or declared void and unenforceable because of lack of jurisdiction or breach of the rules of natural justice.

In *City Inns Ltd* v. *Shepherd Construction Ltd* (2001) the onus of proof following the adjudication was considered in the context of a dispute concerning the interpretation of a clause which required the contractor to notify the architect, on receipt of any instructions, of the effect on the contract sum, the completion date and any anticipated loss and expense. It was held that an adjudicator's decision in relation to an extension of time did not affect the onus of proof in subsequent litigation or arbitration. This remained with the party claiming the entitlement to the full extension of time to establish its entitlement as a whole, not just that over and above that awarded by the adjudicator. The judge stated:

> 'As has been observed in a number of cases, the function of adjudication, as contemplated in the 1996 Act, is to provide a speedy means of reaching a binding interim determination of disputes arising under construction contracts. It goes no further than that . . . It is, in my view, no part of the function of an adjudicator's decision to reverse the onus of proof in an arbitration or litigation to which the parties require to resort to obtain a final determination of the dispute between them.'

## 16.12 Human rights

Another consideration is the implication of the Human Rights Act 1998. Does this open up an avenue for challenges to adjudicators' decisions? In *Elanay Contracts Ltd* v. *The Vestry* (2001) the judge considered the effects of the European Convention on Human Rights. Article 6 of the Convention states:

'In the determination of his civil rights and obligations . . . everyone is entitled to a fair and public hearing within a reasonable time by an independent and impartial tribunal established by law. The judgment shall be pronounced publicly'.

The Vestry argued that enforcement should not be ordered as the adjudication procedure was unfair. This was partly due to the fact that for much of the time the defendant's key witness was attending hospital visiting his dying mother. The shortness of the proceedings, which were over in 35 days, added to the sense of unfairness.

The judge took a different view. He considered that Article 6 did not apply to statutory adjudication. The reason given was that whilst proceedings before an adjudicator determine questions of civil rights, they are not in any sense a final determination.

In the case of *Austin Hall Building Ltd* v. *Bucklands Securities Ltd* (2001) it was again decided that neither the Human Rights 1998 Act nor the Convention applied. The challenge was that the adjudication system set up by the statute was itself inherently unfair because it did not give sufficient time for either or both parties to present their case; there was no public hearing and pronouncement of the decision.

This is a very important issue. Notwithstanding the decisions by the single judges above, it could be said that it has not been fully argued in any decision from the courts so far. It is possible that an appeal court in particular might take a different view if asked to pronounce upon this question.

## 16.13 Changes in the statutory framework

Adjudication in the form we now understand it was introduced under the 1996 Act, the relevant part of which came into effect in 1998. When it was introduced the Government indicated that it would keep the legislation under review and it would consider changes to the 1996 Act or the Scheme if experience suggested changes were required. This now touches upon a devolved matter and any legislation for Scotland should come from the Scottish Executive rather than Westminster.

In January 2003 the Scottish Executive issued a consultation paper 'Improving Adjudication in the Construction Industry'. In May 2004 it issued its report on the consultation, with proposals. Basically, it took the view that most of the perceived problems could be dealt with by providing guidance to adjudicators. The only area in which legislative intervention was thought necessary was to give express power to adjudicators to correct errors in decisions. Unfortunately, by the time the Scottish Executive had issued its proposals many thought that things had moved on and adjudication needed a more thorough review with more significant statutory changes. Accordingly, all this was overshadowed by an announcement later that year that the UK

Government had asked Sir Michael Latham to lead a review of the workings of the 1996 Act.

After Sir Michael reported, a formal consultation was not started until March 2005. In January 2006 an analysis of the consultation was published setting out various proposals. The Westminster Government is still consulting to decide what action it will take in relation to amendment of the legislation for England and Wales. While the outcome of that is still uncertain at the time of writing, no action has been taken by the Scottish Executive pending the completion of the review in England and Wales.

It is thought that, given the 1996 Act is a UK-wide statute and many businesses operate throughout the UK, it would be appropriate that any material statutory changes should apply both north and south of the border. It should be remembered, however, that there are certain differences between the position in Scotland and that in England and Wales which the Scottish Executive should address as solely Scottish issues.

# Chapter 17
# Arbitration

## 17.1 Introduction

It seems likely that arbitration was known in Scotland before the establishment of the public courts. Its introduction has been described as contemporaneous with the foundation of Scots law, see *MacCallum* v. *Lawrie* (1810).

Recourse to arbitration continued to be frequent, as in most civilised countries, even after regular courts of law had been established, particularly in mercantile matters and in a wide range of cases where the questions at issue were best suited to determination by a person with skill or experience, or where it was hoped to avoid the delay, expense and publicity of procedure in the courts of law.

For a time the utility of the process was at risk of being lost, because the courts had come to accept that an arbiter's award was open to challenge on the ground of iniquity in the Judge or *enorm lesion* (i.e. considerable injury) of a party. This meant that an award was for all practical purposes open to review upon its merits at the discretion of the court in every case.

The 25th Act of the Articles of Regulation 1695 was made in order to deal with the situation, to the effect that the court would not sustain the reduction of any decree arbitral upon any cause or reason whatsoever unless that of corruption, bribery or falsehood, be alleged against the arbiter who pronounced the same. The effect of this 25th Act was to restore to the agreement to submit to arbitration what has been described as its natural force and vigour and to secure for an arbiter's award the conclusive finality which it was said was the object of parties to confer upon it when they originally agreed to this procedure.

It is only in recent times that the position established in 1695, whereby an arbiter's decision was final both in fact and in law, has come to be modified by the introduction of a procedure whereby an arbiter may be required at any stage in the arbitration to state a case for the opinion of the Court of Session on any question of law arising in the arbitration, see section 3 of the Administration of Justice (Scotland) Act 1972.

Arbitration has been the traditional means of obtaining a final decision on disputes in the construction industry for decades. This is because arbitration procedure can be well suited to the types of dispute that arise under construction contracts. This has been reflected in standard form contracts, such as those produced by JCT, SBCC and ICE, which have required disputes to be resolved by arbitration. However, the absence of modern and comprehensive arbitration legislation for Scotland has been held out as one of the reasons why fewer and fewer disputes are being referred to arbitration in Scotland. This has resulted in greater recourse to the courts for a final decision either after or without recourse to adjudication. Indeed, for the first time, the SBC requires parties to choose arbitration, failing which disputes are to be determined by the Court. In the past, the default position has always been in favour of arbitration. Given the disquiet in some quarters concerning the quality of some adjudicators' decisions and the need to have a means of obtaining a final rather than interim decision in some construction disputes without going through the courts, it is thought that there is likely to be a revival in construction arbitration if there is legislative reform.

### 17.1.1 Definition of arbitration

Arbitration has been defined as the method of procedure by which parties who are in dispute with each other agree to submit their dispute to the decision of one or more persons, traditionally in Scotland described as 'arbiters', rather than resort to the courts of law. Elsewhere the generally used term is 'arbitrator'.

### 17.1.2 Elements of ordinary arbitration

The essential elements of an ordinary arbitration are: two or more parties; a dispute or question; resolved by this method under an agreement entered into voluntarily to refer to a third party, the arbiter; the arbiter's jurisdiction is limited by the terms of the reference and he is subject to the supervision of the ordinary courts; and the arbiter must decide the dispute or question submitted to him by means of one or more decrees arbitral (awards). It will thus be apparent that, in the ordinary case, arbitration arises out of contract.

> 'The law of Scotland has, from the earliest time, permitted private parties to exclude the merits of any dispute between them from the consideration of the court by simply naming their arbiter ... It deprives the Court of jurisdiction to enquire into and decide the merits of the case, while it leaves the Court free to entertain the suit, and pronounce a decree in conformity with the award of the arbiter. Should the arbitration from any cause prove abortive the full jurisdiction of the Court will revive, to the effect of enabling it to hear and determine the action upon its merits'.

See *Hamlyn & Co. v. Talisker Distillery Co.* (1894).

### 17.1.3  Absence of codified statutory framework for control of arbitration

Unlike that of other countries, including England and Wales, the law of arbitration in Scotland is based almost entirely on the common law developed over the centuries since the 25th Act of the Articles of Regulations 1695 and has been only marginally affected by statute.

The most important statutory provisions are:

- Section 2 of the Arbitration (Scotland) Act 1894 – which gives the Court of Session and Sheriff Court the power to appoint an arbiter should the parties fail to agree on a particular person.
- Section 3 of the Administration of Justice (Scotland) Act 1972 – which gives an arbiter the power to state a case, on the application of either party, on a point of law, to the Court of Session in order to obtain its opinion. While the arbiter has a discretion to decide whether or not to state a case, if he refuses to do so he must provide a statement of his reasons and the Court of Session may still direct that he must state a case for its opinion. The power to state a case may be excluded by the parties in which event the only remedy open to a party dissatisfied with the outcome is to seek judicial review or reduction but these remedies are only available in very limited and unusual circumstances, discussed below.
- Section 66 of the Law Reform (Miscellaneous Provisions) (Scotland) Act 1990 – which effectively adopts the UNCITRAL Model Law on International Commercial Arbitration for international arbitrations held in Scotland.

The lack of a codifying statute setting out a modern and comprehensive Scots law on arbitration has been the subject of much controversy and has been stated as the principal reason for the decline of commercial arbitration in Scotland in recent years. The then UK Government set up the Dervaird committee to review and recommend changes to provide a modern and effective arbitration framework in Scotland. In 1996, the committee produced a report and draft Arbitration Bill which has subsequently been updated. However, to date no parliamentary time has been found to pass new legislation. This is now a devolved matter and any legislation would have to be enacted by the Scottish Parliament at Holyrood.

Many of the recognised deficiencies in the present Scots law of arbitration including the absence of a common law power to award damages or to award interest before the date of decree arbitral have had to be addressed by practical means. Arbiters have to be given appropriate powers by the parties (a) in the arbitration clause itself, (b) in the Deed of Appointment or Submission or (c) by adopting a set of Rules such as the Scottish Arbitration Code 1999 promulgated by the Scottish Council for International Arbitration, SBCC and the Chartered Institute of Arbitrators (Scottish Branch). A variation of the 1999 Code is the Scottish Construction Arbitration Code 2005 which is based on the 1999 Code with certain modifications introducing (a) a timescale for initial procedure, (b) a relatively short times-cale for a decision, (c) a move away from court style written pleadings, (d) a presumption against producing draft decisions and (e) safeguards regarding arbitrators' fees. Clearly, the parties have to agree that one of the Codes or other such arbitration rules should apply to their arbitration.

Accordingly, it is important to note that such Rules do not just set out purely procedural rules for the conduct of an arbitration. They alter the legal rights and obligations of the parties and the terms of Rules should be considered carefully before adopting any in whole or in part. Some, such as the Codes, for example, give rise to uncertainty as to the rules of evidence to be applied in the arbitration and very seriously restrict the scope for intervention by the Courts.

### 17.1.4. Statutory arbitrations

There are statutes, for example, in relation to agricultural issues, compensation or compulsory acquisition of property where Parliament has decided that these issues should be settled by arbitration. The legal implications of these statutory arbitrations as they affect the rights and duties of all parties concerned are the same, apart from the specialities provided for in the statute, as if the arbitration was one which proceeded under a private contract.

### 17.1.5 UNCITRAL Model Law

One major advantage of the Scottish system of arbitration is that by section 66 of the Law Reform (Miscellaneous Provisions) (Scotland) Act 1990, Scotland adopted the UNCITRAL Model Law in respect of all international commercial arbitrations. Any party considering raising an arbitration in Scotland can now be clear that the rules to be followed are contained in this Model Law. Furthermore, any parties to an arbitration which is not classed as an international commercial arbitration may still derive the benefits of the Model Law by agreeing that the provisions of the Model Law will apply.

The Model Law, with certain modifications to adapt it for application in Scotland, is set out in Schedule 7 to the 1990 Act. The scope of the Model Law is defined by article 1, sub-paragraph 3 and is worth quoting:

'An arbitration is international if:

the parties to an arbitration agreement have, at the time of the conclusion of that agreement, their place of business in different States, or one of the following places is situated outside the State in which the parties have their place of business;

(i)  the place of arbitration if determined in, or pursuant to, the arbitration agreement; and

(ii)  any place where a substantial part of the obligations of the commercial relationship is to be performed or the place with which the subject-matter of the dispute is most closely connected.'

Scotland is defined as a 'State' for the purposes of the 1990 Act. Accordingly a commercial arbitration between a Scottish and non-Scottish legal entity (including an English legal entity) may well be an international commercial arbitration to which the Model Law will apply.

## 17.1.6 Contractual nature of arbitration

Apart from the legislative provisions mentioned earlier the effect of legislation upon the Scottish system of arbitration is very limited. The decision whether or not to choose arbitration over court proceedings is entirely one for the parties and the entire procedure is a matter which may be dealt with contractually between the parties. They may agree at the outset of their relationship that should any disputes arise they will refer them to arbitration; they may agree when a dispute arises that it should be resolved by arbitration; or, they may agree after the commencement of a court action that they would rather proceed by way of arbitration. However, once the parties have reached agreement to refer certain disputes to arbitration then either party may enforce this agreement and a Scottish court normally has no discretion but to sist (suspend procedure) the court action for arbitration, see *Sanderson* v. *Armour* (1922).

## 17.1.7 Arbitrable issues

Every matter may be made the subject of arbitration with regard to which the parties have a dispute and over which they possess a sufficient power of disposal. This general statement includes matters arising out of many different types of contract including contracts relating to land and structures erected on land (heritable property) including building contracts.

The right to arbitrate may be lost if the court process is used in a way which evidences an intention not to arbitrate. Such actions may found a plea of waiver, see *Inverclyde Mearns Housing Society* v. *Lawrence Construction Co. Ltd* (1989).

Only questions which the parties could, if they wished, determine for themselves by a legally binding contract may be submitted to ordinary arbitration. Certain questions may not be referred to arbitration, for example, matters in which the public have an interest such as the status of parties (paternity, legitimacy, marriage, divorce, domicile). There cannot be an arbitration on whether someone has committed a crime. Further, certain transactions are illegal and are not enforceable and therefore cannot be referred to arbitration.

An arbiter may consider the question of fraud in any case where the incidental determination of this point is necessary in order to settle the real question at issue, see *Earl of Kintore* v. *Union Bank of Scotland* (1863). The question of whether or not there is an arbitrable dispute which must be referred to arbitration arises with great frequency out of many different contracts and has produced a large number of cases.

### 17.1.8 Scope of arbitration

The scope of the dispute referred to arbitration will depend upon what the parties have actually agreed. Thus an arbiter will have jurisdiction and power only in relation to those specific questions which the parties have agreed to submit to him. It can be seen therefore that a court may still have jurisdiction in a dispute where certain questions have been referred to arbitration but the determination of those questions does not resolve the dispute. In such circumstances, the court may still pronounce a decree in the action provided its judgment is in line with the awards of any arbiter, see *Hamlyn & Co.* v. *Talisker Distillery Co.* (1894). Such situations arise frequently in civil actions and it is common for courts to sist actions until questions referred to arbitration are resolved. It should also be clear from this that simply because a party raises a court action it does not lose its rights to refer a dispute to arbitration. A party may, for example, raise proceedings in order to carry out diligence on the dependence.

### 17.1.9 Relationship with courts

In Scotland, subject to the Stated Case procedure, there is no appeal to a court of law against the decision of an arbiter either on points of law or on questions of fact. Thus a court, in Scotland, cannot simply review the merits of an arbiter's decision. The only remedies available to any party to an arbitration are either to have the award reduced or to have the decision (or the arbiter's conduct prior to the publication of his decision) judicially reviewed. Judicial review and reduction are discussed more fully below.

The arbiter exercises a subordinate jurisdiction to the courts under their supervision by virtue of their residual powers. Specific examples of the support of the arbitration process by the courts are citation of witnesses; recovery of documents; warrant to execute diligence on the dependence of associated proceedings; enforcement of decrees arbitral, interim, part and final; Stated Case under section 3 of the Administration of

Justice (Scotland) Act 1972; suspension and interdict; and reduction and judicial review.

## 17.2 Arbitration proceedings

### 17.2.1 Submission to arbitration

Where parties have made provision for arbitration proceedings by some form of clause in their contract then normally provision will also have been made as to the rules to be followed, the powers of the arbiter and so forth. Such a clause can normally be brought into operation by the serving by one party of a Preliminary Notice on the other party requiring arbitration on the matters in dispute. However, parties need to be careful to follow any particular contractual requirements for commencing an arbitration. The prerequisites in ICE Conditions are particularly tortuous. However, the court will be slow to take an overly technical approach regarding notices seeking arbitration, see the decision of the Inner House of the Court of Session in *Scrabster Harbour Trust* v. *Mowlem plc* (2005).

There are four matters that, as a minimum, should be covered in the Preliminary Notice (these words have a significance in the context of the law of prescription). These are:

- that a dispute exists between the parties properly designed and the nature of the dispute;
- that the parties either have now agreed or are bound to submit the dispute to an arbiter for resolution;
- that the dispute falls within the scope of the arbitration clause; and
- that the addressee i.e. the other party should agree who the arbiter should be within, say, 14 days or an appointing authority will be approached to make the appointment.

Where no such clause exists in the original contract but the parties subsequently agree to refer their differences to arbitration, the proceedings are raised by way of a submission to arbitration. There is no standard form of submission necessary provided the parties to the dispute clearly express their decision to refer the dispute to arbitration and also to be bound by the arbiter's award.

A Deed of Appointment (where there is an arbitration clause in the underlying contract) or Deed of Submission (where there is no such clause) usually deals with the appointment of the arbiter; the endurance of the appointment; the arbiter's powers (e.g. including the power to award damages and interest); and the exclusion, if the parties so agree, of section 3 of the Administration of Justice (Scotland) Act 1972.

A submission to arbitration may be specific in that it is limited to one or more identified issues or it may be general in that it relates to all disputes outstanding between the parties.

## 17.2.2 Choice of arbiter

After the parties submit to arbitration the next stage, if it has not already been agreed, is the appointment of an arbiter. Again this is normally a matter of agreement between the parties. Any person selected is entitled to act provided he is reasonably qualified to deal with the issues and he has no interest which would affect his ability to act impartially. The arbiter may be chosen by the parties when they originally agreed to refer disputes to arbitration or he may not be chosen until the dispute actually arises.

If no agreement or concurrence in the appointment of an arbiter is reached, then either party may apply to the Court of Session or appropriate Sheriff Court requesting the appointment of an arbiter, see section 2 of the Arbitration (Scotland) Act 1894. Alternatively the arbitration clause or submission to arbitration may provide a formula for appointment of an arbiter, for example, that he be appointed by a particular professional body.

Many different organisations in Scotland do act as appointing authorities and a few of them also provide rules for conduct of arbitrations which the parties may choose to adopt. Appointing authorities include the Scottish Council for International Arbitration, SBCC, the Chartered Institute of Arbitrators (Scottish Branch) and professional organisations such as the Faculty of Advocates, the Law Society of Scotland, the Royal Incorporation of Architects in Scotland and the Royal Institution of Chartered Surveyors in Scotland.

Once an arbiter has been appointed, it is necessary that he accept the appointment. This he can do simply by a signed letter or in more formal cases by a Minute of Acceptance.

With regard to the arbiter's terms and conditions, it is proper for the arbiter to state his position before he accepts the appointment in order that parties are clear as to his terms, particularly in relation to his fees. It is now clear that an arbiter does not act gratuitously and is entitled to be paid for acting. It is sensible to have the arbiter's terms and conditions of appointment and his powers regulated by agreement from the outset in order to avoid any doubt.

Having accepted the appointment, it continues until the issues in the submission are resolved. The arbiter cannot refuse to act without good reason.

Having accepted appointment, the arbiter, if he wishes, may appoint a Clerk who is normally a solicitor. The Clerk's duties involve safe custody of pleadings and productions (the process); advice to the arbiter on procedure and substantive law; advice on drafting Interlocutors (procedural orders) and awards; provision of office facilities; provision of a channel of communication between parties and arbiter; administrative assistance for hire of rooms and arrangements for all hearings; provision to arbiter of works of reference; taking notes of evidence as led; and assistance with any Stated Case, including ensuring compliance with the Rules of Court.

The arbiter may also wish to appoint an assessor. His role is to provide independent advice to the arbiter upon a genuine area of expertise in which the arbiter is neither qualified nor experienced. His duties are to attend hearings, acquaint himself with the issues and to supply his views in an appropriate manner.

Consent to employment of an assessor is required from the parties as his employment will entail expense. His opinion should be a component but a separate part of the reasons. Fairness dictates that the parties should have available to them the material upon which the arbiter has relied in coming to his decision and it would be normal practice for the parties to be able to make representations to an assessor and then comment upon his report.

### 17.2.3  Procedure

The parties to an arbitration may agree in their submissions the procedure to be adopted or adopt all or some of the rules on arbitration as laid down by, for example, the Law Society of Scotland or any other arbitration regulating organisation. Otherwise the procedure in any arbitration is regulated solely by the arbiter using his common law powers, although he will obviously take the interests and agreement of the parties into account. He must ensure that there are no irregularities with the proceedings. In Scotland, it has been suggested that an arbiter's obligations are to act fairly; with reasonable diligence; with reasonable care and such special skill as he or she professes; in accordance with Law; and in accordance with the provisions of the contract of submission and deed implementing it, in particular ensuring that the issues submitted for decision are exhausted and their limits observed.

The arbiter has the power to decide if and when hearings will take place and all other procedural matters. There is no requirement in arbitration for written pleadings to be submitted but the arbiter usually requires them. Pleadings normally take the form of a Statement of Claim containing the contentions of fact and law of the Claimants and Answers thereto by the Respondents.

Assuming written pleadings are required, the arbiter has the authority to decide whether to allow adjustment of the pleadings and if so, for how long, and whether to allow amendment of the pleadings after the end of the adjustment period. Although these matters are within the arbiter's discretion, procedure is normally a matter discussed between the arbiter and the parties involved. If written pleadings are used, the rules of pleading apply, see *Rogerson Roofing Ltd* v. *Hall & Tawse Scotland Ltd* (2000).

### 17.2.4 Evidence

In relation to the rules of evidence, it is sometimes forgotten that, except insofar as parties make specific provision for the rules of evidence which are to apply in their arbitration, the rules in the Civil Evidence (Scotland) Act 1988 apply to arbitrations.

### 17.2.5 Hearing on legal issues or debate

Sometimes the dispute between the parties may relate solely to a matter of law and it is not necessary to hear evidence from witnesses, for example, a dispute relating to the interpretation of the terms of a contract. In such cases the arbiter will fix a hearing on legal issues (sometimes called 'a debate') at which the parties will make representations to the arbiter on the law and thereafter the arbiter will proceed in the same manner as set out below where there has been a hearing of evidence.

### 17.2.6 Witnesses

Where the arbitration is not one where it is agreed that the arbiter should proceed on the basis of 'documents only', an arbiter may allow witnesses to be heard. However, one shortcoming of his powers is the fact that he cannot force witnesses to appear nor force production of physical items of evidence. In such circumstances, if the parties wish this then they are required to petition the Court of Session for such an order. This is normally granted quickly and as a matter of routine. If such a court order is obtained, then failure to comply with it is contempt of court.

### 17.2.7 Proof

In relation to the procedure at the proof (trial) at which evidence is led, this is again a matter for the arbiter's discretion. He is only constrained by the fact that he must allow the parties a fair hearing and his decision must be just and proper. Therefore he is normally bound to hear all the evidence of the parties before making his award, especially in cases where the dispute is in relation to questions of fact.

Once all the evidence has been led by the parties, they normally make submissions to the arbiter as to how they see the factual and legal position in the particular case. These are similar to submissions in a court action.

### 17.2.8 The decree arbitral or award

After the proof is concluded, the arbiter will consider matters and thereafter issue his decree arbitral or award. Before issuing such decree arbitral or award, an arbiter normally issues a note of his proposed findings. This step in the proceedings is carried out as it allows parties an opportunity to seek a Stated Case in order to obtain an opinion of the Court of Session on a point of law if necessary. Once the arbiter issues his final award, the parties may not challenge his decision except by way of reduction or judicial review. These remedies are open in only limited and unusual circumstances. Thus all the issues referred to the arbiter are finally and conclusively resolved by the final award.

An arbiter's decree arbitral or award should ideally be in self-proving form and should deal fully with all the matters submitted to him by the parties. It is not necessary to give reasons for his decision unless the express terms of the reference require this but modern practice dictates that he should do so in a separate note.

The award of an arbiter derives its authority from the fact that all the parties to the arbitration have agreed to be bound by the arbiter's decision when they submitted the dispute(s) to arbitration. Should a party fail to comply with an award there are usually two possibilities for enforcement. Firstly, the parties may have agreed in their submission that the award can be registered for execution and thus a party can simply go ahead and enforce the award in the same way as a court judgment. Secondly, there may be no such agreement and thus it will be necessary to petition the court for an order to implement the award (usually a decree conform) which will give the award the force of a court decree

### 17.2.9 The law applicable to the arbitration

Where there is a relevant provision in the contract this will determine the procedural law which is applicable to the arbitration proceedings. Where there is no such provision then it is the law of the place where the arbitration proceedings are held. In Scotland, it appears to be an open question as to whether the parties may choose a procedural law different from the law of the place where the proceedings take place.

Under Schedule 8 of the Civil Jurisdiction and Judgments Act 1982, the Scottish Courts have jurisdiction in proceedings concerning an arbitration which is conducted in Scotland or in which the procedure is governed by Scots law. One must distinguish the law applicable to the contract (i.e. the one which determines the substantive rights and obligations of the parties) from the procedural law applicable to the arbitration proceedings.

## 17.3 Arbiter's powers

The main disadvantage of the current Scottish system of arbitration is the lack of powers possessed by arbiters. As arbiters are simply appointed by the parties to a dispute then the powers they possess are limited to those matters which are agreed between the parties or implied by law. Thus they can have no power over matters which fall outwith the relationship between the parties. For example, an arbiter cannot compel third parties to become parties to the proceedings unless the third party itself agrees.

Some of the most important limitations of the powers of arbiters are as follows; the arbiter has no power to award damages (and therefore interest on damages) unless expressly given, see *Blaikie* v. *Aberdeen Railway Co.* (1852). This is considered in detail, below at section 17.7. As a general rule, an arbiter has no power to award interest from a date earlier than his decree arbitral or award. This is considered in detail, below at section 17.6. In Scotland the arbiter has no power to order rectification of a contract. Only a Court has jurisdiction to do so. It is unclear as to whether an arbiter has power to pronounce a decree by default where one submitter invites the arbiter to proceed and the other party ignores the arbiter. In such circumstances, it may be sensible for an arbiter to hear evidence on liability and quantum, see *Hunter* v. *Milburn* (1869).

Rules such as the Scottish Arbitration Code (or similar rules), if used, will assist in overcoming difficulties in relation to the powers of arbiters but as indicated earlier, care should be taken as to the extent of their use.

## 17.4 Termination of arbitration contracts and proceedings

Upon the issue of the final award, the arbiter is *functus officio* provided he deals with all the matters referred to him. If the submission contains an expiry date, it will expire upon that day being reached. If the expiry date is left blank in the agreement to refer, the effect is not in doubt. Unless there has been a valid prorogation, that is an extension of the duration of the submission, the primary obligations under the contract expire at the end of a year and a day. However, the submission can continue by express or implied agreement of the parties. The position where the submitter or arbiter dies should be covered by a provision in the submission. An arbitration can terminate by agreement or by abandonment.

## 17.5 Decrees arbitral

### 17.5.1 Types of decree arbitral

There are three principal types of decree arbitral or award recognised by Scots Law: interim awards; part awards; and final awards.

An interim award is one in which the arbiter makes a determination on the matters covered by it but only on a provisional basis. This means that such an award is subject to recall or alteration by a subsequent interim or final award. There is some doubt as to whether an arbiter has an implied power to make interim awards at common law. Where the parties wish the arbiter to have a power to make interim awards, this should be expressly conferred. An award which is intended to be interim should be clearly specified as such in the award itself.

A part award is one in which the arbiter makes a determination which is conclusive and irrevocable in respect of part only of the matters submitted to him. Here, also, there is doubt as to whether an arbiter has power to make part awards at common law. On occasion the Courts have been prepared to hold that such a power is implied in the submission, see *Lyle* v. *Falconer* (1842). However, accordingly, if parties wish the arbiter to have such a power, it should be expressly conferred.

A final award is one where the arbiter makes an irrevocable decision on a matter or matters covered by the award. It is important to note that an award which irrevocably decides only part of the subject matter of the arbitration is a final award. The phrase 'final award' is also used to describe an award in which all matters submitted to the arbiter have been determined.

If the award is 'a final award', it should narrate if any interim awards have been made and the extent to which these are to be upheld or varied. This should be done with care in order to prevent any suggestion of ambiguity. Any part awards should also be appropriately narrated.

Conditional and alternative awards are also possible in certain circumstances, but these are unusual. Provided the arbiter is empowered to do so he may pronounce an alternative award. Conditional awards introduce a condition which must be satisfied before the award can take effect and will be enforceable if the condition can be worked out without having to return to the arbiter, see *Duffus* v. *Petrie* (1838).

### 17.5.2 Style of awards

It appears to be the case that the use of a particular style of written award is not required by law. The forms used have evolved from the practice of arbitration over the centuries. In Scotland decrees arbitral can be traced back to at least the year 1492.

The form of a Scottish decree arbitral usually comprises three principal elements: the introductory or narrative clause; the adjudication clause; and the testing clause.

The introductory or narrative clause narrates the parties to the arbitration, the name and appointment of the arbiter, the contract which has given rise to the submission, the questions submitted to the arbiter for determination and the history of the proceedings before the arbiter leading up to the award.

The adjudication clause narrates the decision of the arbiter upon the matters submitted to him. The award should clearly narrate the type of award which is being made, whether it is final, interim or part.

In Scotland, the reasons of the arbiter for reaching his award should not be included as part of the award itself but should be appended in the form of a Note of Reasons.

Where the submission requires that the arbiter states reasons for his award, the arbiter must provide them. In the absence of such a requirement, there is no legal obligation upon him to do so. However, where it is reasonable for an arbiter to do so, modern practice dictates that he should give his reasons for reaching his decision.

The testing clause should narrate the particulars as required in any other self-proving deed, namely, the date and place of signature of the decree arbitral and the name and designation of the witness.

### 17.5.3 Validity and form of decree arbitral

For a decree arbitral or award to be valid it must satisfy legal requirements as to (a) form and (b) substance.

It appears that it is not competent to prove an award by the oath of an arbiter, see *Ferri* v. *Mitchell & Others* (1824). Accordingly, for all practical purposes, it can be stated that a decree arbitral must be in writing and signed by the arbiter.

Under the Requirements of Writing (Scotland) Act 1995, all that is required for a document to be formally valid is for that document to have been signed by the granter. The circumstances which give rise to a document being regarded as 'self-proving' are considered above in Chapter 3.

The award must be issued. This may be done by delivering the principal or a certified copy to either of the parties (see *Gray & Woodrow* v. *McNair* (1831)); or by registering the principal in the books of a court for preservation and execution (see *Gray & Woodrow*); or by delivering it to the clerk in circumstances indicating that it is to be held for the parties (see *McQuaker* v. *Phoenix Assurance* (1859)).

### 17.5.4 Substantive requirements

To be valid, a decree arbitral must satisfy certain substantive requirements. These can be summarised as follows:

#### A decree arbitral must be complete

In so far as possible, any decree arbitral should be self-contained and self-explanatory. It should not depend upon any outside deeds or documents. Where an arbiter finds it necessary to make reference to other deeds or documents in the body of the decree arbitral, such deeds or documents must be clearly identified.

**The decree arbitral must be certain**

Where the decree arbitral provides for payment of a sum of money, the arbiter must fix the precise amount to be paid. Any directions as to acts which are to be performed or the deeds which are to be executed should be sufficiently clear and precise to enable a decree for specific implement to be obtained if the award requires to be enforced through the courts. Once the arbiter has exhausted the submission by issuing the award, he is *functus officio*. It is incompetent to ask him to provide his interpretation of the award. That is a matter of construction for the courts, not a matter upon which evidence can be lead. It is perhaps true to say that it is impossible to frame an award in such precise and unambiguous terms that it cannot under any circumstances give rise to dispute. However, the courts will give an award a liberal and sensible construction and they will be more inclined to uphold it than to set it aside.

**A decree arbitral must be exhaustive of the reference**

It is the object of the decree arbitral to decide the matters which have been referred to the arbiter and to bring the submission to an end. It should leave none of the disputed matters undecided unless power has been given to pronounce part awards. The failure of the arbiter to exhaust the submission will render a decree arbitral liable to reduction. There is a presumption in favour of the validity of the award. While it has been held that silence on a particular point will not necessarily lead to an inference that an arbiter has failed to deal with a particular matter, an arbiter should endeavour to frame the award in such a way that he states his decision under reference to each of the points which have been submitted to him.

**A decree arbitral must not be *ultra fines compromissi***

The decree arbitral must not stray beyond the terms of the matters detailed in the submission. The arbiter acts *ultra fines compromissi* in deciding any matter which has not been referred to him by the parties in the submission. Where it is possible to separate the elements of a decree arbitral which are *ultra fines compromissi* from those which are within the terms of the reference, the decree arbitral may be set aside as to the matters which are *ultra fines compromissi* and affirmed in respect of those matters which are *intra fines compromissi*. That rule requires to be qualified because, where it is clear that a decision or any part of the decision which is *intra fines compromissi* was influenced by the decision on the matters which are *ultra fines compromissi* the whole award will be reduced. Difficult situations may arise where it is clear during the course of the arbitration that the real point at issue is not the same as that which has been asked in the submission. The arbiter should be careful to confine himself to the questions put to him unless the parties expressly confer power upon him to deal with further matters.

### An award must be possible and consistent

Where an arbiter makes an award which is not itself capable of being performed, such award is not enforceable against the party against whom it is made, because a party cannot be forced to do something which it is impossible for him to do. Where an award is inconsistent within itself it is open to reduction.

## 17.6 *Awards of interest*

It is important to note that different considerations apply in determining what awards of interest can be made by an arbiter when compared with those considerations which apply before the courts. The first question which requires to be addressed is what are the powers of an arbiter to deal with questions of interest? It is a matter for the parties to ensure that any issue relating to interest is put before the arbiter for his decision. However, if we exclude arbitrations in which the contract or the deed of submission make specific provision in relation to interest, does the arbiter have power to deal with interest? In a Stated Case before the Second Division which dealt with this area of the law, it was argued against the claimants in the arbitration that the arbiter had no implied power at common law to award interest, see *Farrans (Construction) Ltd. v. Dunfermline District Council* (1988). In that case, their Lordships did not take the opportunity which was offered to them to approve a general rule of law that an arbiter does have such implied power. The court considered that they were not required to do so because they were happy that on a proper construction of the deed of submission entered into between the parties, the arbiter had been empowered to award interest.

Some assistance is, however, available from remarks made by Lord Dunpark in *John G McGregor (Contractors) Ltd v. Grampian Regional Council* (1991). In that case, the Joint Deed of Submission made no provision for the arbiter to award interest but the Claimants sought interest from the commencement of the arbitration. The court held that the arbiter had no power to award interest before the date of the decree arbitral but Lord Dunpark observed:

> 'I have no doubt that an arbiter has an implied power to award interest on sums found due from the date of his final decree until payment but, in the absence of any express agreement that he shall have power to award interest on principal sums prior to that date, I do not consider that such a power may be implied.'

Where an arbiter has power to deal with questions of interest, whether by express power in the original contract, or by express power in the deed of submission or other agreement of the parties or due to an implied power at common law, we must consider the rate at which interest runs.

It is trite to say that if there is a contractual or agreed rate of interest then that is the rate at which interest should be sought and awarded in any decree arbitral. The arbiter, like the court, should not re-write the bargain entered into between the parties, see *Bank of Scotland* v. *Davis* (1982).

Accordingly, at what rate should an arbiter award interest? There is authority for the proposition that an arbiter is entitled to award interest at the judicial rate. This is again to be found in the *Farrans Construction Ltd* case referred to above. In that case the respondents argued that the arbiter should not have awarded interest at the then judicial rate of fifteen per cent *per annum*. The argument ran that the rate of interest should reflect what could reasonably be expected by way of return in the course of commerce or business and that in the relevant period, interest rates generally had been much lower than the judicial rate. Accordingly the respondents moved the Court to find that the arbiter should have awarded a rate of interest less than fifteen per cent *per annum*.

The Court rejected all such arguments, stating that there was no sound basis for arguing that an arbiter was not entitled to rely upon the judicial rate then existing as being a reasonable rate to award on any decree arbitral. The rate of interest awarded was a matter within the arbiter's discretion. However, their Lordships did not lay down a general rule that an arbiter should award the judicial rate. There is no basis to be found in that case for the belief that if, in appropriate circumstances, the arbiter awarded less or more than the prevailing judicial rate that would be regarded as an error in law.

The rate of interest awarded remains a matter within the discretion of the arbiter provided that such discretion is exercised reasonably after taking into account all the relevant circumstances.

It does not appear to be settled if an arbiter can award interest based on a specified standard which may fluctuate but there seems to be no proper basis in principle as to why that should not be possible.

The next question to be considered is what is the date from which interest runs on an arbiter's award? As has been stated previously an arbiter does not have power to award interest from a date earlier than his decree arbitral unless he has been given such power by the parties. If such power has been granted, what is the date from which interest should run on any principal sum awarded? Under Scots Law, except in certain special cases, the starting point appears to be has there been 'wrongful withholding', see *Farrans Construction Ltd, Carmichael* v. *Caledonian Railway Company* (1870) and *Dean Warwick Ltd* v. *Borthwick* (1983).

In *Elliot* v. *Combustion Engineering Ltd* (1997) a court action was raised in 1987 for payment of certain sums allegedly due but the matter was subsequently sisted for arbitration. The arbiter awarded interest on certain sums from 1982. The court held that the power conferred on the arbiter in the deed of submission to award interest to the claimant was only to award it if the claimant was legally entitled to it, that the general rule was that interest ran on contractual debts from judicial demand in court proceedings (the 'wrongful withholding') and there was no wide discretion conferred on the court nor on the arbiter to determine the date untrammelled by legal rules. Accordingly, as the claimant's claim did not fall within any recognised qualification or exception to the general rule he was not entitled to interest from 1982 as awarded by the arbiter. He was only entitled to interest from the date of judicial demand in 1987.

## 17.7  Awards of damages

An arbiter does not have power to make an award of damages unless he is specifically empowered to do so by the parties, see *Aberdeen Railway Co.* v. *Blaikie Bros.* (1852) and *North British Railway Co.* v. *Newburgh & North Fife Railway Co.* (1891). If such power is given to the arbiter, he should also be given specific power to award interest on any damages awarded.

   This is a standard power which is usually included in (a) the arbitration clause in the underlying contract or (b) expressly in the deed of appointment or submission or (c) by using Rules which include such a power, for example, the Scottish Arbitration Code 1999. This position is to be contrasted with the powers of courts to award interest on damages which are now governed by statute, see section 1 of the Interest on Damages (Scotland) Act 1958, as amended by section 1 of the Interest on Damages (Scotland) Act 1971.

## 17.8  Awards of expenses

   In formal submissions a clause is usually and properly inserted empowering the arbiter to deal with the question of expenses. The power has been said in the past to be implied in any submission, see *Pollich* v. *Heatley* (1910). Matters are different where there is express provision in the submission, see *Grampian Regional Council* v. *John G McGregor (Contractors) Ltd* (1994).

   If there are specific provisions relating to expenses in the submission, an arbiter must adhere strictly to them. Any award of expenses must be made prior to the issue of the decree arbitral terminating the arbitration because thereafter the arbiter has no power to bind the parties, see *Jack* v. *King* (1932).

   If an arbiter exercises his discretion in awarding expenses in a judicious manner the courts will not interfere even if they would have come to a different decision in the circumstances, see *McArdle* v. *J and R Howie Ltd* (1927). However the main and overriding principle to be applied in respect of an award of expenses is that expenses follow success, that is, an arbiter should award the expenses of the submission to the party who is successful.

An arbiter, like a judge, must have material upon which, if he does not follow the usual rule of awarding expenses to the successful party, he can take any other course of action, see *Feeney* v. *Fife Coal Board* (1918).

In England circumstances which are regarded as justifying departure, wholly or partially, from the general rule that expenses follow success are:

- failure by the otherwise successful party in a matter in issue in the submission on which a large amount of time had been spent during the arbitration hearing;
- extravagance in the employment of professional advisers or in the calling of witnesses; or
- unreasonable or obstructive behaviour of the successful party which has increased the expense of proceedings to the unsuccessful party.

It is clear that some modification of the application of the general rule on expenses could be justified in such circumstances. It is arguable that building and engineering cases call for an approach which recognises that each issue may be looked at individually so that one party may succeed on one point but not on another so that there is mixed success and that this should be reflected in separate awards of expenses reflecting separate and independent successes or even neutral outcomes where it would be fair and reasonable for each party to bear its own expenses or a share of the arbiter's fee and outlays.

## 17.9 The stated case

### 17.9.1 Introduction

Until 1973, the decision of an arbiter was final both on questions of law and of fact. However, Section 3(1) of the Administration of Justice (Scotland) Act 1972 provided:

> 'Subject to express provision to the contrary in an agreement to refer to arbitration, the arbiter or oversman may, on the application of a party to the arbitration, and shall, if the Court of Session on such an application so directs, at any stage in the arbitration state a case for the opinion of that Court on any question of law arising in the arbitration.'

In the debate on the bill, the Government spokesperson said 'While accepting that the relative speed and finality of arbitration proceedings should not lightly be discarded, it is the Government's view that where an arbiter had made a patent error in law, it should be possible to correct that error on appeal'.

If that was what was desired, the 1972 Act, in the view of many, has singularly failed to achieve it. The Stated Case procedure is slow, ponderous and expensive and the subject of possible law reform.

The form of wording in the 1972 Act renders it incompetent to seek a stated case once the final award is made. This is very important. The root problem is the wording used in the Act 'at any stage in the arbitration', which has been judicially determined to mean that the question could not be stated once the decision had been made, see *Fairlie Yacht Slip* v. *Lumsden* (1977). This has led to the practice of issuing any decision in draft in order to allow parties to decide if they wish to ask the arbiter to state a case. This can give rise to difficulties in practice where representations are made on drafts and changes are made thereto, see *Mowlem (Scotland) Ltd* v. *Inverclyde Council* (2003).

The procedure involved in a Stated Case is set out in Chapter 41 of the Rules of the Court of Session. On the appropriate use of the procedure, see the comments of Lord President Hope (as he then was) in *ERDC Construction Ltd* v. *H M Love & Co. (No.2)* (1997).

### 17.9.2 No right of appeal to the House of Lords

It has been held by the House of Lords that the opinion of the court upon questions of law given upon consideration of a case stated under s.3(1) of the 1972 Act did not constitute a judgment within the meaning of s.40(1) of the Court of Session Act 1988 or an 'order or judgment' within the meaning of section 3 of the Appellate Jurisdiction Act 1876, both of which allow appeals from the Court of Session to the House of Lords in certain circumstances, see *John G McGregor (Contractors) Ltd* v. *Grampian Regional Council* (1991).

For a case which went to the House of Lords and where the point of competency was not taken, see *Scott Lithgow Ltd* v. *Secretary of State for Defence* (1989).

### 17.9.3 EU law

It appears unlikely that an arbiter has power under Article 177 of the EU Treaty to obtain a ruling from the Court of Justice on a point of EU law, see *Nord Deutsche Hochseefischerei GmbH* v. *Reederei* (1982). If the arbiter has power to state a case the proper course may be for him to state a case on the question for the opinion of the Court of Session, where he considers that a decision on it is necessary to enable him to give judgment, leaving it to that court to decide whether or not to refer the matter to the Court of Justice.

### 17.9.4 Arbiter postponing stating a case

In the case of *Edmund Nuttall Ltd* v. *AMEC Projects Ltd* (1993) the court considered the circumstances in which an arbiter declined to state a case on the ground that it was expedient that the facts should be ascertained before their application was determined, as permitted, in terms of Rule 41.7.

It was held that while s.3(1) conferred a right to obtain a stated case from an arbiter if the Court so directed, it was inappropriate for the court to be required to entertain questions of law which the arbiter had decided he was not going to decide for the time being, and it was consistent with the existing law and practice which related only to timing and procedure, to give the arbiter a discretion on the receipt of an application to state a case to postpone further consideration of the application until the facts had been ascertained.

## 17.10 Judicial review

### 17.10.1 Introduction

The Court of Session has jurisdiction to exercise supervision over the work of inferior tribunals. The court's supervisory jurisdiction does not proceed upon a public/private law distinction and judicial review as now developed applies to both areas of law, see *West* v. *Secretary of State for Scotland* (1992).

Chapter 58 of the Court of Session Rules regulates the procedure. A person must be able to show both title and interest to enforce the right claimed in order to have *locus standi*, e.g. a party to an arbitration. The petitioner for judicial review may seek interdict, including interim interdict, suspension, reduction or removal. The grounds can be procedural irregularity, as in *Shanks & McEwan Ltd* v. *Mifflin* (1993); fraud, corruption, acting *ultra vires* and special or exceptional reasons. Grounds for refusal of the petition include delay, a failure to make full and frank disclosure, a failure to pursue an alternative remedy, see *Tarmac Econowaste Ltd* v. *Assessor for Lothian* (1991), lack of *locus standi* and lack of a *prima facie* case. Unlike an application for a stated case under s.3(1) of the 1972 Act, no preliminary step in the arbitration requires to be taken before presenting a petition for judicial review of the actions of the arbiter.

### 17.10.2 Jurisdiction

Subject to the court insisting on the use of s.3(1) of the 1972 Act, the award of an arbiter is subject to the supervisory jurisdiction of the Court of Session. An arbiter remains subject to judicial review in the exercise of the court's supervisory jurisdiction, see *ERDC Construction Ltd* v. *H M Love & Co. (No.2)* (1997).

## 17.11 Reduction

### 17.11.1 Competency and procedure

Reduction of an award after issue can be sought either by means of an action of reduction or as a defence to an action of implement. It appears that an action of reduction is not competent where a party seeks to set aside interim orders or proposed findings of an arbiter on the ground that the party can still seek his remedy from the arbiter until the arbiter makes his final award. It therefore appears to be the case that reduction is not competent until an arbiter has issued a final award, except perhaps where the arbiter has made interim awards for payment.

Although an arbiter may properly be called as a defender to an action, for such interest as he may have, an arbiter need not enter appearance to defend the action unless there are statements reflecting on his conduct of the arbitration.

In a hearing in an action of reduction, an arbiter cannot give evidence as to what he meant when he made the award, see *Reid* v. *Walker* (1826). However, an arbiter can give evidence on what took place in front of him, which was the *res gestae* of the proceedings and his notes taken at the time can also be used for that purpose.

### 17.11.2  Partial reduction

Where an award is challenged but only part of it is open to objection, it is competent to reduce the bad part, leaving the remainder standing, if the two parts are separable. If the two parts are inseparable, the whole award must be set aside, see *Reid* v. *Walker* (1826) and *Miller & Son* v. *Oliver & Boyd* (1903).

In certain clear-cut circumstances, partial reduction may be possible as, for example, in *Adams* v. *Great North of Scotland Railway Company* (1889) where an arbiter gave a decree for a larger sum in name of penalties than was claimed by the party in whose favour a decree was granted, and the court reduced the decree in respect of the excess.

### 17.11.3  Effect of reduction

The effect of reduction of an arbiter's decree takes the parties back to square one. They will be required to submit their dispute once again to arbitration. For the parties in dispute, this is perhaps one of the most unsatisfactory aspects of the remedy of reduction.

### 17.11.4  Grounds of reduction

#### Breach of natural justice

Natural justice is a word often misunderstood by non-lawyers. It is perhaps best seen as an implied condition in the submission that the arbiter will conform to those standards of fair and impartial conduct which are implicit in arriving at a just decision.

One aspect of the arbiter's obligation is that he must allow the parties to receive a fair and impartial hearing. In particular he must not hear only one side while denying the other party the opportunity to present its case, see *Mitchell* v. *Cable* (1848) and *Barrs* v. *Inland Revenue* (1959).

Where an arbiter's award was based on information other than comparables provided by parties, this constituted misconduct. The arbiter was not entitled to withhold from the parties particulars of comparables relied on, see *Fountain Forestry Holdings Ltd* v. *Sparkes* (1989).

The other aspect of the requirements of natural justice is that parties are entitled to have their disputes decided by a non-biased judge. The arbiter must not have any interest which would disqualify him from acting. The law relating to a disqualifying interest has been summarised in the case of *Wildridge* v. *Anderson* (1897) where Lord Moncrieff stated:

'1.   As a general rule a pecuniary interest, if direct and individual, will disqualify, however small it may be.

2.   An interest although not pecuniary may also disqualify, but the interest in that case must be substantial.

3.   Where the interest which is said to disqualify is not pecuniary, and is neither substantial nor calculated to cause bias in the mind of the judge, it will be disregarded, especially if to disqualify the judge would be productive of a grave public inconvenience.'

An award by an arbiter is only open to challenge on the ground that the arbiter had a disqualifying interest if that interest was not known to the party impugning the award at the date of his agreement to enter into arbitration or if the interest arose thereafter, see *Sellar* v. *Highland Railway Company* (1919) and *Magistrates of Edinburgh* v. *Lownie* (1903). It has also been said that there is an implied condition in a submission to arbitration that the arbiter should be in a position to approach the questions submitted to him with an open mind. The arbiter is to determine the matter in dispute in a judicial spirit, see *Crawford Brothers* v. *Commissioners of Northern Lighthouses* (1925).

### Failure to give effect to judgment of the courts

A further ground for the challenge of an arbiter's decision is that he has failed to give effect to the judgment of the court on the question of law which has been the subject of a Stated Case, see *Mitchell-Gill* v. *Buchan* (1921) which was concerned with a statutory arbitration.

### Award not properly executed

In *Mackenzie* v. *Girvan* (1840) it was held that it was not competent for the court to review or set aside an award where it is 'clear of its terms, correct in its form, and embracing nothing which was not referred, and exhausting all that was referred'. However, it is necessary to add to this list the requirement of proper execution. Where a submission to arbitration is a formally valid document, the award which follows thereon should also be a formally valid document. An informal award may therefore be open to challenge as in the case of *McLaren* v. *Aikman* (1939), where it was held that an arbiter's formal valuation was not binding on the defender as it was not a formal award, and the court treated the informal valuation as being merely a provisional finding. Under the Requirements of Writing (Scotland) Act 1995, all that is required for a document to be formally valid is for that document to have been signed by the granter.

### Grounds of challenge relating to procedure

#### (1)   Bribery

It is likely that 'bribery' involves receipt by an arbiter of an inducement in money or money's worth from one of the parties. There is little case law on this matter as it is rare in occurrence and in any event almost impossible to prove. In one case, *Mitchell* v. *Fulton* (1715), an arbiter's award was set aside by the court where he had accepted the gratuitous assignation of debts due to one party.

#### (2)   Falsehood

The term falsehood probably covers dishonesty, deceit and untruthfulness by the arbiter or the parties. It may include a forged submission or award (see *Hardy* v. *Hardy* (1724)) and also an arbiter concocting the narrative of the proceedings in his award.

#### (3)   Corruption

There is little authority as to what is 'corruption', see *Duff* v. *Pirie* (1883). It appears it is not corruption for an arbiter to ask each party in turn for a loan, see *Morissons* v. *Thomson's Trustees* (1880). One wonders whether or not the same conclusion would be reached today.

#### (4)   Misconduct

This is likely to be procedural misconduct, i.e. not conducting the arbitration in a fair and even handed way.

As has already been made clear, the statutory provisions contained in the Articles of Regulation of 1695 still have the force of statute. Although the wording of the Articles of Regulation appears to be very restrictive, they are not exhaustive of the grounds on which the parties may seek reduction of an arbiter's award, see *Adams* v. *The Great North of Scotland Railway Company* (1890).

# Chapter 18
# Tax

## 18.1 Value Added Tax

### 18.1.1 Introduction

Value Added Tax ('VAT') is regulated by the Value Added Tax Act 1994, the Value Added Tax Regulations 1995 and a number of other VAT regulations. It is enforced and administered by HM Revenue and Customs ('HMRC').

Most supplies relating to the construction of buildings are standard rated for VAT purposes. Some supplies are zero-rated or subject to the lower rate of 5 per cent. These are considered in section 18.1.2 below.

### 18.1.2 Zero-rated and reduced rate supplies

The following supplies are zero-rated:

- Supplies in the course of the construction of a dwelling;
- Supplies in the course of the construction of a building to be used for a relevant residential or charitable purpose (in which case a certificate has to be issued by the employer); and
- Approved alterations to protected buildings.

Zero-rating does not apply to the services of architects, surveyors or other professionals, unless these costs are included in the cost of a design and build contract. The reduced rate of 5 per cent applies to residential conversions and to the renovation and alteration of buildings which have been empty for three or more years. Full details of the extent of zero-rating and the requirement for certificates can be found in VAT Notice 708 *Buildings and Construction*.

### 18.1.3 Design and build contracts

Where the design, construction and materials are supplied under a single contract which does not separately identify the design element, there is a single composite supply which can be zero-rated or subject to the reduced rate of 5 per cent.

### 18.1.4 VAT liability of supplies by sub-contractors

Supplies by sub-contractors follow the VAT status of the main contract in contracts relating to residential properties. For supplies in relation to the construction of relevant residential or charitable buildings, however, only the main contractor can zero-rate their supplies. Sub-contractors have to charge VAT on their supplies.

### 18.1.5 The VAT-inclusive rule

If a contract is silent about VAT, then any sums mentioned in it are deemed to be VAT-inclusive, and the contractor will be unable to charge VAT in addition to the contract sum. The contractor will, however, be obliged to account for VAT to HMRC out of the contract sum, and will therefore be out of pocket. The contractor should therefore ensure that the contract provides for VAT to be payable in addition to the contract sum. VAT is also chargeable in relation to any non-cash consideration. It is essential that the contract specifies that VAT is payable in relation to both cash and non-cash consideration.

### 18.1.6 Set-off

Even though contracts may provide for set-off, it cannot be assumed that VAT will only be chargeable on the net amount. The nature of the supplies must be considered carefully, to ensure that the correct amount of VAT is charged.

### 18.1.7 The need for VAT invoices

Those paying for construction services need to ensure that they have a VAT invoice in order to recover the input tax which they have incurred. The contract must therefore provide for a VAT invoice (or an authenticated receipt) to be supplied, or for the self-billing invoice procedure to be used.

### 18.1.8 Time of supply – when VAT must be accounted for

The time of supply dictates when the party making the supply has to account to HMRC for the VAT. It also specifies when the party paying for the supply can recover the input tax. The time of supply can often be difficult to determine in construction contracts because of the complex payment mechanisms used and because of the rules which apply for stage payment contracts.

### 18.1.9  Single and stage payment contracts

Contracts where a single sum is payable follow the normal rules for VAT, i.e. VAT is chargeable when all of the work is complete, or when a VAT invoice is issued if that is earlier.

If the contract provides for stage payments or interim payments to be made, the tax point is the date on which payment is received, or the date an invoice is issued, if that is earlier. Care has to be taken not to issue a VAT invoice any earlier than is necessary, as this will trigger a liability to account to HMRC for VAT.

There is generally no tax point when the work is completed, subject to special anti-avoidance rules which apply in some cases.

### 18.1.10  Retention payments

The time of supply for retention payments is delayed until payment is received or a VAT invoice is issued, whichever is earlier. The VAT liability for retention payments follows the status of the main contract (i.e. if supplies under the main contract are zero-rated, any retention payments will also be zero-rated).

### 18.1.11  Self-billing arrangements

Self-billing generally arises where the main contractor issues invoices on behalf of a sub-contractor. Instead of the sub-contractor issuing a VAT invoice, the main contractor makes out a VAT invoice on behalf of the sub-contractor, and sends a copy of it to the sub-contractor with the payment. HMRC and the suppliers in question have to agree to the arrangements, and suppliers must also agree not to issue VAT invoices in relation to the transactions for which self-billing has been applied. The tax points under self-billing are the same as for normal VAT invoices for stage payment contracts. For single payment contracts the issue of a self-billing invoice creates a tax point. A self-billing invoice can be used to support a claim for input VAT.

### 18.1.12  Authenticated receipts

The authenticated receipts procedure allows a main contractor to prepare a receipt for supplies received which is sent to the sub-contractor along with payment. The receipt is only valid for VAT purposes once the sub-contractor has authenticated it. This means that no tax point is created until the receipt is authenticated. The authenticated receipt is used instead of a VAT invoice in order to reclaim VAT. The customer and the supplier have to agree to use the procedure, and the supplier must not issue VAT invoices.

## 18.1.13 Disputes

As explained below, in some circumstances payments to settle disputes are outside the scope of VAT. This is not always the case, however, as many disputes relate to payment for supplies made under the contract.

Payments made to settle a dispute out of court once proceedings have been commenced are treated as follows:

- if the payment is compensatory, and does not relate directly to supplies of goods and services, then the payment is outside the scope of VAT and no VAT is chargeable;
- if the payment is consideration for a specific supply of goods or services, the payment is subject to VAT.

This treatment is generally accepted as applying also in cases where proceedings have not yet commenced, and to cases involving arbitration and adjudication.

It can frequently be difficult to determine whether a payment is compensatory or whether it relates to supplies of services. Care should be taken not to assume that any payment resulting from a dispute will be VAT free. In complex cases, it may be necessary to seek a ruling from HMRC.

The VAT-inclusive rule should be borne in mind in relation to the settlement of disputes. In drawing up agreements to settle court actions or arbitration or adjudication proceedings, VAT should not be overlooked and, where appropriate, agreements should provide for the payment of VAT in addition to the settlement sum and ensure that a VAT invoice is provided to the payer.

## 18.1.14 Liquidated damages

Payments under liquidated damages clauses are not treated as payments for a supply for VAT purposes and no VAT is chargeable on them. This applies whether the amount payable is specified as a fixed sum or whether it is arrived at by way of a formula. If a payment for a supply under a contract is set off against a liquidated damages payment, VAT will still be chargeable in relation to the supply.

## 18.1.15 The SBC provisions

Clause 4.6 of the SBC provides that the Contract Sum is exclusive of VAT and in relation to any payment to the Contractor the Employer is also obliged to pay the amount of any VAT properly chargeable in respect of it. If after the Base Date the supply of goods and services to the Employer becomes exempt from VAT, there is to be paid to the Contractor an amount equal to the amount of input tax on the supply to the Contractor of goods and services which contribute to the Works but which as a consequence of that exemption the Contractor cannot recover, see clause 4.6.2.

## 18.2 The Construction Industry Scheme

### 18.2.1 Introduction

A new construction industry scheme ('CIS') was introduced by the Finance Act 2004 sections 57 to 77 and the Income Tax (Construction Industry Scheme) Regulations 2005 and applies to payments made on or after 6 April 2007. References to regulations in this section are to the 2005 Regulations.

The CIS applies to payments by contractors to self-employed sub-contractors in relation to construction operations. The terms 'contractor' and 'sub-contractor' have particular meanings in the CIS, but these do not necessarily correspond with the way these terms are used in the industry.

For CIS purposes, a contractor is merely a person who pays another person (a sub-contractor) for construction services, and a sub-contractor is a person who receives payment. It follows that for CIS purposes, the employer under a building contract would be the contractor, and the main contractor would be a sub-contractor. Similarly, a sub-contractor could be a contractor for CIS purposes.

The CIS does not apply to employment contracts. If a contract is an employment contract, the contractor is obliged to apply PAYE and deduct income tax and National Insurance Contributions (NIC) from the payments made, and account to HMRC for employer's NIC.

Under the CIS, before making a payment to which the CIS applies, the contractor must verify the payment status of the sub-contractor with HMRC and either:

- pay the sub-contractor gross, if the sub-contractor is registered for gross payment;
- pay the sub-contractor under deduction of tax at the lower rate of 20 per cent if the sub-contractor is registered for payment under deduction; or
- pay the sub-contractor under deduction of tax at the higher rate of 30 per cent if the sub-contractor is not registered or cannot be 'matched' by HMRC's systems.

Payments for materials are not covered by the CIS. The main differences between the old CIS and the new scheme are:

- electronic verification of sub-contractors with HMRC has replaced tax certificates and registration cards;

- under the new CIS there are two rates of deduction – a lower rate of 20 per cent for sub-contractors registered with HMRC and a higher rate of 30 per cent for unregistered sub-contractors;
- monthly returns have been introduced in place of vouchers; and
- a monthly declaration must be made by contractors that none of the payments included in the monthly return relate to employment contracts.

The differences between the old and new schemes mean that the CIS clauses in existing contracts which are based on the old scheme will not readily apply to the new scheme. Consideration should be given to amending contracts to deal with the new scheme where that is possible.

The new CIS applies to all payments made on or after 6 April 2007, regardless of when the work was carried out. This means that contractors must verify the payment status of sub-contractors in relation to retention payments paid after 6 April 2007 but relating to pre-April 2007 contracts

### 18.2.2 Employed or self-employed

The CIS only applies to self-employed sub-contractors. It is the responsibility of the contractor to consider the employment status of sub-contractors before any payments are made. If a sub-contractor is an employee for tax purposes, then PAYE should be operated and tax and NIC should be deducted from payments made.

If the contractor treats a sub-contractor as self employed and makes payments under the CIS, but it transpires that the sub-contractor is actually an employee, the contractor is liable for the income tax and employee's NIC which should have been deducted under PAYE and the employer's NIC which should have been paid to HMRC.

Contractors should be aware that the distinction between a self-employed sub-contractor and an employee is not straightforward. HMRC do not consider themselves to be bound by decisions of the Employment Tribunal, and vice versa.

The question of employment status is particularly important under the new CIS, because of the requirement for the contractor to make an employment status declaration each month. There is a penalty of £3,000 for each incorrect return made. In addition, making an incorrect return, including making an incorrect employment status declaration, could lead to cancellation of gross payment status (see section 18.2.7 below).

It is vital, therefore, that contractors have mechanisms in place to assess the employment status of each new sub-contractor, both at the start of the engagement and on an on-going basis. Contractors should ensure that they are in a position to demonstrate to HMRC that these checks have been carried out.

Under the old CIS, the fact that a person held a CIS 4 registration card did not mean that HMRC had accepted that he was self-employed. It merely meant that he had registered with HMRC as receiving payments for construction operations.

Unfortunately many contractors did not appreciate that the CIS 4 was not a guarantee of self-employed status, and simply applied the CIS deduction in circumstances where the individual was actually an employee so that PAYE should be applied. Similar problems may arise under the new CIS in relation to the verification process. The verification process merely confirms the payment status of the individual, not their employment status.

### 18.2.3 Deemed contractors

Contractors for the purposes of the CIS include not just construction companies and building firms but can also include 'deemed contractors', i.e. businesses whose main trade is not construction related but whose expenditure on construction operations exceeds certain prescribed limits (currently £1 million on average over a three-year period).

This brings within the scheme bodies such as government departments, local authorities and many businesses normally known in the industry as 'clients'. Expenditure on business premises for the deemed contractor's own use is excluded from the CIS from 6 April 2007 (although it was included before that date).

### 18.2.4 Verification

The verification process involves the contractor checking with HMRC the payment status of the sub-contractor, i.e. whether tax should be deducted and at what rate.

It should be noted that the verification process only verifies payment status and not employment status. It is the responsibility of the contractor to determine whether the sub-contractor is employed or self-employed.

Before commencing the verification process, the contractor must first decide whether the sub-contractor is employed or self-employed. If the sub-contractor is an employee, the contractor must apply PAYE and deduct income tax and employee's NIC and account for employer's NIC. If the sub-contractor is self-employed, the contractor should verify his payment status.

Verification by HMRC will establish whether the sub-contractor is registered for gross payment; registered for payment under deduction at the lower rate of 20 per cent; or not registered, in which case the higher rate of 30 per cent applies. Contractors can verify sub-contractors by telephone, or over the internet. The fact that HMRC have verified that a sub-contractor can be paid gross or under deduction at the lower rate does not mean that HMRC have verified that the sub-contractor is self-employed.

There are transitional rules which mean that contractors need not verify sub-contractors to whom payments had been made in the two years prior to the introduction of new CIS. Most contractors are in practice not relying on the transitional rules and are verifying all sub-contractors with HMRC even if payments have been made under the old CIS.

### 18.2.5 Higher and lower rates of deduction

There are two rates of deduction. Deduction at the standard rate is 20 per cent and this applies to sub-contractors who are registered with HMRC but are not registered for gross payment. Deduction at the higher rate applies if the sub-contractor is not registered with HMRC. This is at the rate of 30 per cent, which creates an incentive for sub-contractors to register with HMRC.

HMRC advise that the higher rate of deduction applies if the sub-contractor has not registered or cannot be 'matched' on HMRC's system, and will continue until the sub-contractor has contacted HMRC in order to register or resolve the matching problem. In other words, sub-contractors may suffer deduction at the higher rate because their records cannot be traced on HMRC's system, rather than because they have not registered. The cash flow implications for sub-contractors suffering the higher rate deduction may be severe.

Contracts should therefore contain provisions requiring CIS contractors to carry out the verification procedure expeditiously, and to advise sub-contractors of the outcome of the verification procedures, so that sub-contractors can deal with any problems arising.

### 18.2.6 Registration for gross payment

Contractors are required to pass a number of tests before being registered for gross payment, including a turnover test and a compliance test. The compliance test requires the contractor and all its directors to file all tax returns and make all tax payments on time over a 12-month period. There is provision for a small number of failures to be disregarded.

### 18.2.7 Cancellation of registration for gross payment

HMRC can cancel registration for gross payment if:

- the sub-contractor fails the compliance test or the turnover test;
- the sub-contractor makes any incorrect return under the new CIS; or
- HMRC become aware that the original registration was obtained using false information.

HMRC check the compliance record of contractors once a year, and look at the compliance record for the previous 12 months. If a contractor fails the compliance test, HMRC issue a notice of cancellation, and the registration for gross payment is cancelled from three months after the date of the notice, thereby allowing time for an appeal to be made against the cancellation.

A registration for deduction at the lower rate can also be cancelled by HMRC if they believe that any of the documents provided to obtain the registration is false or incorrect.

Contracts should require CIS sub-contractors to notify contractors as soon as registration for gross payment has been cancelled, or if HMRC have issued a notice that it is to be cancelled. They should also require CIS contractors to notify sub-contractors if they are advised by HMRC of a cancellation of registration for gross payment or for payment under deduction at the lower rate, so that the sub-contractor can take steps to remedy the position if appropriate.

### 18.2.8 Monthly returns and the Employment Status Declaration

Contractors must complete monthly returns detailing all payments to sub-contractors. The monthly return includes the 'Employment Status Declaration', i.e. a declaration by the contractor that:

- none of the contracts to which the return relates is a contract of employment;
- the contractor has complied with the verification procedure in relation to each person to whom a payment included on the return has been made; and
- all the information required for the return has been included.

In other words, the contractor is bound to keep the employment status of his sub-contractors constantly under review. There are penalties for incorrect returns (including making an incorrect Employment Status Declaration) of £3,000 per return. Contractors should therefore set up systems to ensure that the employment status of sub-contractors is considered both at the beginning of the engagement and on an on-going basis.

### 18.2.9 Payment and Deduction Statements

Contractors must supply details to sub-contractors of what has been paid and what tax has been deducted in a Payment and Deduction Statement. Payment and Deduction Statements must be issued at least once a month, or can be made for each payment if more frequently. They can be supplied in writing or by fax, or electronically if the sub-contractor agrees. The contract should address the way in which Payment and Deduction Statements must be supplied.

## 18.2.10 Retentions

The CIS applies on a payment basis. Where part of the contract price is retained by way of a retention, the contractor must consider the CIS position at the date on which the payment is actually made, and cannot pay gross if the sub-contractor is not registered for gross payment at the time the payment is made, even if they were registered at the time the work was carried out.

## 18.2.11 Nominees

If a contractor asks for payment to be made to a nominee, payment can only be made gross if both the nominee and the sub-contractor are registered for gross payment. If the nominee is not registered for gross payment, payment must be made under deduction of tax at the appropriate rate.

## 18.2.12 Materials

The CIS deduction only applies to the labour element of the payment and not to the part representing the direct cost of materials to the sub-contractor. 'Direct cost' means the amount which the sub-contractor can demonstrate was paid in respect of the materials.

If the sub-contractor cannot demonstrate the amount paid for materials, the contractor is entitled to estimate the amount. Since the sub-contractor may often be passing on the cost of materials to the contractor subject to a mark-up, the sub-contractor may be reluctant to disclose the actual cost of materials to the contractor. Nevertheless, the legislation is very clear on this point, and only the direct cost of materials can be excluded from the CIS deduction.

## 18.2.13 Travelling expenses

Travelling and accommodation and subsistence paid as part of a contract for construction operations is treated as being part of the cost of the labour element of the price and is therefore subject to the CIS deduction. This would not apply if the contractor entered into a separate arrangement with a hotel or travel company as that contract would not be a contract for construction operations.

## 18.2.14 VAT

The CIS deduction is applied to the payment exclusive of VAT. Thus the sub-contractor's gross payment as detailed on the monthly return should be the amount due before VAT is added.

## 18.2.15  CITB levy

The CIS deduction applies to payments made under contracts rather than payments due. Consequently, if the contractor withholds amounts from payments to sub-contractors in respect of public liability insurance or other administrative charges, the CIS deduction should be applied to the net amount.

## 18.2.16  The scope of construction operations

Before the CIS will apply, there must be in place a contract relating to construction operations in terms of which a sub-contractor is supplying services to a contractor.

For the purposes of the CIS, the term 'construction operations' is defined by section 74 of the Finance Act 1974. That definition is, for all practical purposes the same as the definition contained within s.105(1) of the 1996 Act (see section 1.2.2 above).

Expenditure on construction operations for the purposes of the CIS includes expenditure on repairs and maintenance as well as on alterations or other new work.

The installation of systems of heating, lighting, air-conditioning, ventilation, power supply, drainage, sanitation, water supply or fire protection is included within the scope of the CIS, whether within buildings or outside, but not repairs to these types of systems.

The internal cleaning of buildings and structures is within the CIS. Cleaning is only within the scope of the CIS if it is carried out in the course of, or on completion of, construction work. The external cleaning of buildings and structures is excluded. The routine cleaning of existing commercial or industrial premises not undergoing construction work is not within the scope of the CIS.

## 18.2.17  Exemptions from CIS

A number of matters are specifically excluded from the operation of the CIS.

### Reverse premium on grant of lease

It is fairly common that a landlord provides an inducement to a tenant to take a lease by paying the tenant a capital sum towards the tenant's fitting out costs which is conditional on the fitting out being undertaken by the tenant. Although, on the face of it, this is a payment under a contract which relates to construction operations, it is specifically excluded from the new CIS by regulation 20. It should be noted that reverse premiums were not excluded from the scope of the old CIS scheme.

### Artistic works

The 'making, installation and repair of artistic works, being sculptures, murals and other works which are wholly artistic in nature' is excluded from the CIS. It should be noted that this does not include the installation of stained glass windows, ornamental gates and balustrades, and decorative tiling.

### Temporary structures

Whilst the CIS applies to the construction, alteration, repair, extension, demolition or dismantling of buildings or structures (whether permanent or not), including offshore installations, HMRC has agreed that certain temporary structures (broadly speaking, those which will not remain in place for more than two months) fall outside the scope of the scheme. Examples of these include exhibition stands; film and TV sets; theatre sets; marquees; portacabins and portable offices.

### Business premises exemption for deemed contractors

Expenditure by deemed contractors (see section 18.2.3 above) on repair or construction of premises for their own use is excluded from the CIS.

### PFI

Payments by public bodies to PFI project companies are excluded from the CIS under the exception contained in regulation 23.

### Charities

Payments by charities are excluded from the CIS by regulation 24.

### 18.2.18 The SBC provisions

In terms of clause 4.7 of the SBC, where it is stated in the Contract Particulars that the Employer is a 'contractor' for the purposes of the CIS or if at any time up to the payment of the Final Certificate the Employer becomes a 'contractor', the obligations of the Employer to make any payment under the contract are subject to the provisions of the CIS.

# Chapter 19
# Health and Safety

## 19.1 Introduction

The issue of health and safety is a significant one in the construction industry. It is an industry that is inherently dangerous by virtue of the nature of the site environment and the operations carried out thereon. It is also an industry that has a poor record in relation to accidents. Whilst employers (in the construction sense) and sub-contractors have duties in respect of health and safety, the most significant responsibilities in this field will fall upon the contractor, in their role as employer in the employer/employee sense.

A detailed examination of the law of health and safety is beyond the scope of this book. We will, however, consider in some detail the primary statute and the most significant subordinate legislation from the point of view of the construction industry.

## 19.2 Common law

At common law, employers have an obligation to provide competent staff, adequate material, a proper system of work, effective supervision and a safe place of work, see *Wilsons and Clyde Coal Co. Ltd* v. *English* (1938). They also have a duty to instruct and to take steps to ensure that instructions are carried out, see *McWilliams* v. *Sir William Arrol & Co. Ltd and Another* (1962).

The law insofar as it relates to health and safety has a relevance both in a civil and criminal context. Notwithstanding the fact that much, indeed the vast majority, of the law of health and safety at work in Scotland is to be found in statutory materials, the common law still has a relevance.

That relevance is particularly notable in civil cases. The relevance is highlighted by section 47 of the Health and Safety at Work etc. Act 1974 (which we will refer to as 'the 1974 Act'). In terms of that section, the 1974 Act does not confer a right of action in civil proceedings in respect of failures to comply with any duty imposed by sections 2 to 7, which we consider in detail below. That provision is contained within s.47(1)(a), however, it falls to be compared and contrasted with s.47(2) whereby a breach of duty imposed by health and safety regulations shall, so far as it causes damage, be actionable, except insofar as the regulations provide otherwise.

Accordingly, in many civil cases, the common law is still of relevance, the basic duty of the employer being to take reasonable care that the employee is not exposed to unnecessary risk, see *Longworth* v. *Coppas International (UK) Ltd* (1985).

It has been suggested that the duty breaks down into three basic parts, namely, that the employer is required to provide and maintain suitable materials (i.e. plant, machinery and equipment); to keep his premises safe and devise and operate a safe system of working; and to exercise care in the selection of competent fellow employees.

## 19.3 Health and Safety at Work etc. Act 1974

### 19.3.1 General

The current starting point in relation to health and safety legislation is the Health and Safety at Work etc. Act 1974. This creates duties which are incumbent on employers (in the employer/employee sense as opposed to the construction sense), employees, persons in control of premises and designers and manufacturers of articles and substances. The sections imposing these duties are considered below, along with a number of the other significant provisions of the 1974 Act.

### 19.3.2 Section 2

The principal duties incumbent upon employers, insofar as their own employees are concerned, are contained within section 2 of the 1974 Act, namely to:

- ensure, so far as is reasonably practicable, the health and safety and welfare of their employees (see s.2(1));
- ensure the provision and maintenance of plant and systems of work that are, so far as is reasonably practicable, safe and without risks to health (see s.2(2)(a));
- provide safe systems for the use, storage and transport of articles and substances, so far as is reasonably practicable (see s.2(2)(b));
- provide such information, instruction, training and supervision as is necessary to ensure the health and safety at work of employees, so far as is reasonably practicable (see s.2(2)(c));
- maintain a safe place of work and provide safe access to and egress from that place of work, so far as is reasonably practicable (see s.2(2)(d));
- provide and maintain a working environment that is, so far as is reasonably practicable, safe, without risks to health, and adequate as regards facilities and arrangements for employees' welfare at work (see s.2(2)(e)); and

- provide and maintain a written statement of safety detailed in the safety policy of that company and the arrangements for implementing it (see s.2(3)).

It has been observed that the general duties under the 1974 Act are deliberately similar to the duties of care giving rise to civil liability at common law. The general duties are to be found in sections 2 to 7 of the 1974 Act.

The general duty laid down by s.2(1), and the more specific duties laid down in s.2(2)(a) to (e), set out in statutory form the common law obligations owed by employers to their employees, see *West Bromwich Building Society v. Townsend* (1983).

### 19.3.3 Section 3

Section 3 of the 1974 Act sets out the general duties of employers and the self-employed to persons other than their employees.

By virtue of sections 1 and 2, virtually identical duties are imposed on employers and self-employed persons, whereby each is required to conduct their undertaking in such a way as to ensure, so far as is reasonably practicable, that persons not in their employment who may be affected by their work are not exposed to risks to their health or safety. It should be noted that s.3(2) also imposes a duty on self employed persons to ensure, again so far as is reasonably practicable, that they, themselves, are not exposed to risks.

Like section 2, this section imposes absolute criminal liability, subject only to the defence of reasonable practicability, which defence relates only to measures necessary to avert the risk.

Particularly crucial in terms of this section is the phrase 'conduct their undertaking'. It was believed that an employer did not conduct his undertaking if he employed an independent contractor to do the relevant work, provided the employer neither exercised any control over the work nor was under any duty to do so. That was the substance of the decision of the English High Court in *RMC Roadstone Products Ltd* v. *Jester* (1994).

Whilst the decision in *RMC Roadstone Products Ltd* has not been expressly overruled, it was, however, doubted in the case that sets out the present state of the law in England, namely, *R* v. *Associated Octel Ltd* (1996), a decision of the House of Lords. Whilst not binding in Scotland, there is nothing to suggest that the courts in Scotland would view matters differently.

In *Associated Octel Ltd*, the appellant company, which operated a chemical plant, engaged a firm of specialist contractors to carry out annual maintenance and repair work. As part of the scheduled work, the contractors had to repair the lining of a tank within the chlorine plant, which involved grinding down the damaged areas of the tank, cleaning the dust from the surfaces with acetone and applying fibreglass matting to rebuild those areas. While the specialist contractor's employee was inside the tank the bulb of the light he was using broke and the electric current caused the acetone vapour to ignite. There was a flash fire and explosion, which badly burned the employee.

Associated Octel were charged with, and convicted of, an offence under the 1974 Act of failing to discharge the duty imposed on it by section 3, to conduct their business in such a way as to ensure, so far as is reasonably practicable, that persons not in its employment who might be affected thereby were not exposed to risks to their health or safety.

Associated Octel appealed, unsuccessfully, against the conviction. The Court of Appeal held that the word 'undertaking' in s.3(1) of the 1974 Act meant 'enterprise' or 'business' and, in the particular circumstances of the case, the cleaning, repair and maintenance of plant, machinery and buildings necessary for carrying on the employer's business were part of the conduct of their undertaking for the purposes of s.3(1), whether it was done by the employer's own employees or by independent contractors.

Accordingly, if there was a risk of injury to the health and safety of persons not employed by the employer, whether to the contractor's men or members of the public, and if there was actual injury as the result of the conduct of that operation, there was *prima facie* liability, subject to the defence of reasonable practicability.

It was further held that the question of control might well be relevant to the issue of whether it was reasonably practicable for the employer to give instructions on how the work was to be done and what safety measures were to be taken and, in each case, the question was one of fact and degree.

There was a subsequent (again unsuccessful) appeal to the House of Lords, who held that if an employer engaged an independent contractor to do work which formed part of the employer's undertaking, the employer was required by s.3(1) to stipulate for whatever conditions were reasonably practicable to avoid risk to the contractor's employees. Whether or not the employer was in a position to exercise control over work carried out by an independent contractor was not the decisive question under section 3, which is whether the activity in question could be described as part of the employer's undertaking, which will be a question of fact in each case.

### 19.3.4 Section 4

Section 4 imposes a duty on persons in control of, or concerned with, premises to ensure, again so far as is reasonably practicable, the safety of persons on those premises. The duty does not extend to employees. It covers 'non-employees' who use non-domestic premises made available to them as a place of work or as a place where they may use plant or substances provided for their use there. A similar duty is found in s.2(d) of the 1974 Act in respect of employees.

In terms of s.4(2), it is the duty of each person who has, to any extent, control of premises to which this section applies to take such measures as is reasonable for a person in his position to take to ensure, so far as is reasonably practicable, that the premises are safe and without risks to health.

Section 2 imposes an absolute duty, subject only to the limited qualification 'so far as is reasonably practicable', see *Mailer* v. *Austin Rover Group* (1989). This does not require the duty holder to take precautions against unknown and unexpected events.

The phrase 'person who has, to any extent, control of premises' has a wide meaning. Instructive in this regard is the case of *T Kilroe & Sons Ltd* v. *Gower* (1983). In that case, the appellant had obtained a contract to demolish large factory premises. In order to fulfil this contract, it had entered into an agreement with experienced demolition contractors to provide the bulk of the labour and execute much of the work on a profit-sharing arrangement. The factory inspectors discovered that asbestos de-lagging from pipes in the boiler house of the factory was taking place with the doors of the premises unsealed and opened and with no proper provision having been made for showering and decontamination of the workers involved. The appellants were convicted of failing to discharge their duty under s.4(2) of the 1974 Act.

The appellants appealed on the basis (a) that the boiler house was a separate entity from the rest of the site and that since the work therein was being exclusively carried out by the demolition contractor and its employees, the appellant did not have any, or any sufficient, control of the premises to bring it within the section; and (b) that in any event, it was not in breach of its duties since it had taken such steps as was reasonable for it to take by employing experienced demolition contractors to undertake the works.

The appeal was dismissed. It was held that there was no justification for treating the boiler house as a separate entity, even though it was a separate building. The contract was for the demolition of the whole site and in the absence of any evidence that the boiler house had been treated in some way as separate from the rest of the site, the premises referred to the whole site. It was also held that where there was such an obvious risk to health, even if the appellant believed that the demolition contractors were experts in asbestos stripping (which, on the evidence, the court did not accept), as soon as they observed the lack of expertise they should have acted, if necessary, by removing the demolition contractor from the work and assuming overall control themselves.

The difficulty with any authority relative to the 1974 Act is that, inevitably, each case turns, to a significant degree, on their own facts and circumstances. In each case, what is 'reasonably practicable' will differ. This term is considered below in section 19.3.13.

### 19.3.5 Section 7

Section 7 of the 1974 Act imposes a duty on employees to take reasonable care for their own health and safety at work, as well as for other persons who might be affected by their acts or omissions.

### 19.3.6 Section 15

Section 15 of the 1974 Act is the provision whereby health and safety regulations can be made. The relevance of subordinate legislation in the field of health and safety cannot be overstated. A plethora of regulations exist, sometimes covering esoteric and obscure industries and operations. An examination of these is beyond the scope of this book.

### 19.3.7 Section 20

The day-to-day enforcement of health and safety legislation falls to enforcing authorities. Essentially, these are either the Health & Safety Executive (HSE) or, in certain limited cases, local authorities. By virtue of section 19, enforcing authorities are entitled to appoint inspectors who are to be such persons having suitable qualifications as the authority thinks necessary for carrying into effect the relevant statutory provisions within its field of responsibility.

The powers of inspectors are wide ranging and are to be found in section 20 of the 1974 Act. The specific powers are to be found in s.20(2).

### 19.3.8 Section 21

If an inspector is of the opinion that a person is either contravening one or more of the relevant statutory provisions or has contravened one or more of those provisions in circumstances that make it likely that the contravention will continue or be repeated, he may serve upon that person what is known as an improvement notice.

The notice is required to state the opinion of the inspector in relation to the contravention, specify the provision or provisions involved, give particulars of the reasons why he is of that opinion and require the recipient of the notice to remedy the contravention or, as the case may be, the matter which is occasioning it, within such period as may be specified in the notice. In the case of an improvement notice that period can end no earlier than the period within which an appeal against the notice can be brought.

### 19.3.9 Section 22

This provision deals with the giving of prohibition notices. It applies to any activities which are being, or are likely to be, carried on by or under the control of any person, being activities to or in relation to which any of the relevant statutory provisions apply or will, if the activities are so carried on, apply. The section applies where an inspector is of the opinion that, as carried on or likely to be carried on, activities involve or, as the case may be, will involve a risk of serious personal injury.

The prohibition notice requires to state that the inspector is of that opinion; specify the matters which in his opinion give rise to or, as the case may be, will give rise to the said risk; specify any relevant statutory provisions that are being, or will be, contravened; and direct that the activities to which the notice relates shall not be carried on unless the matter specified in the notice and any associated contraventions have been remedied.

A direction contained in a prohibition notice shall take effect either at the end of the period specified in the notice, or, if the notice so declares, immediately.

## 19.3.10 Section 24

This section deals with appeals against improvement or prohibition notices.

The right of appeal is to an employment tribunal. On appeal, the tribunal may either cancel or affirm the notice and, if it affirms the notice, it may do so either in its original form or with such modifications as the tribunal thinks appropriate in the circumstances.

In hearing such an appeal, an employment tribunal does have the power to deal with the question of expenses.

In the case of an improvement notice, the bringing of the appeal has the effect of suspending the operation of the notice until the appeal is disposed of. In the case of a prohibition notice, the bringing of the appeal only has that effect if, on the application of the appellant, the tribunal so directs. Essentially, without such a direction from the tribunal, an appeal against the prohibition notice does not suspend the operation of the notice.

## 19.3.11 Section 33

Section 33 of the 1974 Act sets out offences. The provision is both extensive and complex.

Seventeen separate offences are set out in s.33(1). These include failing to discharge a duty imposed by sections 2 to 7 of the 1974 Act; contravening any health and safety regulation; contravening any requirement imposed by an inspector; obstructing inspectors in the exercise or performance of their powers or duties; contravening any requirement or prohibition imposed by an improvement notice or a prohibition notice; and falsely pretending to be an inspector.

Penalties for offences under the 1974 Act are now prescribed by s.33(1A), s.33(2) and s.33(2A). In terms of monetary penalty, on conviction on summary complaint, the maximum fine is presently £20,000. On conviction on indictment, the available fine is unlimited. A number of offences only allow the imposition of a fine not exceeding level 5 on the standard scale (presently £5,000).

Imprisonment is an option open to the court in certain circumstances. On summary conviction, the maximum available term is one of six months.

On conviction on indictment, the maximum available term is one of two years.

### 19.3.12  Section 37

The provisions of Section 37 are worthy of note. Where an offence under any of the relevant statutory provisions committed by a body corporate is proved to have been committed with the consent or connivance of, or to have been attributable to any neglect on the part of, any director, manager, secretary or other similar officer of the body corporate or a person who was purporting to act in any such capacity, that person, as well as the body corporate, shall be guilty of that offence and is liable to be proceeded against and punished accordingly. An example of this is *Armour* v. *Skeen* (1977).

### 19.3.13  Practicable and reasonably practicable

The concepts of 'practicability' and 'reasonable practicability' arise regularly in both the 1974 Act and also in many health and safety regulations made under the 1974 Act. It is, in fact, the latter concept that is infinitely more commonplace.

Neither term is defined in the 1974 Act, or elsewhere. The *Oxford English Dictionary* definition of 'practicable', i.e. that which is capable of being carried out in action or that which is feasible, was applied by the Court of Appeal in *Lee* v. *Nursery Furnishings Ltd* (1945). Prefixing 'practicable' with 'reasonably' creates a qualification whereby the extent of the risk requires to be balanced against the measures necessary to avert that risk, a form of cost benefit analysis, see *Sharp* v. *Coltness Iron Co. Ltd* (1937) and *Edwards* v. *NCB* (1949) subsequently approved by the House of Lords in *Marshall* v. *Gotham Co. Ltd* (1954).

What is reasonably practicable depends upon whether the time, trouble and expense of precautions suggested are disproportionate to the risk involved. What is reasonable for a large undertaking may be unreasonable for a small undertaking. It should be noted that 'reasonably practicable' has been held to have a narrower meaning than 'physically possible', see the decision of the Court of Appeal in *Marshall* v. *Gotham Co. Ltd* (1953).

## 19.4  The Construction (Design and Management) Regulations 2007

### 19.4.1  Introduction

The Construction (Design and Management) Regulations 2007 ('the 2007 Regulations') came into force on 6 April 2007.

The 2007 Regulations revoke and replace the Construction (Design and Management) Regulations 1994 ('the 1994 Regulations') and revoke and re-enact with modifications the Construction (Health, Safety and Welfare) Regulations 1996.

The 2007 Regulations implement, in Great Britain, the requirements of Directive 92/57/EEC on the implementation of minimum safety and health requirements at temporary or mobile construction sites, save for those requirements which were implemented by the Work at Height Regulations 2005.

The 2007 Regulations are divided into five parts. Part 1 deals with the formalities of citation and commencement, interpretation and application; Part 2 sets out the general management duties which apply to construction projects; Part 3 sets out additional duties imposed where the project is notifiable; Part 4 deals with the duties relating to health and safety on construction sites; and Part 5 deals with the general matters of civil liability, enforcement, transitional provisions and revocations and amendments.

### 19.4.2  Regulation 4

No person on whom the Regulations place the duty shall appoint or engage a CDM co-ordinator, designer, principal contractor or contractor unless he has taken reasonable steps to ensure that the person to be appointed or engaged is competent.

In a similar vein, no person can accept an appointment or engagement unless they are competent. The Approved Code of Practice for the 2007 Regulations states that, to be competent, an organisation or individual must have sufficient knowledge of the specific task to be undertaken and the risks which the work will entail; and have sufficient experience and ability to carry out their duties in relation to the project; and to recognise their limitations and take appropriate action in order to prevent harm to those carrying out construction work, or those affected by the work.

Satisfying oneself as to competence means making reasonable enquiries to check that the organisation or individual is competent to do the relevant work and can allocate adequate resources to it.

For notifiable projects (see section 19.4.11 below), a key duty of the CDM co-ordinator is to advise clients about competence of designers and contractors, including the principal contractor.

### 19.4.3  Co-operation, co-ordination and the general principles of prevention

Regulation 5 requires that every person concerned in a project, on whom a duty is placed by the Regulations, shall seek the co-operation of any other person concerned in any project involving construction work at the same or an adjoining site and co-operate with any person concerned in any project involving construction work at the same or an adjoining site. Every person concerned in the project who is working under the control of another person shall report to that person anything which he is aware is likely to endanger the health or safety of himself or others.

By virtue of regulation 6, all persons concerned in a project on whom a duty is placed by the Regulations, shall co-ordinate their activities with one another in a manner which ensures, so far as is reasonably practicable, the health and safety of persons carrying out the construction work and affected by the construction work.

Regulation 7(1) requires every person on whom a duty is placed by the Regulations in relation to the design, planning and preparation of a project to take account of the general principles of prevention in the performance of those duties during all stages of the project. In similar, although slightly different terms, regulation 7(2) requires every person on whom a duty is placed by the Regulations in relation to the construction phase of a project to ensure, so far as is reasonably practicable, that the general principles of prevention are applied in the carrying out of the construction work.

The general principles of prevention are to be found in Schedule 1 to the Management of Health and Safety at Work Regulations 1999. They are as follows:

- avoiding risks;
- evaluating the risks which cannot be avoided;
- combating the risks at source;
- adapting the work to the individual, especially as regards the design of workplaces, the choice of work equipment and the choice of working and production methods, with a view, in particular, to alleviating monotonous work and work at a predetermined work-rate and to reducing their effect on health;
- adapting to technical progress;
- replacing the dangerous by the non-dangerous or the less dangerous;
- developing a coherent overall prevention policy which covers technology, organisation of work, working conditions, social relationships and the influence of factors relating to the working environment;
- giving collective protective measures priority over individual protective measures; and
- giving appropriate instructions to employees.

### 19.4.4 Election by clients

Regulation 8 provides that where there is more than one client in relation to a project, if one or more of such clients elect in writing to be treated for the purposes of the Regulations as the only client or clients, no other client who has agreed in writing to such election shall be subject thereafter to any duty owed by a client under the Regulations, save for certain duties that relate to information in their possession (see regulations 5(1)(b), 10(1), 15 and 17(1)).

### 19.4.5 Regulation 9

Regulation 9 sets out the client's duty in relation to arrangements for managing projects. A client is an organisation or individual for whom a construction project is carried out. Clients only have duties when the project is associated with a business or other undertaking (whether for profit or not). This can include, for example, local authorities, school governors, insurance companies and project originators on private finance initiative projects. Domestic clients are a special case and do not have duties under the 2007 Regulations.

Every client is required to take reasonable steps to ensure that the arrangements made for managing the project (including the allocation of sufficient time and other resources) by persons with a duty under the 2007 Regulations (including the client himself) are suitable to ensure that:

- the construction work can be carried out so far as is reasonably practicable without risk to the health and safety of any person;
- the requirements of Schedule 2 to the Regulations (which sets out the welfare facilities that contractors are obliged to provide), are complied with in respect of any person carrying out the construction work;
- any structure designed for use as a workplace has been designed taking account of the provisions of the Workplace (Health, Safety and Welfare) Regulations 1992 which relate to the design of, and materials used in, structures.

The client is obliged to take steps to ensure that the arrangements made for managing the project are maintained and reviewed throughout the project.

### 19.4.6 Regulation 10

Regulation 10 sets out the client's duty in relation to the provision of information. Every client is obliged to ensure that every person designing the structure and every contractor who has been, or may be, appointed by the client is promptly provided with pre-construction information.

By virtue of regulation 10(2), the pre-construction information consists of all of the information in the client's possession (or which is reasonably obtainable), which is relevant to the person to whom the client provides it, including:

- any information about or affecting the site of the construction work;
- any information concerning the proposed use of the structures as a workplace;
- the minimum amount of time before the construction phase which will be allowed to the contractors appointed by the client for planning and preparation for construction works; and
- any information in any existing health and safety file.

Generally speaking, the purpose of providing such information is to ensure, so far as is reasonably practicable, the health and safety of persons engaged in the construction works; those liable to be affected by the way in which it is carried out; and those who will use the structure as a workplace. It is also to assist the persons to whom the information is provided (i.e. the designers and the contractors) to perform their duties under the Regulations and to determine the resources required to manage the project.

### 19.4.7  Duties of designers

The duties of designers are to be found in regulation 11. Designers are those who have a trade or business which involves them in preparing designs for construction work, including variations. This includes preparing drawings, design details, specifications, bills of quantities and the specification (or prohibition) of articles and substances, as well as all the related analysis, calculations and preparatory work. This includes also arranging for employees or other people under their control to prepare designs relating to a structure or part of a structure.

Designers therefore include architects, civil and structural engineers, building surveyors, landscape architects, other consultants, manufacturers and design practices (of whatever discipline) contributing to, or having an overall responsibility for, any part of the design, for example, drainage engineers designing the drainage for a new development.

The definition does, however, go much further if one considers paragraph 116 of the Approved Code of Practice. That suggests that designers could include quantity surveyors who insist on specific materials; clients who stipulate a particular layout for a new building; building services designers or others designing plant which forms part of the permanent structure (including lifts, heating, ventilation and electrical systems); those purchasing materials where the choice has been left open; temporary works engineers; interior designers, including shop fitters who also develop the design, heritage organisations who specify how work is to be done in detail; and those determining how buildings and structures are altered.

The first point to make is that, by virtue of regulation 4(1)(b) a designer shall not accept an appointment as such unless he is competent. Once the designer is satisfied that he is able to do the job, he still cannot commence work in relation to a project unless any client for the project is aware of his duties under the Regulations.

Once the designer starts designing (or modifying a design) he has to avoid foreseeable risk to the health and safety of persons in five defined categories, namely those:

(1)   carrying out construction work;

(2)   liable to be affected by construction work;

(3)   cleaning any window or any transparent or translucent wall, ceiling or roof in or on a structure;

(4)   maintaining the permanent fixtures and fittings of a structure; or

(5)   using a structure designed as a workplace.

In preparing the design, the designer shall eliminate hazards which may give rise to risks; and reduce risks from any remaining hazards, and in doing so shall give collective measures priority over individual measures. In preparing the design, the designer is obliged to take all reasonable steps to provide with it sufficient information about aspects of the design of the structure or its construction or maintenance as will adequately assist clients, other designers and contractors to comply with their duties under the Regulations.

### 19.4.8  Designs prepared or modified outside Great Britain

As the Regulations apply to Great Britain, the possibility of the design being prepared or modified somewhere else is dealt with by regulation 12. In those circumstances, the party who commissions the design, if they are established within Great Britain, or if they are not so established, any client for the project, is required to ensure that regulation 11 (duties of designers) is complied with.

### 19.4.9  Duties of contractors

Contractors are those who actually do the construction work and are, thus, those most at risk of injury and ill-health. Anyone who directly employs or engages construction workers or controls or manages construction work is a contractor for the purposes of the 2007 Regulations. This includes companies that use their own workforce to do construction work on their own premises.

   As with designers, no contractor shall carry out construction work in relation to a project unless any client for the project is aware of his duties under the Regulations. As with designers, the contractor should not accept an appointment unless they regard themselves as competent to carry it through. Contractors are obliged to plan, manage and monitor construction work carried out by them or under their control in a way which ensures that, so far as is reasonably practicable, it is carried out without risks to health and safety.

   Contractors are required to ensure that any contractor they engage is informed of the minimum amount of time which they will be allowed for planning and preparation before they begin work.

   Regulation 13(4) sets out requirements in respect of the provision of information and training for every worker carrying out the construction work. This includes:

- suitable site induction, where not provided by any principal contractor;
- information on the risks to the worker's health and safety, whether brought out by a risk assessment under regulation 3 of the Management of Health and Safety at Work Regulations 1999 or arising out of the conduct by another contractor of his undertaking;
- the measures which have been identified by the contractor in consequence of the risk assessment as measures he needs to take to comply with the requirements and prohibitions imposed upon him by or under the relevant statutory provisions;
- any site rules;
- the procedures to be followed in the event of serious and imminent danger to workers; and
- the identity of the persons nominated to implement those procedures.

A specific duty is set out, in regulation 13(6), regarding the prevention of access to site by unauthorised persons. Work cannot start unless reasonable steps have been taken in that regard. Lastly, by virtue of regulation 13(7) provision is made in relation to welfare facilities. These are set out in Schedule 2 to the Regulations.

### 19.4.10  Part 3

Part 3 sets out the additional duties which arise where a project is notifiable. What this actually means is considered below. In such circumstances additional duties are incumbent upon clients, designers and contractors. Perhaps more importantly, however, it introduces us to the CDM co-ordinator and the principal contractor, which roles are considered in detail below.

### 19.4.11  Notifiable projects

By virtue of regulation 2(3), for the purpose of the 2007 Regulations, a project is notifiable if the construction phase is likely to involve more than 30 days; or 500 person days (e.g. 50 people working for over 10 days) of construction work. All days on which construction work takes place count towards the period of construction work. Holidays and weekends do not count if no construction work takes place on these days.

### 19.4.12  Client's duties on notifiable projects

Where a project is notifiable, the client is obliged to appoint a CDM co-ordinator as soon as is practicable after initial design work or other preparation for construction work has begun. After appointing a CDM co-ordinator, the client is obliged to appoint a principal contractor as soon as is practicable after the client knows enough about the project to be able to select a suitable person for such appointment.

The appointments of the CDM co-ordinator and principal contractor are to be changed or renewed as necessary to ensure that there is, at all times until the end of the construction phase, a CDM co-ordinator and principal contractor. For so long as either or both of these appointments are not made, the client is deemed to have been appointed as CDM co-ordinator or principal contractor, or both. By virtue of regulation 15, where the project is notifiable, the client is obliged to promptly provide the CDM co-ordinator with the pre-construction information envisaged by regulation 10(2).

By virtue of regulation 16, where the project is notifiable, the client is required to ensure that the construction phase does not start unless the principal contractor has prepared a construction phase plan (see section 19.4.16 below) and he is satisfied that the requirements in respect of the provision of welfare facilities will be complied with during the construction phase.

Lastly, in relation to the clients' additional duties, by virtue of regulation 17, the client is required to ensure that the CDM co-ordinator is provided with all the health and safety information in the client's possession (or which is reasonably obtainable) relating to the project which is likely to be needed for inclusion in the health and safety file.

Where a single health and safety file relates to more than one project, site or structure, or where it includes other related information, the client is required to ensure that the information relating to each site or structure can be easily identified.

After the construction phase, the client is to take reasonable steps to ensure that the information in the health and safety file is kept available for inspection by any person who may need it to comply with the relevant statutory provisions; and is revised as often as may be appropriate to incorporate any relevant new information.

In the context of developers, regulation 17(4) is significant. If a client disposes of his entire interest in the structure, delivering the health and safety file to the person who acquires his interest in it and ensuring that he is aware of the nature and purpose of the file, is sufficient compliance with regulation 17(3) (i.e. the obligation set out above to keep the health and safety file available for inspection etc.).

### 19.4.13  Additional duties of designers and contractors

Insofar as designers are concerned, by virtue of regulation 18, where a project is notifiable, no designer can commence work (other than initial design work) in relation to the project unless a CDM co-ordinator has been appointed for the project.

The designer is required to take all reasonable steps to provide with his design sufficient information about aspects of the design of the structure or its construction or maintenance as will adequately assist the CDM co-ordinator to comply with his duties under the Regulations, including his duties in relation to the health and safety file.

Insofar as contractors are concerned, by virtue of regulation 19, where a project is notifiable, no contractor shall carry out construction work in relation to the project unless:

- he has been provided with the names of the CDM co-ordinator and principal contractor;
- he has been given access to such part of the construction phase plan as is relevant to the work to be performed by him, containing sufficient detail in relation to such work; and
- notice of the project has been given to HSE.

Additional obligations are created by regulation 19(2). Every contractor shall promptly provide the principal contractor with any information which might affect the health and safety of any person carrying out construction work, or of any person who may be affected by it, which might justify a review of the construction phase plan; or which has been identified for inclusion in the health and safety file.

Every contractor is obliged to promptly identify any contractor whom he appoints or engages in his turn in connection with the project to the principal contractor. Every contractor shall comply with any directions of the principal contractor and any site rules. Lastly, every contractor shall promptly provide the principal contractor with the information in relation to any death, injury, condition or dangerous occurrence which the contractor is required to notify or report under the Reporting of Injuries, Diseases and Dangerous Occurrences Regulations 1995.

Three further duties are imposed around the construction phase plan. Every contractor shall take all reasonable steps to ensure that the construction work is carried out in accordance with the construction phase plan; shall take appropriate action to ensure health and safety where it is not possible to comply with the construction phase plan in any particular case; and shall notify the principal contractor of any significant finding which requires the construction phase plan to be altered or added to.

### 19.4.14 The CDM co-ordinator

The role of CDM co-ordinator is a new one created by the 2007 Regulations. The role of planning supervisor, created by the 1994 Regulations, has gone.

The role of CDM co-ordinator is to provide the client with a key project adviser in respect of construction health and safety risk management matters. They should assist and advise the client on the appointment of competent contractors and the adequacy of management arrangements; ensure proper co-ordination of the health and safety aspects of the design process; facilitate good communication and co-operation between project team members and prepare the health and safety file.

CDM co-ordinators must give suitable and sufficient advice and assistance to clients in order to help them to comply with their duties under the Regulations, in particular, the duty to appoint competent designers and contractors and the duty to ensure that adequate arrangements are in place for managing the project.

They are also obliged to ensure that suitable arrangements are made and implemented for the co-ordination of health and safety measures during planning and preparation of the construction phase, including facilitating co-operation and co-ordination between persons concerned in the project and the application of the general principles of prevention.

They are required to liaise with the principal contractor regarding the contents of the health and safety file, the information which the principal contractor needs to prepare the construction phase plan and any design development which may affect planning and management of the construction work.

The CDM co-ordinator is required to take all reasonable steps to identify and collect the pre-construction information; to promptly provide, in a convenient form, to every person designing the structure and every contractor who has been or may be appointed by the client such pre-construction information in his possession as is relevant to each; to take all reasonable steps to ensure that designers comply with their duties under regulations 11 and 18(2); to take all reasonable steps to ensure co-operation between designers and the principal contractor during the construction phase in relation to any design or change to a design; to prepare, where none exists, and otherwise review and update the health and safety file ; and at the end of the construction phase to pass the health and safety file to the client.

The duty to notify the project to HSE falls upon the CDM co-ordinator by virtue of regulation 21(1). The particulars to be notified to HSE are set out in Schedule 1 to the 2007 Regulations.

### 19.4.15 Duties of the principal contractor

The duties incumbent upon the principal contractor are set out in regulations 22, 23 and 24.

The key duty of principal contractors is to properly plan, manage and co-ordinate work during the construction phase in order that risks are properly controlled. There can only be one principal contractor for a project at any one time. However, sometime two or more projects take place on a site at the same time. This can occur if different clients commission adjacent work, or if a client procures two truly independent, unrelated packages of work which do not rely upon one another for their viability or completion. Where overlapping projects are running on a single construction site, it is usually best to appoint one principal contractor for all of them. If this is not done, all the principal contractors must co-operate and their plans must take account of the interfaces, for example, in traffic management.

The principal contractor for the project shall plan, manage and monitor the construction phase in a way which ensures that, so far as is reasonably practicable, it is carried out without risks to health or safety. This includes facilitating co-operation and co-ordination between persons concerned in the project and the application of the general principles of prevention.

The further duties imposed upon the principal contractor are:

- to liaise with the CDM co-ordinator during the construction phase in relation to any design or change to a design;
- to ensure that the requisite welfare facilities are provided throughout the construction phase;
- where necessary for health and safety, to draw up rules which are appropriate to the construction site and the activities on it;
- to give reasonable directions to any contractors so far as is necessary to enable the principal contractor to comply with his duties under the Regulations;
- to ensure that every contractor is informed of the minimum amount of time which will be allowed to him for planning and preparation before he begins construction work;
- where necessary, to consult a contractor before finalising such part of the construction phase plan as is relevant to the work to be performed by him;
- to ensure that every contractor is given, before he begins construction work and in sufficient time to enable him to properly prepare for that work, access to such part of the construction phase plan as is relevant to the work to be performed by him;
- to ensure that every contractor is given, before he begins work and in sufficient time, such further information as he needs to comply punctually with his obligation in respect of welfare facilities and to carry out the work to be performed by him without risk, so far as is reasonably practicable, to the health and safety of any person;
- to identify to each contractor the information relating to the contractor's activity which is likely to be required by the CDM co-ordinator for inclusion in the health and safety file and to ensure that such information is promptly provided to the CDM co-ordinator;
- to ensure that the particulars required to be in the notice to the HSE are displayed in a readable condition in a position where they can be read by any worker engaged in the construction work;
- to take reasonable steps to prevent access by unauthorised persons to the construction site;
- to take reasonable steps to ensure that every worker carrying out construction work is provided with a suitable site induction and with suitable information and training for the particular work to be carried out by him.

### 19.4.16 Construction phase plan

The construction phase plan should set out the way in which the construction phase will be managed, identifying the main health and safety issues arising. It should be specific and should not simply be an accumulation of generic risk assessments or method statements. It requires to be tailored for the project to which it relates. The matters that ought to be contained within the construction phase plan are set out in detail in Appendix 3 to the Approved Code of Practice to the 2007 Regulations.

The duties of the principal contractor in relation to the construction phase plan are contained in regulation 23. Before the start of the construction phase, the principal contractor is obliged to prepare a construction phase plan which is sufficient to ensure that the construction phase is planned, managed and monitored in a way which enables the construction work to be started, so far as is reasonably practicable, without risk to health or safety, and which pays adequate regard to the information provided by the designer and the pre-construction information provided through the CDM co-ordinator.

From time to time, and as often as may be appropriate throughout the project, the principal contractor is obliged to update, review, revise and refine the construction phase plan so that it continues to be sufficient to ensure that the construction phase is planned, managed and monitored in a way which enables the construction work to be carried out without risk to health and safety, again insofar as is reasonably practicable.

Lastly, the principal contractor is obliged to ensure that the construction phase plan is implemented in a way which will ensure, so far is reasonably practicable, the health and safety of all persons carrying out the construction work and all persons who may be affected by that work.

The principal contractor is obliged to take reasonable steps to ensure that the construction phase plan identifies the risks to health and safety arising from the construction work, including the risks specific to the particular type of construction work concerned, and includes suitable and sufficient measures to address such risks, including site rules.

### 19.4.17 Health and safety file

To be completed and handed over to the employer at the end of the project, the health and safety file should contain relevant information in relation to the structure which will be of assistance in relation to any future project carried out to it. As will have been noted above, clients, designers, principal contractors, other contractors and CDM co-ordinators all have duties incumbent upon them under the 2007 Regulations in relation to the health and safety file.

### 19.4.18 Co-operation and consultation with workers

Regulation 24 imposes three specific duties relative to co-operation and consultation with workers.

Firstly, the principal contractor is required to make and maintain arrangements which will enable him and the workers engaged in the construction work to co-operate effectively in promoting and developing measures to ensure the health, safety and welfare of the workers and then checking the effectiveness of such measures.

Secondly, the principal contractor is obliged to consult those workers (or their representatives) in good time on matters connected with the project which may affect health, safety or welfare, so far as they or their representatives are not so consulted on those matters by any employer of theirs.

Thirdly, the principal contractor is obliged to ensure that such workers or their representatives can inspect and take copies of any information which the principal contractor has which relate to the planning and management of the project, or which otherwise may affect their health, safety or welfare. In this regard, qualifications do exist in relation to certain matters, see regulation 24(c)(i) to (v).

### 19.4.19 Part 4

Part 4 of the Regulations sets out the duties relating to health and safety on construction sites. It deals with a wide range of matters, namely, safe places of work; good order and site security; stability of structures; demolition or dismantling; use of explosives; excavations; cofferdams and caissons; reports of inspections; energy distribution installations; prevention of drowning; traffic routes; vehicles; prevention of risk from fire; emergency procedures; emergency routes and exits; fire detection and fire fighting; fresh air; temperature and weather protection; and lighting. A detailed consideration of Part 4 is outwith the scope of this book.

### 19.4.20 Civil liability

The position in relation to civil liability is regulated in Part 5 of the 2007 Regulations and, in particular, by regulation 45.

The position has changed, somewhat, from that which subsisted under the 1994 Regulations. In those, only regulation 10 (start of construction phase) and regulation 16(1) (requirements on principal contractor) could confer a right of action.

Of the 2007 Regulations, the obligations imposed by regulations 9(1)(b); 13(6) and (7); 16; 21(1)(c) and (l); 25(1), (2) and (4); 26 to 44; and Schedule 2 can confer a right of action in civil proceedings, insofar as the relevant duties apply for the protection of a person who is not an employee of the person on whom the duty is placed.

### 19.4.21 Transitional arrangements

By virtue of regulation 47(1), the 2007 Regulations apply in relation to projects which had commenced prior to their coming into force (on 6 April 2007), with certain modifications.

CDM co-ordinators and principal contractors require to be appointed as soon as is practicable.

It will be noted that practicable is not prefixed by 'reasonably'. Any planning supervisor or principal contractor appointed under regulation 6 of the 1994 Regulations shall, in the absence of an express appointment by the client, be treated for the purposes of regulation 47(2) as having been appointed as the CDM co-ordinator or the principal contractor.

Where a client appoints any previously appointed planning supervisor or principal contractor to the CDM co-ordinator or principal contractor role under the 2007 Regulations, the client is required within 12 months of the 2007 Regulations coming into force, to take reasonable steps to ensure that any CDM co-ordinator or principal contractor so appointed is competent within the meaning of regulation 4(2). Similarly, anyone treated as having been appointed as CDM co-ordinator or principal contractor pursuant to regulation 47(4) has 12 months to ensure their own competence.

By virtue of regulation 47(6), any agent appointed by a client under regulation 4 of the 1994 Regulations may, if requested by the client and if he himself consents, continue to act as agent of that client. This is very much a transitional provision, there being no 'agency' appointments available under the 2007 Regulations.

In the event that the agent does continue to act, they shall be subject to such requirements and prohibitions as are placed by the 2007 Regulations on their client, unless or until such time as the agency appointment is revoked by the client, the project comes to an end or (in very much the worst case scenario) five years elapse from the coming into force of the 2007 Regulations, whichever arises first.

## 19.5  *The SBC provisions*

Under clause 2.1 of the Standard Building Contract (SBC), the Contractor is under an obligation to carry out and complete the Works in compliance with the Construction Phase Plan and the Statutory Requirements in relation to the Works. Implicitly, this will include all health and safety legislation insofar as it is relevant to the work.

Each party to the contract is required, by virtue of clause 3.25, to comply with the 2007 Regulations. This includes clause 3.25.2 whereby the

Contractor is obliged, while they remain Principal Contractor, to ensure that the Health and Safety Plan as developed by them is received by the Employer before construction work is commenced and that any subsequent amendment to it by the Contractor is notified to the Employer.

Whilst they are Principal Contractor, the Contractor must ensure that welfare facilities complying with Schedule 2 of the 2007 Regulations are provided from the commencement of construction work until the end of the construction phase. Where the Contractor is not the principal contractor, they are obliged to promptly inform the Principal Contractor of the identity of each sub-contractor that they appoint and of each sub-sub-contractor appointment notified to them.

The contractor is also required, under clause 3.25.4, to provide, and ensure that any sub-contractor provides, to the CDM co-ordinator such information as the CDM co-ordinator reasonably requires for the preparation of the health and safety file. This requirement must be complied with before practical completion can be certified, see clause 2.30.

Under clause 3.26, if the Employer appoints a successor to the Contractor as Principal Contractor, the Contractor is required, at no cost to the Employer, to comply with all reasonable requirements of the new Principal Contractor to the extent necessary for compliance with the 2007 Regulations. No extension of time is given in respect of such compliance.

# Tables of Cases

The following abbreviations of Reports are used:

| | |
|---|---|
| AC | Law Reports, Appeal Cases |
| All ER | All England Law Reports |
| BLR | Building Law Reports |
| CH | Law Reports, Chancery |
| CILL | Construction Industry Law Letter |
| CLD | Construction Law Digest |
| Con LR | Construction Law Reports |
| Const LJ | Construction Law Journal |
| CSIH | Court of Session Inner House |
| CSOH | Court of Session Outer House |
| D | Dunlop's Session Cases 1838–62 |
| DLR | Dominion Law Reports |
| ECR | European Court Reports |
| EGLR | Estate Gazette Law Reports |
| EuLR | European Law Reports |
| EWCA | England and Wales Court of Appeal Cases |
| EWHC | England and Wales High Court Cases |
| F | Fraser's Session Cases 1898–1906 |
| FC | Faculty Collection |
| FCR | Family Court Reports |
| GWD | Greens Weekly Digest |
| H&N | Hurlstone & Norman |
| Hudson's BC | Hudson's Building Contracts |
| Lloyd's Rep | Lloyd's Law Reports |
| M | Macpherson's Session Cases 1862–73 |
| Macq | Macqueens Scotch Appeal Cases |
| Mor | Morison's Dictionary of Decisions |
| PD | Law Reports, Probate Division |
| PNLR | Professional Negligence Law Reports |
| QB | Law Reports, Queens Bench |
| SLR | Scottish Law Reporter |
| S | P Shaw's Session Cases 1821–38 |
| SC | Session Cases 1907– |
| SCLR | Scottish Civil Law Reports |
| Sh Ct Rep | Sheriff Court Reports |

# Table of Statutes

# Table of Statutory Instruments

# Table of References

*JCT Standard Form of Building Contract (1998 Edition) and the Standard Building Contract with Quantities for Use in Scotland SBC/Q/Scot (Revised May 2006)*

## Table of References to the Design and Build Contract for Use in Scotland, DB/Scot 2005 (Revised May 2006)

# Index